"The Church desperately needs compe
pose fashionable lies and errors for wh;
to forgotten truths that earlier genera
Christopher Malloy does exactly that.'

—**Edward Feser**
Professor of Philosophy, Pasadena City College

"The Church's enemies are pressing in from every side—and often from within.
Professor Malloy helps us to deflate their manifold errors and heresies by way of
the sharpest of all double-edged swords. Highly recommended."

—**C. C. Pecknold**
The Catholic University of America

"Are Catholics indoctrinated by the Church in America? They seem rather to
be undoctrinated and even misdoctrinated! Malloy, in plain language, explains
what doctrine is, its necessary role in the Church, and why so many Catholic
teachings are ignored, contested, or denied today."

—**Guy Mansini, O.S.B.**
Ave Maria University

"The past few decades have seen much confusion by the diffusion of false doctrines that menace Catholic faith. Christopher J. Malloy exposes them in a
clear, comprehensible way—not only for theologians and pastors, but also for
the interested public at large."

—**Prof. Dr. Manfred Hauke**
University of Lugano (Switzerland)

"The last fifty-five years has seen a growth and diffusion of heresy that is
without precedent. Every article of the Faith and the very foundations of
Christian morality have been under attack, not only from professors but
from priests and prelates of the highest ranks in the Church. Christopher
Malloy has written a book of courage and clarity that will reanimate the
hope of every Catholic who strives to be faithful to the gospel of Christ
in His one true Church."

—**Fr. John Saward**
Senior Research Fellow, Blackfriars, University of Oxford

"In the nineteenth century, when St. John Henry Newman dared to criticize
reactionary ecclesiastical trends, he had to do so subtly and mainly in private
correspondence. After the Second Vatican Council, more room has been given
for critical voices, both on the left and on the right. In fidelity to the Second

Vatican Council and in full communion with the Church, Malloy's basic question is: Are doctrines that the Catholic Church has held for centuries, solemn doctrines of faith and morals, going to crumble and even be repudiated? Is the Church going to become a liberal Christian denomination? His answer is no, but the urgent tone and forceful content of his prescriptions remind us why this conversation—which, in a certain way, occupies all serious theologians today even when they do not agree with Malloy in every respect—cannot be suppressed or bottled up."

—**Matthew Levering**
James N. and Mary D. Perry Jr. Chair of Theology,
Mundelein Seminary

"In a book that is both powerfully argued and richly documented, Christopher Malloy dispels the theological confusions that most centrally afflict the Catholic Church today. In a time when so many faithful Catholics are disturbed by reckless and sloppy teaching, Malloy's sober clarity is especially needed."

—**Robert C. Koons**
Professor of Philosophy, University of Texas

"The great merit of this book lies in its close diagnosis of the difference between theological evolutionism and the orthodox unfolding of doctrine through history. Looking through this lens, Christopher Malloy has done a signal service in outlining for us the critical issues facing the practice of theology in the modern Church. This work will be of use to anyone wishing to understand the current state of Catholic theology in its relation to the Church and the world. It is a sobering read but one that shines with rays of hope for the future. Collected here in this approachable volume one finds incisive criticism coupled with rigor and clarity. Malloy does the heavy lifting in order truly to demonstrate a 'holistic' approach to the difficult problems and troubling situations facing faithful Catholics."

—**Donald Prudlo**
Warren Professor of Catholic Studies, University of Tulsa

"Christopher Malloy's illuminating book gives a timely account of the current crisis in fidelity and orthodoxy in the Catholic Church. On key issues, from the nature of the Church to justification, salvation, and marriage, Malloy surveys the historical Magisterium from Nicaea to Vatican II, giving an eloquent exposition of Church teaching while exploring with insight the roots of its rejection not only in contemporary culture but in the theology of the last sixty years."

—**Thomas Pink**
Professor of Philosophy, King's College, London

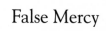

False Mercy

Christopher J. Malloy

False Mercy
Recent Heresies Distorting
Catholic Truth

SOPHIA INSTITUTE PRESS
Manchester, New Hampshire

Sophia Institute Press

Box 5284, Manchester, NH 03108

1-800-888-9344

www.SophiaInstitute.com

Sophia Institute Press® is a registered trademark of Sophia Institute.

paperback ISBN 978-1-64413-418-4

ebook ISBN 978-1-64413-419-1

Library of Congress Control Number: 2021942834

First printing

To Mary, destroyer of all heresies

I testify to you this day that I am innocent of the blood of all of you, for I did not shrink from declaring to you the whole counsel of God. Take heed to yourselves and to all the flock, in which the Holy Spirit has made you guardians, to feed the church of the Lord which he obtained with his own blood. I know that after my departure fierce wolves will come in among you, not sparing the flock; and from among your own selves will arise men speaking perverse things, to draw away the disciples after them. Therefore be alert.

—St. Paul to the Ephesians (Acts 20:26–31)

Contents

Preface

This book is a guide for orthodox Catholics who want to know what they must believe and what they must reject about certain errors threatening the Faith today. As a professor of theology, I hear regularly from undergraduate and graduate students, friends, and acquaintances of all ages that things Catholic are confusing. Even bright students feel bewildered. Many *want* to hold the Catholic Faith, but they are getting different messages. This person says this; that person says that. On top of it all, certain media, renegade theologians, and confused theologians are twisting out of context soundbites from Pope Francis and other recent popes and defending strange claims foreign to the Catholic Faith.

So, what should we believe? Whom should we believe? Is everything up for grabs? Is the Catholic Faith changing? In a nutshell, no; dogmas and infallible teachings do not change. There is legitimate development in doctrinal expression, and there are legitimate differences in the understanding of the mysteries, but the Faith is one and does not change. This theological study addresses these concerns and anxieties in an accessible way. Though it is not an academic book, there are plenty of supporting notes for further research.

We face a new modernism that has been wildly successful. The new modernism has its leaders, its unwittingly supportive laborers, and others caught in the undertow of confusion. The leaders allege that a doctrinal revolution is warranted by the Second Vatican Council, adducing as supposed evidence doctrinal developments and certain pastorally chosen changes in communication strategy. Now, legitimate developments do not constitute revolution, nor do prudential changes in communication strategy. Examples of prudential changes include addressing magisterial documents to the world and not just to Catholics; treating part but not all of the truth on this or that topic; employing less precise language; including few if any condemnations; identifying the elements of truth in heretical or erroneous teachings; issuing lengthy texts; and treating renegades with remarkable patience. These policies can be seen as part of a strategy to foster conversations with non-Catholics and to inspire loving obedience in Catholics. In conversation with a stranger or someone unfamiliar with or recalcitrant toward the Faith, it can help to start with common ground, not to be too incisive or technical, to evoke interest in further conversation, and so forth.

Some theologians take as their sufficient point of departure the documents from the Second Vatican Council and thus forget crucial doctrines from the past not articulated by the council. But the genuine conversational skills just mentioned call for completion with already taught doctrines in the great tradition. On the opposite extreme, modernists call for a completion of the wrong kind. They call for a completion of revision. For the modernists, Vatican II was the beginning of a revolutionary break from the great tradition. Both those who take their sole orientation from the texts of Vatican II, forgetting crucial truths of the Catholic tradition, and those who champion the "event" of the council as a radical rejection of the past are mistaken. Vatican II does not warrant either the forgetting or the renunciation of doctrine and tradition. Rather, it requires the remembrance of both, as Paul VI expressly noted only a month after the council.[1]

We need to affirm the entire truth. Communication is sharing truth so as to form friendships. Friendships are built upon shared truth, in which friends take mutual delight. Christian friendships are centered on the Truth who sets us free. Therefore, a full strategy of communication

[1] See Paul VI, General Audience, January 12, 1966.

requires—eventually and in the right way—that we come around to certain difficult truths that our interlocutor rejects and that have been unexpressed for some time. But the modernists interpret silence on a portion of the truth as denial of past doctrine, ambiguity as an opportunity to reject the Church's precise definitions, the absence of condemnation as approval of errors long condemned, and wordiness as an excuse to forget doctrine.

Besieged by the success of the new modernists, we have become dizzy and disoriented. In imitation of the Good Shepherd, we went out, searching for lost friends so as to bring them home, conversing with them in a friendly manner.[2] All the while, we employed these methods of invitation. But our memory, being weak, has at length failed many of us; we have forgotten perennial teachings. As a result, we have ourselves become like these lost friends, like lost sheep. As if speaking prophetically, Leo XIII exhorted, "Let it be far from anyone's mind to suppress for any reason any doctrine that has been handed down. Such a policy would tend rather to separate Catholics from the Church than to bring in those who differ."[3] Today, we need refreshment. We need direction home. We need the whole truth. We need clarity. We need errors pointed out and rejected. We need rebels to be disciplined lest, as ravenous wolves disguised as models of virtue, they seduce the young and impressionable away from the Catholic Faith.

But there is hope. We *can* be Catholic today. We *can* confess the full Faith. We do not need to take the word of errant theologians as Gospel

---

[2] See Leo XIII, encyclical *Testem benevolentiae* (January 22, 1899), art. 25, Papal Encyclicals, https://www.papalencyclicals.net/Leo13/l13teste.htm.

[3] Leo XIII, *Testem benevolentiae*, art. 6. Apparently, Cardinal Spellman contended that the task of the Second Vatican Council was "to teach the members of the Church, rather than those outside of it." Similarly, Bishop Grotti is reported to have counseled at the council, "Hiding the truth hurts both us and those separated from us. It hurts us, because we appear as hypocrites. It hurts those who are separated from us because it makes them appear weak and capable of being offended by the truth." See Ralph M. Wiltgen, *The Rhine Flows into the Tiber: A History of Vatican II* (Rockford, IL: TAN Books, 1978), 94–95.

truth if their word contradicts the deposit of faith. Their footnotes are no bulwark against dogma. Contrary to the rebels, silence is not denial, recent ambiguity does not annul prior precision, and lack of condemnation is not approbation. The Church has weathered great and terrible storms before. She can weather this storm too. The gates of Hell will not prevail against her.

As its title suggests, this book is directed against errors and heresies that are currently afflicting us. Some of these are ancient errors that have returned to haunt us; some have arisen only lately. The official definition of heresy, employed by those with the authority to judge persons in the public forum of the Church, is obstinate doubt or denial on a matter of divine and Catholic Faith. In this book, however, the term "heresy" is used broadly, indicating simply the incompatibility of some claim with the Catholic Faith. The term is not meant to indicate culpability, especially in our situation, which, with precious little correction from the pastors, teems with an air of undisciplined "free thinking." Theologians distinguish formal and material heresy. Material heresy involves holding some claim that contradicts the deposit of faith, whether or not one is aware of the contradiction. Formal heresy requires rejecting the authority of God revealing. Those who have never had faith cannot commit formal heresy. Now, Catholics have the blessing and responsibility of knowing that God's revealing authority is mediated through the Church's teaching authority, or Magisterium. So, objectively speaking, for a Catholic to reject an infallible dogma of the Church is to be guilty of formal heresy. The proper Church authorities judge public expressions of such heresy.

Sometimes, however, people simply make mistakes. Little children confuse the Virginal Conception of Jesus with the Immaculate Conception of Mary. Some pious Catholics *think* that God changes or they picture Him as changing. These are the mistakes of untrained believers. Even trained theologians make mistakes, often innocently. Theologians are nonetheless expected to grow in awareness of the deposit of faith and are held to a higher bar of accountability. They should be aware of and affirm the basic doctrines and dogmas of the Church. Theologians unaware of a basic doctrine or dogma are incompetent, and their mistakes can lead others into error. Such error can wreak havoc in life.

Given the situation we are in, it is understandable, although lamentable, that some of us are ignorant of our tradition; hopefully, each of us is trying to remedy this deficit. But theologians who deliberately doubt or deny such doctrines are in formal error or heresy. Their lack of faith renders them blind guides. When errors are published, it is a service of charity to point them out publicly; God alone knows the culpability. Of course, when they reason about matters not yet doctrinally settled, such as grace and free will, theologians can easily make various mistakes. For all that, their theology is not formally heretical or unorthodox. Further, dogmas concern deep mysteries, and theologians can unwittingly make mistakes as they attempt to fathom these realities. It goes without saying that theologians should presume one another's goodwill regarding mistakes about deep mysteries — provided these mistakes are not blatant contradictions of infallible teachings — or about matters not doctrinally settled, even while vigorously debating the truth or error of their claims.

I consider it a duty and an honor to defend basic Catholic teachings, since they are truly liberating. Truth sets us free. In pursuit of this task, I am privileged to have a mandatum from my local ordinary, the Most Reverend Edward J. Burns, so as to teach Catholic theology at the University of Dallas. This mandatum requires certain commitments: teaching according to authentic Catholic doctrine and refraining from putting forth as Catholic teaching anything contrary to the Magisterium of the Church, refraining from openly criticizing or ridiculing the teaching authority of the Church, and refraining from living in a manifest way contrary to the teachings of the Magisterium of the Church. Although a sinner, I am committed to living according to the Church's teachings. Although a fallible thinker, I am committed to teaching authentic Catholic doctrine and not presenting anything contrary to this as Catholic teaching. Finally, I am committed to honoring, defending, and upholding the teaching authority of the Church. This authority demands irrevocable acceptance of all the infallible teachings of the Church and submission of mind and heart to the noninfallible doctrine, according to the degree of authority accorded them. This book stands firmly in defense of these responsibilities.

For whatever is true and useful in this book, I give thanks to God. For whatever is unfruitful or erroneous, I welcome correction.

Introduction

"What's going on?" A friend of mine recently asked me this question after Sunday Mass. He was holding one of his children and had a troubled expression. I had no idea what he meant. Puzzled, I looked behind me, searching the cafeteria for some commotion. Finding nothing unusual, I turned back toward him. "What?" I asked. "In the Church," he clarified. "What's going on in the Church?" I replied, "Yes, what *is* going on?"

These are strange days for the Catholic Church and for the world. A deadly virus, emanating from Communist China, has threatened the lives and health of millions around the world. Many nations have responded with crippling lockdowns. In the United States, a variety of sexual devian-cies are now sanctioned by the Supreme Court's dubious interpretations of the U.S. Constitution. Protests and riots have called for, and sometimes achieved, states of lawlessness. In the Catholic Church, some priests and bishops — hierarchical members of the Church that Jesus Christ instituted to divinize the human race — have engaged in or covered up horrific acts against minors. But, as revolting as these scandals and this tumult are, they pale in comparison with another scandal.

The greatest scandal in the Church is the failure of more than a few hierarchs and theologians to teach clearly the whole Catholic truth and nothing but the truth. Some of these are simply misled by the confusion of our age; others are protagonists of revolution and chaos. In both cases, their failure correlates with a grave crisis of faith. A majority of Catholics in the United States no longer practice their Faith regularly. A majority no longer assent to a number of Church teachings, especially on topics that affect individual lifestyles. Many Catholics think that the Church's teachings can change or should change. That non-Catholics don't hold some Catholic teachings is understandable. When Catholics do not affirm basic Catholic teachings, there is a problem.

Such Catholics are of two sorts: those who consciously reject the teachings and those who are unaware of or confused about them. The former group comprises rebels, whose continuance in the Church is a danger to the flock. In the time of Pius X, such heretics lay hidden, so as to avoid condemnation as they spread their errors. These were the modernists of old. Recently, new modernists have come out of the woodwork. They propagate their errors with bravado because they are not disciplined. The latter group is composed of good-willed but confused or ignorant Catholics. They are confused about two things. As a general matter, they mistakenly worry that the Church *might* water down, alter, or reject her perennial teachings. They worry that doctrine can *evolve*. Doctrinal evolutionism is the notion that an older doctrine, while useful and true in the past, is now extinct (not useful) and even false. Doctrinal evolutionism also includes the belief that newer dogmas were not already present in the original deposit of faith; rather, newer dogmas result from new "inspirations." Doctrinal evolutionism is a heresy in itself and also a fountainhead of individual heresies. On specific matters, these confused faithful do not know what truths they must believe and what errors they must reject.

As a result of this twofold confusion, good-willed Catholics struggle to fulfill their baptismal obligation to confess the entire Catholic Faith. Their debility inhibits their capacity to love God and neighbor. After all, we cannot love what we do not know. Nor can we love a neighbor rightly if we don't know his true good. Charity is the greatest theological virtue, to be sure (see 1 Cor. 13), yet charity depends on the truth of faith. We can have faith without charity; it will not save us, but it remains true faith and presents us with a correct map of reality. We cannot, however, have charity without faith. Warm feelings of love are not charity but only sentiments. Sentiments fade.

Introduction

As confused as we find ourselves today, it was not always this way. For centuries, the Catholic Church had been a bastion of clarity. Yes, heretics arose and led many astray. The bishops of entire nations abandoned the Church overnight. And we have always had moral corruption with us. Yet in past times, heresies, schism, and apostasy were normally discernible *as* rebellions. Only infrequently was there global doubt as to whether rebellion or a legitimate development was underway. Only a few times in history did half-truths, errors, and heresies linger within the very ranks of the hierarchy and among the faithful, either being unchecked by competent authority or being fostered by the abuse of office. For the past five centuries, Catholics and the public could count on the Church's stability. Catholics were proud of it, and some non-Catholics admired it from afar. Objectors could always count on the target of their doubt or ire to remain the same. Five or six decades ago, however, the confusion that accosts us began to set in. Once released, it spread like a contagion.

What is to blame for this crisis of faith? Surely, many factors are at work. Some of these factors are external to the Church's governance and thus not in the hands of hierarchs. The sexual and cultural revolutions have no doubt played significant parts. The spirit of the world has enticed many Catholics with its seductive allure. Intellectual movements have for centuries been warring against God and His Christ. Since Catholics are human, these trials affect the way Catholicism is lived. Other factors are internal to the Church and thus under the control and responsibility of the hierarchy. Poor parochial catechesis is one factor. Bland liturgies are another. The breakdown of neighborhoods — a cultural phenomenon — negatively impacted parish life in America. Another factor is the forgetting of doctrine by those of goodwill who suffer from incomplete formation. Worse, there is the infidelity of some theologians to their mandate and even of some bishops to their episcopal office and some priests to their pastoral office. Although some bishops, faithful to charity, have taught the whole truth clearly, others have not. For instance, some bishops have failed to teach and defend the full substance of perennial Catholic truth. Others have taught with ambiguous language, leaving the faithful in doubt about matters that, although already settled doc-trinally, the world disputes. Still others have uttered doctrines foreign to the Faith. Furthermore, few bishops discipline renegade theologians and priests who espouse and promulgate heresy.

What are the widest effects of this crisis? Just as the faithful are confused about the Catholic Faith, so is the public at large. Bystanders ask whether the Church still believes what she preached for centuries. Some of these observers—who long found something admirable in the Church—sense a loss. My wife's Jewish midwife, superb at her craft, recently offered us something like condolences over the state of the Church. Others rejoice. Elton John, for example, has exulted in the confusion insofar as he takes it to have ratified his unnatural lifestyle. Hence, his pain at a recent, precise statement on same-sex unions (see the statement of the Congregation for the Doctrine of the Faith issued March 15, 2021). On the superficial level, the world rejoices to hear leading prelates celebrate perversity and hide, water down, or abandon Catholic truths.

On a deeper level, however, the world is saddened by the theft of the Gospel's illumination, power, and calling. Worse, the world is even angered. Why? The natural desire for happiness cannot find fulfillment outside of God. The world senses this. Further, the world shall never forget the absolute and exclusive claims that the Catholic Church has faithfully upheld for two millennia. Deep down, the world recognizes that bishops and priests who espouse doctrinal evolutionism are being hypocritical. They are teaching what is foreign to their office, which demands fidelity to the Church's unchanging Faith.

Some define "hypocrisy" as preaching one thing while doing another. This is not the truest form of hypocrisy but only the ordinary human sin-fulness of a leader. The truest meaning of hypocrisy is to pretend fidelity while rejecting the Faith; leaders who fail to fulfill their teaching office are guilty of the gravest form of hypocrisy. They display themselves as loving, but they withhold food from the flock, or they leave the flock to wander in search of nourishing pastures; some feed the sheep poison. It is one thing to sin in weakness while preaching the truth. It is quite another to twist the Faith into conformity with one's own sinfulness.

This latter hypocrisy traps both its perpetrators and those misled by them. We have always had sinful preachers who teach the Faith clearly while failing to live it out. They are not real hypocrites because they believe what they teach and teach what they believe. They are morally weak and sinful, but they do not speak so as to deceive. They teach the truth. They help others journey toward happier ways of life and, ultimately, toward Heaven. Would that we had more men willing to be hypocrites in this way! Those who promote heresy, by contrast, usher people toward misery. Some heretics appear as lambs outwardly, but their heresy makes them ravenous wolves inwardly.

Some readers might be asking, "Are things really as bad as you say?" Some are rosier than I about the current state of affairs. They remain hopefully skeptical when they hear stories of doom. Hope is a virtue. We must always hope. Yet hope must also be grounded in truth. Despair hides from truth. Anecdotal evidence is insufficient for those who have no personal experience of the crisis. Hard data might speak more persuasively.

Data on Catholic Beliefs and Practices

We have data on Catholic beliefs and practices in the United States. We also have data on changes in beliefs and practices through time. Finally, we have recent data on the success or failure of various religious groups to attract more adherents than they repel. Thus, we can study the current crisis within a larger historical context.

Catholic Beliefs Today

Let us begin with the beliefs of Catholics in the United States today. According to a Pew study in 2019, only 50 percent of Catholics in the United States know the teaching of the Church on transubstantiation.[4] Of those who know this teaching, 44 percent regard the teaching to be

---

4 "What Americans Know about Religion," Pew Research Center, July 23, 2019, https://www.pewforum.org/2019/07/23/what-americans-know -about-religion.

false. So 69 percent of Catholics believe that the bread and wine are only symbols of the Body and Blood of Jesus Christ.[5] Now, the Eucharist is the center of our entire religion. When someone's faith in the Eucharist flags, his Catholicity is dead or dying.

Data also show that the majority of Catholics today think that the Faith can and should change.[6] Doctrinal evolutionism, part of the heresy of modernism, dominates Catholic opinion polls. For example, 76 percent think that the Church should change her infallible condemnation of artificial birth control; 62 percent think that the Church should allow divorced Catholics who have "remarried" without an annulment to receive the Eucharist; 61 percent think that those who are cohabiting should be allowed to receive the Eucharist; 59 percent of Catholics reject the infallible teaching that the Church has no authority to ordain women; 46 percent reject the infallible teaching that marriage is by definition a heterosexual covenant. Truly, it would be lamentable if even 10 percent of Catholics thought the Church's teachings can or should change. It is beyond tragic that the majority do.

Importantly, the current lack of faith in Catholic teachings is part of a downward trend. For instance, in 1987, 66 percent thought that one could be a good Catholic without accepting the infallible teaching on contraception. That is, 66 percent believed that one could deny infallible teaching and yet be a good Catholic. In 1999, that figure grew to 72 percent.[7] In 2019, as we saw above, 76 percent of Catholics thought the Church *should* change her condemnation of contraception. The starting point at 66 percent was bad enough; the trajectory is alarming. Again,

---

[5] Gregory A. Smith, "Just One-Third of U.S. Catholics Agree with Their Church That Eucharist Is the Body, Blood of Christ," Pew Research Center, August 5, 2019, https://www.pewresearch.org/fact-tank/2019/08/05/transubstantiation-eucharist-u-s-catholics.

[6] Benjamin Wormald, "Chapter 4: Expectations of the Church," Pew Research Center, September 2, 2015, https://www.pewforum.org/2015/09/02/chapter-4-expectations-of-the-church/#catholic-desires-for-change.

[7] Kenneth C. Jones, *Index of Leading Catholic Indicators: The Church Since Vatican II* (Saint Louis: Oriens, 2003), 77.

in 1987, 39 percent of Catholics thought one could be a good Catholic while disobeying the Church's condemnation of abortion. This figure alone is tragic. Alas, by 1999, it grew to 53 percent.

Trends in Catholic Practices

Have these downward trends persisted for a long time? When did they begin? Unfortunately, there is no adequate diachronic study — a study of changes through time — of the faith of Catholics in Church teachings over a long time. So we cannot as yet get a definite picture of trends in the past hundred years regarding faith in the Real Presence and in moral teachings.

Nonetheless, we do have reliable data on important Catholic *practices* for the past seventy-five to a hundred years. Examination of the trends regarding these practices might give us some clues. Kenneth Jones presents useful data in his book *Index of Leading Catholic Indicators: The Church Since Vatican II*. Jones works mostly but not exclusively from the *Official Catholic Directory* (OCD). Georgetown's Center for Applied Research in the Apostolate (CARA) also uses many figures from the *OCD* and offers a helpful FAQ page, updated frequently, on its website.[8] CARA has a reputation for reliability. Unfortunately, its data go back only to 1970. In contrast, Jones goes back to 1920. Can we use both sets of data to study one and the same trend? To do so is not ideal; nonetheless, the following considerations show that it is reasonable to do so. Jones and CARA often agree on figures from certain years. When their numbers diverge, they do so non-systematically: sometimes Jones's figures are slightly higher, and sometimes CARA's figures are slightly higher. Thus, the discrepancies tend to cancel each other out. Furthermore, in every case, the size of the discrepancies pales in comparison with the size of the gross numbers. Finally, both sets of data agree on the overall rate

---

[8] "Frequently Requested Church Statistics," Center for Applied Research in the Apostolate (CARA), https://cara.georgetown.edu/frequently-requested-church-statistics. I am using figures from CARA updated as of July 21, 2020.

of change. Since CARA is reliable and updates its numbers regularly, however, I have decided to favor CARA's data from 1970 forward.[9]

What figures should we examine first? To decide, we must acknowledge the radicalness of Catholic life. Its centerpiece is the Mass, the consumption of the Body and Blood of Jesus Christ, the only Savior of the world. This is no ordinary claim. The universal road of heroism for Catholics is saintly charity, which any Catholic in a valid state of life can undertake. As the Second Vatican Council reminded us, God's call to holiness is universal. Moreover, non-Catholics can obtain and grow in holiness as well, although they face obstacles from heresies and from a lack of crucial means of sanctification.[10] Although the call to holiness is universal, the measure of a society is the stature of its heroes. There are objectively heroic ways of being a Catholic. Chief among these are the way of the priesthood and the way of religious vows. A society is healthy if its noblest ideals are pursued with zeal. For the Catholic Church, key signs of vitality include the number of those committed to, or in training for, the priestly life or the religious life. Of course, the married life is increasingly scorned, so the married life is becoming more and more heroic relative to the culture. For that matter, just *being* a man or a woman is becoming more and more heroic. Thus, we should

---

[9] Although CARA is working from the *OCD*, in my experience even CARA's numbers change. Further, the 2015 *OCD* shows a different figure for the number of adult Baptisms (44,544) than does CARA (42,751).

[10] For those Catholics who doubt this claim, holding that only card-carrying Catholics can be sanctified and saved, I would refer to two sources. First, there is the Decree of the Holy Office from 1949. See Heinrich Denzinger and Peter Hünermann, *Compendium of Creeds, Definitions, and Declarations on Matters of Faith and Morals*, 43rd ed., ed. Robert Fastiggi and Anne Englund Nash (San Francisco: Ignatius Press, 2012), nos. 3866–3873. When citing from this edition, I will use the standard abbreviation "DH" and include the paragraph numbers: here, DH 3866–3873. Second, consult the fine work of Joseph Clifford Fenton, "The Theological Proof for the Necessity of the Catholic Church: Parts I–III," in *The Church of Christ: A Collection of Essays by Monsignor Joseph C. Fenton*, ed. Christian Washburn (Tacoma: Cluny Media, 2016), 141–202.

also take stock of the practices of the ordinary Catholic, some of whom reach heights of holiness. We have data regarding trends in the number of Catholic marriages and in the rates of weekly Mass attendance. All these data will help us determine the health of the Church in the United States over the past hundred years. We will begin with the priestly and religious life.

In 1920, there were 17 million Catholics in the United States. In 2002, there were 65 million.[11] The number of Catholics recognized in the OCD began to plateau in 2002, rising to only 68 million by 2018.[12] So, from 1920 to 2018, the Catholic population increased by 400 percent. As the number of Catholics expands, the number of priests serving them should likewise expand, *if* the Church is healthy and has adequate financial means. Catholics in America gained the financial means throughout the course of the twentieth century. So, if the Church was healthy, we should have seen steady growth from 1920 to 2018. What actually happened? There was fairly steady growth for forty-five years. In 1920, there were 21,019 priests. From 1920 to 1965, there were almost 1,000 more priests added to the total each year. In 1965, however, growth came almost to a halt. The number of priests plateaued for fifteen years at about 59,000. After 1980, the number of priests steadily declined. In 1990, there were only 52,124 priests. In 2010, there were about 40,000.[13] By 2019, the number fell to about 36,000. As a result, there are fewer priests now than there were in 1945, despite nearly a threefold growth in the Catholic population. The year 1965 marked the end of steady growth and the beginning of a stagnation leading to a steady decline.

---

[11] Jones, *Index*, 11. The chief source for Jones is the volumes of the OCD.

[12] See on the CARA website "Frequently Requested Church Statistics," (FRCS) which incorporates figures from the OCD, https://cara.georgetown.edu/frequently-requested-church-statistics. I found that the OCD reports 71,128,395 in 2015, whereas CARA reports 68,100,000.

[13] I use the data from Jones, *Index*, 15, for the years up to 1965. I use CARA for 1970 onward. Once again, Jones's and CARA's figures are in sufficient agreement overall. They are both working from the OCD.

Priests

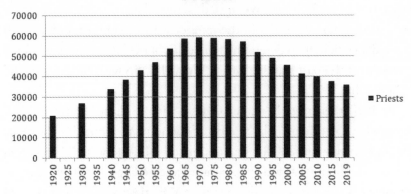

Figure 1 (data from Jones and CARA)

The number of seminarians in the United States tells a more dismal story.[14] In 1920, there were almost 9,000 seminarians. In 1930, there were 16,000. The deviancies of the roaring twenties did not inhibit a large increase in the number of those willing to commit their lives to Christ. The next decade saw modest growth of 5 percent. Perhaps the depression discouraged vocations. At any rate, from 1940 until 1965, the number of seminarians increased steadily, capping at 49,000. After 1965, the number plummeted. By 1970, there were only 28,800 seminarians, a drop of more than 40 percent in just five years. By 1975, the number dropped another 37.5 percent to 18,000. By 1980, it dropped 26 percent to 13,200. Ten years later, the figure dropped 53 percent to 6,200. In 2015, only 4,785 men were seminarians.[15] The number of seminarians grew steadily from 1920 until 1965, but from 1965 to 2002, the number dropped 90 percent. Despite this catastrophic decline since 1965, the Catholic population grew by 43 percent.

---

[14] For data, I am relying on Jones through 1995 and the OCD from 2000 through 2015. This is certainly not ideal, but the numbers do dovetail with sufficient proximity to yield a basic and harmonious narrative.

[15] OCD, 2015.

Seminarians

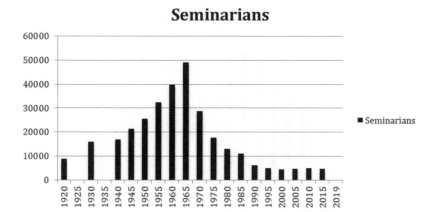

Figure 2 (data from Jones and OCD)

The year 1965 was a tragic watershed. There was modest growth during the first decade of the third millennium. While every generation is filled with sinners, not every generation strives to follow Christ's call. Before 1965, the heavenly homeland inspired many a young man to abandon the promise of life with a woman and children for the life of priestly sacrifice. Now, few men seek to trek those heights.

Pursuit of the heavenly homeland is yet more radical in the religious life. Those who follow this path are like those who sell all that they own to buy a pearl of great price. What happened to religious vocations in the last seventy-five years? Part of this story is woven into the above data on seminarians. The number of religious seminarians — those in the religious life — more than doubled from 1945 to 1965. From 1965 to 1985, however, the number plunged by over 83 percent.[16] The other part of the religious-seminarians story is the number of brothers and sisters. In 1945, there were 6,594 brothers. This number grew steadily until it peaked at 12,271 in 1965. A downward trend began the following year. By 1975, there were only 8,635 brothers. By 2010, there were only 4,690 brothers. In 2019, there were but 3,931. From the high in 1965 to the

---

[16] Jones, *Index*, 31.

Brothers

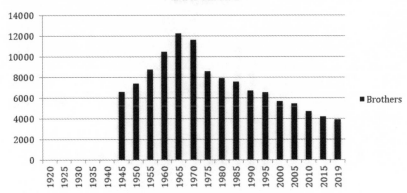

Figure 3 (data from Jones)

year 2019, the number dropped by more than 67 percent.[17] Once again, 1965 was the watershed.

The story of women religious is even more tragic. In 1945, there were 138,079 sisters in the United States. The number of women religious increased 7 percent every five years until its high point in 1965, when there were 179,954 sisters. By 1970, that number decreased 11 percent to 160,931. From 1970 to 1975, the number decreased 16 percent to 135,225. By 2010, there were only 57,544 women religious in the United States.[18] In 2019, there were but 42,441 sisters. From 1965 to 2019, the number of sisters declined by 76 percent.[19]

Each of the above sectors of Church life indicates that since 1965 the worldly mindset, with which each of us is born, has not been effectively converted by the noble call of the Gospel, at least not in the United

---

[17] Ibid., 35. For statistics regarding recent years, see also FRCS.

[18] See Jones, *Index*, 37.

[19] A recent CARA report on the data from the OCD confirms these statistics, placing the exact peak at 1966. See Erick Berrelleza, S.J., Mary L. Gautier, and Mark M. Gray, *Population Trends among Religious Institutes of Women*, CARA Special Report (Washington, DC: CARA at Georgetown University, 2014), https://cara.georgetown.edu/wp-content/uploads/2018/06/Women_Religious_Fall2014_FINAL.pdf.

Sisters

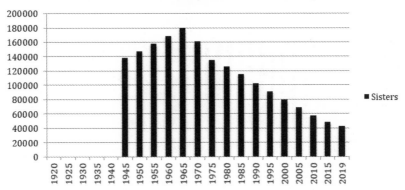

Figure 4 (data from Jones and CARA)

States. We have not fostered ardent charity and magnanimity. As insiders know, we have shunned virility and stunted spiritual growth.

The ordinary way of Catholic life, sacramental marriage, has also imploded in the past fifty years. In 1945, there were 249,140 Catholic marriages celebrated; in 1955, there were 313,652; in 1965, there were 352,458. The number peaked in 1970 with 426,309.[20] The spike from 1965 to 1970 is noteworthy. Two explanations might account for this. First, 20,000 men left the seminary in that period. Second, the baby boomers came of age. At any rate, after 1970, the number of Catholic marriages declined. In 1975, there were only 369,131.[21] In 1995, only 294,144 Catholic marriages were celebrated.[22] In 2010, only 168,400 were celebrated, and in 2019, only 137,885.[23] While the Catholic population grew about 40 percent, the number of Catholic marriages decreased by 67 percent from its high in 1970. These numbers do not promise an increase in Catholic children growing up in stable Catholic households.

---

[20] This is CARA's figure, although Jones has 417,271. See Jones, *Index*, 69.
[21] From CARA; compare with 385,029 from Jones. See Jones, *Index*, 69.
[22] Jones has 305,385. See Jones, *Index*, 69.
[23] See FRCS.

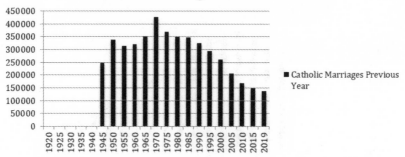

Catholic Marriages Previous Year

Figure 5 (data from Jones and CARA)

The number of those who attend Mass weekly has also decreased. Jones and CARA offer corroborating data on the trend downward, but the latter source presents a more drastic picture. Kenneth Jones, using Gallup surveys, reports that in 1940, roughly 65 percent of American Catholics attended Mass weekly. The percentage increased to about 72 percent in 1950.[24] Jones indicates that in 1975, only 52 percent attended Mass weekly. Georgetown's CARA project paints a bleaker picture. According to CARA, 42 percent attended Mass weekly in 1975, declining to 32.5 percent in 1990, 24.2 percent in 2010, and only 21.1 percent in 2019.[25]

Both Jones and CARA show that the situation is grim. Which is more accurate? The Gallup data, which Jones used, come from surveys rather than on-site measurements. In 1994, Mark Chaves and James Cavendish conducted a smaller study with on-site measurements with headcounts. The CARA data for 1995 approximate this 1994 study.[26] Thus, the percentages that Jones reported may be higher than the percentages of actual attendees. Still, both Jones and CARA show steady trends downward. Finally, in an examination of thirteen dioceses in the

[24] See Jones, *Index*, 73.
[25] See FRCS.
[26] See Jones, *Index*, 73–74.

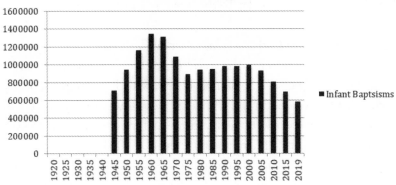

Figure 6 (data from Jones and CARA)

United States, Stephen Bullivant observes that the downward trend accelerated as of 2002.[27]

The number of infant Baptisms in the Church follows a similar trajectory. In 1945, while many men were fighting overseas, there were 710,648 infant Baptisms. In 1950, there were 943,443, and in 1955, there were 1,161,304. The number peaked in 1960 with 1,344,576. In 1965, the number dropped slightly to 1,310,413. It dropped significantly in 1970 to 1,089,000. It dropped to 894,992 in 1975. It then rose to about 990,000 in 1990. It rose again in 2000 to 996,199. Then, it dropped to 929,545 in 2005. In 2010, it dropped to 806,138. In 2015, it dropped again to 693,914. In 2019, it dropped to 582,331. Broadly speaking, the watershed year for infant Baptisms was 1960.

A healthy society maintains in its citizens robust support for its founding premises. In a healthy society, sufficient numbers of its members affirm and express their patriotism, remain willing to defend it even at the cost of life, and pursue activities that support its well-being. The foregoing statistics establish definitively that the Catholic Church in the United

---

[27] See Stephen Bullivant, *Mass Exodus: Catholic Disaffiliation in Britain and America since Vatican II* (Oxford, UK: Oxford University Press, 2019), 229–231.

States is sick in both respects. There are also negative data regarding the Catholic Church worldwide. To these we now briefly turn.

Select Data Regarding Catholic Trends Worldwide
The Catholic population in the world more than doubled from 1970 to 2017. During that period, the number of priests worldwide did not decline nearly as badly as it did in the United States. However, the number did not increase, as we would hope, but decreased from 419,000 to 414,000. The number of sisters fell significantly, from 1,000,000 in 1970 to 650,000 in 2017. That is a drop of 35 percent. In the same period, the number of brothers declined 35 percent, from 79,500 to 51,500. Finally, the number of marriages between two Catholics also declined by 35 percent, from 3.3 million to 2.1 million. There was one inspiring statistic worldwide: the number of graduate-level seminarians more than doubled, from 24,000 in 1975 to 56,000 in 2017. The bulk of this increase took place during the Pontificate of John Paul II. I cannot find world statistics for the years prior to 1970.

Healthy and vibrant societies foster growth and creativity within their members, and this invariably deepens the population's allegiance and loyalty. It also attracts new adherents. A healthy society attracts others, whereas a sick society repels its own. Regarding the metric of attractiveness, is the Catholic Church in the United States healthy or sick? We have data to answer this question.

Data on the Attractiveness of the Catholic Church
We can assess the effective attractiveness of the Catholic Church by examining the numbers of those who join her as adults, leaving their familial religion. Two distinct studies can help us, one of which is diachronic. Georgetown's CARA studied the trajectory in the number of non-Christians who were baptized as Catholics, beginning in 1970. Jones tracked the data from 1930 through 2002. For the years of overlap, Jones and CARA have roughly similar figures.[28] Jones's figures show steady

---

[28] The 2015 *OCD* shows a different figure for the number of adult baptisms (44,544) than does CARA (42,751).

Adult Baptisms

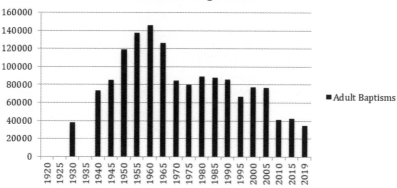

Figure 7 (data from Jones and CARA)

growth from 1930 until 1960. In 1930, there were more than 38,000 adult baptisms into the Church. In 1940, the number grew to 73,000; in 1950, there were more than 119,000, and in 1960, there were more than 146,000. This is significant growth. All that changes in the next ten years. From 1960 to 1970, the number plummeted 42 percent, never to recover. In 1970, there were only 84,000 adult baptisms into the Church. The number hovered at roughly that figure for twenty years. Thereafter, the number declined to 41,000 in 2010 and only 35,138 in 2019.[29] All the while, the nation's population expanded. The watershed year was 1960.

A second study is by Pew Research Center, which investigated net gains to losses in membership of various "religious" groups. Pew's 2014 study, titled "Religious Switching," targets the ratio of persons entering to persons leaving this or that religious group during the period 2007–2014. The study does not include the number of those who enter the religious group from birth or shortly thereafter, thereby eliminating the issue of fertility rates affecting growth or decline. Nor does the study treat Judaism or Islam; it treats only a variety of Christian groups as well as the religiously unaffiliated. Pew's work adds dimensions not covered by CARA. First,

[29] See FRCS.

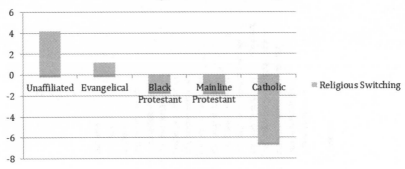

Figure 8 (data from Pew)

Pew studies not only non-Christian adults being baptized as Catholics but also those already baptized who go on to join the Church. Second, Pew compares this number with those who decide to leave. Third, Pew studies five groups, helping us to compare the attractiveness of the Catholic Church with that of other groups. Of the groups studied, only one is experiencing significant overall gains, the "religiously unaffiliated." For every person who leaves this category, 4.2 persons "join." Among Evangelicals, for every person who leaves, 1.2 persons join. These two groups are experiencing gains. Black Protestant communities are experiencing notable net declines: they lose 1.6 members for every one they gain. The group Pew calls "Mainline Protestants" are losing 1.7 members for every one they gain. What of the Catholic Church? For every person who joins the Catholic Church, 6.5 persons leave.[30] You read correctly; the Church in America is hemorrhaging adherents.

Pew's data is corroborated by evidence from another study. In 2016, Public Religion Research Institute (PRRI) conducted a similar study with a smaller sample. Its results approximate those of Pew. PRRI found in 2016 that, on average, 12.8 persons had left the Catholic Church for every 2.5

---

[30] See "Religious Switching" in 2014 Religious Landscape Study of the Pew Research Center. Available at https://www.pewforum.org/2015/05/12/chapter-2-religious-switching-and-intermarriage.

that had entered. This is worse than a 5-to-1 ratio of losses to gains.[31] What do former Catholics become? PRRI indicates that 49 percent of them become religiously unaffiliated.[32] As the Catholic Church hemorrhages, the religiously unaffiliated group grows by leaps and bounds. The Catholic Church appears to be the biggest single supplier of religiously unaffiliated persons. Moreover, PRRI shows that the rate of hemorrhaging is increasing. In 2007, the net loss to gain was 3.9 to 1.[33] A New York Times–CBS poll taken in 1987 claimed that the net losses to gains for the Catholic Church in the United States was 3 to 1.[34] According to these studies, the trend of religious switching gets worse from 1987 to 2016.

We must take stock of all this information. The data from this and the previous section indicate "signs of the times."[35] The Second Vatican Council asks Catholics to interpret the signs of the times in the light of the Gospel. What do these signs tell us?

Changes in Strategy, Policy, and Communication

The dramatic demographic reversals mentioned above pivot on or near 1965. Before that year, there was steady growth. After that year, there was decline. Now, the most significant event for the Catholic Church in that year was

---

[31] Betsy Cooper, Daniel Cox, Rachel Lienesch, and Robert P. Jones, "Exodus: Why Americans Are Leaving Religion—and Why They're Unlikely to Come Back," Public Religion Research Institute, September 22, 2016, https://www.prri.org/research/prri-rns-poll-nones-atheist-leaving-religion.

[32] Daniel Cox and Joanna Piacenza, "A Profile of Former Catholics in the U.S.," Public Religion Research Institute, September 3, 2015, https://www.prri.org/spotlight/profile-of-the-american-former-catholic.

[33] Joseph Liu, "Chapter 2: Changes in Americans' Religious Affiliation," Pew Research Center, February 1, 2008, https://www.pewforum.org/2008/02/01/chapter-2-changes-in-americans-religious-affiliation/#the-dynamics-of-religious-change.

[34] See Bullivant, 221, citing Adam Clymer, "Poll Finds Catholics Defecting from Church," *New York Times*, September 10, 1987, B10.

[35] *Gaudium et spes*, art. 4, in *Vatican Council II*, ed. Austin Flannery (Northport, NY: Costello Publishing, 1975). I have used this translation throughout except where otherwise indicated.

the papal ratification of the Second Vatican Council. This council enacted significant changes, not in doctrine but in strategy, pastoral policy, and communication. Further, despite the notable differences among the popes after the council, each one has continued to espouse and employ those innovations. Is there a causal connection between the decline in the Church's vitality and these changes inaugurated at the Second Vatican Council?

The simple correlation between these trends and the council does not by itself prove causation. To argue "X happened after Y; therefore, X was caused by Y" is a logical fallacy.[36] Let's say that the Cubs won the 2016 World Series the evening after I tweeted, "Cubs'll clobber Kluber" (Kluber being the unbeatable pitcher whom they clobbered the third time around). Obviously, my tweet was not the cause of their victory. So the simple fact that the radical shift in these trends happened after Vatican II does not allow us to assign a causal relationship by itself without further evidence. Still, my tweet was obviously a superficial and inefficacious event. The Second Vatican Council was not a superficial and inefficacious event.

Now, it is not the task of this book to establish a causal connection on a matter so complex. Instead, this book seeks to clarify the truth about several Catholic doctrines that many people now doubt because of current confusions. Still, a few words are in order, since the causal question is relevant to my argument. Readers who want to explore the question of causation should consult, among other works, Stephen Bullivant's *Mass Exodus: Catholic Disaffiliation in Britain and America Since Vatican II*. Bullivant offers a measured approach toward his subject. He points out that this matter is much more complicated than many make out. We all know that great cultural shifts date from that era. These no doubt have caused some decline. Bullivant notes the possibility that the changes enacted by the council helped retain some Catholics and attract new ones even though they may have repelled others. Perhaps some of the reforms were helpful while others were not. Perhaps some things would have been worse without the council. Moreover, as many note, we need to distinguish the real council—its texts—from what some allege to be the "spirit" or "event" of the council.

---

[36] This is the *post hoc ergo propter hoc* fallacy.

Granting these points, Bullivant suggests evidence for a causal connection yielding a net loss. He highlights negative trends *unique* to Catholicism.[37] There are notable differences between the changing health of the Catholic Church and that of peer institutions. Gallup tracked the weekly worship attendance statistics for Catholics *and* for Protestants from 1955 through 2018. These data allow us to determine how Protestant and Catholic communities differently handled the cultural pressures. From 1955 to 2018, Protestant attendance has remained fairly steady, going from 42 percent up to 45 percent after a low point in 1965. By contrast, Catholic attendance has steadily declined. It was 75 percent in 1955, 67 percent in 1965, 54 percent in 1975, and 39 percent in 2018. This difference in changes in worship attendance in the United States is mirrored by drops in membership. Gallup measured the rates of membership among Protestants and among Catholics for the years 1998–2000, 2008–2010, and 2018–2020. Protestant communities went from 73 percent to 72 percent to 64 percent. The Catholic Church went from 76 percent to 73 percent to 48 percent. The overall drop in membership among Catholics from 2000 to 2020 is 18 percent, which is twice that among Protestants.[38] If the causal factors were largely the cultural trends, we would not see such diversity in changes. Note also that the experience of radical changes from 2010 to 2020, between which years we see a dramatic drop in membership, echoes that of the late 1960s and early 1970s. The Catholic Church has not weathered the recent storms as well as Protestant communities. Recall also that in the roaring twenties the number of seminarians grew significantly. The Church was able to thrive during prosperous and increasingly decadent times by proclaiming the full truth with clarity. We should also recall Pew's 2014 study of religious switching. The data in that study show beyond doubt that the Catholic

---

[37] See Bullivant, 260–261.

[38] See Jeffrey M. Jones, "U.S. Church Membership Falls Below Majority for First Time," Gallup, March 29, 2021, https://news.gallup.com/poll/341963/church-membership-falls-below-majority-first-time.aspx?utm_source=newsletter&utm_medium=email&utm_campaign=newsletter_axiosam&stream=top.

Church in America is currently doing far worse than the Evangelicals
and the mainstream Protestant groups. The Church is doing worse than
mainline Protestant denominations by 380 percent. Data such as these
suggest that sustained practice of the communication-strategy changes
of the Catholic Church has proven unfruitful in the United States.

What exactly are the practices and policies that date back to 1965? As
earlier indicated, in 1965, the Magisterium adopted significant changes
in strategy, pastoral policy, and communication. These changes cannot
be summed up in a pithy phrase, but we will note some salient aspects of
some of them in the chapters that follow. Here, however, we will mention only the following notable methodological policy changes practiced
since 1965: (1) The Church has often drafted doctrinal statements with
a strong eye toward their reception by the *world* and not simply with an
eye to the instruction of Catholics.[39] Notable exceptions prove the rule.[40]
(2) Accordingly, the Church has presented some but not all aspects of her
teaching concerning various topics.[41] (3) The Church has preferred biblical and modern expressions to precise modes of expression that had been
employed for centuries (e.g., technical philosophical terms, Scholastic
language, etc.). Concerning this point, we must note that the Church
has often tried to express her dogmas not merely in technical but also in
widely understandable and and inspiring language. This approach also
helps the Church stay close to her biblical and patristic roots. Technical
language was used to disambiguate truth from heresy when heretics hid
behind vague statements. (4) Further, at times the Church has employed
language that is vague, less precise, and sometimes ambiguous.[42] We may
note that previous councils sometimes did the same, especially when

---

[39] She speaks "to the faithful and to the whole human race." *Lumen gentium*
(1964), art. 1; DH 4101.
[40] One can think of the declaration *Ad tuendam fidem* (1998) by John
Paul II, of Benedict XVI's *Summorum Pontificum*, or of announcements
concerning indulgences, etc.
[41] "It does not, however, have it in mind to give a complete doctrine on
Mary." *Lumen gentium*, art. 54; DH 4174.
[42] We will see examples in chapters 4, 5, and 10.

a legitimately disputed matter was not as yet resolved. This approach sometimes gives opportunity for new insight; for example, Vatican II profoundly compares the Church to a sacrament. (5) The Church has rarely issued condemnations of errors but has offered instead descriptive expressions of the Faith.[43] (6) These positive expositions have often been quite lengthy. Compare, for instance, Vatican I's treatment of the Church with that of Vatican II. Now, sometimes this very length has allowed a *fuller* exposition of a mystery than would a simple definition or anathema. For example, *Lumen gentium* explored many of the marvelous aspects of the complex mystery of the Church, also advancing doctrine on the episcopate, just as *Dei verbum* explored the historical aspects of revelation. (7) The Church has stressed the positive about human existence, culture, other religions, and the world, treating the negative in passing. (8) The Church has rarely disciplined heretics and renegades.

Now, many, if not all, of the new strategic decisions and policies are, for a purpose and for a season, acceptable in themselves. Globally, such an approach can be likened to the skill with which to begin a difficult conversation with someone who is unfamiliar with or skeptical about one's views. Pope Leo XIII approved a limited employment of this manner of approach in America:

> If, among the different ways of preaching the word of God that one sometimes seems to be preferable, which [is] directed to non-Catholics, not in churches, but in some suitable place, in such wise that controversy is not sought, but friendly conference, such a method is certainly without fault.... For we think that there are many in your country who are separated from Catholic truth more by ignorance than by ill-will, who might perchance more easily be drawn to the one fold of Christ if this truth be set forth to them in a friendly and familiar way.[44]

---

[43] See John XXIII, opening address of the Second Vatican Council, October 12, 1962.

[44] Leo XIII, *Testem benevolentiae*, art. 25.

False Mercy

Stating a portion of the truth can sometimes be more effective than stating the whole truth. Furthermore, no council should be burdened with the job of repeating everything already taught on a topic. Surely, presenting the world at large with the most attractive and immediately acceptable depiction of the Catholic Faith can win attention and a second hearing. The faith *is* beautiful, and the scriptural narratives show us that our Faith is concrete and real, not abstract. Few people are prepared to understand, much less enjoy, Scholastic language. The use of modern expressions can help contemporaries receive the Church's heritage. Honey attracts more flies than vinegar. Jesus didn't go around grousing; He preached the kingdom. For example, He accompanied the woman at the well and brought her toward a fuller appreciation of His identity. Similarly, St. Paul urged us to meditate on "whatever is true, whatever is pure" (see Phil. 4:8), and he used pagan writings to preach (Acts 17:22ff). For his part, St. Augustine found admirable insights among the heathen, as did St. Thomas Aquinas. St. John Henry Newman found elements of truth in world religions. Psychologically, it is healthy to understand error in the light of truth and evil in the light of the good. Such an approach can foster joy, which is proper to the Gospel. I trace my own conversion to the enthusiasm of John Paul II, which was inspired in part by these aspects of the recent council. His attitude inspired others who helped propel me into the Faith and more deeply into its adventure.

So we can consider these strategies as exemplifying characteristics of conversation that invite further discussion and consideration. These strategies yielded some positive effects. Still, in light of the data treated above and in light of the confusion that the faithful are experiencing about their Faith, it is reasonable to ask whether sustaining these strategic changes in a monolithic way remains prudent today. (Note that I am not considering here legitimate developments in doctrine, some of which will be indicated in later chapters. Legitimate development of doctrine can never be the intrinsic cause of a bad effect.) Cannot continued silence on half the truth be misunderstood as a denial of truth? Cannot routine imprecision and ambiguity of language give the appearance of noncommitment and even substantive change? Cannot wordiness obfuscate attention to crucial truths, especially those doubted or disputed by the world? Cannot the sole focus on positive messages cause us to lower our guard against errors and heresies? Cannot the failure to condemn current errors imply that they are not grave? Cannot the refusal to discipline renegades signal approval of their causes? Cannot the abandonment of customary modes of expression be mistaken for abandonment of substance?

In fact, renegade theologians have deceptively argued that these new strategies support doctrinal revolution; for them, the council did not go far enough. It was an event that marked the beginning of a new Catholic order. And, more frequently than not, these scholars have done so with impunity. For example, Hermann J. Pottmeyer, a theology professor in Germany, depicts Vatican II as a "rebellion against centralization." He likens Vatican II to a "building site" that shows only the foundations of a future edifice destined to replace the old edifice — namely, the "nineteenth- and twentieth-century Vatican centralization," rooted in Vatican I, which stood in the way of Vatican II's progressive project. Today, "While the building erected by centralization awaits demolition, as the old St. Peter's Basilica did in its day, the four supporting pillars of a renewed church and a renewed ecclesiology wait to be crowned by the dome that draws them into unity."[45] What? Are we to liken Vatican I to an inconvenient eyesore that wastes space and needs to be demolished? Other theologians have unwittingly supported the cause of these rebels, taking marching orders from the leaders of the new modernism. Still others have been caught in the undertow of this movement. Even some on the side of the angels take almost their sole orientation from the council, neglecting to gain adequate formation from the great tradition so as to interpret the council in the manner Paul VI indicated.

Cannot a reasonable person infer some causal connection between sustained and monolithic practice of the above-noted policies in our concrete situation and the measurable loss of faith among Catholics?

---

[45] Hermann J. Pottmeyer, *Towards a Papacy in Communion: Perspectives from Vatican Councils I & II*, trans. Matthew J. O'Connell (New York: Crossroad, 1998), 110–11. Massimo Faggioli of Villanova twice cites this passage favorably in his *Vatican II: The Battle for Meaning* (New York: Paulist Press, 2012), 98 and 124.

False Mercy

Pope Leo XIII once critiqued those Americans who erroneously urged that "in order to more easily attract those who differ from her, the Church should shape her teachings more in accord with the spirit of the age and relax some of her ancient severity and make some concessions to new opinions."[46] A great lover of the flock, he warned: "Let it be far from anyone's mind to suppress for any reason any doctrine that has been handed down. Such a policy would tend rather to separate Catholics from the Church than to bring in those who differ."[47]

Now, loss of faith weakens the desire to carry out Catholic duties; it dampens the courage to live heroically. Charity and fervor grow cold. The revolutionaries have succeeded in watering down Catholicism. This lukewarm version of Catholicism espouses the general error of doctrinal evolutionism as well as specific doctrinal errors. The specific errors that afflict us today contradict one crucial and overarching message of true Catholicism: earthly life is a pilgrimage of preparation for union with God, which is conditional upon a life of holiness, which is made possible only through Jesus Christ, who founded the Catholic Church as instrument of salvation.

Can watered-down Catholicism inspire zeal for greatness? No. If watered-down Catholicism were true, one could simply bank on Heaven while either (1) enjoying life on Earth with its many pleasantries—the bourgeois dream—or (2) working militantly for the elusive promise of a better future—the Marxist delusion of liberation theology. In either case, why attend the Sacrifice of the Mass for this message? Why leave father and mother, wife and children to seek the kingdom? Why believe in Hell when frolicking about in the weeds is a guilt-free alternative? While infants are slaughtered, why believe that Christ paid a price for us so that we might be forgiven and attain salvation? Why bother about fidelity in marriage? Why refrain from perverse sexual pleasure? Why risk reputation and neck in service of the Gospel? Why encourage Muslim neighbors to convert to Christ, true Prophet and true God? Why cling

---

[46] Leo XIII, *Testem benevolentiae*, art. 4.
[47] Ibid., art. 6.

to "old truths" if truth can change at the whim of an errant bishop or a renegade priest?

Watered-down Catholicism cannot do it for us. We need the full Catholic truth taught clearly. *We need a Catholic huddle!* I draw the analogy from American football. A team can take press conferences after the game, but during the game, team leaders need to strategize and speak clearly to players on their team. Similarly, Catholics need the bishops to speak *to them*, not merely to the world. The analogy is not perfect, since the Catholic "team" is *for* the salvation of all; it is not an opponent of other teams. But if we do not know what salvation is or how to get there or get others there, then *who* can be saved? Needy and hungry, Catholics need bishops to speak the *whole* truth, not just parts of it. Confused by conflicting messages, they need their bishops to speak plainly and unambiguously. Bewildered by innovations, they need their bishops to induct them into the doctrinal language of the ages, even if it is at first unfamiliar. Seduced by worldly spirits, Catholics need bishops to condemn errors and heresies, for these are grave obstacles that undermine genuine faith, true charity, and eternal salvation. Wavering Catholics need their pastors to give them confidence that Catholic truth is knowable and unchanging. Catholics need bishops who remember that their primary duty as protectors of the Faith is to communicate with the Catholic faithful.

Further, the world itself needs the whole truth, for only in truth is there freedom, love, and friendship. Above all, we must *never* adapt the truth of Christ to the perverse appetites of the world. The Gnostics falsely claimed that Christ *adapted* the truth to the erroneous preconceptions of His hearers. As Irenaeus rightly retorted, to do that would not be the act of a healing physician.[48] Only truth, the fullness of truth, will guide us to the waters of life. We need not lose the grace of tact. Gracefulness, tact, prudence, cheerfulness, and charity are always needful. Truth barked out of an angry mouth can be frightening. But sentiment without truth is not love.

---

[48] See Irenaeus, *Against Heresies*, bk. III, chap. 5.

False Mercy

Clarity and Orthodoxy Lead to Positive Results

As Catholic common sense — the *sensus fidelium* — indicates, a partial and ambiguous proclamation of Catholic truth naturally leads to a sickening of the Faith. The data confirm this judgment by indicating a correlation between an incomplete, ambiguous proclamation of the truth and unhealthy demographic results. Conversely, there is evidence that suggests a correlation between healthy vital signs and comprehensive, clear, orthodox teaching, coupled with traditional piety. There are dioceses and religious orders that (1) embrace Catholic orthodoxy enthusiastically and live the traditional expressions of piety more fervently and that (2) have experienced notable increases in vocations. To be sure, this corroborating evidence is not complete. However, it does contribute toward a fuller understanding by providing a counterpoint to the negative overall trends.

We can point to religious orders that are committed to the Church's perennial teaching and to authentic worship of God and discipleship of Jesus Christ. In the United States, the Dominican Sisters of Mary, Mother of the Eucharist is a religious order formed in 1997. While relatively new, they have 97 sisters who have made final profession as of 2020. They have 41 sisters in formation. The average age of a sister in this community is only 32. They are young; they are healthy. These are remarkable figures for such a newly formed community. They are a ray of hope.

The community from which these sisters originated — the Dominican Sisters of the Congregation of St. Cecilia, otherwise known as the "Nashville Dominicans" — has also experienced steady growth since the early 1980s. The Nashville Dominicans had an explosion of growth from 2000 through 2010.[49] It is widely known that both communities live their discipleship of Christ joyfully and embrace all the teachings of the Catholic Church enthusiastically.

Another group of sisters that zealously embraces the traditional acts of devotion in the Catholic Church is the Religious Sisters of Mercy in

---

[49] See Berrelleza, Gautier, and Gray, *Population Trends*, 5.

Alma, Michigan. This community has experienced steady growth from the early 1970s.

These cases are evidence that supports the judgment of Catholic common sense: where the teachings and traditional practices of the Church are embraced unambiguously and with joy, there should be growth and vitality.[50]

Unsurprisingly, *America*, a Jesuit-run magazine, does not agree.[51] In its pages, Patricia Wittberg attempts to explain away the positive trends experienced in more traditional communities of women religious. She adduces as evidence that the raw number of new vocations to traditional women's religious communities — those in the Council of Major Superiors of Women Religious (CMSWR) — is the same as that to the progressive women's religious communities — those in the Leadership Conference of Women Religious (LCWR).[52] Each set of congregations, Wittberg relates,

---

[50] Ibid.

[51] The Jesuit magazine *America* publishes articles that defend women's ordination and provides a platform for their controversial editor-at-large, Fr. James Martin, S.J.

[52] Patricia Wittberg, "Reality Check: A Fact-Based Assessment of U.S. Religious Life," *America*, August 13, 2012, https://www.americamagazine. org/issue/5148/100/reality-check. A quick examination of the websites for each group reveals that the sisters belonging to CMSWR congregations enjoy wearing the religious habit, whereas those belonging to LCWR congregations do not. Clothing speaks loudly. At any rate, the anecdotal argument made here is supported by data. In a recent study out of Canada, professional researchers claim, "Whatever the underlying explanation, theological conservatism of both clergy and congregants are significant predictors of growth in this sample of growing and declining mainline Protestant churches in southern Ontario, even after controlling for a wide range of other relevant church- and individual-level factors. This finding, based as it is on a detailed quantitative and qualitative examination of an understudied group of churches, clergy and congregants, represents a significant, if preliminary, contribution to research on religion in Canada." See David Millard Haskell, Kevin N. Flatt, and Stephanie Burgoyne, "Theology Matters: Comparing the Traits of Growing and Declining Mainline Protestant Church Attendees and Clergy," *Review of Religious Research* 58 (2016): 539.

had exactly 73 new candidates in the year 2009. She concludes from this that there is no significant correlation between vitality and being traditional. There is a significant problem in Wittberg's argument, however. There are more religious communities in the LCWR (173) than there are in the CMSWR. The LCWR, although dying, represents the majority of nuns in the United States; its congregations collectively are wealthy with many resources. The CMSWR congregations are far fewer. Merely because the total number of candidates is the same for each group does not indicate equivalent vitality. Since the fewer orthodox communities are attracting 73 young women, they are showing greater vitality than the progressive congregations. Wittberg herself notes that the median number of entrants into any LCWR community was only 1, while that into any CMSWR community was 4. Thus, each CMSWR community is, on average, 400 percent more attractive. We should, of course, hope and pray for more robust health in the traditional congregations, but we can thank God that they are experiencing real growth. We should also note that each of the traditional congregations follows the texts of the Second Vatican Council. They do not use the council as an excuse to evade the great Catholic tradition. They do not foist an alien "spirit" on the council.

As for priestly vocations, some dioceses have had noteworthy success. The Diocese of Wichita, for example, recently experienced a 20 percent growth in their priestly population within just two years.[53] What a counterpoint to the shrinking populations of priests in most dioceses! Among the explanations that the diocese has given for this growth is the large number of chapels dedicated to perpetual adoration. The diocese is known for its love of the teachings of the Catholic Church. The priests also have a great spirit of collegiality. Wichita is a largely rural diocese made up of small towns where the parish is the center of social activity. Here it is unsurprising that the more conservative culture is friendly to

---

[53] Mary Farrow, "What's the Secret Sauce in Wichita's Vocations Boom?" Catholic News Agency, June 7, 2018, https://www.catholicnewsagency.com/news/whats-the-secret-sauce-in-wichitas-vocations-boom-46562.

religious vocations. Orthodox teaching in schools and catechesis in parishes play a role. The diocese also sponsors popular programs for young people to help them discern whether they have a vocation. Finally, the diocese has a policy of funding Catholic elementary schools by Sunday donations, so that the poor may attend. What a model for every diocese in the nation! Ultimately, the Church will not see a rise in vocations until she proactively invests in her young people.

Those familiar with the "East Coast Dominicans"—the Province of St. Joseph—also know that they have experienced a sustained explosion in vocations for two or more decades. They are rock-solid in orthodoxy, stress virtuous living and a beautiful liturgy, and live their vocation joyfully. Growing pains occasioned for them the blessing of a massive addition to their house of formation.

Finally, we can point to the success of explicitly traditionalist movements. The Priestly Fraternity of St. Peter (FSSP), for example, has sustained good numbers for a long time. From 1990 to 1994, their seminary in Wigratzbad averaged more than 60 seminarians per year. After they expanded to America, their numbers rose. From 1995 to 2000, they grew steadily each year, topping out at about 135 seminarians. From 2001 to 2008 (the year in which they added a seminary in Sydney), their numbers held even at about 110 seminarians. From 2010 to the present, they have averaged more than 140 seminarians. Moreover, scores and scores of families are moving closer to parishes staffed by the FSSP. One sees a very young population in these traditional parishes; the boisterous cries of babes bring hope and solace even during Mass. I have been grateful to God for my membership in an FSSP parish. I can trust the homilies to deliver the Catholic Faith and not venture into errors or worthless speculations. Further, the traditional liturgy attracts worshippers from many ethnic and racial backgrounds, highlighting how the Church is universal and how the Mass, when celebrated properly, can enrich parish life in many ways.

These positive trends in communities that embrace the teachings of the Church contrast radically with the declining trends that exist overall in the United States. Such contrasting trends suggest that authentic

Catholicism is attractive, whereas watered-down Catholicism is repugnant. What is worse is that there may have been, in some places, concerted efforts to thwart good and healthy vocations. Archbishop Eldin Curtiss of Omaha claimed in 1996 that there is no crisis in vocations, only a crisis in faith. He added that dissenters place obstacles in the path of good vocations:

> I personally think the vocation "crisis" in this country is more artificial and contrived than many people realize. When dioceses and religious communities are unambiguous about ordained priesthood and vowed religious life as the Church defines these calls; when there is strong support for vocations, and a minimum of dissent about the male celibate priesthood and religious life loyal to the Magisterium; when bishop, priests, Religious and lay people are united in vocation ministry—then there are documented increases in the numbers of candidates who respond to the call.
>
> It seems to me that the vocation "crisis" is precipitated and continued by people who want to change the Church's agenda, by people who do not support orthodox candidates loyal to the Magisterial teaching of the Pope and bishops, and by people who actually discourage viable candidates from seeking priesthood and vowed religious life as the Church defines the ministries.
>
> I am personally aware of certain vocation directors, vocation teams and evaluation boards who turn away candidates who do not support the possibility of ordaining women or who defend the Church's teaching about artificial birth control, or who exhibit a strong piety toward certain devotions, such as the Rosary.[54]

He continues:

> And the same people who precipitate a decline in vocations by their negative actions call for the ordination of married men and

---

[54] Archbishop Elden Curtiss, "Crisis in Vocations? What Crisis?" *Christian Order* (March 1996), https://www.ewtn.com/catholicism/library/crisis-in-vocations-what-crisis-3905.

women to replace the vocations they have discouraged. They have a death wish for ordained priesthood and vowed religious life as the Church defines them. They undermine the vocation ministry they are supposed to champion.[55]

I concur with the archbishop. People I know experienced firsthand the contagion of sodomy in seminaries of the 1980s and 1990s and the witch-like laughter of progressives dismissing the traditional teachings of great popes such as Pius XII. Who would want to follow weak and effeminate men, who refuse to preach the Gospel, into the priesthood? And what woman would want to leave the opportunity of a wonderful marriage for life as an angry, plain-clothed nun campaigning for "social justice"?

Even though analyzing statistics to determine causal factors is not a simple process, the statistics verify what common sense tells us: where there is love of the whole truth and traditional worship, there should be growth. We were made for God, not for the world.

Overview and Structure of the Book

The present book aims to present clearly certain teachings that are questioned today, especially those associated with a central claim of Catholicism that life is a pilgrimage in response to God's love, either toward Heaven or toward Hell. To serve this end, the book identifies and refutes some heresies and errors that call these truths into question. Now, the "modernists" who espouse these heresies pretend to find justification for their mistakes in some recent magisterial statements that are incomplete or ambiguous; they conveniently ignore or even reject clear teachings opposed to their agenda. This book exposes the futility of the modernist strategy. It does so by practicing a "hermeneutic of continuity" in a specific mode.

The "hermeneutic of continuity" is a phrase coined by Pope Benedict XVI to help explain how we should interpret the Second Vatican Council. In his Christmas address to the Curia in 2005, Benedict observed that

---

[55] Ibid.

some theologians read Vatican II as though it were in "discontinuity and rupture" from the Church's great tradition. Today's modernists do exactly that: they justify their dilution or distortion of dogma by attributing a false meaning to the conciliar documents. As we shall see, this method of abusing the council leads to errors in the Faith and even to heresy. Pope Benedict rejected this misinterpretation of the council. He also criticized those who, rightly loving the great tradition, simply reject the texts as a total rupture. (Such theologians should *not* be confused with those faithful scholars who accept the texts according to their authority, interpret them in light of the great tradition, appreciate their contributions, and yet find here or there some detrimental weaknesses of ambiguity, imprecision, incompleteness, overenthusiastic optimism, or the like. Joseph Cardinal Ratzinger did not hesitate to criticize some documents, even though he was generally highly appreciative of the council.) The theologians who simply reject the documents resist new developments. Benedict counseled instead a "'hermeneutic of reform,' of renewal in the continuity of the one subject-Church."[56] He was identifying how to discern authentic dogmatic development. As we shall see in the next chapter, genuine dogmatic development never involves dilution or distortion of infallible teachings. These teachings remain forever true. We may never depart from them. Adopting Benedict's terminology and direction, faithful theologians contrast the "hermeneutic of rupture" with the "hermeneutic of continuity." The latter hermeneutic allows for theological development in understanding of the unchanging Faith while insisting on the perpetual validity of dogmas and infallible doctrines that articulate the one deposit of faith.

In the face of the new modernism, the hermeneutic of continuity should be exercised in two modes: the exegetical mode and the preservative mode. The exegetical mode attempts to show how newer statements can be interpreted to be in continuity with the constant and unchanging Faith. The exegetical mode is laudable and has been widely adopted. Still,

[56] See Pope Benedict XVI, Christmas Message to the Roman Curia, December 22, 2005.

it is also cumbersome. Further, it focuses on exegesis of recent statements, not on the very Faith itself. But the Faith itself is more important than expressions of it. Further, this very Faith is in jeopardy because of the new modernists and the benign forgetfulness of doctrine. Therefore, another mode of the hermeneutic of continuity is needed: the preservative mode. This mode focuses on the perennial Faith and defends it against all distortion or dilution. Its axiom can be expressed as follows: no Catholic has any excuse to water down, distort, or renounce past infallible teachings. This is why it would be pure abuse to use any recent magisterial statement—even if ambiguous, imprecise, unclear, or incomplete—in such a way as to reject or distort past infallible teaching. The preservative mode is clear and straightforward. Since the task of the present book is to help Catholics understand clearly some basic teachings of the Faith that have pastoral and moral implications, it primarily practices the preservative mode of the hermeneutic of continuity. Still, it undertakes the exegetical mode in key places, highlighting thereby some of the contributions of the Second Vatican Council to Catholic life.

Chapter 1 tackles the heresy of doctrinal "evolutionism." This heresy is the fountainhead and offspring of the others that follow. It is the fountainhead because it sets the global expectation that perennial teaching can and perhaps will change. It is the offspring because, when one *thinks* that some doctrine or other has changed, one concludes that doctrines *can* evolve.

Each chapter from 2 through 9 examines a specific heresy or error of watered-down Catholicism. These errors war against a crucial, overarching message of true Catholicism: that earthly life is a journey and a trial, whereby we make our way either to Heaven or to Hell. Each of these heresies espouses a *false* sense of mercy, making it look as though the hard way of Christ is indistinguishable from the easy way of the world. Some admire and praise this false mercy. They call "harsh" anyone who repeats Christ's own words about sin and damnation. They are mistaken. False mercy is destructive. It does not will the true good of the sinner. It fails to help the sinner root out the evil. Meanwhile, sin and evil damage the soul. The sinner needs not only to be loved where he is but also to be led toward a better place. If we simply sit with the sinner and drink beer with him for hours on end, never mentioning the sin, never calling him to conversion, he will continue in his sin. Or perhaps his mind will wander off to the sin that nags at him. He will suffocate in silence before us, wondering whether he can ever escape, while he waits for clarification. When we are falsely merciful, we despair about the sinner. We despair, and we invite him to despair. False mercy emerges from despair. It can also invent presumptuous ways out of the despair, claiming that all shall be saved, or that faith alone justifies, or that one's religion doesn't matter, or that sin is no longer sinful.

Chapters 2 through 9 have similar parts, although not always in the same order. Each identifies a specific error, expounds reasons alleged in its favor, and counters the error with Church teaching and theological argument. Readers will thus be equipped to avoid recent heresies and to assist others in avoiding them. Chapter 10 consists in abbreviated treatments of a number of other heresies and errors. In this way, one can get a basic sense of the scope of the crisis and a basic prescription to remedy this or that error.

Chapter 2 deals with the idle dream of those who hope that Hell is or might be empty. This is an error, and it also suggests that life is not serious. To the contrary, life is serious; it is a glorious calling, and the stakes are extreme. But in case Hell might not be empty, some attempt to seek shelter in Luther's fantasy of justification by faith alone. Chapter 3 critiques Luther's theory and shows why there is no reason for Catholics to accept his error. Chapter 4 treats the theme of Christ as "sinner," Luther's blasphemous reading of Christ's redemptive act in support of his theory of justification. The upshot of these three chapters is that Hell is populated and that obedience to the commandments, not "faith alone," is required for salvation. But clearly, such a life is difficult. So how does God make available salvation in Christ?

Chapters 5 through 7 deal with how God communicates to us His plan of and means for salvation. They discuss the Catholic Church, which embodies the one true religion, founded by Christ on the basis of His redemptive act. Chapter 5 explores the truth that Jesus Christ founded only one Church, the Catholic Church. True, there are other Christian communities that share, to various degrees, in the gifts that characterize Christ's Church. Still, these gifts belong by right to the Catholic Church and thus objectively tend toward the incorporation of non-Catholic Christian communities into the Catholic Church. Chapter 6 argues that the true religion Christ left us is a coherent whole, not a collection of disparate practices. As such, it is practiced *only* in the Catholic Church. True, other religions have some noble elements, as well as grave errors, but Christ founded only the Catholic religion, in which the promises of the Old Covenant are continued and fulfilled. Thus, the noble aspirations of man, awakened differently in this or that culture, are called to submit themselves to the one true religion. In this submission, these noble aspirations can, having been purified and elevated, contribute toward the beautification of the practice of the one true religion. The Greek liturgy came to us not simply from God above but also from a rich cultural heritage.[57] Similarly, we can expect great things to come from the cultural and intellectual beauty in the East and the Middle East, *if* these cultures take on the easy yoke of Christ and shoulder His cross. Clearly, the incorporation of these good things into Catholic devotion and worship depends on the spread of the Catholic Faith. Hence, chapter 7 treats the topic of evangelization, which some dismiss as a sin. In sum, chapters 5 through 7 treat the modernist denial of the exclusive claims of the Catholic Church. Some modernist principles are true while others are false. These chapters disentangle the false from the true so as to recover the perennial truth.

Chapters 8 and 9 deal with yet one more strategy of the modernists: the denial of the sinfulness of sinful actions. This is the final strategy, as it were: just in case Hell is not empty and just in case justification by faith alone is a bust, they propose that the things we used to call sinful are no longer sinful. Because one book is inadequate to cover comprehensively

---

[57] Of course, these gifts of culture are ultimately from God. Still, their "entry" into or effective existence within the practices of the Church is not part and parcel of the institution of the Church in her essence.

the breadth of the crisis, chapter 10 takes up a number of other errors and heresies more briefly so that the reader can appreciate the scope of the problem.

We must trust God that the Catholic Church can weather the current storm. We can gather reasons for hope from the past. The Catholic Church has been shaken many times by various scandals. We have suffered through murderous and lascivious bishops and popes, not to mention despotic and greedy ones. We have even suffered through bishops and popes that courted or neglected to condemn error and heresy. In the fourth century, the Church was rocked by the Arian heresy. So many of the faithful and so many bishops became Arian that, according to St. Jerome, the world groaned to find itself Arian. Today, the world finds the Catholic Church in the midst of a "diabolical disorientation."[58] But just as we survived terrible crises in ages past, so we will survive the present crisis.

The Catholic life is not easy. Who would seek the narrow gate when the yawning gate of worldliness lies close at hand? Who would dare trek the hard path that leads to life when faced with enticing, easy pleasures? To live the Catholic life is not "natural" in the colloquial sense of what comes easy. It is challenging. One must be inspired to live it. One must be called to greatness.

What can help us mount up to such greatness? Watered down Catholicism? Hardly. Only true Catholicism prepares us for greatness. True Catholicism is found where the full truth is spoken clearly and unambiguously in the Catholic huddle. This book is intended to serve the Catholic huddle. It encourages the reader to fulfill his or her baptismal obligation to confess the holy Catholic Faith in its entirety and to refuse to be seduced by those who use ambiguous or incomplete statements to the detriment of that obligation. Thus, it is hoped, the reader will make his way to God's heavenly kingdom, our only true home.

---

[58] The words of Lucia, a seer at Fátima.

1

Dogmas: Here Today, Gone Tomorrow?

Many people today believe or fear that the Catholic Church *can* or *might* change her dogmas. They have this belief largely because of the errors we will detail in the chapters that follow. The new modernist mantra inculcates this feeling: "We used to think *that*. But the Church has changed. Now we think *this*." Martin Sheen portrays this mindset in the remarkable 1973 film *The Conflict*. He plays a young revolutionary priest sent by Rome to reconcile to the Church a breakaway group of traditionalist Irish monks who oppose the radicalization of their religion. We learn from Sheen that "Vatican IV" jettisoned the dogma of transubstantiation. Theological radicals justify their conviction with appeals to the false notion of "dogmatic evolutionism," according to which dogmas develop just as species evolve. Just as an older species must go extinct so that a newer species can evolve, so, the modernists say, older dogmas must give way to newer dogmas in order that the faith life may survive. Sadly, some good theologians get caught in the undertow of this modernism.

This view of doctrinal development is itself heretical. So our current situation involves a combination of two kinds of error: the substantive error of this or that heresy and the methodological error of a false notion of development.

To combat the errors that currently threaten Catholic teaching, we must first correct this false notion of doctrinal evolution. By examining this methodological error that undermines authentic teaching on development, we will get a global view of the problem. To understand the Church's teaching on doctrinal development, we begin with an examination of the deposit of faith and the Magisterium.

The Deposit of Faith

Vatican I makes it clear that revelation involves God's communication to man of His mysteries and decrees: "It pleased his wisdom and goodness to reveal himself and the eternal decrees of his will."[59] Vatican II, elaborating this truth and developing appreciation of the historical dimension, states that this public revelation was accomplished over time, through deeds and words. Furthermore, the council upholds the constant and universal tradition that the historical act of revelation came to a close at the end of the apostolic era. That is, by the end of the apostolic era, God had entrusted to the Catholic Church a deposit of revealed truths to be guarded, explicated, and promulgated. This deposit was found in two expressions or vehicles by which it might be handed on: Sacred Scripture and Sacred Tradition.[60] So the deposit of faith that God gave to the world is *transmitted* to us through Scripture and Tradition. For this reason, Scripture and Tradition have long been called "sources" of revelation.[61]

Now, we embrace as true all the contents of this deposit by the virtue of faith. We accept these contents not because we agree with them individually or find them beautiful. Rather, we accept them in virtue of the authority of God, who is a trustworthy revealer. Our discipleship of Christ leads us, therefore, to accept everything He has said. Of course, those who do not yet accept Him must inquire and look for the appropriate signs of authenticity. But believers who follow Him and

---

[59] *Dei Filius*, chap. 2; DH 3004.
[60] The classical expressions were "sacred scriptures" and "sacred traditions" in the plural.
[61] See chapter 10.

subsequently reject even one of His teachings sin against the Faith and therefore lose the very virtue of faith itself. They accept only what they can see to be true or beautiful. It is no longer enough for them that God has spoken. We shall encounter this point again in greater detail in chapter 7.

Obviously, it is difficult to interpret these sources of revelation for a number of reasons. For its part, Scripture contains many passages that are difficult to understand. What does "God hardened Pharaoh's heart" mean? What did Jesus mean when He said, in the same breath, "Eat my flesh" and "The flesh is of no avail"? These difficulties are not problems. They conceal great treasures, but they require faithful explication. They promise rich rewards if mined with faith and humility. So Scripture re-quires interpretative care.

For its part, Tradition is not written down; it is the entire deposit as handed down in various ways other than the inspired Scriptures. Thus, Tradition is in some senses even more difficult to interpret than Scripture. We can, however, discern the contents of Tradition through witnesses to or expressions of it. The writings of the Church Fathers bear witness to Tradition, as do the liturgical and sacramental institutions. The holiness of the saints also gives witness to Tradition. So the Sacred Tradition does come to written expression; we call it "non-written" in the sense that it is not Scripture itself. We do not claim, therefore, that the expressions of Tradition, such as the writings of the Fathers, are inspired. Finally, both Scripture and Tradition deal with great mysteries. Granted, even a young child can make a real act of faith in God, in the Incarnation, and in the Eucharist; yet even the brightest of men struggle to grasp the mysteries of the Faith and this or that passage of Scripture.

Since the sources of revelation are difficult of interpretation, we need assistance. God wishes us to understand His revelation in a manner sufficient to direct our lives to Him in a human way. Catholics believe that God has entrusted an interpretative helper to mankind, so that all might rightly fathom His revelation as the times and circumstances of life change. This helper is the Magisterium, hierarchical communion with which is integral to living Catholicism well.

False Mercy

The Magisterium and Doctrine

Magisterial Words versus Words of a Magisterial Official

The Magisterium is the teaching office of the Church. Those who exercise the ministry of this office are the pope and the bishops in communion with him. Does this mean that everything these persons do is "magisterial"? No. Not everything that comes out of the mouth of a member of the Magisterium is magisterial and has magisterial authority.

It can happen that one who occupies a magisterial office speaks or writes as a "private person" and not as a member of that office. The phrase "acting as private person" does not mean, "acting secretly." It means acting *outside* the office one holds, even if the act is publicized. In recent memory, magisterial authorities have acted in both ways, as have secular authorities. Sometimes a politician tweets or offers an interview; such acts are not authoritative acts. They are merely acts of a man who happens to be a politician; they are personal opinions, even if publicly aired. Similarly, a Church official can publicize his personal opinions. When so acting, he is speaking merely as a private person. We must distinguish authoritative words from words that happen to come from a person in authority or, in this case, a member of the Magisterium.[62] Magisterial words are authoritative; words of one who happens to occupy a magisterial office are not authoritative. In the case of the pope, we distinguish papal words from words of a pope. Words of a pope are the words of a man who happens to be pope. Papal words are authoritative; mere words of a pope are not.

"Words of a pope" and "words of a magisterial official" are more pervasive today than they used to be. It used to be that one who occupied such an office limited his public expressions to acts of his office. There were reasons for this practice: dying to self and serving others. Another reason was to preserve the mark of authority, lest truly authoritative

---

[62] Although, when taken widely, the expression "words of one who happens to be a member of the Magisterium" includes both magisterial and nonmagisterial words, I reserve this phrase to indicate only those words that are nonmagisterial.

statements be ignored together with nonauthoritative statements. One can think of Pius XII as an example. He seemed to act and speak to the world only as a public person, hardly ever as a private person. Because of this approach, most of the words of Pius XII were papal words. To be sure, he had his confidences with friends, but he did not project personal views publicly. More recently, popes have projected their personal views publicly, perhaps to show a personal touch and win the affection of the people, even for the sake of Christ. Consequently, the world has heard many words of a pope that are not papal words. Because of this new practice, we must draw the distinction. Thus, I will use "words of a pope" in the restricted sense of those nonauthoritative words of a man who happens to be pope.

Consider some examples of this phenomenon. In 1994, John Paul II published a book titled *Crossing the Threshold of Hope*. This book contains the personal opinions of John Paul II. Since he was such an engaging and popular figure, the book sold wildly. Still, it bears no papal authority. To treat it as authoritative would be an abuse of Catholic theology and would cheapen the currency of magisterial words.

More recently, Pope Benedict XVI published a multivolume work titled *Jesus of Nazareth*. Thankfully, in the foreword, the pope explicitly stated that the work is not an authoritative act of the Magisterium but simply the expression of his mind as a private theologian. Thus, readers are free to agree or disagree with him.

Most recently, Pope Francis has allowed others to interview him and publish the results. He has also expressed his personal views *ex tempore* on a wide range of topics. These interviews do not constitute authoritative acts of the Magisterium. They are words of a pope, not papal words. Moreover, some journalists have had the temerity to report private conversations with the pope to the world. Such words are even further removed from papal authority; they are sheer rumors because they lack corroboration. Eugenio Scalfari's alleged interviews with Pope Francis are notable examples. Scalfari, an atheist journalist who cofounded the newspaper *la Repubblica*, has published several such interviews. Scalfari's interviews have caused massive confusion in the public, to the detriment of the Faith. Catholics can console themselves with the knowledge that these are not papal words but instead rumors about words of a pope.

The authentic Magisterium involves *only* magisterial words; it does not involve "words of a magisterial official" in the restricted sense. When it comes to the pope in particular, the authentic Magisterium involves only papal words, not words of a pope. Of course, it is possible that some words of a pope may be useful and helpful. Still, they remain nonauthoritative. A responsible theologian will treat them accordingly. Having drawn this crucial distinction, we can now turn to magisterial words.

Infallible Teachings

Some magisterial words are infallible, and some are not. Catholics can be certain of an infallible teaching because it has the divine guarantee of truth. Consequently, Catholics must give an irrevocable assent of the mind to infallible teachings. Assent means holding something certainly to be true. Since an infallible truth has the guarantee of truth, our assent to infallible teachings has the character of being certain and irrevocable.[63] If the teaching regards the contents of the deposit itself, then the irrevocable assent is a matter of faith. Obstinate doubt or denial on such matters is heresy. If the teaching regards something related to the deposit, then the assent is not one of faith but of rational obedience rooted in faith.

Infallible teachings can be either affirmative or negative. An affirmative infallible teaching presents a truth that Catholics must affirm with certainty. A negative infallible teaching proscribes an error that they must reject with certainty. The beauty of infallible teachings is the certainty they give about specific claims. For example, we are certain that Jesus is both human and divine yet one person. We are certain that the Eucharist is the true Body and Blood of Jesus. We are certain that abortion is gravely evil.

---

[63] We might later become infidels, but in our acts of faith we assent without reservation.

In what ways are infallible teachings promulgated? The Magisterium proclaims infallible teachings in two ways. First, the magisterial office can be exercised in an *extraordinary* manner when used, not in the ordinary course of daily teaching, but on a specific occasion with the special note of infallibility. An extraordinary exercise of the office produces a definition, a precise formula to which Catholics are forever bound to assent. This exercise can occur in one of two ways: either in an ecumenical council or by the pope himself acting *ex cathedra*.

A valid ecumenical council is a gathering of all Catholic bishops able to attend, convoked and confirmed by the pope.[64] To be sure, not everything in every ecumenical council is an exercise of the extraordinary Magisterium. When reading the documents of an ecumenical council, one needs to use discernment. First, magisterial teaching concerns faith and morals, either directly or indirectly.[65] For example, the person and natures of Christ pertain to faith, and teachings on human sexuality pertain to morals. On the other hand, many applications of moral principles to specific policy decisions are not matters of faith and morals. For example, what the minimum wage should be is a matter of legitimate debate outside the scope of the magisterial office. Whether this or that nation should have this or that kind of border security is a matter of legitimate debate. How to ensure that all have access to the health care of some given culture in accordance with the demands of human dignity is a matter of legitimate debate. Second, one can look for key words. Expressions such as "If anyone holds X, let him be anathema"

---

[64] The task of convoking and confirming is now practiced by the pope expressly. In early times, it was practiced only tacitly.

[65] A teaching that directly regards the Faith is one that treats any matter divinely revealed, that is, any matter *within* the deposit of faith. A teaching that indirectly regards the Faith treats a matter that only *pertains* to the Faith but is not *within* the deposit (or is not yet known as being in the deposit). For example, God did not reveal anything about the Anglican priesthood, but Pope Leo XIII, in defending true priesthood, declared infallibly that Anglican orders are null and void. The justification for his declaration is that the Anglicans used an invalid formula for ordination for such a long period that no valid priestly orders remained.

and "We define that Y" are obvious key words that indicate infallible teachings that are to be held definitively. The latter expression—"we define" or "we declare"—is an affirmative one, presenting what must be held. The former expression—"let him be anathema"—is a negative one, condemning an error. To be anathema is to be cursed by God; someone anathematized is invited to repent but is currently under judgment. The saying goes back to St. Paul. Although an apostle of great authority, Paul subjected himself to the Gospel. He even commanded his flock *not* to assent to *anything* that contradicted the Gospel he had preached *in the past*. He wrote, "Even if we, or an angel from heaven, should preach to you a gospel contrary to that which we preached to you, let him be accursed" (Gal. 1:8).

In some cases, an ecumenical council issues a declaration and then closes with a statement referring to the entire declaration as being a matter of infallible teaching. These documents consist in numerous infallible teachings. A case in point is the Sixth Session of the Council of Trent, which ends a lengthy treatment of the various truths of justification with this statement: "No one can be justified unless he faithfully and firmly accepts this Catholic doctrine on justification."[66]

A papal document can also contain an extraordinary use of the magisterial office. Such an exercise is said to be *ex cathedra*, which means "from the chair or seat of authority." Which papal teachings have been issued with this authority? To find out, we can examine papal documents in the same way that we examined ecumenical councils, looking for teachings on faith and morals and also looking for the key words indicating an extraordinary exercise of the office. To be sure, we do not expect an extraordinary use of magisterial power in the typical papal document, whereas we do in most ecumenical councils. When a papal document contains expressions such as, "We declare and define . . . ," it indicates an infallible exercise of the extraordinary Magisterium.[67]

---

[66] Trent, Session VI, chap. 16; DH 1550.

[67] The 1983 *Code of Canon Law* specifies that, to be *ex cathedra*, the teaching must be clearly presented as "irreformable." The pope is not "under" this

Today, there are excellent reference books that identify many infallible teachings. For a layperson or an untrained theologian, the best resource is a tried-and-true manual of dogmatics. Such a manual indicates which teachings are, and which are not, of infallible authority; it also indicates lower levels of authority. Thus, it responsibly inducts the Catholic into a fuller and more articulated reception of the deposit of faith. To this end, I highly recommend Ludwig Ott's *Fundamentals of Catholic Dogma*. This text is dated, to be sure. It is nonetheless quite accurate; it is also up to date in terms of infallible teachings, because the Church has not exercised the infallibility of her extraordinary Magisterium since Pope Pius XII declared that Mary was assumed into Heaven after her earthly life. So a copy of Ludwig Ott's book can help readers be current on infallible teachings of the Church taught by the extraordinary Magisterium. I also recommend John Hardon's *The Catholic Catechism: A Contemporary Catechism of the Teachings of the Catholic Church*; it is clear and accessible. And, of course, the *Catechism of the Council of Trent* is of value and also clear. The new *Catechism* is useful for those trained in theology.

I should note that catechisms are not vehicles by which new doctrines are promulgated; rather, they are expressions of already established doctrines. For those who desire to obtain the promulgating documents, it can help to have a copy of Denzinger, named after a German theologian who compiled a set of magisterial teachings throughout Church history, numbering and arranging them in chronological order. Unfortunately, there is no perfect edition of Denzinger for the following reasons: only some, not all, magisterial teachings are selected in any edition. Further, some newer editions include documents that have no doctrinal authority at all and likewise fail to include some key texts on doctrines that contemporaries have forgotten.[68] Still, since most people use the newer

---

law, but it can be helpful if contemporary popes abide by it. Importantly, this canon does not govern past papal pronouncements. There are infallible *ex cathedra* statements before Pius IX.

[68] This is the case with the forty-third edition, published in English by Ignatius Press, from which I am citing. See Christian Washburn's critical review of this work in *Nova et Vetera* 12 (2014): 597–600. An older

editions, the newer numbering system will be cited below. Finally, we may consult universally used creeds since these enjoy infallible status. The Nicene-Constantinopolitan creed is a case in point. The "Athanasian," or *Quicumque*, creed, is another. There are, as well, professions of faith endorsed by the Church's highest authority.

The second way in which the Magisterium teaches doctrines infallibly is less remarkable and less easy to peg. This is the so-called *ordinary and universal* exercise of magisterial authority. Following my retired but venerable colleague at the University of Dallas, Mark Lowery, I call this OUM for short. A teaching of the OUM concerns a matter of faith and morals, either directly or indirectly, repeated over a sufficient length of time by a moral unanimity of the bishops in union with the pope when they teach something as being a matter of faith or morals. If, for instance, the overwhelming majority of bishops in union with the popes, over a period of centuries, puts forward some teaching as a matter of faith and morals, then that teaching calls for an irrevocable assent because it is an infallible teaching. Of course, the OUM does not produce a definition or precise formula, because the infallible authority is not concentrated in one act on one occasion. Rather, the accumulation of witnesses to the teaching indicates to us that the teaching is in fact infallible or certainly true. We do not have a definition, one neat formula, but we can affirm the truth itself. The condemnation of artificial contraception as gravely evil is a case in point.

Can we specify an exact timeframe and the exact degree of moral unanimity required to identify a teaching as infallible by the OUM? Unfortunately, we cannot. Thus, the identification of such teachings is not without difficulty. Some teachings adequately meet the criteria for any theologian who is not recalcitrant. It suffices if, for several

---

edition that restricts itself to doctrinal documents is *The Sources of Catholic Dogma* (Fitzwilliam, NH: Loreto, 1955). In that this older edition presents only doctrinal teachings, it is recommendable. The weaknesses of this edition are that the translations are sometimes awkward and that it does not include anything since 1955.

centuries, many popes and the moral unanimity of bishops were to teach something as a matter of faith and morals. If they were to do so for only sixty to seventy years, we would probably not have sufficient warrant to consider the teaching infallible. Another factor to consider is the wording and framing devices employed. When, for instance, the Church issues pastoral instructions, the very framing device — pastoral instruction — indicates something of lesser doctrinal authority than a statement found in, and thus framed as, a "dogmatic decree." The various documents of the Second Vatican Council offer a set of examples. Some of these documents are presented as "dogmatic constitutions," some as "constitutions," some as "pastoral constitutions," some as "decrees," and some as "declarations."

Noninfallible Teachings

All other magisterial teachings are noninfallible. That is, the Church does not require that Catholics irrevocably assent to these other teachings. Rather, the Church requires that Catholics accept the teaching inwardly (and outwardly, of course). The technical expression is "religious submission of mind and will." We are asked to embrace these teachings as being taught "opinionatively," to use an apt expression of the great American theologian Joseph Clifford Fenton.[69] Catholics accept such a teaching for the present, even though it is not impossible for it to be in some way erroneous. Although not infallible, such teachings are authoritative. These teachings can be found in papal decrees and in decrees of the Congregation for the Doctrine of the Faith (CDF), which used to be called the Holy Office. They can even be found in ecumenical councils. The Second Vatican Council abounds with noninfallible teachings. In fact, this council is unique in that it did not issue infallible teachings by an extraordinary exercise of the magisterial office,[70] nor did it anathematize

---

[69] See Joseph Clifford Fenton, "The *Humani Generis* and the Holy Father's Ordinary Magisterium," in *The Church of Christ*, 110–123.

[70] See Paul VI, General Audience, January 12, 1966. As the pope indicates, the council must not be conceived as a rupture from Catholic doctrine.

heresies. Still, other ecumenical councils also contain some statements that are doctrinally authoritative but not infallible.

The category "noninfallible" admits of varying shades or degrees. By repetition and stress, these teachings can take on more weight. We say that they are not infallible because there is insufficient magisterial warrant for them now to be taken as certainly true. It is not Catholic practice, nor is it fitting, to say that they are "fallible." The preferred term is "noninfallible." It accords better with the way in which we are to receive these teachings. Since they are authoritative indications issued by the authority Christ has established, these teachings deserve religious submission of mind and will. Now, this duty is a general but not an absolute rule. An expert or trained theologian knows that the first duty is to the deposit of faith. If a noninfallible teaching appeared to be in tension with the deposit, the theologian's duty to be faithful to the deposit remains. This is true Catholic fidelity, not disobedience and dissent. There is a strict duty never to depart from infallible teachings already promulgated. No excuse could justify departing from this duty. The dissenters of the 1960s and the 1970s rejected the past infallible teachings.

Thankfully, Christ's Church is indefectible. This means that members of the hierarchy, despite their flaws, cannot definitively lead her into error over the long run. Consequently, we should not expect members of the Magisterium to be in error for a long time. Teaching error authoritatively should, if it happens, be rare and relatively short-lived. So we should not treat noninfallible teachings with the cavalier attitude that they are here today and gone tomorrow. Rather, we should give them the submission due to them.

Noninfallible teachings can have greater or lesser authority. Sometimes they are long established; such are, as it were, near the threshold of infallibility. All things being equal, long-standing teachings have a greater weight of authority than shorter-lived teachings. Unambiguous teachings help clarify ambiguous ones. Precise teachings help clarify imprecise ones.

Finally, the lowest rung of magisterial teachings is that regarding contingent and changing matters. Normally, such teachings are simply guidelines that are good rules to follow and safe practices to keep. They can be timely warnings about current errors, for instance. Because of their concreteness and contingency, however, they may not be of long use for the Church, which must last until the end of time.

Having discussed the deposit of faith and the Magisterium, we can now turn to authentic development of doctrine.

Organic Development of Doctrine

The Impossibility of Change or Diminution of Doctrine Once Taught
If infallible dogmas could change or evolve, then what the Church held as definitively true in the past could be rejected as false in the future. As noted above, this notion of development is itself heretical. Some Catholics embrace it mistakenly. Others know better. Of these, few are so bold as to hold doctrinal evolutionism explicitly and publicly. Most entertain doctrinal evolution implicitly because they concretely think that this or that dogma can change. Their error causes real damage to the faithful.

We can detect their error in the way they speak about Church teaching. Some, for instance, describe the Church's infallible teachings as "positions" or "policies." They hold that prohibitions against contraceptive sex and women's ordination are just "policies." What does this view of Church teachings imply? Well, a "policy" is a debatable and changeable position of a governing authority. Since a policy can change, those who present Church teaching as policy imply that doctrine can change. One can understand the secular media using this language, although the depiction is still lamentable. It is irresponsible and scandalous for theologians or Church officials to express themselves in this way, whether or not they subscribe to the false notion implicit in the expression.

Church teaching may not be treated as policy for two reasons. First, to do so confuses the office of teaching truth with the office of legislating on prudential matters. There is no immutable law about when to fast, how long to fast, and what constitutes a fast. The Church must make determinations on these matters according to the prudence of her officials. These determinations can, one must admit, be imprudent at times. Does this mean we should buck imprudent decisions? No, it does not. Having only prudent policies is not as great a good as having real authority to determine these matters and enjoying the fruitfulness of real unity in action that emerges therefrom. It would be chaos if Catholics measured obedience by their private determinations of what is prudent regarding ecclesiastical law. So, even if a mere one-hour fast before receiving Communion were an imprudently lax law, or if a fast that excludes everything, including water, from midnight until reception of the Eucharist were imprudently strict, nonetheless, having one authority to make the call and thus to unite the Church Militant is by far a greater good than allowing all and sundry to determine for themselves how to act in such matters. In short, the Church sometimes issues laws that one might reasonably wish were different. These are, to use a profane word that is inept in matters sacred, "policies." By contrast, what the Church teaches infallibly is simply true and must be accepted by all.

Second, since the authority to legislate is superior to the laws is-sued, couching doctrine in terms of policy implies that the doctrinal teachings of the Church are under the Church's authority. That is false; the Magisterium is a *servant* of revelation, not a source of revelation; the Magisterium merely *indicates* what God has revealed. As Vatican II states, "This teaching office is not above the Word of God, but serves it, teaching only what has been handed on, listening to it devoutly, guard-ing it scrupulously, and explaining it faithfully in accord with a divine commission and with the help of the Holy Spirit."[71] As a result of these two confusions, one who construes doctrine as policy can come to opine that just as the Church had once "infallibly" taught "X," she can at some later date teach "Not X." As a result, the very meaning of "infallible" is annihilated.

We might ask why it is that some today consider doctrines to be changeable policy. As hinted above, a partial cause is the number of doctrinal teachings that people commonly *think* have been changed. The rest of this book will offer evidence in this regard. Another cause is a misunderstanding of the purpose and accomplishments of Vatican II. In

---

[71] *Dei verbum*, art. 10; DH 4214.

his opening address at the council, John XXIII stated, "For this deposit of faith, or truths which are contained in our time-honored teaching is one thing; the manner in which these truths are set forth (with their meaning preserved intact) is something else."[72] Some misunderstood this statement to mean that the pope desired to change dogmas. Pope John's speech does not warrant this reading.

Authentic Principles of Organic Development of Dogma
What does the Church teach about doctrinal development? The Church herself gives us some clear guidelines. The most important text of relevance is Vatican I's *Dei Filius*:

> The doctrine of faith that God has revealed has not been proposed like a philosophical system to be perfected by human ingenuity; rather, it has been committed to the spouse of Christ as a divine trust to be faithfully kept and infallibly declared. Hence also that meaning of the sacred dogmas is perpetually to be retained which our Holy Mother Church has once declared, and there must never be a deviation from that meaning on the specious ground and title of a more profound understanding. "Therefore, let there be growth in understanding, knowledge, and wisdom, in each and all, in individuals and in the whole Church, at all times and in the progress of ages, but only within the proper limits, i.e., within the same dogma, the same meaning, the same judgment."[73]

---

[72] This English translation leaves something to be desired. The Latin clearly conveys the words of the First Vatican Council accurately regarding the same doctrine, the same sense, and the same judgment.

[73] *Dei Filius*, chap. 4; DH 3020. As for Karl Rahner's notion of dogma, it would take too many pages to add a treatment here. I would simply cite the criticism of a competent scholar who is sympathetic to Rahner's project: "The question remains open whether, in the light of the relativization of all human propositions, dogmatic or otherwise, Rahner's notion of infallible dogma is anything other than the verbal affirmation of a reality that does not in fact exist in any meaningful way," Patrick Burke, *Reinterpreting Rahner: A Critical Study of his Major Themes* (New York: Fordham

This passage presents a number of crucial truths. (1) Revelation is a *deposit*, a gift from God. It is not the product of human understanding. (2) The Church is charged not to "grow" the deposit but to preserve and protect it. Conservative language is required *because* the deposit is a divine gift, not a human achievement. (3) Of course, we *are* called to grow in understanding of the deposit, to enter into its pith and marrow, both individually and collectively. This growth in understanding does not constitute an "addition" to the deposit. (4) Growth in understanding must be faithful both to the original deposit and to prior dogmas. One never has excuse to deny past dogmas or to abandon part of the deposit of faith. So no newer teaching can displace the older teaching or the deposit itself. Newer teaching can make more precise articulation of what was previously held but with less explicit precision. Newer teaching can also approach the same deposit from a different vantage point, drawing out the riches of the deposit.

As correlative to its positive teaching, Vatican I condemns the notion that newer teachings displace older ones:

> If anyone says that, as science progresses, at times a sense is to be given to dogmas proposed by the Church different from the one that the Church has understood and understands, let him be anathema.[74]

Once a teaching has been defined infallibly, every Catholic has an obligation to assent to it in its entirety. Under no pretext whatsoever may one deny, alter, or water down the full truth once defined.

University Press, 2002), 225. Burke's analysis is acute, and such analysis is required, since Rahner is so elusive. Among the telltale warning signs in Rahner's corpus is his conviction that no new infallible dogma is possible in our age of pluralism. Karl Rahner, "On the Concept of Infallibility in Catholic Theology," in *Theological Investigations*, vol. 14, trans. David Bourke (New York: Seabury Press, 1976), 71–75. Another warning sign is his advice to those struggling with a dogma to rid themselves of the burden of the dogma by ignoring it. Karl Rahner, "The Faith of the Christian and the Doctrine of the Church," *Theological Investigations* 14:37.

74 Ibid., canon 3; DH 3043.

If true doctrinal development never involves alteration or denial of past dogma, what is the *development?* Dogmatic development is the movement from what is implicitly contained in the deposit of faith to an explicit statement of the same mystery. An *implicit* presence is *not* a mere vague possibility. It is a real presence that, when contemplated with a precise line of inquiry, ultimately necessitates a certain answer, an answer that renders what is implicit to be explicit. (The process can take many centuries.)

The deposit of faith is a mystery entrusted to us to fathom. This mystery does not change. As we understand it, we can formulate our understanding in truth claims or statements. These statements express in articulated fashion the truths that the deposit really contains in a denser and compact way. Dogmas articulate distinctly what is compactly present in the deposit, so there is growth from the deposit to a dogma. Likewise, there is growth from one dogma to another.

The Church teaches that three distinct but related labors serve as causes of this growth or development.[75] First, there is the theological labor of contemplation and study of the mysteries treasured in the heart. Second, there is the experience of the mysteries by those sanctified in Christ. Third, there is the genuine preaching of the bishops. By these efforts, believers enter the doors of the mysteries and strive to fathom the unfathomable.

Once developments have occurred, we can describe the intellectual movement from an earlier to a later dogmatic formulation. We can identify three broad categories of such movement. Firstly, the earlier statements (either in Scripture and Tradition or in dogma) sometimes logically entail the subsequent ones in a straightforward and deductive manner. For example, if we believe that Jesus is a man we implicitly believe that He has a human will, since every man has a human will. Secondly, earlier statements (or scriptural passages) at other times contain a great

---

[75] See *Dei verbum*, art. 8; DH 4210. See also Guy Mansini, *Fundamental Theology* (Washington, DC: Catholic University of America Press, 2018), 126–131.

variety of disparate witnesses to some single truth; the upshot of these variegated witnesses can be expressed in a simpler, more unified way in a later dogma.[76] For example, the statement "the Son is consubstantial with the Father" is a precise and articulate way of putting together the upshot of the manifold New Testament witness to Christ in terms of his preexistent identity. By the way, the simpler statement does not do away with the rich variety that preceded it. Both must be kept. Thirdly, there are times when newer teaching can bring to light something to which little attention had previously been given. The newer teaching may emerge from a new vantage point with regard to the same mystery. For example, the dogma of transubstantiation puts in precise words the *change* of the sacramental species. Whereas Catholics had always held the Real Presence to emerge, they had not attended to the very nature of the *change* itself by which that Real Presence is brought about.

In *no* case of authentic development does the newer teaching water down or contradict the older teaching; rather, the newer teaching makes a statement not previously made. Quite often, the newer teaching is a further *precision* on what was inchoately taught before. After a newer teaching that is infallible is promulgated, one must hold *both* the newer teaching and the older teaching.

Illustration of Some Dogmatic Developments
Our current crisis calls for a more thorough examination of the development of dogma. If we study more closely a line of theological development on, for example, the person and natures of Christ, we can learn quite a bit about how to handle the current crisis. In this section, we are tracing one line of development that is clearer than other developments. It thus serves as a good point of departure. We will see herein two examples of movement: deductive inference and developments from many pointers

---

[76] This is not to say that the prior statements are less useful. In fact, the prior statements are often rich in ways that are lacking in later statements. On the other hand, the later statement captures the upshot of the prior statements. Thus, both the earlier and the later statements are useful.

to a single upshot. In a later section, we will investigate a third and more difficult set of cases that also exemplify movement.

At the Council of Nicaea (AD 325), the Church defined that the Son of God is "true God" and "consubstantial with the Father." Neither of these assertions is found explicitly in Scripture. However, the Scriptures really present the Son as God as worthy of worship, as knowing minds and hearts, as working miracles by His power, as instituting a new law, as Lord of the Sabbath, as offering Himself up for our redemption and divinization, and so forth. This variegated set of truths has a necessary upshot: Jesus is "true God." Someone who is educated in sound philosophy can also ask a precise question about this Son: "Is He *consubstantial* with the Father?" That is, is the Son of the same identical nature as the Father? The disciple of Christ believes in only one God and confesses the Son to be fully God. Since there is only one God, there is only one substance of divinity. Since there is only one substance of divinity, the Son must be consubstantial with the Father. As we see, the dogmas of Nicaea do not violate or add truths to Scripture. Rather, they encapsulate precisely the real upshot of the scriptural narratives concerning our Savior. Since Nicaea states explicitly what Scripture teaches implicitly, Nicaea represents an authentic development of dogma. This kind of development is, in fact, an example of multiple pointers converging into a single formulation. Now, this precision in teaching did not bring reflection to an end. Rather, it provoked the need for another precise teaching, because it raised new questions.

In the wake of Nicaea, some came to think that if the Son is indeed God, He cannot be fully human, for, as they thought, no person can have two minds! Since they accepted Nicaea, they denied the full humanity of the Son. They held that the divine Son plays the role of the human mind, so that Jesus does not have a human mind. At the Council of Constantinople (AD 381), the Church responded: the Son of God has a human mind. The reasoning was simple: the Son really became man, as John 1:14 states. Nicaea did not dispense with Scripture, nor did Constantinople dispense with Nicaea. Like Nicaea, Constantinople's teaching stated in explicit terms what follows from scriptural teaching in various ways. Since Scripture teaches that Jesus is human, it implies that He has a human mind, because every man has a human mind. Scripture also teaches that the Son marveled at His hearers' lack of faith (Mark 6:6). Now, "to marvel" involves knowing enough to recognize something as puzzling but not knowing that something exhaustively or comprehensively. To recognize a puzzle, one must be intelligent. To be unable to comprehend, one must be a creature. So only a created intellect can marvel. Therefore, Jesus can marvel about something only if He has a created mind. Again, Jesus asks, "Who was it that touched me?" (Luke 8:45). To ask a rational question on the basis of sensory knowledge demonstrates a specifically human intellect. Thus, the incarnate Son had a human intellect. Thus, what we see with Constantinople is an example of a doctrinal development from many pointers to a precise upshot. Constantinople made explicit the mystery that the Scriptures implicitly contain. Constantinople did not replace the rich and manifold scriptural witness to our Lord's life. We must still ponder our Lord's questioning and marveling. Constantinople did promulgate a real and genuine truth, which, if we ponder it, can yield rich rewards. He humanly thinks of us.

As we can see, this development of dogma marched forward without retracting a step. However, this truth is difficult to fathom. Those who insisted on removing the mystery confined it within their own imaginations, finding contradictions where there were none. As did the previous heretics, these, too, could not fathom that one person would have two minds, a divine mind and a human mind. Instead of denying the human mind, they chose to deny the unity of Christ's person. They affirmed two truths: that the Son is true God with a divine mind and that Jesus is true man with a human mind. But they lost the very unity of Jesus Christ as one person! These heretics held that the Son is one person and the man Jesus another person. Consequently, they lost sight of the Incarnation itself. These were the Nestorians. According to them, the Son of God did not *become* flesh; He did not become the Son of David. Instead, the Son of God "teamed up with" or "dwelled within" the Son of David. They saw the term "the Christ" as a tag team inclusive of two persons, the divine

Son of God and the human Son of David. Their heresy is eminently rational. Indeed, it is rationalistic. It is not an absurd heresy; it is simply false and heretical. Their desire to affirm only what they could clearly see to be rational confined them within the limits of reason; eventually, they denied the *mystery* of the Incarnation.

The true sons of the Church—e.g., Cyril of Alexandria—knew how deadly this heresy was. It struck at the very heart of the scriptural narrative: "And the Word *was made* flesh" (see John 1:14, emphasis added). If the Word was made flesh, then that very Word truly became human. The Nestorians, by contrast, held that the Word "linked up with" the flesh. They held that the Word "dwelled within" the man Jesus. In short, for the Nestorians, Jesus was a great prophet but not the very Son of God. Consequently, they held that Mary was only the Mother of Jesus but not the Mother of God. Ingeniously, they cloaked their heresy with ambiguity: they called Mary "Mother of the Christ." Why? For them, "the Christ" was a tag-team term that included two saving figures, Jesus the man and the divine Son of God. Since "the Christ" was for them a label that applies to both saving figures, Mary is "Mother of the Christ" insofar as she is mother of one part of the tag team. As the saints knew, the Nestorian heresy represented an overthrow of the entire foundation of Christianity. In the Eucharist, we would not be receiving the life-giving flesh of God but the flesh of a mere man. What was at stake was the very starting point of Christianity.

So the Council of Ephesus condemned Nestorianism in 431. It taught that there is but "one hypostasis" or person, the eternal Son of God who became man. Since the same person is eternal God and also man, what we say about either nature we are really saying about the same one person who has two natures. Hence, since Mary is the mother of that very person according to His human nature, she is the Mother of the Son of God. Since the Son of God is true God, Mary is the Mother of God. To deny this Marian dogma is to deny the Incarnation itself. Ephesus shows us that to get Mary right helps us get Christ right: Mary crushes heresies. Note that the Nestorians claimed to be faithful to the recent council! They claimed to take shelter in recent magisterial words. In fact, they denied something ancient and basic, something going back to the first century—namely, the Christian belief that the Word *became* flesh. The Nestorians preferred an easy, rational picture over the mystery. They were unfaithful to the treasure of the Faith. Were there "good elements" in their heresy? Of course! These elements, however, are found already in the Church's Faith; in the Nestorian portrait, they are *yoked* to heresy. The Marian and Christological developments of dogma at Ephesus also exemplify the second kind of movement mentioned above. They move from the many pointers—the unity of Christ as indicated throughout Scripture and Mary as the Mother of *the Lord*—to the one upshot.

Predictably, some heretics used the Council of Ephesus to deny the distinction of Christ's two natures, divine and human. It is as though they rallied to the cause of the recent council and scoffed at the clarity of Constantinople. Using the dogma of "one hypostasis" or person in Christ, they portrayed Christ as a "blend" of two natures. In the Council of Chalcedon (AD 451), the Church condemned these confused heretics, stressing that the two natures remain "without confusion or change."[77]

Also predictably, Nestorians used Chalcedon in order to reject the Council of Ephesus! These Nestorians proclaimed themselves vindicated by Chalcedon, the hot new council. Of course, their use of this latest of councils was treacherous. Chalcedon gave them no support whatsoever. Later followers of Nestorius, the neo-Nestorians, continued his misrepresentation of Chalcedon for a century. These were, we should note, difficult times. Finally, the Church condemned them at the Second Council of Constantinople in 553. This condemnation was essentially a reaffirmation of prior dogma.

As if that weren't enough, proponents of a heresy related to that condemned at Chalcedon arose in the wake of Constantinople II. Chalcedon taught that Jesus had a perfect or integral human nature. Certain heretics abused Constantinople II so as to claim that Jesus had only one

---

[77] DH 302.

will (monothelitism). Their heresy implied that Jesus had no human will. Foremost among these was Sergius, patriarch of Constantinople. The dispute transformed into high drama for two reasons. First, they used false ecumenism and political expediency as partial defenses of their error. False ecumenism is anchored not in complementary expressions of truth but in substantive doctrinal compromise. These heretics complained that the Christians who rejected Chalcedon might come back to the Church if the Church would only allow one to say that Jesus has only one will. This false ecumenical gesture would help the empire regain its strength to fight the Persians and the rising tide of new heretics from Arabia, the Muslims. Second, the pope himself failed to condemn the heresy. Indeed, he seemed to give the heretics protection. In a letter of response to Sergius, who had sought his assistance, Pope Honorius declared that Christ possesses only *one* will, not two wills.[78] Good theologians knew, to the contrary, that since Christ has two rational natures, divine and human, he has also two wills. Thus, Honorius's statement contradicted what we can *deduce* from Scripture and prior dogmas. The proper response of a good theologian at the time was to hold fast to what Scripture and the prior dogmas *imply*—namely, that Christ had two wills. Some say that Honorius was only a confused theologian; they say that he was only teaching that Christ's human will was not opposed to his divine will, as though Honorius simply said that Christ was not "divided" in heart. That may be the case. The common good of the Church, however, was at stake. Regarding this good, the document itself was at best highly misleading. Worse, Sergius and the other heretics used his very document as justification for their heresy. So, even if Pope Honorius did not formally commit an act of heresy with his statement, his very words were used as an excuse for heresy. Subsequent popes had to condemn the notion that Christ had only one will. In 680, Pope Agatho officially declared that Christ had *two* wills, definitively rejecting the teaching that Pope Honorius seemed to hold.[79] The Third Ecumenical Council of Constantinople endorsed

---

[78] DH 487.
[79] DH 544.

Agatho's teaching.[80] The same council also condemned Pope Honorius himself with the following words:

> After having investigated the dogmatic letters written by Sergius, the former patriarch of the God-protected and imperial city ... to Honorius, then pope of elder Rome, and in like manner also the letter written in reply by that one, that is, Honorius, to the same Sergius, and after having discovered that these are entirely alien to the apostolic teachings and to the decisions of the holy councils and to all the eminent holy Fathers but instead follow the false teachings of the heretics, these we entirely reject as soul-destroying.[81]

The council continued, "We have seen fit to banish from the holy Church of God and to anathematize Honorius, the former pope of the elder Rome, because we have discovered in the letters written by him to Sergius that he followed in everything the opinion of that one and confirmed his impious dogma."[82] In his papal ratification of the acts of this council, Pope Leo II concurred with the condemnation of Honorius but moderated the claim:

> And, in like manner, we anathematize the inventers of the new error: namely, Theodore, Bishop of Pharan, Cyrus of Alexandria, Sergius, Phyrrus ... and also Honorius, who did not purify this apostolic Church by the doctrine of the apostolic tradition, but rather attempted to subvert the immaculate faith by profane treason.[83]

These words stand as a monument for all time that no pope may deny, alter, or water down the holy and Catholic Faith.

The example of the heresy (or bad theology) of Honorius shows us several things. First, we may not use a false understanding of ecumenism

---

[80] See DH 553.
[81] DH 550.
[82] DH 552.
[83] DH 563.

as an excuse to compromise on the Faith. Second, we may not use errant papal words, much less errant words of a pope, as an excuse to deny the deposit. Third, a man who was pope has been condemned. Fourth, if we accept the deposit in faith, some truths deductively follow, and we must accept these also.

Notice how the Christological development in these six councils added precision at every step. Truth adds upon truth. Doctrinal development is not doctrinal "evolution." According to the theory of evolution, older forms go extinct and disappear. The newer forms of biological species, because they are more excellent than the older forms, do not contain the older forms. In doctrinal development, by contrast, the older truths remain forever. Newer teaching does not replace older teachings. Organic development of dogma can loosely be illustrated by analogy with the development of a tree. One tree remains the same over time, but it develops from having a small trunk and short, sparse limbs and twigs to a thicker trunk with many limbs that are wide at their beginning but branch out again and again, ramifying into smaller and more delicate parts. Similarly, an article of faith, such as the Incarnation, can be treated with greater and greater precision, each precision more delicate and refined, although the original statements, generic as they were, remain entirely true: Jesus is true God, Jesus is true man, Jesus is one person, Jesus retains two natures, Jesus has a free human will, Jesus has a human heart, and so on.

Principles for Navigating Alleged Cases of Doctrinal Evolution
As a result of the foregoing reflections, we can suggest *some* interpretative principles regarding claims of alleged doctrinal *evolution* in recent statements from magisterial figures. This list of principles is designed precisely with an eye to the preservative mode of the hermeneutic of continuity in the face of confusion. It is not an exhaustive list of principles for the discernment of all cases of legitimate doctrinal development.

What should we do when someone alleges that the Magisterium has just taught P, Q, or R, when these appear novel and disconsonant with the deposit of faith? First, we should make sure that the statement is indeed a magisterial statement. If it is merely a rumor, it should be treated as such. If it is only the word of a magisterial figure (a private phone call or an off-the-cuff remark), it is not authoritative. Only magisterial words are authoritative.

Second, we should, above all, cling fast to the Church's dogmas and infallible teachings. We must guard them both firmly and inviolably. Dogmas are, when the term is used precisely, infallible teachings taught in a neat definition issued by an extraordinary exercise of the Magisterium. The very words of dogmas deserve our respect and fidelity, and, of course, the truth claim itself, which could be expressed also in a different formula, must be held with certainty to be true. Teachings that are infallible in virtue of the OUM do not have a specific definition enunciating them. Still, they are truths that must forever be held. Both dogmas and OUM infallible teachings form anchors for our assent. We must irrevocably assent to the truth of both sets. Nor do we ever have excuse for setting aside or altering or watering down these truths. No further magisterial statement, no words of a pope, no supposed scientific theory, no rumor, nothing can ever excuse the Catholic from leaving any dogmas and infallible truths behind. Someone may complain: "How stifling! This shackles us to the past." To the contrary! This unites us to the Truth, which is one and never changes. So this notion of development is a great boon. In a shifting world whose foundations are buckling, we have something we can bank on.

These first two principles are so important that I repeat them for stress. But what should we do about cases of *apparent* change or evolution?

Third, if the past teaching is infallible, we must never invent an excuse to abandon it, even if a newer teaching appears to contradict it. If we were to abandon the past infallible teaching, we would be abandoning Christ's own voice. We never have any excuse for that—period! Keeping this in mind, we could practice the exegetical mode of the hermeneutic of continuity, making a good effort to interpret the newer teaching in light of the infallible older teaching. It may be, for example, that the newer teaching presents only half the truth; it may be imprecise or ambiguous or something of the sort. In such a case, silence is not denial; ambiguous expressions do not cancel unambiguous, infallible teachings. Theologians may work to show how the new expression really remains faithful to the past. In such a case, there really is no *development* of doctrine; rather, there is an imprecise or vague statement that could be clarified. (In normal times, we do this clarification spontaneously in our minds: we do not nitpick. In times of confusion, it helps to get explicit about what must be held.)

If the past teaching is only noninfallible and a newer teaching seems to contradict it, what should we do? Fourth, as the Magisterium itself teaches, we must accord its teachings the degree of authority they call for. This authority is signaled by repetition, stress, and so forth. If the past teaching had been repeated for a very long time with great stress, while the newer teaching has been issued only recently and in pastoral statements, then the burden of obligation is to cling to the past teaching. Can a newer teaching abrogate an older teaching? It is possible, but the Church fosters in us the expectation that abrogation should be quite rare, since the Church enjoys the note of indefectibility. Furthermore, because of the danger of scandal and confusion, a newer teaching should be clearly presented as abrogating the prior teaching with the authority sufficient to do so. Otherwise, our very fidelity to the prior teaching would put us in a difficult situation. Pastors would not want to do that.

These third and fourth principles point to an area that is quite sensitive and not easy to navigate, to be sure. Our rule of discernment should be to *expect real continuity* with the past. Continuity is demanded in the case of infallible teachings and dogmas. Continuity should be *expected* even in the case of noninfallible teachings, especially those that are well established.

Fifth, Pope Pius XII gives us yet another criterion in magisterial teaching, that of *clarity*. He teaches, "It is clear how false is a procedure that would attempt to explain what is clear by means of what is obscure. Indeed the very opposite procedure must be used."[84] This teaching of Pius

---

[84] Pius XII, *Humani generis* (1950), art. 21; DH 3886.

XII is crucial. He is teaching that in a disputation about what we should believe, we should begin with the clear, not the obscure. This teaching implies further that we should begin with what is precise, clear, and unambiguous, not with what is imprecise, unclear, and ambiguous. This is the heart of his teaching, and it behooves us to heed it.

Now, until very recently, magisterial teaching used to *gain* in precision and clarity as history moved forward. The historical trajectory of magisterial teaching used to be from imprecise to precise, from vague to specific, from ambiguous or polyvalent to unambiguous. The Christological development traced above is a case in point. Obviously, if the historical trajectory is from imprecise to precise, then recent statements should serve as the proximate guides to the interpretation of more ancient statements. The more recent statement can be said to have greater "articulation" than the more ancient statement. Thus, when we need to focus on the exact point at dispute with a more articulate question, we need to have recourse to the most precise statement on the subject. Insofar as the general trajectory of Church teaching is from imprecise to precise, theologians have usually been better served by more recent statements than by older statements.

That's how it was up through Pius XII's lifetime. Back then, one could generally say that recent pronouncements were more precise than past ones. Unsurprisingly, then, Pius XII also counseled that in the case of a question about meaning, one should begin with the more recent statements of the Magisterium and work one's way backward through tradition in order to grasp what prior formulations strove to express.[85] One would at

---

[85] This is not an exercise in anachronism. It requires the suppleness of the intellectual historian to see two things. On the one hand, he notes the absence of the explicit precision in the earlier formulas; he notes the serious struggles. On the other hand, he reads those struggles in the light of faith. That is, he does not foist a precise heresy upon an imprecise formula. For example, St. Cyril used the formula "one nature of the Incarnate Word." Clearly, we see the lack of Chalcedon's precision: two natures in one person. However, Cyril was by no means proposing the monophysitism of Eutyches (one blended nature from two sources), which Chalcedon condemned. To foist heresy upon Cyril would be the

length come to the sources of revelation. Pius lays out this itinerary—from recent to ancient—because, to his mind, the recent Magisterium made more precise statements than the earlier doctrines and Scripture. He was urging scholars *not* to use the polyvalence (ambiguity) of Scripture to undercut the definitive precision of later formulas, which (because infallible) are correct interpretations of the earlier formulas. Now, if the later formula is, in fact, more precise, clearer, less ambiguous, and more complete, then we should begin with the more recent statement.

As I noted in the introduction, however, some recent magisterial statements are, in comparison with some prior statements, polyvalent, ambiguous, imprecise, vague, and incomplete. In cases such as these, a prudent theologian will, in the course of a doubt or debate, have recourse to the most precise, unambiguous, clear, and complete statement. It would be folly to abandon precision for imprecision, the unambiguous for the ambiguous, the complete for the incomplete, and the infallible for the noninfallible. Moreover, we must not, as modernists do, take silence as denial. The argument from silence is invalid and unbecoming a Catholic theologian. Recent statements often cannot repeat everything taught previously on a given topic. It would be tedious to have to repeat all Church teachings in every ecumenical council. Given that the Church forever retains all her past dogmas and infallible teachings, there really is no need to repeat past teachings on every conceivable occasion. Of course, in a culture that puts the past up for grabs and erases its memory of history, a little bit of repetition can serve as a timely, pastoral reminder. If a shepherd truly wants to feed his flock, he will do so.

The foregoing principles can help us navigate current difficulties. Certain people are claiming that, because a recent pope said something ambiguous, we are now free to adhere merely to the ambiguity, even if the prior Magisterium taught about the matter infallibly. This way of proceeding is not Catholic. We do not believe the pope is an oracle

---

anachronism. Anachronism is avoided, finally, by close scrutiny of Cyril's reasoning about the properties of Christ, which demonstrates, illatively, that he affirmed the full humanity of Christ.

who can reverse infallible teachings and dogmas. Therefore, we should never allow an ambiguous or incomplete statement to dislodge from us our conviction in what has already been taught infallibly.

Subtler Developments: New Perspectives on the Same Mystery
The developments noted above are accepted widely by Christians. At least in hindsight, as it were, they seem straightforward. Other developments are subtler. In the face of these, an outsider might object that what Catholics call development is actually a perversion. In the face of this complaint, two reactions might result. One person might reject Catholicism because, allegedly, it leaves the Bible or Tradition behind. Another person might embrace Catholic modernism, which fully admits that it leaves old truths behind in favor of novel positions. For a Catholic, neither reaction is healthy. Further, with care, a Catholic can defend the legitimacy of such subtle developments. In this section, we consider three examples of subtler development, which an outsider might mistakenly call ruptures. The first might look like an addition; the next two might look like contradictions of past teaching. In fact, each development involves a new perspective on the same mystery or a new use of an older term.

1. A New, Higher Insight into the Mystery:
The Immaculate Conception

In 1854, Pope Pius IX defined the dogma of the Immaculate Conception, according to which Mary never existed in a state of sin; she did not inherit original sin; rather, God preserved her from this on account of Christ's foreseen merits. Some Christians, especially Protestants, complain that this teaching is in error and constitutes a claim alien to the deposit of faith. To the contrary, Mary's Immaculate Conception is not an addition to revelation; rather, it is implicitly, albeit not explicitly, found in Scripture.

Still, the way in which Mary's Immaculate Conception is implicit in Scripture is *diverse* from the way in which Jesus' intellect, will, and heart are implicit in Church teaching and Scripture. As we have seen, once we recognize that Jesus is fully human, a simple deduction shows us the truth that He has an intellect, a will, and a heart. To be sure, drawing out this deduction can take a long time, because one has to face difficulties. (Study, prayer, and episcopal teaching are the wellsprings of the effort.) It is not an easy matter to affirm that Jesus is one person and yet has two intellects! If that straightforward deductive move can take a century or more, the kind of movement involved in recognizing Mary's Immaculate Conception is more demanding. For centuries, some of the greatest theological minds could not recognize this truth, even when explicit questions were asked about it. The Immaculate Conception is "implicit" in a different way. Scripture and Tradition witness to this truth in a manifold, variegated way.

Here, I will trace the path of development that led to the dogma. My focus is not Mariology but a subtle form of dogmatic development that rested on a collective, historical exercise of what John Henry Newman called the "illative sense."[86] The illative sense is an intellectual skill or virtue whereby one has the knack to follow the evidence of a manifold and variegated set of testimonies to the right conclusion and to arrive at it with certainty. None of the individual pieces of evidence constitutes a demonstration; yet, taken together in their variety, they warrant not just a probable opinion but certainty. The example Newman used to illustrate his thesis was his certainty that England is an island. He had never walked around England, yet he was absolutely certain that it is in island. His evidences were many and various: his mother's testimony, the testimony of maps, the testimony of England's history, personal experience of the shore being only so many miles away, and so forth. In the face of so many and varied testimonies, a person of sound judgment concludes with certainty that England is an island. We can apply Newman's theory of the illative sense to the case of the Immaculate Conception in a historical and collective exercise of this skill.

---

[86] See John Henry Newman, *An Essay in Aid of a Grammar of Assent* (Notre Dame, IN: University of Notre Dame Press, 1979). Applying Newman's notion of the illative sense, Guy Mansini characterizes the movement toward the Marian definition as an exercise of the illative sense. This seems to me spot on. See Mansini, *Fundamental Theology*, 127–128.

False Mercy

Perhaps the central text for the Immaculate Conception is the angelic salutation of Mary: "Hail, full of grace" (Luke 1:28). Gabriel does not use Mary's name but, rather, identifies her with a *quality*, "full of grace," as though making that quality her name. We call this a substantive use of an adjectival word. The word in Greek is the participle *kecharitomene*; it is a perfect passive participle in the feminine gender. The verbal root of the participle, *charitein*, means "to favor," that is, to confer grace.[87] That the participle is *passive* indicates divine action. God is the hidden agent who gives grace, and Mary is the beneficiary who receives the grace on account of God's favor or love. That the participle is in the *perfect* tense means that the action—being given grace—has been perfectly accomplished at the moment of the angelic salutation. In short, it means that Mary is at that time perfectly graced. ("Perfect" does not mean she cannot increase in grace; Christ increased in grace. It means, rather, that the grace she had was full in its measure at that stage according to the divine plan.)

This is no little privilege. St. Jerome pondered this greeting and tried to render it faithfully in Latin. He came up with the phrase *plena gratia*, which means "endowed with full grace" or "full of grace." Until relatively recently, even Protestant translations rendered the phrase this way. The course of Catholic history can be seen as the course of a deeper and deeper fathoming of this mysterious text. This history did not unfold in isolation from other Marian privileges. The doctrine of Mary's divine maternity—Ephesus's dogma that she is Mother of God—played the most important role. Once the Church's members fathomed that Mary was truly the Mother of God, they turned toward a deeper appreciation of Mary's holiness.

---

[87] We see here an interconnection of dogmas. Protestants understand "favor" as indicating simply an attitude of God toward us. Catholics pursue the divine favor to its conclusion, understanding that if God favors or loves anyone, He wills his good. Since He wills his good, He also gives grace, because God's love is not empty. This grace that God gives transforms the interior man, making him truly holy in God's sight. Thus, if Luke 1:28 means "highly favored" it really implies "having been graced."

Theologians pondering Mary's privileges drank deeply from the spiritual meaning of the Old Testament. They came to see that Mary is the reality that is typified by the pure vessel of gold, the Holy Ark of the Covenant, which no one is to touch. The enigma of the first couple's sin, and the mystery of God's promise of redemption, were also objects of contemplation. Theologians pondered the enmity that God prophesied between the woman and the ancient serpent. This prophecy was announced in Genesis 3:15 but recapitulated in Revelation 12. What would happen if we were to conceive of this enmity as being perfect? What trajectory of thought would emerge? Satan's vomit aimed to destroy the human race through the contagion of original sin (Rev. 12:15). How does a holy person escape from original sin? When does a very holy and privileged one do so?

There was also another factor at play. When one begins to stammer the truth that God became man and fathoms that Mary is therefore the Mother of the God-man, one enters a journey of exploration. One begins to ask God, "Who is this woman?" As the Church meditated on these mysteries for centuries, a trajectory emerged. The Venerable Bede provided an impetus. He studied the episode in which Mary greets Elizabeth and the baby John jumps in his mother's womb. Bede concluded that John must have been sanctified *at* that moment, for the Holy Spirit came down upon Elizabeth at that time and John then leapt for joy. Now, John was the greatest of prophets, but even the least in the kingdom of Heaven is greater than he. And of those in the kingdom of Heaven, Mary is the greatest. So, in the wake of Bede's insight, theologians began to speculate when Mary was first sanctified. Surely, God would have sanctified His own mother earlier than He did His forerunner. At this point, we can almost anticipate a "race" to identify the earliest moment of Mary's redemption. This race took place in Britain and in the Latin West.

The above labors are both theological and experiential. Theologians pondered with their minds, yes. But they also prayed with their hearts. Meanwhile, another factor was at play, an influence from the East. Here, we touch on the liturgy. Since the liturgy is the concern of bishops, we will be noting the influence of episcopal preaching in the broad sense.

False Mercy

From as early as the sixth century, the East had been celebrating the feast of Mary's conception; many Eastern theologians had lost any desire to assert any sin in Mary. This feast made its way to Sicily and then to Britain. It was appreciated in light of the movement inaugurated by Bede's insight. Mary was eventually celebrated by some as "immaculately conceived." The faithful were eager to light candles and process in honor of Mary immaculate. These efforts took place under the care of bishops. Who refused to join the processions? Great theological minds. They challenged these celebrations with the concern that Mary, daughter of Adam, needed to be saved by Jesus. If she was saved, they asked, how could she have been free of original sin? Bernard, Thomas, and Bonaventure all stumbled upon this question. From their vantage point, they could see no alternative: either Mary was redeemed by Christ and not conceived immaculate, or she was conceived immaculate and not redeemed. It was Duns Scotus who achieved a higher vantage point on the mystery and offered the convincing response: Mary was saved by being *preserved* from original sin. Further, she was so preserved *by* an application of Christ's redemption. Thus, she was saved by Christ's work and yet never suffered the stain of original sin. Centuries of pondering, contemplation, prayer, and theological labor bore fruit at last. The Catholic Magisterium supported this claim more and more as the centuries passed and finally defined it dogmatically.

So, whereas there is no explicit teaching on the Immaculate Conception in Scripture, a Catholic can appreciate that it is implicitly taught therein by a variety of witnesses. These, when read by the prudent judgment of a faithful mind in the right historical circumstances, offer to the Church a theological proposal. The Holy Catholic Church, the sole authoritative interpreter of the mysteries of Christ, eventually pronounced on this proposal, concluding definitively that it is a true reading of revelation. In this act, the Church ushers us all the more deeply into the mystery of Christ's power.

As hinted above, the dogma does not contradict Paul's teaching in Romans 5 that all those who are begotten of Adam are *due* to inherit original sin in virtue of their descent from him. It did take theological acumen to achieve insight into this point. We can contemplate the harmony of the Immaculate Conception and original sin as follows. Consider Mary as someone *about* to be conceived. She does not yet exist, but she will exist tomorrow, when she will be conceived. We are considering her as a possible future human person. In this regard, she is someone to be begotten of Adam. Now, as one to be begotten of Adam, Mary is *due* to inherit original sin. Was she *actually* begotten in sin? No, she was not. The power of God intervened and prevented what was *due* to her from becoming actual in her. Surely, God is *able* to do such a thing. Was He *willing* to do so? Yes, He was. For a good reason, God in His wisdom prevented Mary from contracting original sin. God chose her as the tabernacle of His humanity. How fitting to preserve this tabernacle, not simply for Mary's sake but primarily for the sake of His Son.

So the Catholic dogma is that Mary was redeemed from Adam's fault in the most perfect way. She was *preserved* from contracting that woeful inheritance. This preservation does not mean that Jesus did not save Mary. On the contrary, she was redeemed, as all men are redeemed, *because* of the merits of Christ. These merits are applied to all redeemed people, whether before or after Christ. With respect to those who came before Christ, we say that God redeemed them on account of the foreseen merits of Christ. It is not that God is in time so as to see beforehand. But God's application of merits to Abraham depends on what we consider to be God's "foreknowledge" of Christ's merits. God, who sees all time, can apply the merits of a future act before that act takes place. Like Abraham, Mary existed before Christ offered up His sacrifice. Still, no one is saved except in the name of Jesus. Similarly, we confess that Mary was redeemed in view of the *foreseen* merits of Christ. The difference between Abraham and Mary is that, whereas Abraham was redeemed after having inherited original sin, Mary was redeemed by being preserved from original sin. Christ's death was a very powerful redemption.

How on earth can a Catholic "prove" this mystery to a Protestant who relies only on Scripture and his own interpretation? It is an uphill battle, to be sure. I suggest that the most important thing in the *theological* discussion of this issue with a Protestant is to help him enter into the deep and patient reading of Scripture so prized in the Catholic tradition.

We do not read the Scriptures in a way that superficially passes over the mysteries they contain. Rather, we dwell with the texts. We listen to the great theologians of the past who have plumbed the depths of Scripture. We approach with pious humility, feet unshod, in awe and wonder.

Now, in order to inculcate these attitudes in a Protestant, a prior task is often in order. One must help him see that the Catholic Church is the one true Church instituted by Christ. While there is evidence to support this claim, it can be obscured in our day. Once a rock of constancy, the Church today appears to be tossed by the waves of controversy and indecision. Even so, human weakness cannot alter God's plans for His people. Acknowledging the divine origins of the Church is a priority for Catholics because God established the Church to save souls. By this discipleship, a Catholic follows Christ wherever He leads, and He leads His sheep through His voice on Earth, the one, holy, catholic, and apostolic Church.

The case of the Immaculate Conception helps us to see that doctrines develop in nondeductive ways, that the Church gathers insight into the manifold witness of Scripture and Tradition over the course of time and through many labors. This insight is fostered by study, by the savor of faithful experience, and by the preaching of holy pastors.[88] In this process, the Church helps us to fathom more profoundly the original teaching of Scripture. We have not abandoned or added to Scripture; rather, we have entered more deeply into its chambers. Scripture is like a great and inspiring cathedral. Too much to take in at one glance. Thanks be to God for His Church, which guides our steps.

2. Development through Change of Context:
Naturally Good Works

In her first several centuries, the Church taught that we can do nothing good without the grace of God.[89] After the Reformation, the Church

---

[88] See *Dei verbum*, art. 8; DH 4210.

[89] See the Second Synod of Orange at DH 377. Although this was merely a regional African synod, it has nonetheless been received by the universal Magisterium as authoritative.

taught that we *can* do some good things without the grace of God.[90] Is this a contradiction? As mischievously stated above, perhaps; but in fact, close investigation shows that the teachings do not contradict each other. Rather, the Church approached the matter of human action from a new vantage point and thereby added precision to a prior teaching. In short, the precise topic shifted. In earlier centuries, the Church was teaching that no *salvifically* good works are possible without grace. She still teaches this. In later centuries, the Church taught that *naturally* good works, albeit not salvific, are possible without grace. In other words, she taught that not every naturally good act requires grace. In earlier centuries she did not deny this. Thus, there is no contradiction; rather, there is growth and further precision. We can show this if we study the matter in greater depth.

It is the constant teaching of the Church, following our Lord (John 15:5), that we can do nothing salvifically good without grace. A salvifically good act is meritorious of Heaven; it really leads us toward Heaven because it is a holy act rooted in charity. Now, the Church did not use the expression "salvifically good work" in her earlier declaration in the Second Synod of Orange (AD 529). She simply said that we can do "nothing good" without grace. Those who understand the context know that the Church was referring precisely to *salvifically* good deeds. The Church was not saying that everything a sinner does is sinful. In fact, the theologian whose work was behind that synod was St. Augustine, and he clearly taught that pagans and sinners can and do perform acts that are not sinful. He said of these acts that not only are they not sinful, but not to do them would be sinful.[91] It would never have occurred to any of the bishops involved in the teaching to think that every last act of an unjustified person, including sleeping, is a sin. However, this thought did occur to Martin Luther, who was the first to dream that we sin in every act.

---

[90] See Pius V's condemnation of Michael Baius at DH 1925 and 1927.
[91] See Augustine, *On the Spirit and the Letter*, chap. 48 (*PL* 44:230). See also Augustine, Sermon 349, 1 (*Enchiridion Patristicum*, par. 1528).

False Mercy

Luther's assertion was echoed by later Catholic theologians espousing heresies. Michael Baius (d. 1589) said that every work of an unjustified person is a sin. The Church condemned this claim. The Church taught, to the contrary, that an unjustified person *can*, without grace, do some things that are *naturally good*. A mobster in the state of sin can, for example, help another person cross the street. A habitually lascivious young man can call his mom on Mother's Day out of genuine concern for her physical and emotional welfare. Such acts are naturally good, even though they are not salvifically good. They are not salvifically good because the person committing them is living in a state of sin. When living in a state of sin, one does *not* have sanctifying grace and charity in one's heart. As a result, one has very limited resources for acting well. Further, *only* by the power of sanctifying grace and charity can any of our actions be "proportionate to" or "meritorious of" the good of eternal salvation. So, without sanctifying grace and charity, we cannot take steps closer to Heaven. Without charity, we cannot perform any salvifically good acts. Importantly, however, by refraining from sin, we can make ourselves less indisposed to grace. But in order to obtain grace and charity after having committed a mortal sin, we must repent by a conscious and free act, and such repentance requires God's grace. Unless sinners repent and are justified, they will not go to Heaven, despite their "naturally good" acts. These acts—calling mom and helping a person cross the street—are good on a human level, but they are not acts of a divinized son of God. When committing these acts, the mortal sinner does not have sanctifying grace. He does not have sanctifying grace because he decided some time previously to choose a finite good as his last end and has refused to repent of it.

Why did the Church bother teaching about naturally good acts when such acts will not save anyone? It is a simple acknowledgment by the Church that we are not *totally* corrupted. Not everything we freely choose to do is morally evil. When an evil politician—who, through his legislative acts, attacks true marriage—tucks his child into bed at night, he is not doing evil. When the abortionist pays his home's electric bill, he is not doing evil. In short, those in the state of sin *do not sin in their every free act*, much less in their unfree or unconscious acts. Liberals who drink coffee at Starbucks but hate the Catholic Church might at least find this Catholic teaching to be more balanced, or less unbalanced, than that of Luther, whose extremism Baius imitated. This difference between Catholicism and Lutheranism shows that the Catholic Church appreciates *reason*. Conversing with friends, having a drink in moderation, playing softball, knitting a blanket, planting a tree for the environment, and the like are naturally good acts.

The development that took place on good works helps us see that the Church can treat in two contexts two subjects that are related but not identical. Put another way, she can approach the same matter in a new way. The earlier claims were focused on salvation, the only good that lasts; the later claims regard human action from a new vantage point. In treating the second topic, the Church added refinement to earlier claims. It would be erroneous to read the earlier claim that salvific acts require grace as already eliminating the possibility of the later acknowledgment that not every act of a sinner is sinful. In virtue of the development, two distinct but related doctrines are taught.

3. DEVELOPMENT THROUGH NEW TERMINOLOGY:
THE HYPOSTASIS OF THE SON

In the third century, the Church taught that the Son of God was *not* a "hypostasis" distinct from the Father.[92] In the fourth century, she taught that the Son *is* a "hypostasis" distinct from the Father.[93] To an outsider, the change looks like an obvious contradiction. It was not. The very meaning of the term "hypostasis" changed from one context to the next. In the earlier teaching, the term "hypostasis" meant something like "a being." Since Christians are monotheists, they have always held that there is only one God. So, when the term "hypostasis" means "a being," there clearly can be only one hypostasis in God. According to this usage of the term, the Son is not a "hypostasis" (i.e., a God) distinct from God the

[92] See the Council of Nicaea at DH 126.
[93] See, for example, the Synod at the Lateran at DH 501.

Father! But the meaning of the term shifted. It came to mean a distinct person, a distinct *bearer* of some nature. Thus, if there is a distinct bearer of the divine nature, there is a distinct "hypostasis." Since the Father generates the Son and sends the Son into the world, the Father is distinct from the Son. They share the same nature and are the same God, but they are distinct one from the other. Thus, according to this usage, the Father is one hypostasis and the Son is another hypostasis. They are distinct hypostases. The Church's earlier teaching that the Son is not "another being" from the Father does not contradict the Church's later teaching that the Son is "another person" from the Father. In a book on Trinitarian theology we could explore this issue at greater length, but this exposition helps us see that sometimes the meaning of a term shifts. Can the meaning ever remain constant? Yes. Insofar as the Catholic Church guides a whole body of people, she can use her authority to define the very meaning of terms. Consequently, she can instruct her people to employ that meaning. In this way, creeds and catechisms lend verbal stability to the tradition over time.

This case of development helps us appreciate that the meanings of words *can* change. If the Church wishes to use the newer public meaning of the term, she can reformulate a prior teaching. The truth claims in the two formulae are not contradictory; they can be identical or, as in the present case, complementary. None of the above objections is an instance of evolution or change. So none of the above examples is proof of doctrinal alteration.

Conclusion

Dogmatic development is the fruit of contemplative study in a heart that treasures God's mysteries, of the experience of the saints in prayer, and of the preaching of the bishops. Specific developments occur in various ways. In some cases, a dogma draws out a conclusion by way of deduction from the deposit. In some cases, a dogma arises from a sound but supple judgment concerning a multitude of testimonies in Scripture and Tradition. In some cases, a new approach to the same mystery can yield new insights about that mystery. New contexts and new meanings of terms occasion new dogmas.

In no case is a new formulation of dogma a distortion of or addition to the deposit of faith. Rather, a dogma is a precise statement of the mystery contained in the deposit or of a truth pertinent to that deposit. In each case, a dogma is an indication of what the Church has always believed based on the treasured twofold witness to Christ: Scripture and Tradition. She advances forward by cultivating a deepened insight into the same mystery.

Modernists claim that dogmas evolve, casting out the old in favor of the new. The Church rejects this notion as heresy. We must not let the modernists steer us toward a hermeneutic of rupture and discontinuity. Following the guidance of Pope Benedict XVI, we must practice a hermeneutic of continuity. In its exegetical mode, the hermeneutic of continuity helps us appreciate the Church's deeper insights as she advances in contemplation of the same deposit. Just as the development from the Old Testament to the New Testament was good, just as the development from Nicaea to Constantinople III was good, so are later developments. Dogma can and does develop. We shall encounter the exegetical mode of the hermeneutic of continuity in chapters 5 through 8. In its preservative mode, the hermeneutic of continuity helps us keep faith with the ancient teaching, which is forever true. Accordingly, our axiom remains firmly in place: we never have any excuse to water down, distort, or reject past infallible teachings. Having examined the basic elements of the Church's teaching on dogmatic development, we can now turn to specific errors and heresies. First, we turn to the fantasy of an empty Hell, by which our pilgrimage is made farcical.

2

Hell: An Empty Threat?

Some people do not think of the afterlife as a real possibility. Hence, the specter of an early death due to a virus such as COVID-19 is terrifying. On the other hand, the threat of eternal damnation does not bother them. In fact, such a prospect is no longer a major player in the decisions many people make, especially in the West. Those who do not believe in life after death often want to drink the cup of earthly enjoyment to its dregs, be it sensual pleasure or companionship with others or excellence in work. After this cup has delivered its promise, they hope to toss their aging bodies aside. Others, however, believe in the afterlife, but they cheer themselves with the Disney-like fantasy of an afterlife of rose petals, sunshine, and calm shorelines. Few people today act as though Hell is a real possibility.

One reason for the lack of concern of both groups is widespread loss of genuine faith. If the supernatural does not exist, there can be no Hell. Another reason is a falsification of divine mercy. This falsification is rooted in theological errors. Some theologians categorically deny that there is a Hell at all. They claim that the possibility of Hell is incompatible with a good and powerful God. The University of Notre Dame's David Bentley Hart is a notable recent example. Others, such as Peter C. Phan of Georgetown, toy with the idea of reincarnation: Christian faith "*may* accept the theory of reincarnation at least for those individuals whose lives do not possess a genuine history of freedom."[94] Since, however, the Scriptures and Catholic teaching are clear that Hell is not only possible but exists, few Catholic theologians are as frank as Hart. Instead of tackling the dogma of Hell directly, a number of Hell deniers strike it from the side. They do so in two ways. Some contend that, although Hell exists, it is practically impossible that anyone will go there. Others contend that those who go to what we call "Hell" will end up leaving Hell one way or another. They will either convert to God or annihilate themselves. We will treat both errors in turn, beginning with the latter.

The Error of Annihilationism

Popular Version
Eugenio Scalfari, atheist and provocateur, claimed in *la Repubblica* (March 2018) that Pope Francis told him that no humans suffer eternally in Hell. Instead, the supposedly "damned" eventually annihilate themselves. If you don't exist, you cannot be punished. Thus, according to Scalfari, Pope Francis denied that there is an everlasting punishment.[95] Scalfari had already attributed a similar claim to Pope Francis in 2015. Scalfari then alleged that, in response to a question about the fate of deceased souls, Pope Francis said, "There is no punishment, but rather the annihilation

---

94   Peter C. Phan, "Contemporary Context and Issues in Eschatology," *Theological Studies* 55 (1994): 530. For David Bentley Hart's argument against the possibility of Hell, see his *That All Shall Be Saved* (New Haven: Yale University Press, 2019). Hart's argument is engaging; were there more room, it would be good to address it. Suffice it to say that Hart has no explanation for the origin of evil. For him, it is as though evil just happens, while God is working on making the world a better place. Meanwhile, the question threatening his entire outlook is this: Why did not God create the world so that no evil would arise? In virtue of this difficulty, I find that Hart's thought is less Christian than neo-Platonist.

95   See Eugenio Scalfari, "Il Papa: 'È un onore essere chiamato rivoluzionario,'" *la Repubblica*, March 28, 2018, https://rep.repubblica.it/pwa/esclusiva/2018/03/28/news/il_papa_e_un_onore_essere_chiamato_rivoluzionario_-192479298/?ref=RHPPRB-BH-I0-C4-P1-S1.4-T1.

of that soul. All the others will participate in the beatitude of living in the presence of the Father."[96]

Given Scalfari's reports, are Catholics permitted to believe that souls are annihilated rather than damned? No, they are not. First, Catholics must recognize that Scalfari's claims are not papal words. They are not even "words of a pope." Rather, they are *alleged* words of a pope. Thus, they have no authority whatsoever. Second, we must not contradict Catholic dogma. Therefore, we must shun completely everything that contradicts Catholic dogma. In 2018, the Vatican did issue a statement to the effect that the pope met with Scalfari but did not offer an interview. Thus, the Vatican noted, Scalfari's words are but his own reconstruction of the discussion.[97] An explicit renunciation of annihilationism would have cleared up confusion for good-willed Catholics and would have defended them from modernist subversions of the Faith.

But in any case, on such matters, Catholics must take their lead from the infallible teachings and dogmas of the Faith. We believe that Hell exists. But all that God does is good and just. Therefore, the punishment of Hell is good and just. Further, we believe that Hell is already populated by demons. And demons are people too! Finally, we believe that, if any human souls are in Hell, they will never get out, just as no demons will get out. There is no such thing as the "annihilation" of the soul. There is no such thing as repenting of mortal sin after death. These ideas are pure fantasy. With tragic irony, these falsehoods lead souls to the Hell we are told is fake.

Scalfari obviously paid no attention to Pope Francis's severe warning to the men and women of the mafia:

> Please, change your lives, convert, stop, cease to do evil! We are praying for you. Convert, I ask it on my knees; it is for your own

---

[96] Eugenio Scalfari, "Quel che Francesco può dire all'Europa dei non credenti," *la Repubblica*, March 15, 2015, https://www.repubblica.it/politica/2015/03/15/news/quel_che_francesco_puo_dire_all_europa_dei_non_credenti-109542750/.

[97] Letter of the Press Office of the Vatican, March 29, 2018.

good. This life you are living now, it won't bring you pleasure, it won't give you joy, it won't bring you happiness. The power, the money, that you possess now from so many dirty transactions, from so many mafia crimes, is blood-stained money, it is power soaked in blood, and you cannot take it with you to the next life. Convert, there is still time, so that you don't end up in hell. That is what awaits you if you continue on this path.[98]

Deeper Theological Version

Why would anyone deny that souls suffer in Hell? To find an answer, we should consult a professional theological defense of the idea. If a professional defense does not work, neither will a less sophisticated and retrograde one. I will consider a robust theological argument to the effect that there is no Hell but rather *either* self-annihilation of the soul *or* conversion of the soul.[99] In this argument, annihilation is defined as a human person's disintegration. It is a person's ceasing to be a person, the end of a process that leaves only the bare traces of the old self. Accordingly, the souls of those in this "Hell" are not forever doomed. Rather, they can either repent or "annihilate themselves." Proponents of self-annihilation propose several interdependent arguments.

One argument is rooted in a patristic insight that sin is a *diminishment* or privation of the good. If sin is a diminishment of the good, then whatever is sinful is also good. So even the damned in Hell have *some* good in them. This patristic doctrine is true, yet the annihilationist misunderstands it, thinking that it entails that Hell cannot exist. He asserts without warrant that any rational creature that has some goodness can repent. So the annihilationist reasons, if there is some good present in the "damned," then the "damned" can repent.

---

[98] Francis, Address, March 21, 2014.

[99] See Paul Griffiths, "Self-Annihilation or Damnation? A Disputable Question in Christian Eschatology," *Pro Ecclesia* 16 (2007): 416–444. For another account by a Catholic, see Robert Wild, *A Catholic Reading Guide to Conditional Immortality: The Third Alternative to Hell and Universalism* (Eugene, OR: Resource Publications, 2016).

If they repent, they will no longer be damned. This is what you might call a "back door" out of Hell. The annihilationist further posits that whoever completely lacks the ability to repent has no goodness at all. But whoever has no goodness at all ceases to exist as a human; only remnants of a human remain.

The annihilationist also tackles this issue from the point of view of our dependence on God for existence. If we were to be totally bereft of God, we could not exist. So far, so good. Problematically, the annihilationist defines Hell as the total absence of God. If Hell is the total absence of God, then Hell cannot manage to exist. The annihilationist further charms us: if Hell *did* manage to exist, it would not entirely lack God's presence. But if it did not entirely lack God's presence, it would have some good in it. If it had some good in it, the souls detained there could repent and get out. According to this reasoning, a Hell of eternal punishment without hope of change is a contradiction in terms. Accordingly, after death, those who die in mortal sin either repent or "annihilate" themselves. Poof. So easy. Why didn't old Augustine recognize this magic trick when he had all the intellectual wherewithal at his disposal?

Evaluation

The annihilationist thesis is erroneous. The implication of the position — that Hell is not possible — contradicts the dogma of the Church that Hell is real. Since Hell exists, it must be possible. Thus, annihilationism entails a contradiction of the Faith.

Moreover, key theses in the arguments are erroneous. First, the annihilationist teaches that those who are in "Hell" can eventually escape its punishment, either by conversion or by annihilation. To the contrary, it is the solemn and constant teaching of the Catholic Church that the *punishment* of the damned lasts forever. This doctrine necessarily implies that the damned exist forever. The following teaching of Pope Pelagius I in 557 affirms the reality of eternal punishment:

> The wicked, however, remaining by their own choice as "vessels of wrath fit for destruction" [Rom. 9:22], who either did not know

the way of the Lord, or, knowing it, abandoned it when seduced by various transgressions, he will hand over by a most just judgment to the punishment of eternal and inextinguishable fire, so that they may burn without end.[100]

Pope Innocent III reaffirmed this teaching in 1201 and at Lateran IV in 1215.[101] Similarly, the First Council of Lyons solemnly taught in 1245: "If anyone dies in mortal sin without repentance, beyond any doubt, he will be tortured forever by the flames of everlasting hell."[102] The Church continues to teach this doctrine.[103] Thus, the Church in her ordinary and universal Magisterium and in her extraordinary Magisterium teaches infallibly that the punishment of Hell lasts forever.

Now, punishment cannot exist unless the person being punished exists, because punishment is the condition of a person undergoing punishment. Indeed, as the patristics teach us, punishment is a *privation* of the good, inflicted on account of guilt. But a privation exists only in an existing subject. The privation is the deprivation in that subject of some due good. So, if the punishment exists forever, so does the person being punished. By denying this, the annihilationist commits an error against a theologically certain conclusion.[104]

How do annihilationists respond to these criticisms? Their arguments transform into a hydra of weak responses. For example, they suggest that "eternal punishment" means only that there is an eternal "absence" of the vision of God because the supposedly damned person no longer exists. Since the "damned" person has annihilated himself, the remnant scraps of his former self eternally "lack" the vision. This response is vacuous.

---

[100] DH 443

[101] DH 780 and 801.

[102] DH 839.

[103] *Catechism of the Catholic Church* (CCC), pars. 1033–1035.

[104] The conclusion is only "theologically certain" because we have to add a premise: punishment can exist only if a punished person exists. Those who deny a theologically certain doctrine imply heresy but do not in that act commit heresy. Instead, they practice very bad theology. Suchlike errors endanger the Faith itself.

There is no meaningful "lack" where there is no relevant being there to experience this lack. If your dog Fido dies, the pile of meat that the worms are eating does not "lack" your affection as master. Fido the dog no longer exists! Since he no longer exists, he cannot lack anything. Now, Hell is the punishment of damned persons. If there exist no damned persons, the punishment does not exist. If it does not exist, it cannot be everlasting. So this response falls apart. Eternal punishment necessarily correlates with eternal existence of the punished.

Second, Catholic teaching implies the impossibility of the self-annihilation of the soul. The Church teaches that the soul is *immortal*. The Fifth Lateran Council declares:

> We condemn and reprove all those who assert that the intellectual soul is mortal or that it is one and the same in all men or who raise doubts in this matter. The intellectual soul is not only truly, of itself and essentially, the form of the human body [as in the Council of Vienne] ... but it is also immortal and, according to the great number of bodies into which it is individually infused, it can be, must be, and is multiplied.[105]

Note that this dogma treats the very "nature of the rational soul."[106] So this quality of immortality belongs to the nature of the soul. Since the soul is by nature immortal, it is by nature not able to disintegrate into "remnant parts." The Church teaches the former and thus implies the latter. Moreover, the same council condemns as false any philosophy purporting to prove the mortality of the soul. In addition, Roman congregations under Popes Gregory XVI and Pius IX declared that reason can prove the *spirituality* of the soul.[107] Pope Leo XIII in his encyclical against Masonry and naturalism declared that we can know of the soul's spirituality and immortality by the natural light of reason.[108] Pius XI de-

---

[105] DH 1440.
[106] DH 1440.
[107] DH 2766 and 2812.
[108] See Leo XIII, *Humanum genus* (1884), arts. 17–18.

clared that man "has a spiritual and immortal soul."[109] Vatican II reiterated this teaching in *Gaudium et spes*, art. 14. Paul VI reaffirmed it again in *Solemni hac liturgia*, art. 8. Thus, this teaching is constant and universal. It is one of the infallible truths that must be affirmed by all Catholics. But the annihilationists claim that we can annihilate even our souls. If we could annihilate them, our souls would not be immortal.

How do annihilationists respond? They fabricate the idea that the Church teaches merely that souls are *conditionally* immortal. They say that something that does not *have* to cease to exist is "conditionally immortal"; in other words, it *can* go on forever *if* it meets a condition. This reading of the Magisterium will not suffice. It runs contrary to the very sense in which these texts have been understood by commentators throughout the centuries. This interpretation is an "interpolation," by which the annihilationists inject foreign material into the dogma. They alone, if we would believe them, have unlocked the key to death and thus freed us from our soul's spiritual nature. What a boon for sinners! Here today and gone tomorrow: "Come, therefore, let us enjoy the good things that exist" (Wisd. 2:6). Let us sin today and annihilate ourselves tomorrow—perhaps, we might even repent! These are erroneous thoughts that lead us into sin (see Wisd. 2:21). They are scandalous in the proper sense of the term. As Justin the Martyr states, "If [death] issued in insensibility, [it] would be a godsend to all the wicked."[110]

As we have seen, the annihilationists even try to find support in odd readings of Augustine. Their notion of "conditional immortality" does not square with Augustine's understanding of immortality. Augustine was clear that Adam, as a man, in the state of original justice, was *not* immortal. Why? Because it was not impossible that he, being a rational animal, could die; God was preserving him from the necessity of death, but death was not an impossibility. In fact, *should* he sin, biological death would become an eventuality. So Augustine reserved the word

---

[109] DH 3771.

[110] Justin Martyr, *First Apology*, in *Ante-Nicene Fathers*, vol. 1, trans. Philip Schaff et al. (Peabody, MA: Hendrickson Publishers, 1994), 168–169.

"immortal" exclusively for life that *cannot* perish.[111] Importantly, however, Augustine did ascribe immortality to the soul. Although the soul can lose the graced life that comes from God, it never loses its capacity for cognition and experience entirely. Indeed, in the everlasting condemnation, the soul is quite cognizant.[112] Let the annihilationists drink in that sobriety.

Furthermore, the Fifth Lateran Council expressly states that our Lord teaches the immortality of the soul when He says, "Do not fear those who kill the body but *cannot* kill the soul" (Matt. 10:28, emphasis mine). It is not possible to kill the soul. You cannot "annihilate" your soul. This same council *teaches* the link between eternal punishment and the immortality of the soul. Thus, the Church herself guarantees the theological conclusion that the immortality of the soul is implicitly revealed in the revelation of eternal punishment.[113] As though anticipating the error of annihilationism, the *Catechism of the Catholic Church* defines "immortality" by apposition in the following statement: the soul "is immortal: it does not perish when it separates from the body at death."[114] The notion of "conditional immortality" is a figment of the imagination. Better to heed Hamlet's haunt: "What dreams may come, when we have shuffled off this mortal coil?"

Finally, we should note that the annihilationist position is contrary to reason. The soul is an immaterial principle of existence that subsists of itself. Now, only material things can be corrupted or cease to exist by change. The stuff of the apple is eaten; it ceases to be the stuff of an apple and now is the stuff of a human. A goat is eaten by a lion; what was the stuff of a goat is now the stuff of a lion, and the remnants are stuff of worms, and so forth. The concrete corporeal thing has ceased to exist. But the soul is immaterial. It is not a composite of matter and form,

---

[111] See Augustine, *City of God*, bk. 13, chaps. 1–2.

[112] See ibid., 21.

[113] See Fifth Lateran Council, Session VIII, December 19, 1513, in Norman P. Tanner, ed., *Decrees of the Ecumenical Councils*, vol. 1 (London: Sheed & Ward, 1990), 605–606.

[114] CCC 366.

such that its material aspect could lose its form by corruption. Thus, the soul cannot be corrupted by any activity. We can kill our bodies, but we cannot kill our souls. To be sure, God can annihilate our souls by withdrawing existence from them. But there is nothing we can do to our souls to render them no longer human souls. We're "stuck," so to speak. God created us by His love, and He invites us to His mercy. Let us not insult Him by our absurdities and heresies.

Conclusion

Whether the odd remarks of high-ranking prelates or the irresponsible work of recent theologians are the cause or not, many people have the sense that the Catholic Church no longer thinks that Hell is a big deal. As a result, life has been gutted of its seriousness. Our biggest concerns now seem to be plastics, youth unemployment, policies of extraction, and unjust police brutality. While these are real concerns that need to be addressed, they are not priorities of the Gospel. Instead, the New Testament begins with the Baptist's warning cry: "Who warned you to flee from the wrath to come?" (Matt. 3:7). If we neglect this foundational question, we know not what to live for. Why not either indulge in the pleasantries of the world or become angry rioters who pillage and destroy? If we do heed this cry, we can be transformed into people of love who work prudently to make the world a more just place *by* orienting it to Heaven above all things.

Some people admit the possibility of Hell but think of it as an irrelevant possibility. Hell exists, they say, but, practically speaking, no one will go there. A professor at Notre Dame once said to us students, "None of us is smart enough to commit a mortal sin." Well, if you're not smart enough to commit a mortal sin, you certainly can't go to Hell either. I remember thinking to myself, in my sinful youth, "That's awesome. Let's sin, and sin boldly!" But living along the lines of that poisonous advice left me empty. Receiving the Eucharist while in that state made me feel terrible. What deplorable advice. Deep down, I felt that something was wrong, that I had been lied to. To this issue of a real Hell that is nonetheless most likely vacant we now turn.

The Error of a Possibly Empty Hell

Popular Confusion

A full presentation of the Catholic teaching on this topic calls for attention both to mercy and to justice. We must attend both to the hope of repentance and to the reality of judgment and condemnation. Just as it is imbalanced for a priest to preach only fire and brimstone, so it is imbalanced for a prelate to stress divine mercy to the point of eclipsing divine justice and human sinfulness.

Recent popes have issued statements that some have taken to suggest that Hell is empty. John Paul II, in his personal work *Crossing the Threshold of Hope*, asks about damnation: "To what degree is it realized in life beyond the grave?"[115] He responds by noting that the matter is a mystery. Then he immediately cites 1 Timothy 2:3–4, "God ... desires all men to be saved." When *Crossing the Threshold* was published, I was involved in an unofficial ecumenical dialogue in Washington, DC. One of the members of the dialogue was a cultured and brilliant Baptist pastor who worked on Capitol Hill. He lamented the presence of this passage in a book he considered otherwise decent. I lamented with him. Why? In the above passage, John Paul II, a heroic man, seemed to muse on the possibility that all men may be saved. He thus seemed to neglect the following words of our Lord: "The gate is narrow and the way is hard, that leads to life, and those who find it are few" (Matt. 7:14). At any rate, how should a Catholic receive these reflections of John Paul II? Above all, a Catholic should recognize that they are only the pope's personal reflections. These are not papal words but words of a pope.

More recently, Pope Francis has made statements that seem to touch on this issue. On February 15, 2015, Francis stated, "The way of the Church is not to condemn anyone for eternity."[116] Some have taken this to mean that Francis rejects Hell. Such a reading ignores the context: the statement regards the Church's power to make ecclesiastical judgments.

---

[115] John Paul II, *Crossing the Threshold of Hope*, 73.
[116] Francis, homily, February 15, 2015.

Obviously, the Church has no power to cast anyone into Hell. Rather, God casts sinners into Hell. So this statement does not deny the dogma of Hell. A clarification would help us smelly sheep find verdant pastures and living water.

Two years earlier, Pope Francis had said, "God never condemns, he only loves and saves."[117] Some, taking this statement on its own, seem to think that it denies the possibility of Hell. Even if it did, Catholics know that they are obliged to cling to dogma. The context shows that Pope Francis meant to insist that the *sinner*, not God, makes himself worthy of condemnation. Still, to avoid confusion let us remember that the Catholic Church does indeed believe that God condemns unrepentant sinners to hell (see Matt. 7:23) while she rejects the idea that God causes anyone to sin (so-called double predestination).

In a General Audience of December 11, 2013, Pope Francis taught that Jesus judges us in love and that therefore all fear and hesitation should fade away. Again, Pope Francis described the Last Judgment as an encounter with the merciful Jesus. He did not mention the justice and judgment of Christ. He concluded, "Everything will be saved. Everything."[118] Some take this statement to mean that no intellectual creature (no person) goes to Hell. Such a reading would contradict the constant and universal Catholic teaching that demons are in Hell. Since demons are people too, no Catholic has any excuse to use this statement to hold that Hell is empty. A full presentation of the Last Judgment includes both mercy and justice.

On another occasion, in his post-synodal exhortation *Amoris laetitia*, Pope Francis declared, "No one can be condemned forever, because that is not the logic of the Gospel."[119] How should a Catholic react to this claim? Once again, no Catholic has an excuse for denying the existence of Hell. And once again, Pope Francis is here speaking of the *Church's* authority. The Church has no authority to condemn anyone to Hell. The Church

---

[117] Francis, Way of the Cross, Colosseum, March 29, 2013.

[118] Francis, General Audience, October 11, 2017.

[119] Francis, *Amoris laetitia* (2016), art. 297.

does, however, have the power to excommunicate. So Francis may be referring to excommunication and related penalties. Without question, the Church always holds out hope for those whom she excommunicates. There are two purposes of excommunication. Above all, it is intended to safeguard the *common good* of the whole Church, protecting the flock from the excommunicated person or his errors. It is also intended for the good of the excommunicated person. Excommunication tells a person that his sin is serious and requires repentance. Reconciliation before death is possible. In that sense, the Church does not condemn someone irrevocably. We can see Francis reminding us of this. The reminder does not annihilate Hell.

On another occasion, Pope Francis claimed that God never abandons his children. In a General Audience of May 9, 2018, he stated,

> The seal of Baptism is never lost! "Father, but if a person becomes an infamous brigand, who kills people, who inflicts injustice, does the seal not disappear?" No. To his own shame a child of God is the person who does these things; but the seal does not go away. And he continues to be a child of God, who opposes God; but God never disowns his children. Do you understand this last point? God never disowns his children. Shall we all repeat it together? "God never disowns his children." A little louder, because either I am hearing impaired or I did not understand: [they repeat, louder] "God never disowns his children." There, that was better.[120]

The core truth within this message is the first statement, "the seal of Baptism is never lost." In fact, the permanence of the baptismal character is a dogma of the Church. But what does this dogma mean, and what does it not mean? It does not mean that every baptized person will go to Heaven or that it is impossible for a baptized person to be damned in Hell. Damnation is possible for the baptized; a damned Christian retains the seal of Baptism, but it does him no good. Rather, the seal entitles him to greater punishment, for it is a sign of the abundant grace that

---

[120] Francis, General Audience, May 9, 2018.

was offered to him during his life. During the pilgrim life of the believer, God offers the graces necessary for salvation. After death, those who alienated themselves from God's graces are cast out as lifeless branches and tormented forever in the flames of Hell. Christ Himself will disown these souls, saying, "I never knew you; depart from me, you evildoers" (Matt. 7:23).[121] This is our Catholic Faith. This is crucial knowledge given to us that we cannot afford to forget.

The popular misconception many Catholics have—that Hell is empty or practically empty—has its deeper roots in the works of recent Catholic theologians. Foremost among these are the works of Karl Rahner, S.J., and Hans Urs von Balthasar. As inspection shows, Balthasar makes a more elaborate case than does Rahner, and he is widely respected by many devout Catholics. Further, Rahner's arguments rest upon his theory of the supernatural existential, which has grave weaknesses.[122] For these reasons, I consider only Balthasar's arguments here.

Hans Urs von Balthasar's Hope

Balthasar asks, "What may we hope for?" His question is whether we may hope that all human beings will be saved. Many who popularize Balthasar's message, including high-profile bishops, hone in on this narrow question: "*May* we *hope* that *all humans* will be saved?" The question has two appealing characteristics. First, it is tentative: "May we hope?" Second, it regards only humans, not demons. If we reduce the whole issue

---

[121] Even John Paul II describes God's response to unrepentant sin as "God's rejection of man" in his *Crossing the Threshold of Hope*, 70.

[122] For a popular critique of Rahner's project, see Christopher J. Malloy, "Rahner: The Withering of Faith," in *"Faith Once for All Delivered": Tradition and Doctrinal Authority in the Catholic Church*, ed. Kevin Flannery and Robert Dodaro (forthcoming). Rahner also puts forth a theory he calls the "supernatural existential." It is far too complicated to present here, but it is one of the major pillars of his entire work. Almost all of the opinions of Rahner mentioned below rest on this theory. For my critical academic analysis of his theory, see Christopher J. Malloy, "Rahner's Supernatural Existential: What *Is* It?" *Freiburger Zeitschrift für Philosophie und Theologie* 63 (2016): 402–421.

to this very narrow formulation of the question, we will fail to notice the full scope of Balthasar's apparatus in defense of his answer. Add to these characteristics the following mistaken decoy: Balthasar and his disciples point out that the Church has never dogmatically declared that any man is in Hell. The recipe of these three factors attracts many readers to Balthasar's alluring question. To address this issue thoroughly, we must examine the various argumentative engines that propel Balthasar's thinking on this topic. After doing that, we can finally return to the question about Hell's population and what we may hope about it.

We should begin by noting the important truths that Balthasar highlights for us. Above all, it is Catholic doctrine that everyone who is alive is redeemable. Every living person, no matter how enmeshed in sin, *can* repent. (Apparently, that would include the sundry antichrists who have accosted the Church through the ages, even the final one, whenever he may appear.) The most aberrant sexual deviant, who freely got himself into his various levels of degradation, can still repent. The most hardened racist who opposes the advancement of races other than his own can still repent. The greedy miser who pays inhuman salaries and threatens starved laborers with unemployment can still repent. Only death closes off the possibility of conversion. Death, the separation of the rational soul from the body (not necessarily brain or cardiac "death"), is the moment after which conversion from hostility to friendship with God, from sin to grace, is no longer possible.

Of course, there is a crucial fact that Balthasar glosses over *in places where it should be stressed*—namely, that those who fail to repent soon after committing a mortal sin enter into a state of impenitence. This hardened state of the heart can grow worse. Impenitence makes conversion ever more difficult. It thus anticipates the state of the damned, for whom there is no hope. Catholic doctrine thus offers a balance: the mercy of God toward the living and the real threat of sin leading to impenitence, a foretaste of damnation. To stress the mercy of God for the living is *simply Catholic truth*. It is fruitless to paint a dire picture of sin and then leave the hearers flailing in anguish and guilt. Just because the world has forgotten about justice does not mean that we can take His vengeance into our hands. It puts people off. Our message must lead to hope, to deeper trust that God, as a loving Father, wants our salvation. This mercy led Christ to shed His blood even for the worst of sinners. Jesus Himself exemplified the ways in which we should become a people of mercy, reaching out toward the spiritually poor as well as the materially poor, toward the possessed, toward the lascivious, toward murderers, and even toward Judas. If He asked Peter to forgive seventy times seven times, how much more magnanimous will our Savior be?

I do not recommend that untrained theologians read Balthasar. In my opinion, there are too many errors in his work. These errors are obstacles to the Faith. Still, his work is very engaging and attractive, even *enticing*. It is attractive especially for the pious. Why? Because Balthasar calls on each of us to repent and to pray and mortify ourselves for sinners. He lauds God as beautiful. He also has many genuine, deep insights. No one can object to these strengths! Moreover, Balthasar was a literary genius; his works are often hymns. Finally, he has many profound and startling insights. But in his arguments for hope in an empty Hell, Balthasar goes astray. To these we now turn.

One of Balthasar's arguments is scriptural. He holds that every text in Scripture that appears to indicate future damnation of guilty humans is simply a *warning*. No such text, he counsels, should be read as a prophecy of the damnation of any human being. No such text indicates an actual outcome; each indicates only a *possible* outcome. Thus, although Scripture apparently presents us with two distinct groups in the future, the saved and the damned, such texts are simply warnings that there *might* be a group of damned as well as that of the saints. Here, in a rare moment, Balthasar cites favorably a modernist principle of Karl Rahner.[123] Given

---

[123] For Balthasar's endorsement of Rahner's approach, see *Dare We Hope "That All Men Be Saved"?* trans. David Kip and Lothar Krauth, 2nd ed. (San Francisco: Ignatius Press, 2014), 20. Balthasar is frequently at antipodes from Rahner. He would not agree with Rahner's wider claim that any future scriptural revelation, however veiled in symbolism, is only an extrapolation from our present situation: "Man's knowledge of the future still to come, even his revealed knowledge, is confined to such prospects as

that, for Balthasar, Scripture does not prophecy the damnation of men, how should we read it? We should read it as people "under judgment" who (1) just might sin mortally without repenting and yet (2) are inspired by hope in God's mercy. Most popularizers stop here. The thesis seems humble, hopeful, and sober. The popularizers tend to ignore Balthasar's supporting arguments. I will examine this thesis only after examining Balthasar's systematic arguments.

Among Balthasar's systematic arguments is, first, that only sheer malice—pure and absolute hatred of God—can condemn someone to Hell. How does he justify this claim? Balthasar portrays sin as a "reality." For him, sin is not just a "privation."[124] In classical terminology, a privation is an absence, *in* someone or something, of a good proper to the kind of thing that someone or something is. For example, blindness is a privation in an animal that should be able to see (e.g., a dog). Blindness is the absence of the ability to see in an animal for whom seeing is natural. The Fathers of the Church unanimously held that sin is a privation of a good in human action; they agreed that sin is not a thing. By contrast, the Gnostics and the Manichaeans held that sin is a thing. Balthasar rejects the patristic tradition and holds that sin is a reality. For Balthasar, sin is a loathsome thing in us. Balthasar further claims that Jesus removes this reality of sin from us and takes it upon Himself. As a result, Balthasar believes, the sinner has been freed from the awful burden of sin, if only he will let Jesus carry it away from him.[125] After Jesus' redeeming act,

---

can be derived from the reading of his present eschatological experience." See Karl Rahner, "On the Hermeneutics of Eschatological Statements," in *Theological Investigations*, vol. 4, trans. Kevin Smyth (Baltimore: Helicon Press, 1966), 334. Rahner is here at one with the modernists.

[124] Balthasar, *Dare We Hope*, 107–108. See also Hans Urs von Balthasar, *Mysterium Paschale*, trans. Aidan Nichols (Grand Rapids, MI: Eerdmans, 1990), 173, and Hans Urs von Balthasar, *Theo-Drama: Theological Dramatic Theory*, vol. 5, *The Last Act*, trans. Graham Harrison (San Francisco: Ignatius Press, 1998), 314. The implication may be found in Hans Urs von Balthasar, *Theo-Logic*, vol. 2, *Truth of God*, trans. Adrian Walker (San Francisco: Ignatius Press, 2004), 323.

[125] See Balthasar, *Theo-Drama*, vol. 5, 260–261, 267, and 314.

Balthasar argues, Jesus shed the terrible burden of the reality of sin; as a result, the pure essence of sin came to exist on its own. All the sins of the world came to exist in one "place," as it were; they became a heaping lump of pure malice, an existing *Non serviam* (I will not serve)" to God. Jesus' redemptive act now calls to us: "Let me take your sin away from you." What will we do in response? Will we allow this redeeming act to save us? If we allow it, Christ will take away the malice of our sin and leave everything else. So, if there is anything in us that is not pure malice, it will remain and we shall be saved. Only if we identify ourselves with the malice that Christ takes away will we be damned, for, in such a case, we would *be* a pure no to God and would thus be irredeemable. If there is any ounce of non-malice in us, we shall be redeemed.[126] Only those who are identical with their sin are not saved.[127] That's a very high bar for damnation.[128]

Second, Balthasar asks whether such a sin—pure and unrepented malice—is possible. He admits that it is possible in the abstract.[129] But, he holds, such a sin is, concretely speaking, highly unlikely.[130] In support of this claim, Balthasar draws from the tradition of moral theology. He reminds us that our wills are ordered to the "good as such." Everything we do, we do under the aspect of the good.[131] Therefore, sin is a contradiction against our very essence. We must grant that this moral tradition is true. The problem is how Balthasar reads it. The moral tradition holds that our acts seek out the good *in general*; that is, we act toward what has at

---

[126] See Balthasar, *Theo-Drama*, vol. 5, 296–297.

[127] Ibid. , 287–288 and 298.

[128] In *Spe salvi* (2007), Pope Benedict XVI seems to give the impression of such a high bar as well. In article 45, he describes some people as "utterly pure" and others as "totally destroyed their desire for truth and readiness to love." Then, in article 46, he adds, "Yet we know from experience that neither case is normal." Only members of the second group, he seems to say, go to Hell.

[129] See Balthasar, *Theo-Drama*, vol. 5, 285–90.

[130] Ibid., 298 and 314; Hans Urs von Balthasar, *Theo-Drama*, vol. 4, *The Action*, trans. Graham Harrison (San Francisco: Ignatius, 1994), 350.

[131] Ibid., 300–301 and 307.

least the *appearance* of attractiveness. The moral tradition does not hold that our acts stretch out only toward real goods. When one person hates another and acts on that hate, there is nothing *morally* good about the act. But the person hating sees the act as attractive insofar as it achieves his own ends. Perhaps he loves his own honor or freedom from punishment. The little child might hate her parents when she is disciplined for doing serious mischief. The attractiveness of the apparent good does not render the act of hatred morally good in the slightest.

Back to Balthasar. He seems to reify this orientation of the will to the good as such. As a result, he posits that sinning takes more and more effort the more you do it. You grow weary sinning. So, he suggests, you will likely give up sinning eventually. Sin contradicts what you *really* are. Maybe you can swing a sinful lifestyle for a week, a few months, a number of years. But eventually you will give up, since you cannot keep contradicting who you really are. (Abstractly, you might; concretely, you won't.) What will win out in the end, feeble sin or a robust essence oriented to the good? Eventually, Balthasar opines, sin will wear itself out, and we will cease to do evil.[132]

Third, Balthasar on occasion rejects the idea that our eternal fate is determined by the state in which we die. Following up on his first strategy, he contends that if there was one moment in our lives in which we exhibited genuine love, then there is something about us that is salvageable: "We must realize that what is placed in the scales is not the mere final state of a life but this life in its totality." He continues, "We must ask whether a negative fundamental decision, even if it is chronologically the last in a particular life, can have expressed itself in all life situations without exception."[133] These musings imply that even if we die in the state of sin, we can be saved because of that one act of charity in the past. Thankfully, Balthasar cancels out these musings in other places in which he claims not to imply conversion after death. For example, he states that he does not want to "imply that a further 'conversion' is still

[132] Ibid., 304.
[133] Ibid., 296.

possible at the Judgment, after death."[134] We are left with a contradiction. What is Balthasar saying? One thing he seems to deny: a single mortal sin, if unrepented, causes damnation.

Fourth, in case the second strategy fails, Balthasar plays a stronger card, that of the divine will. God's will is infinite, whereas man's will is only finite. Thus, Balthasar holds, God's will *can* overcome our finite will. If God's will can overcome all rebellion, surely He is good enough *actually* to overcome it. Consider these citations:

> "Unless God's demands" on his Son "were divine in character, unless God's acts were unsurpassable, each one surpassing the other, the work of redemption on the Cross could be surpassed by man's negation. But when God makes demands of God he makes sure that God always overtakes man, that grace has more weight than sin, that the redemption is complete."[135]

> There is no longer any possibility of hearing any word of God without thereby coming to the Son.[136]

> If all sins are undercut and undergirded by God's infinite love, it suggests that sin, evil, must be finite and must come to an end in the love that envelops it.[137]

In short, for Balthasar, God's infinite and benevolent will precludes the possibility of a sinner remaining forever unrepentant.

Fifth, following through on that fourth argument, Balthasar *reformulates* his initial question. His initial question was "May we hope" that all men are saved? A reader might take Balthasar to mean: May we hope that every sinner will at length accept the forgiving mercy of God and repent? So understood, the uncertainty about this hope is only on the side of the result: whether the sinner accepts God's grace and repents.

---

[134] Ibid., 297, and *Dare We Hope*, 145.
[135] Balthasar, *Theo-Drama*, vol. 5, 280.
[136] Ibid., 281.
[137] Ibid., 283.

The abundance of God's grace working for this result is a given. But Balthasar will not let the question take this form only. Rather, he places the uncertainty on the side of God's predestining will. He asks whether God will *allow* finite men to defeat His infinite will: "The question is whether God, with respect to his plan of salvation, ultimately depends, and wants to depend, upon man's choice; or whether his freedom, which wills only salvation and is absolute, might not remain above things human, created, and therefore relative."[138] As the trustworthy theologian Fr. Thomas J. White has argued, Balthasar is not asking us to hope that every sinner will repent; rather, he is asking us to hope that God *predestines* all to glory in an unconditional way.[139]

Sixth, Balthasar mocks the traditional distinction, which dates back at least to John Damascene in the eighth century, between God's antecedent will (by which He wills all to be saved) and His consequent will (by which He wills that only those who die in grace be saved). Balthasar taunts anyone who dares to uphold this distinction, making it seem as though anyone who does must believe that God is weak. That is, whoever believes that God's antecedent will that all be saved can be thwarted by sin must believe in a weak God:

> Here one cannot get by without making distinctions that, while retaining the notion of God's benevolent will, nevertheless allow it to be frustrated by man's wickedness.... Permit us, Lord, to make a small distinction in your will.... But what about Jesus' triumphant words when he looks forward to the effect of his Passion: "Now shall the ruler of this world be cast out ..."? Oh, he will perhaps attempt to draw them all but will not succeed in holding them all. "Be of good cheer, I have overcome *the world*" (John 16:33). Unfortunately, only half of it, despite your efforts, Lord.[140]

---

[138] *Dare We Hope*, 6–7. For further references, see *Dare We Hope*, 166ff.

[139] Thomas Joseph White, "Von Balthasar and Journet on the Universal Possibility of Salvation and the Twofold Will of God," *Nova et Vetera* 4 (2006): 633–666.

[140] *Dare We Hope*, 146–147.

Balthasar's argument against the distinction amounts to sarcasm. Sarcasm against what? Against the tradition of sacred theology! This literary tactic is part of a practice. Balthasar labels all who hold that Hell exists and is populated as "infernalists." This is nothing but vilification.

Seventh, Balthasar at times extends his hope to the "already" damned. That is, he argues that God's power extends into Hell itself to make the damned convert from the mortal sin in which they died. Now, Catholic dogma is that those who die in sin go straight to everlasting Hell. Since Hell is everlasting, the damned cannot convert. As we have noted, in his better moments, Balthasar does express agreement with that particular dogma. What, then, is his real position? The occasions of his extension of hope to the damned are linked with his thesis that Christ descended into the Hell of the damned.[141] He contends that no matter how far from God one has gone or could go, Christ is already there, offering His redeeming grace.[142] The following citations show this:

> Sin's impatience, as the sum of all world-historical sinful impatience against God, is finally exhausted in comparison to the patience of the Son of God. His patience undergirds sin and lifts it off its hinges.... But this is precisely how he disturbs the absolute loneliness that the sinner strives for: the sinner who wants to be "dammed" by God now rediscovers God in loneliness—but this time he rediscovers God in the absolute impotence of love. For now God has placed himself in solidarity with those who have damned themselves, entering into nontime in a way we could never anticipate. The verse of the psalm: "If I make my bed in Sheol, thou art there!" (Ps. 139:8) thus receives a whole new meaning. And even the battle cry "God is dead"—that self-asserting diktat of the sinner who is finished with God—gains a whole new meaning that God himself has established. Creaturely

---

[141] See especially Hans Urs von Balthasar, "The Descent into Hell," in *Explorations in Theology*, vol. 4, trans. Edward Oakes (San Francisco: Ignatius Press, 1995), 407–412. See also *Theo-Drama*, vol. 5, 311ff.

[142] See *Theo-Drama*, vol. 4, 311.

freedom is respected but is still overtaken by God at the end of the Passion and once more undergirded (*"inferno profundior,"* as Pope Gregory the Great put it). Only in absolute weakness does God want to give each freedom created by him the gift of a love that breaks out of every dungeon and dissolves every constriction: in solidarity, from within, with [those who] refuse all solidarity.[143]

How will the Judge behave toward those who come before him as ones who have turned away, who appear in the Gospel parables and other logia of Jesus as the ones whom he 'does not know'.... We do not know.... [He won't overpower freedom.] ... It remains, however, to consider whether it is still not open to God to encounter the sinner who has turned away from him in the impotent form of the crucified brother who has been abandoned by God, and indeed in such a way that it becomes clear to the one who has turned away from God that: this One beside me who has been forsaken by God (like myself) has been abandoned by God for my sake. Now there can be no more talk of doing violence to freedom if God appears in the loneliness of the one who has chosen the total loneliness of living only for himself (or perhaps one should say: who thinks that is how he has chosen) and shows himself to be as the One who is still lonelier than the sinner. In order to see this, we must recall what was said at the outset, according to which the world has been founded in advance with all its freely chosen destinies in view of the mystery of the self-surrendering Son of God: whose descent is a priori deeper than the depths any lost person in the world can reach. Even what we call "hell"—although it is indeed the place of reprobation—is still even more a christological place.[144]

Balthasar concludes: "Hell, then, is transformed by the Cross: grace penetrates to the point where damnation was. Redemption penetrates to the

---

[143] *Explorations in Theology,* vol. 4, 421–422.
[144] Ibid., vol. 4, 456–457.

point where there was definitive judgment."[145] Because of God's redeeming action, Hell becomes Purgatory:

He has transformed "the path of man's destiny" into the "path of obedience of the eternal Son", and so "he brings comfort to this place of hopelessness, fire to this place of iciness, mercifulness to this place of justice" and "purgatory" to this place of hell.[146]

Properly speaking, therefore, purgatory comes into existence on Holy Saturday, when the Son walks through "hell", introducing the element of mercy into the condition of those who are justly lost.[147]

The dream of Hell turning into Purgatory sounds like one part of the annihilationist error.

Eighth, Balthasar is thus forced to redefine the "eternity" of Hell. He invents the notion of "eternal punishment" as something that does not necessarily last forever but that is "infinitely intense." With this novelty, Balthasar dismisses the bothersome notion of "everlasting" punishment and asserts that the Church teaches only an infinitely "intense" punishment. So, he implies, it is not heresy to hold that Hell is not everlasting.[148] Some proponents of hopeful universalism also point to the scholarly claim that the English translation for "eternal" should be "ages and ages" or "long-lasting." They say that the Bible does not say, unequivocally, that Hell's punishment is "eternal."

Ninth, Balthasar occasionally weaves into his narrative the contention that Hell is even impossible. He writes, "It would be rewarding here to listen a bit to Gustave Martelet, S.J., 'If God is love, as the New Testament teaches us, hell must be impossible. At the least, it represents a supreme anomaly.'" Balthasar cites Martelet's further comments to the effect that the Gospels never present unrepented sin "as a credible possibility that

---

[145] Balthasar, *Theo-Logic*, vol. 2, 355. See this in the context of pages 345–361.
[146] Balthasar, *Theo-Drama*, vol. 5, 313–314.
[147] Ibid., 363.
[148] Ibid., 309.

Jesus could be satisfied to accept. For hell is the real absurdity."[149] To ears weakened by worldliness and by the heresies of weak-kneed prelates, how could this not sound like extremely welcome good news? This world of darkness is ruled by a prince whose spirit has put the justice of God on trial and found it guilty. The worldly spirit will not tolerate the God of justice. The world limits God to His mercy and love, banishing from Him all retributive justice.[150] Now, Balthasar does admit here that the sinner might remain obstinate. He notes, however, that such would be possible only with the permission of God.[151] And yet, as we have seen, Balthasar's very hope is that God does not permit this at all.[152]

Tenth, Balthasar's final argument is that God would be infinitely and tragically grieved if anyone were damned. If God permitted man to sin impenitently, then God's infinite will for salvation would be forever frustrated.[153] As a result, God would live a tragic sadness eternally.[154] Of course, eternal tragedy is not likely. Thus, Balthasar submits, it is infinitely improbable that Hell is populated.

From the foregoing, it should be clear that Balthasar does not simply point out that there is no dogma stating that any particular person is in Hell. Rather, he argues in sundry ways against the likelihood and even the very possibility of Hell. I have registered some criticism in passing, but I must now do so more incisively.

---

[149] *Dare We Hope*, 37–38n10, citing Gustave Martelet, *L'au-delà retrouvé: Christologie des fins dernières* (Paris: Desclée, 1974), 181ff.

[150] Consider, for example, the words of Pope Francis: "If I embrace [God's] love then I am saved, if I refuse it, then I am condemned, not by him, but my own self, because God never condemns, he only loves and saves." Pope Francis, "Way of the Cross," March 29, 2013. The quotation might be taken to mean that the first cause in the line of evil is the sinner. Taken thus, it is true. If it were taken in the sense that God never judges and punishes in response to the sinful initiative of the sinner, who can remain impenitent until death, it would be false.

[151] *Dare We Hope*, 41.

[152] Ibid., 166–167.

[153] Ibid., 190–191.

[154] See Balthasar, *Theo-Drama*, vol. 5, 299 and 506ff.

Critique of Balthasar's Arguments

Balthasar's thought on this topic is deeply flawed on many points. At the same time, there is something very attractive in his work. I consider his project to be a tragic failure. It could have been a great project, because Balthasar was a man of consummate genius, erudition, creativity, style, and ostensible piety. It is not impossible for theologians to work from some of the basic lines of thought he pioneered. Still, whoever attempts to hoe that path must do so with prudence and with reverence for the theological tradition and the Church's teachings. A bit of Thomistic discipline and clarity would also go a long way. Sadly, Balthasar did not show such prudence and reverence, nor did he exercise Thomistic discipline. Thus, above all, we must locate where his empty-Hell project fails.

First, we have already mentioned that Hell is populated by demons, who are people too. This is a doctrinal fact. This fact serves to undermine a number of Balthasar's other arguments.

Second, the fact that there are demons in Hell mandates a distinction between the "antecedent divine will" and the "consequent divine will," a distinction Balthasar lambasted with mockery. Orthodox theologians draw this distinction to explain the harmony of two truths, God's will that all be saved and the fact of the damnation of some. They accept the fact of damnation, and they attempt to account for it. Calling them "infernalists" is an ad hominem vilification unbecoming of a gentlemen, let alone a Christian.

St. John Damascene taught us to see how God's singular will regards His human creatures in two respects. Building on John's theology, St. Thomas Aquinas distinguished the two ways in which God's one will regards the sinful person: (1) as a person with a human nature and (2) as a free actor who either has or has not cooperated with grace. The divine will considered in the former way is called the "antecedent divine will," and that considered in the latter way is called the "consequent divine will." John is not claiming that God has two wills. He is claiming that God looks at us in two respects. Antecedently, in virtue of the fact that someone is a person of human nature, God wills that person's salvation. In virtue of this benevolence, God offers that person graces sufficient for salvation. Still, the antecedent divine will is conditional, not absolute; one is free to accept or reject those graces.[155] Consequently, God considers whether the human person has cooperated with those graces. The consequent divine will is absolute because it already includes the condition of the response. If the person has accepted and cooperated with grace, God wills to give him eternal life.[156] If the person has not accepted that grace, God wills the person to be damned.

We can see an analogy to this with the way we consider others. Say I mention that Xavier is a young man who lives in your neighborhood. You don't know him. But, if you were to want something for him, what would it be? Since Xavier is a fellow human being, you would probably wish that he were healthy, happy, and free to move about. But if I specify that he has molested pubescent males, what would you wish for him? You would wish that he were incarcerated; of course, you would hope for his repentance and salvation, but you would also wish that he were imprisoned. So it is with God. To repeat: God has only one will, but his will regards the human person in two ways.

Third, it is false for Balthasar to claim that only sheer malice damns. Any unrepented mortal sin damns. Lyons II dogmatically defines this truth: "As for the souls of those who die in mortal sin or with original sin only, they go down immediately to hell, to be punished, however, with different punishments."[157] In order to merit eternal damnation, you simply need to die in the state of sin. But anyone who commits a single mortal sin and fails to repent dies in mortal sin. This is a terrifying reality; let us not deny this half of the truth. It would be unpastoral to do so.

---

[155] We are speaking here about those with the use of free will. Infants are another matter.

[156] This reading of the consequent will of God is compatible with both the "Thomistic" notion of predestination and with the opposing school of thought, which holds that God's predestination to glory takes into account the cooperation of the person. Of course, on the "Thomistic" theory, one needs to read the "if" clause as a mere correlation with God's decree of predestination, not as a reason for God's decree.

[157] DH 858. See also John Paul II, *Veritatis splendor* (1993), art. 68.

False Mercy

Some people object: "That's not fair! Some people die in car accidents. Should they go to Hell simply because they were caught off guard?" The objection deserves a fourfold response. (1) We should not reject dogma just because it is difficult. The Resurrection is difficult to believe; so is the Eucharist; so, in the age of violent "wokeness," is *forgiveness*. (2) Moreover, we should distinguish the condition for being damned from the state of damnation. Those who are already in Hell are consumed with malice; they are filled with hatred. But to have that quality of hatred is not required for entry into Hell. Some mortal sins look nothing like pure hatred of God. Fornication can dress itself up in attractive garb; so can the subtle gluttony of an Epicurean. But any mortal sin can damn me. (3) Any mortal sin can damn me because malice is implicit in any mortal sin, even though the malice need not be explicit. Hence, we must be watchful and sober, for our enemy goes prowling around, seeking victims to devour. Balthasar's theology invites a lax practice of Christianity, except, perhaps, for those who are already saintly. (4) It is our Lord Himself who warns us with the image of a *thief*, breaking in unexpectedly at night (Luke 12:39). What an odd image! After all, the "thief" is actually Christ, the Master. Why is He a thief? We make Him a thief when we commit mortal sin. We do so because we thereby choose some good besides God to be our ultimate good. We thus put ourselves at enmity with God. As a result, when, upon our death, Christ judges us, He takes from us that to which we wrongfully cling. We have made Him a thief of our idolatry, because we have robbed Him of His honor.

Fourth, contrary to certain lines in Balthasar's thought, the state of our souls at death absolutely determines our everlasting fate. If we die in the state of grace, we shall be saved. If we do not, we shall be damned. I repeat the dogma of Lyons II: "As for the souls of those who die in mortal sin or with original sin only, they go down immediately to hell, to be punished, however, with different punishments."[158] Through Ezekiel, God revealed that a person who repents of his past good way of life and changes for the worse is judged according to his final state (Ezek. 18:19–24). The

---

[158] DH 858. See also *Veritatis splendor*, art. 68.

Israelites complained that God was not being just. God retorted, "When a righteous man turns away from his righteousness and commits iniquity, he shall die for it" (Ezek. 18:26). Conversely, "When a wicked man turns away from the wickedness he has committed and does what is lawful and right, he shall save his life" (Ezek. 18:27). God enables virtue and allows a season for good repentance. If the virtuous man rejects former virtue and becomes a traitor, he deserves punishment. If the wicked man repents of his sin and becomes, by God's grace, a friend, God will faithfully complete his conversion in everlasting glory. How could any lawgiver be more just and merciful?

Fifth, contrary to Balthasar, sin is not a "reality." Evil, as such, cannot exist. All the Fathers of the Church agree on this, and when they so agree, we must hold fast to their reading. Further, the Church proclaimed the following doctrine at the Council of Florence: "There is no such thing as a nature of evil, because all nature, as nature, is good."[159] Why? Because God is the creator of all that exists. So, if evil were to be a thing that exists, God would be its Creator. But God is all good and does no evil. Thus, as the same council proclaims, the Church "firmly believes, professes, and preaches that every creature of God is good."[160] Balthasar's calling sin a "reality" is an extreme opposite of the annihilationist who thinks that evil is pure nothingness. Both of these are errors; both are extreme. The truth lies in the middle that is above both errors.

Balthasar and others fear the opposite extreme, that calling evil a privation makes evil purely illusory. In fact, both the annihilationist and Balthasar subscribe to a false dichotomy: either sin is a reality, or it is nothing at all. We must reject this dichotomy as false. The truth lies elsewhere. As we have seen, there is also a *"privation of a due good."* A "privation" is not a pure absence. It is an absence of some fitting and due quality *in an existing subject*. The absence of what is fitting and due is *unfitting*; the absence is not pure nothingness. For example, to wear a slimy wetsuit to Mass is not nothing, but it is most unfitting. It is the

---

[159] DH 1333.
[160] DH 1350.

absence of proper Mass attire. Recall also the example of blindness. A dog that cannot see is blind. Is blindness a "reality that exists"? No. The dog is what exists. Does that mean blindness is pure nothingness? No, blindness is an absence of sight *in a dog that really exists*. The evil of blindness is not a thing. Rather, the dog is a thing that exists and should be able to see. Blindness is the evil suffered by the dog. Similarly, sin is not an evil thing existing in us. That is a Gnostic notion. Rather, sin is the moral *deformity* in our free action. We are ordered to God, but when we act so as to direct ourselves to some idol, we *fail* to follow through on our order to God. We direct our love solely to an idol or creature. We think that the creature can satisfy our hearts. What exists here? We exist, and our loves exist, and the idols exist. What doesn't exist here? Our right order to God doesn't exist; our love of God doesn't exist. But we should love God above all things. Also, our rightly ordered love of the creature doesn't exist, for we should never love a creature as though it were God. This double disorder or "double lack" of ordered love constitutes the sin. And the double lack really has terrible effects in our lives. How? Our hunger for God is our deepest longing, and only He can fulfill it. So, when we *pervert* that love by directing it to creatures, we end up disordered. We become like a lonely person who treats his poodle as though it were a human friend.

A Balthasarian might say that Balthasar was speaking loosely or poetically. Perhaps he was. It would have helped had he indicated as much. Alas, he did not. And we might ask why not. If he had employed a competent theory distinguishing poetic from literal statements, he could have been more precise. Poetry works by metaphors. Literal statements work by the "proper" meanings of terms, that is, from the full definition. A bear is an animal. When I say, "There is a bear in the forest," I use the term literally or properly. When I say, "Man, he's a real bear," I speak poetically. This distinction is crucial for theology. We can call God both "good" and "rock." When we call Him good, we are speaking properly, because He more than meets the definition of "good," which is something like "attractive because perfect." True, God is good in an infinite way that I cannot comprehend, but He *really is* good. When I call Him "rock," I am speaking improperly, because He has no minerals and shape. What I mean is that He is reliable and strong and so on.

The difference between poetry and proper (sometimes called scientific) theological discourse is enormous. Scholastic theology practiced this difference very carefully. But Balthasar, for all his literary genius, failed to offer and employ any adequate theory articulating this difference. Instead, he simply claimed that "for every likeness between creature and God, there is a greater unlikeness." While the claim is true, it does *not* help us differentiate poetry from proper (or scientific) theological discourse. God is both like and unlike a rock, and God's goodness is both like and unlike that of a pizza or St. Francis. But while we can say that God is really and infinitely good, we cannot say that God is really and infinitely a rock. Metaphorical poetry and proper analogy (scientific theological claims) are very different. Alas, Balthasar's ineptitude in this regard led him astray on many points. Just consider this: citing the alleged mystic Adrienne von Speyer, he spoke of the Son as "surprising" the Father's wildest expectations; he spoke of time and space in God.[161] As a fine Dominican teacher of mine once said: "While poetry is wonderful in its proper place, when you try to make it pass as scientific theology, you lead people astray." But let us return to the critique at hand.

Sixth, Christ did not descend into the Hell of the damned, as Balthasar falsely claimed. Irenaeus excoriated Marcion (a quasi-Gnostic) for holding the same abominable thesis.[162] What, then, does the Apostles' Creed mean when it states, "He descended into hell"? It means, as the good Spanish bishops declared in 633, that Christ came to free the *holy* souls in the underworld.[163] As the Jews already understood, there were two realms of the dead, that of the unjust and that of the just. Christ descended into the Hell of the just. A synod in Rome in 745 condemned a priest named Clement for holding that in His descent Christ delivered the impious from

---

[161] See *Theo-Drama*, vol. 5, 79–80.
[162] See Irenaeus, *Against Heresies*, bk. I, chap. 27, in *Ante-Nicene Fathers*, vol. 1, 352.
[163] DH 485.

Hell.[164] Under Benedict XII in 1341, the Church condemned the Armenian error that Christ destroyed Hell itself.[165] In 1351, Pope Clement VI demanded that the Armenians confess, "By descending into hell, Christ did not destroy the lower hell [of the damned]."[166] The *Roman Catechism* reiterates that Christ came to deliver the holy and just souls.[167] Finally, the new *Catechism* states: "Jesus did not descend into hell to deliver the damned, nor to destroy the hell of damnation, but to free the just who had gone before him."[168] This teaching is constant and universal; thus, it is infallible.

Seventh, the Catholic Church, in her constant teaching, holds that the punishment of Hell is everlasting. In a local synod in Constantinople in 543, the error tentatively promulgated by Origen of Alexandria that Hell comes to an end was condemned.[169] This condemnation of the notion of a temporary Hell has been constantly received and confirmed by the Magisterium throughout the Church's history. For this reason, it is held infallibly. Furthermore, the Church explicitly teaches the everlasting character of Hell. Pope Pelagius I confessed that the damned "burn without end."[170] The ecumenical council, Lateran IV, taught that the wicked receive "perpetual punishment."[171] Lyons I, another ecumenical council, taught, "If anyone dies in mortal sin without repentance, beyond any doubt, he will be tortured forever by the flames of everlasting hell."[172] Consistent with this teaching, Lyons I distinguished hell from purgatory. Regarding purgatorial fire, it declared, "This temporary fire purifies sins, not however mortal or capital [sins] that were not previously remitted by penance, but small and minor [sins] that still weigh

[164] DH 587.
[165] See DH 1011.
[166] DH 1077.
[167] See *Catechism of the Council of Trent*, trans. John A. McHugh and Charles J. Callan (Rockford, IL: TAN Books, 1982), bk. I, art. 5, 62ff.
[168] CCC 633.
[169] See DH 411.
[170] DH 443.
[171] DH 801.
[172] DH 839.

down after death even if during life they were forgiven."[173] Thus, it is contrary to the Faith to teach that Hell is not everlasting. Consequently, to read the Scriptures as though "eternal punishment" is simply and only "long-lasting punishment" is erroneous. Augustine long ago disposed of such a misinterpretation of Scripture by the following argument: the Greek term describing the duration of Heaven is the same as that for Hell. Since Heaven truly is eternal, so is Hell.[174] Moreover, Jude 6 describes the chains of the damned as "eternal" in the strict sense. Finally, as our Lord teaches, the worm never dies and the fire is never extinguished (Mark 9:48). How do you get "merely long lasting" from that? You don't.

Eighth, the Church does not pray for the "unfaithful departed" but only for the "faithful departed." In this vein, Gregory III proclaims, "It will not be permitted to [offer the sacrifice of the Mass] for the impious, even if they were Christian."[175] We may, and we should, pray for the faithful departed, but we do not pray for the unfaithful. Why not? Because they cannot repent. Prayers for them would be futile. Now, if Balthasar's excursions into hope for the damned were justified, we should be praying for the unfaithful as well as the faithful, so that the Hell of the former might become the Purgatory of the latter. Balthasar, in these unfortunate moments, asked for prayers that would contradict our doctrine and our liturgical practice.

Ninth, Balthasar's anxiety — that if one man is damned, God suffers tragedy — is misguided. First of all, God is immutable. The First Vatican Council declares that God is "entirely simple and unchangeable."[176] He is already infinitely perfect and happy in Himself. He gains nothing by our salvation. Rather, He communicates to us a share in His perfect happiness. Further, the Church also teaches dogmatically that God is

---

[173] DH 838.

[174] There remains this difference: Heaven is an eternity of rest in the good, whereas Hell is a relentless confrontation with one evil after another. On this topic, see St. Augustine, *City of God*, trans. Henry Bettenson (New York: Penguin, 1984), bk. 21, chap. 23, 1001–1002.

[175] DH 583.

[176] *Dei Filius*, chap. 1; DH 3001.

utterly free from suffering, which is a component of tragedy.[177] Thus, the opinion that Hell would imply tragedy in God collides with the doctrine on God's immutability and impassibility. Secondly, because demons are damned, we must conclude that if Balthasar is correct, then God is already suffering tragically. Now, Balthasar portrays this possible tragedy as something so terrible as to be unthinkable. But if it were that terrible, demons could not be damned, since God's will for universal salvation includes them. Since demons are damned, this terrible prospect of divine tragedy must be a red herring. When he alleged tragedy in God, was Balthasar being poetic?

The foregoing criticisms show that the theology of Hans Urs von Balthasar is saturated with fundamental problems. Many theologians are distracted from these significant errors because they focus on the narrow contention that the Church has never issued a dogmatic damnation of anyone. True enough! The Church has never issued a dogmatic decree concerning the damnation of a specific person. Nor has she dogmatically decreed in an extraordinary way that some humans are in Hell. These facts do not exonerate Balthasar from the foregoing errors. Nor do they exonerate popularizers who would wish to follow his path in the above matters. I find that these errors are the most consequential and problematic aspect of Balthasar's thought concerning eschatology. (His Trinitarian theology, attractive in many respects, is also deeply flawed, but we cannot treat that here.)

The numbers game—the possibility that there are *no* human beings in Hell—is less central. Still, even this question of the population of Hell has considerable pastoral significance. So we should also examine this question.

Are Some Human Beings Damned?
Are some human beings damned? This question has obvious pastoral relevance. If revelation teaches us that some humans are damned, then the way we live our lives will have to change. If revelation teaches us

---

[177] See DH 284, 367, 800, and 2529.

that many humans are damned, all the more must we change our lives. We must be more God-focused. We must be more willing to leave earthly things behind and take the narrow road toward God. This is not to say that Balthasarians cannot take life seriously. Many of them take it quite seriously and live holy lives. This is a simple commonsense judgment about a reasonable connection of cause and effect, one expressed by Justin Martyr, the book of Wisdom, and the Apostle.

Balthasar's disciples keep pointing to the fact that there is no dogma declaring that any human being is in Hell. They claim that we do not know that any particular individual is damned. So, they reason, it is possible that each individual is saved. They then conclude: therefore, it is possible that all human beings are saved. What should we think of this argument?

First, it is not the business of the Church to demonize. The Church canonizes; she does not demonize. She canonizes saints so that we might know to whom we can reliably pray for effective help. In the days of devil's advocates and moderation in the canonization process, canonizations also helped point out role models. But there would be no conceivable benefit for demonizing anyone. Indeed, relatives and descendants of the demonized might despair of their own salvation if they knew a relative was damned. Further, how would the criteria for demonizing work? Would the damned person have to work some unholy effect on Earth, so that the Church might have certainty about the damnation? The Church *does not* know who the damned are, except if there be revealed data. But not to know who is damned does not entail ignorance *that* some are damned. By contrast, the Church *does* know who some of the blessed are.

Second, the reasoning implicit in the argumentation is invalid. We cannot argue from the premise "for each man, it is possible that he be saved" to the conclusion "it is possible that all men be saved." Why not? The argument attempts to move deductively from a particular truth to a universal truth. But that is an invalid argument. In an argument, our knowledge of the truth of the premises is the *cause* of our knowledge of the truth of the conclusion. In short, the premises cause our certainty regarding the conclusion. Now, a particular truth is limited (for each Chicagoan, it is possible to attend the World Series). A universal truth is unlimited (it is possible for all Chicagoans to attend the World Series). Obviously, you cannot deduce an unlimited truth from a limited truth. Your knowledge that "for each Chicagoan, it is possible to attend the World Series" does not allow you to conclude, "It is possible for all Chicagoans to attend the World Series." In fact, we *know* that not all Chicagoans can attend the World Series. Wrigley Field cannot seat them all. Of course, a reader will object: "Wrigley Field is not big enough, but surely God is big enough to include everyone." True enough! There is no intrinsic limit to the population of Heaven. Because of God's goodness and power, the only limit is *our* refusal to repent. The point is that there is no logical necessity that all might be saved just because each one might be saved. This logical limit reflects the limits of our knowledge. From the initial premise, we simply do not know whether it is possible to hope that all men be saved.

So this raises the question: do we know from any other source whether all men will be saved or even might be saved? We do. The Scriptures abundantly testify that *some human beings will be damned*. Therefore, it is not possible that all men be saved. More precisely, the Scriptures testify that many human beings will be damned.

Jude 5–7 is a primary scriptural witness that some human beings are, at this present moment, suffering eternal condemnation. Jude writes:

> I desire to remind you, though you were once for all fully informed, that he who saved a people out of the land of Egypt, afterward destroyed those who did not believe (τοὺς μὴ πιστεύσαντας ἀπώλεσεν). And the angels that did not keep their own position but left their proper dwelling have been kept by him in eternal chains (δεσμοῖς ἀϊδίοις) in the nether gloom until the judgment of the great day; just as Sodom and Gomorrah and the surrounding cities, which likewise acted immorally and indulged in unnatural lust, serve as an example (πρόκεινται δεῖγμα) by undergoing a punishment of eternal fire (πυρὸς αἰωνίου δίκην ὑπέχουσαι).

In this passage, Jude is warning living people to repent, lest they suffer a terrible fate. He bases his warning on a teaching of *present fact*.[178] In his inerrant letter, he teaches that *right now* the souls of those who died on that fateful day in Sodom and Gomorrah are "undergoing a punishment of eternal fire." These souls serve as an example precisely *because* they are in this state. Jude's point is amplified by his analogy between these damned souls and the demons. Just as the demons are in Hell forever, so will these souls be in Hell forever. Scholars note the sobriety of this document, which contrasts with the wild imaginative speculations of some of the apocalyptic literature of this period.[179] Recall that Balthasar, following Rahner, rests his scriptural arguments on one fundamental premise: all the texts "foretelling" a group of damned humans are simply warnings. As we see from Jude, this interpretation of Scripture is unsustainable. Moreover, this teaching from Jude overthrows Balthasar's hope, which depends on our ignorance of the truth or falsity of the following proposition: "Some human souls are damned." If revelation teaches that some souls are damned, it is erroneous to doubt or deny it. Jude teaches that some souls are damned. Therefore, it is erroneous to contradict this teaching.

---

[178] John Paul II, who unfortunately entertained the notion of the salvation of all men, notes that demons *serve* as a warning by their actual plight. See John Paul II, Wednesday Audience, July 28, 1999. It is worthy of note that in his original address, he claimed that we do not know "whether or which" humans are in Hell. The official statement now reads that we do not know "which" humans are in Hell. See Tim Staples, "Are There Souls in Hell Right Now?" Catholic.com, April 11, 2014, https://www. catholic.com/magazine/online-edition/are-there-souls-in-hell-right-now.

[179] See Jerome H. Neyrey, S.J., "The Epistle of Jude," *New Jerusalem Biblical Commentary*, ed. Raymond E. Brown et al. (Englewood Cliffs, NJ: Prentice-Hall, 1990), 917b. See also Jerome H. Neyrey, S.J., *Two Peter, Jude*, vol. 37c, *The Anchor Bible* (New York: Doubleday, 1993) and Bo Reicke, *The Epistles of James, Peter, and Jude*, vol. 37, *The Anchor Bible* (Garden City, NY: Doubleday and Company, 1964). Researcher Phillip J. Silvia contends that several lines of evidence point to a meteor destroying a civilization in the region about 3,700 years ago. See the program notes for the American Society of Overseas Research meeting of November 2018, specifically page 153.

Jude's teaching has ramifications for our reading of other passages of Scripture. Our Lord solemnly compares the fate of Sodom and Gomorrah to certain cities of his day. Of the cities that reject Him, he says, "Truly, I say to you, it shall be more tolerable on the day of judgment for the land of Sodom and Gomorrah than for that town" (Matt. 10:15). He then applies this principle to concrete cities during His ministry: "And you, Capernaum, will you be exalted to heaven? You shall be brought down to Hades. For if the mighty works done in you had been done in Sodom, it would have remained until this day. But I tell you that it shall be more tolerable on the day of judgment for the land of Sodom than for you" (Matt. 11:23–24). Since (at least some of the) men who died in Sodom on that fateful day are in Hell now, so will men of these other cities be in Hell. This is the straightforward meaning of Scripture.

These texts are not isolated; they form an anthem of sobriety by which our Lord cautions us against worldliness and urges us to faith and repentance. In the Sermon on the Mount, He lets us know how challenging is the way to life: "Enter by the narrow gate; for the gate is wide and the way is easy, that leads to destruction, and those who enter by it are many. For the gate is narrow and the way is hard, that leads to life, and those who find it are few" (Matt. 7:13–14). Note the comparisons. Jesus contrasts "wide" and "narrow," "easy" and "hard," "taking" and "finding," and "many" and "few." The first two pairs of words—wide and narrow, easy and hard—describe the entrance and the path. This contrast awakens us to the fact that, from birth, we are, de facto, on the path of alienation. We have been conceived in original sin, and we find sin close at hand, crouching at our door (see Gen. 4:7). We must *change* in order to find and walk along the path of life. The naïve optimism spawned by revolutionaries at least since 1965 has no place in Catholic sensibility.

The second two pairs of words—take and find, many and few—inform us about the numbers. There are *many* who actually *take* the easy way that leads to damnation. By contrast, there are *few* who even *find*, let alone take, the road that leads to life. Some say that this statement is an example of Hebraic hyperbole. That may be. But we must remember a few things. First, hyperbole is *exaggeration*. If our Lord is exaggerating,

His starting point is a real truth. What truth? Some humans *are* on the way to damnation. If no humans were on the way to damnation, then our Lord would not be exaggerating but lying. Would Truth utter a "noble lie"? Second, even if our Lord is exaggerating to some extent, so as to get the point across, He is portraying *such* an extreme imbalance that, when we adjust it in a search for the more "literal" meaning, we easily conclude that many or even a majority of humans are on the way to damnation. Experiences attests that not so many even find the path to life. They do not find because they do not ask. They do not ask because they do not seek. He who fails to seek the true meaning of life, he who fails to look for the right way to live, he who fails to seek God, cannot be saved. And what if we Christians fail to preach the good news and the truth of human sinfulness?

The two ways show that many are on the path of damnation. Will any continue on that path forever? Not all will. Nor, for that matter, will all who are treading the way of life continue in that way. Our Lord gives absolutely no indication of a universal repentance of all those on the road to damnation. Instead, he reveals the opposite. He teaches that many once on the path of life shall be condemned, thus confirming His comparisons of Capernaum and Sodom:

> Not everyone who says to me, "Lord, Lord," shall enter the kingdom of heaven.... On that day many will say to me, "Lord, Lord, did we not prophesy in your name, and cast out demons in your name, and do many might works in your name?" And then will I declare to them, "I never knew you; depart from me, you evildoers." (Matt. 7:21–23)

Here, Jesus is speaking not of frolicking pagans or greedy loan sharks or the lukewarm. He is speaking of Christians who do remarkable works in His name. Even Christians who do remarkable works will find themselves shut out of the kingdom of Heaven. These are sobering words. So our Lord answers the question: some men *are* damned. Finally, of those of His people who reject Him, Jesus says that the men of Nineveh will condemn them (Matt. 12:41–42).

False Mercy

Jesus' parables also give us evidence that some men are damned. A parable is a fictional depiction of an event presented to the listener. It elicits from the listener attention to certain commonly accepted principles and an application of them to the fictional situation. The power of the parable is that there is an analogy between the things depicted and the listener's situation. Taking cognizance of the analogy, the listener can, at last, apply these principles to his own situation, even to the point of judging himself. Sometimes the analogy between the listener's situation and the fictional narrative is difficult to discern. On several occasions, our Lord makes clear what that analogy is. In doing so He *interprets* His parable. This interpretation thus constitutes a clear presentation of His doctrine.

Jesus' own interpretations of His apocalyptic parables are instructive. In public, He spoke the parable of the sower and the parable of the wheat and the weeds. With His disciples, He explained the meaning of each parable. The meaning of the sower is that the word of God is preached to various kinds of people. Three kinds of people do not accept fruitfully the preached word. Those in the first group hardly pay attention to it before the evil one distracts them. Those in the second group are shallow and capitulate during personal struggles. Those in the third group are too worldly (Matt. 13:18–23).

Jesus' explanation of this parable comes immediately before He introduces the parable of the wheat and the weeds. This latter parable adds depth to the prior one. The drama of our lives is not simply determined by our acceptance or rejection of the Word of God. It is also determined by the conflict between the Son of God and the devil, who sows evil seed. Jesus explains the parable of the wheat and the weeds by identifying the players: the sower is the Son of Man; the good seed is the sons of the kingdom; and the evil seed is the sons of the devil. Finally, He identifies the setting: the harvest is the close of the age. Jesus then clearly depicts this end of the age: "Just as the weeds are gathered and burned with fire, so will it be at the close of the age. The Son of man will send his angels, and they will gather out of his kingdom all causes of sin and all evildoers, and throw them into the furnace of fire; there men will weep and gnash their teeth" (Matt. 13:40–42). Just as there really are various groups that reject Jesus' message, so there are those who imitate the devil's example of rebellion. At the end of time, then, the wicked will be removed from the kingdom. Meanwhile, our Lord commanded His followers not to uproot the weeds recklessly, lest they remove the wheat in the process. The separation will occur at the end. Jesus' exegesis is the clear teaching: some humans will be damned.

In this same context, Jesus added yet another parable about the Last Judgment, that of the net that gathers various kinds of things. At the end, "the angels will come out and separate the evil from the righteous" (Matt. 13:49). What is the moral? Once again, Jesus' *explanation* of the parable clearly teaches that there will be a separation of the good and the evil at the end. The evil will be damned. Since we are dealing with His own exegesis of His parables, we are dealing with clarity: some humans will be damned. (Note that the word "some" does not mean "few"; rather, it simply means "not none." It is a word taken from the rules of logic. So the logical word "some" and the quantitative word "many" are compatible.)

In His descriptions of the end times, Jesus enriches us with details about the actions of these evildoers. Warning us about the final persecutions at the end of time, He prophesies that there will be "*many* false prophets" and that "*most* men's love will grow cold" (Matt. 24:11, 12, emphasis mine). False prophets are not in the state of grace; they are enemies of God, even His bitterest enemies. They produce scandals. They tell half-truths when they should present a full picture. They tell lies when they should be faithful. They are deceptively ambiguous when their yes should mean yes. They thereby lead people into sin. The false prophets of our time say that there is no Hell, that punishment does not last forever, that the souls of the "damned" are annihilated, that Hell is empty. These false prophets are wolves in sheep's clothing. Since Jesus prophesies that there will be false prophets, He prophesies that some will oppose Him and His Church. At the end, there will be seriously wicked men that lead people astray. And, as John Henry Newman teaches us, the end we always have with us.[180]

---

[180] See John Henry Newman, "The Patristical Idea of Antichrist," in *Discussions and Arguments on Various Subjects* (London: Longmans, Green, 1924), 44–108.

False Mercy

We can close with a few more indications of the population of Hell. The book of Revelation teaches clearly that the devil, the false prophet, and the beast will all be in the lake of fire and will be tormented forever (20:10). The book of Wisdom differentiates God's purifying treatment of the just from His wrathful judgment of the wicked (11:9–10). St. Paul prophesies a resurrection of two kinds of people, the just and the unjust (Acts 24:15). The author of the Letter to the Hebrews refers to many ancient Jews being abandoned by God. He cites Psalm 95, in which God says, "'They always go astray in their hearts; they have not known my ways.' As I swore in my wrath, 'They shall *never* enter my rest'" (Heb. 3:10–11, emphasis mine). The author specifies the reason that they will never enter God's rest: "They were unable to enter because of unbelief" and "because of disobedience" (Heb. 3:19; 4:6). Such sins are mortal.

Furthermore, the Last Judgment is the *final* judgment.[181] There is no indication in revelation of an undoing of that judgment. This final judgment is the climax of world history. Further, the finality of this judgment is part of its very meaning. Now, what happens in this judgment? The good and the evil are *separated*. Thus, Scripture commands us to affirm that the evil shall never repent after judgment. There is no basis for extending Purgatory to those judged wicked and damned at this final judgment.

To reduce the foregoing scriptural texts to "warnings" about "possible futures" is to turn the Sacred Scriptures into *myth*. But Christianity is no myth; it is historical and realistic. Yes, it has a universal message of truth meant for all. But that does not mean that it is a philosophy dressed in mythical garb. The Christian message comes to us through real, historical sources. It is not the discovery of the human mind but a gift given to us by God through the prophets and ultimately through Jesus Christ. The Scriptures are about real and historical events.

There is a rule in exegesis: always read the text in the "proper literal sense" (nonmetaphorically) *unless* there is a necessary reason to read it in a metaphorical or figurative sense. This is done to avoid an obvious conflict

---

[181] It begins with the particular judgment and is completed with the universal judgment.

with a truth of reason or a truth of faith. There are, to be sure, symbolic elements in Scripture; all acknowledge this. It was not a mere "talking serpent" that tempted Adam and Eve. It was the evil angel who did so. Scripture employs the figures of a serpent and a dragon because it is a lot more exciting to read about serpents and dragons than about "bodiless spirits" who rebelled. The presence of symbol does not eradicate the facts of history; rather, it helps drive them home. We are not permitted to treat the Bible as mythology.[182] In fact, relative to other literature, the Bible is very slim on extended analogies, which are called "allegories." Other ancient religious works abound in allegories. Now, there is no necessary reason to read in a figurative way the above-cited passages of Scripture that straightforwardly indicate a populated Hell. Hell is not impossible; it is actual and populated by demons. Therefore, there is no warrant to read these passages in the figurative sense. They are not mere warnings; they are prophecies; the warning takes power from the prophecy.

At this point, we can register an important criticism of the Rahnerian scriptural exegesis Balthasar relied upon. For Karl Rahner, none of the eschatological texts constitute a prophecy; rather, each is simply an extrapolation by the author of what *might* happen in the future, given what he experiences now. Present experience indicates two things: the reality of sin and the power and goodness of God, who offers grace. So the biblical authors infer from these two realities that there *might* be two groups. The authors are certain of one group, the saints. They suggest the possibility of a second group, that of the damned. Apart from his theological inference from present experience, the biblical author, for all his inspiration, can tell us nothing: "Man's knowledge of the future still to come, even his revealed knowledge, is confined to such prospects as can be derived from the reading of his present eschatological experience."[183] Again, Rahner writes, "What we know about Christian eschatology is what we know about man's present situation in the history of salvation.

---

[182] Leo XIII, *Providentissimus Deus*, art. 15; Benedict XV, *Spiritus paraclitus*, arts. 50–55; and Pius XII, *Divino afflante Spiritu*, arts. 38–40.

[183] Karl Rahner, "Hermeneutics," *Theologial Investigations* 4, 334.

We do not project something from the future into the present, but rather in man's experience of himself and of God in grace and in Christ we project our Christian present into its future."[184] So much for God's own word: "Behold, the former things have come to pass, and new things I now declare; before they spring forth I tell you of them" (Isa. 42:9). "Who has announced from of old the things to come?" (Isa. 44:7). Does Rahner think God is flippantly asking a rhetorical question? Again, our Lord states, "I tell you this now, before it takes place, that when it does take place you may believe that I am he" (John 13:19). Rahner's principles cannot process the Truth. Vatican I also opposes Rahnerian principles. It teaches that prophecies are proofs of God's omniscience:

> God willed that exterior proofs of his revelation, viz., divine facts, especially miracles and prophecies, should be joined to the interior helps of the Holy Spirit; as they manifestly display the omnipotence and infinite knowledge of God, they are the most certain signs of the divine revelation, adapted to the intelligence of all men.[185]

Rahner's error resembles that of the modernists condemned by Pius X of blessed memory. He writes in *Pascendi*:

> To suit their own theories they note with remarkable ingenuity that, although experience is something belonging to the present, still it may draw its material in like manner from the past and the future inasmuch as the believer by memory *lives* the past over again after the manner of *the present*, and lives the future already by anticipation.[186]

Balthasar, who was not afraid to criticize the towering figure of Rahner, on the topic of the damned unfortunately sided with Rahner's reduction

---

[184] Karl Rahner, *Foundations of Christian Faith: An Introduction to the Idea of Christianity*, trans. William Dych (New York: Crossroad, 1990), 432.

[185] *Dei Filius*, chap. 3; DH 3009.

[186] Pius X, *Pascendi Dominici gregis* (1907), art. 22. See also Leo XIII, *Providentissimus Deus* (1893), art. 10.

of the sacred page to theological reasoning. This hermeneutic hardly suits the text revered by Christians for its prophecies.

We return to an evaluation of Balthasar himself. The Magisterium has long given voice to the sense that some humans are damned. Once again, by "some" I do not mean "a few." "Some" is compatible with both "many" and "most." The upshot is that the Magisterium has given voice to the sense that there are indeed damned humans. One sees this, for example, in some important early synods on predestination. Although these were only local synods, they have continually been read as authentic statements of the Faith of the Church. In 633, the Synod of Toledo declared:

> We have attained remission of sins in order to be resurrected by him in the last days in that flesh in which we now live and likewise in the form in which the Lord was resurrected: some (*alii*) receiving eternal life from him for merits of justice, others (*alii*), the sentence of eternal punishment [for sins].[187]

This teaching was reiterated in a synod against double predestination. The Synod of Quiercy in 853 declared, "The just and good God, however, chose from this same mass of perdition according to his foreknowledge those whom through grace he predestined to life [Rom. 8:29ff.; Eph. 1:11], and he predestined for these eternal life." This synod first distinguishes those who are justified from the rest of humanity, teaching that God justified *some* and implying that He did not justify all. Nor was God being stingy with His grace; rather, that the rest remained unjustified was due to their fault: "The others, whom by the judgment of justice he left in the 'mass of perdition,' however, he knew would perish; but he did not predestine that they would perish; because he is just, however, he predestined eternal punishment for them."[188] There are two elements in Quiercy: (1) God foreknew the fault of some, and (2) God prepared punishment for those whose fault He foreknew. The synod's teaching

---

[187] DH 485.
[188] DH 621.

entails that some are damned. Note that the teachings of Toledo and Quiercy exhibit the mind not only of the Church's bishops but also of the heretics. Both the bishops of the Church and the heretics believed that "some are damned." The difference, however, was that the Church taught that God does not predestine anyone to sin. He does, however, permit humans to sin and to abandon Him forever. The heretics were teaching that God predestines some to sin.

Popes taught what these synods taught. Pope Pelagius I in a confession of faith to King Childebert I in 557, declared:

> The wicked, however, remaining by their own choice as "vessels of wrath fit for destruction" [Rom. 9:22], who either did not know the way of the Lord or, knowing it, abandoned it when seduced by various transgressions, he will hand over by a most just judgment to the punishment of eternal and inextinguishable fire, so that they may burn without end.[189]

The pope implies that there are two groups of men: the saved (whom he treats in what precedes this citation) and the damned. The Fourth Lateran Council reiterates this conviction: "All of them will rise again with their own bodies which they now bear to receive according to their works, whether these have been good or evil, the ones perpetual punishment with the devil and the others everlasting glory with Christ."[190] The Council of Trent teaches that there are some who do not accept the redemption in Christ: "Even though 'Christ died for all,' still not all receive the benefit of his death, but only those to whom the merit of his Passion is imparted."[191] Furthermore, Pope Pius II condemned the following proposition of Zanini de Solcia in 1459: "All Christians are to be saved."[192]

Authoritative catechisms also teach that some men are damned. The *Roman Catechism*, which authentically expresses the mind of the Church,

---

[189] DH 443.
[190] DH 801.
[191] DH 1523.
[192] DH 1362.

gives us the rationale for the Church's use of the words "for you and for many" in the eucharistic canon. It explains:

> The additional words for you and for many are taken, some from Matthew, some from Luke, but were joined together by the Catholic church under the guidance of the Spirit of God. They serve to declare the fruit and advantage of His Passion. For if we look to its value, we must confess that the Redeemer shed His blood for the salvation of all; but if we look to the fruit which mankind have received from it, we shall easily find that it pertains not unto all, but to many of the human race. When therefore (our Lord) said: For you, he meant either those who were present, or those chosen from among the Jewish people, such as were, with the exception of Judas, the disciples with whom He was speaking. When He added, And for many, He wished to be understood to mean the remainder of the elect from among the Jews or Gentiles. With reason, therefore, were the words for all not used, as in this place the fruits of the Passion are alone spoken of, and to the elect only did His Passion bring the fruit of salvation.[193]

This exegesis of the liturgy conveys a twofold meaning. First, insofar as Jesus' prayer is offered for His apostles, it still does not apply in its fruitfulness to Judas. Second, insofar as it is offered for all those in the world, it still does not apply in its fruitfulness to the reprobate, those who fall into and die in the state of sin. The Extraordinary Form of the liturgy supports this reading with its Collect for the Good Friday office, which reads:

> O God, from whom Judas received the punishment of his guilt, and the thief the reward of his confession: grant unto us the full fruit of Thy clemency; that even as in His Passion our Lord Jesus Christ gave to each retribution according to his merits, so having cleared away our former guilt, He may bestow on us the grace of

---

[193] *Catechism of the Council of Trent*, "The Eucharist (Form of the Eucharist)," 227.

his Resurrection, who lives and reigns with you, in the unity of the Holy Spirit, one God forever and ever. Amen.

This collect indicates the eternal damnation of Judas. Finally, the new *Catechism*, citing Acts 24:15, declares that the final resurrection will be "of both the just and the unjust."[194] The resurrection applies to humans only. So, if there is a resurrection of the unjust, then some humans are damned.

In summary, the proposition "some humans are damned" is found in revelation. Are we to interpret all these scriptural passages figuratively? What, then, would become of the sobriety and historical concreteness of our religion? The same proposition is implied in the magisterial teachings of the Church throughout the ages. Are we to chalk this constant implication up to an empty formality: "If, by chance, anyone should die in mortal sin, he *would* go to Hell"?

We should also heed the signs of the times in light of the Gospel. The greatest divinely wrought sign in the last millennium was the Miracle of the Sun at Fátima. Precisely three months before its occurrence, the little children at Fátima stated that there would be a great sign worked by God at midday on October 13, 1917. The media and the powers that be and the common people knew of this prophecy by mid-July 1917. Anti-Catholic secular publications published about it in that very month. Representatives of these publications, as well as atheists, Marxists, and Freemasons went to the site of the predicted event on the "prophesied" day, hoping to quash Catholic superstition in Portugal. It is as though they were salivating to annihilate the old religion. Ten years prior to the Fátima event, the Portuguese government, utterly hostile to Catholicism, had laid claim to all Catholic property. They hoped within a few decades to eliminate all traces of Catholicism. The children were putting these plans in jeopardy. So the opponents of Catholicism awaited this event with baited breath.

All the naysayers were proved foolish. A stupendous celestial miracle occurred: a heavenly disk, which many took to be the sun itself, broke

---

[194] CCC 1038.

through thick clouds, which had been raining torrentially for hours and hours. The disk shot out various colors of the rainbow and spun around astonishingly. All the people could look at it without harm to their eyes. The disk did this for four minutes three distinct times. After the last episode, the disk plunged downward. The crowds thought it would destroy the earth. Some repented; all were terrified. Finally, the disk ascended back into the heavens. The ground, which had been absolutely drenched only minutes before on account of the torrential rains, was left perfectly dry with but a few pools of water as testimony of the rain.

There were about seventy thousand people in attendance: not just pious Catholics but also Protestants and Jews, anti-religious people, skeptics, academics, doctors, lawyers, manual laborers, and so forth. In short, a cross-section of Portugal attended. Some even came from Spain and France. Many were interviewed. Not one person denied the above narrative of the event. Now that is data!

Anyone who studies Fátima is forced to ask many questions: "How on earth could these things have happened at that time? If the U.S. military could not pull off this event even today, what power could have pulled that event off so long ago? And to what end? Did God speak here? Is He asking the world to repent? How should I respond?"

Some of those who did not witness Fátima have tried to explain it away. They explain it as a mass psychosis. Against such naysayers, the great physicist and theologian Stanley Jaki remarks:

Since the event witnessed was undeniable, unbelievers may have felt that it was best to follow the example of such great scoffers at miracles as Hume and Voltaire. They both thought it best not to focus on facts, lest they start looming large and dwarf their inept theories about them.[195]

What is the point of a miracle, especially a great miracle? A miracle *confirms a message*. Humanly speaking, Fátima represents the most *publicly*

[195] Stanely Jaki, *God and the Sun at Fatima* (Royal Oak, MI: Real View Books, 1999), 32.

confirmed message since the crossing of the Red Sea. The Resurrection of Christ is more marvelous in itself, but the numbers of people who bore direct witness to the risen Christ were fewer than those at the Red Sea. Moreover, no prophecy anticipated the Red Sea.

What was the message of Fátima? On July 13, the children were exposed to a hideous sight: the eternal damnation of human souls. So dreadful was the apparition that the children swore they would have died of terror had it lasted a moment longer. Each of them subsequently committed to a life of mortification, prayer, and charity. The upshot of Fátima was this message: repent and believe, because Hell is real and real people go there. We must not love the world as our final home while banking on Heaven as a guarantee. Satan and modernist Catholic prelates and renegade theologians have sold us lies.

Another holy person to testify to the reality of Hell was the great Catholic mystic of mercy, St. Faustina. She had a terrifying vision of Hell, one that resembles Dante's *Inferno*. Her vision confirms John Chrysostom's warning about Hell. Chrysostom had to correct those Christians who were "demythologizing" Hell. These demythologizers asked whether the fire was real or only symbolic. Chrysostom replied that if fire is only a symbol of the pain, we may be sure that the actual pain is far more terrible than mere fire. St. Faustina is the great doctor of divine mercy because she teaches us that no living human is beyond the reach of Christ's redemption. Even the serial rapist who murders his victims, even the despot who orders atomic weapons to be launched against innocents, even the bully who beats up an innocent person because of his race, even these can be forgiven before they die. They cannot be forgiven the guilt of mortal sin afterward. Such a great saint of mercy had this to say about the population of Hell: "What I have written is but a pale shadow of the things I saw. But I noticed one thing: that most of the souls there are those who disbelieved that there is a hell."[196] Hell is real, and real people go there.

---

[196] Faustina Kowalska, *Divine Mercy in my Soul: The Diary of the Servant of God, Sister M. Faustina Kowalska* (Stockbridge, MA: Marian Press, 1987), 741.

Be Disillusioned

Without question, the past five decades have skewed the Catholic sensibility concerning the reality of Hell. We have drifted from our moorings. We are floating aimlessly down the river. We hover free from the solid ground of Earth. We feel dizzy in our sin, lightweight in our stupor. At first, this feeling was one of liberation. We breathed a sigh of relief. Perhaps some old priests from the 1940s and 1950s were a bit too dour. Perhaps the nuns struck us too hard on the wrists. *Perhaps*. But this feeling of liberation was chimerical and transient; it was like the "freedom" a rebellious teen feels who suddenly embraces wantonness. She reimagines Daddy as an evil tyrant. But all liberation from the truth of human nature and morality is a lie. And this lie leads the soul astray. The dream of universal salvation is pure illusion. It is distracting souls interiorly. Having put them to sleep, it invites eternal death. It is also causing chaos exteriorly. Arguments in favor of this dream rest on numerous errors and heresies.

It is high time we return to reality, pick up our crosses, make our way to sacramental Confession, amend our lives, and do penance. Let us stop deceiving ourselves. Let us take stock of the apostle's warning: "The time is coming when people will not endure sound teaching, but having itching ears they will accumulate for themselves teachers to suit their own likings, and will turn away from listening to the truth and wander into myths" (2 Tim. 4:3–4). Let us "be sober, be watchful. [Our] adversary the devil prowls around like a roaring lion, seeking some one to devour" (1 Pet. 5:8).

Hell is real, and real people go there. But why? Why do we believe this? Is it good that some go to Hell? Couldn't God have prevented it? Why did He allow some to ruin their lives? To these questions, we briefly turn.

The Wisdom of the Doctrine of Hell

As Catholics, we follow Jesus Christ and the Church that He established. Our very discipleship points us to the teachings of the Church. Since we have decided to leave all things and follow Him (and we *have* decided to do that, even if we are laypeople), we accept all that Christ teaches us through His Church. As Vatican I teaches, we believe the articles of the Faith "not because the intrinsic truth of things is recognized by the natural light of reason, but because of the authority of God himself who reveals them, who can neither err nor deceive."[197] This dogma of Vatican I we must ever keep dear to our hearts. Why? Because, at times, the truth of the Catholic Faith may challenge us! Nevertheless, we should not buckle. We should remain firm in our Faith, confident that an apparent difficulty has an answer, *even if we cannot now find that answer.*

The situation is even better. When we follow Christ, He gives peace to our hearts. We know we are doing the right thing. We do not know where He is leading us, but we are confident He is doing so. Moreover, we can marvel at the truths of the Catholic Faith. These truths display God's wisdom and goodness. Even if we have difficulty with some of them sometimes, most of us, most of the time, can admire their splendor.

So, what is the wisdom in Christ's teaching on eternal damnation?

First, the doctrine of Hell reminds us that we are free creatures with great responsibility. God has entrusted us to the counsel of our own decision (Sir. 15:14). We are coauthors of our life's narratives. We cannot add one bit of good that is not God's gift, but God brings us into the story as participants of the good in us that He is working to build up. He allows us to refuse His gifts and mar His good work. We can thus decide to fall away from the beautiful script He has planned for us. Such a refusal on our part negatively affects us as individuals. God can, however, draw good from our refusal; He can draw out good for the sake of others. Thus, the script or narrative of world history will be to the glory of God's goodness, even though it is to the shame and ruin of those individuals who refuse to rejoice in it.

Second, the doctrine of Hell reminds us that every mortal sin we commit has something everlasting about it. How so? In any mortal sin, I choose something to be my good, no matter the cost. Say it is committing adultery. The man or woman says, "Just this once, I want this;

---

[197] *Dei Filius*, chap. 3; DH 3008.

I won't think about anything else." So it is; in each act of adultery, the adulterer chooses the pleasure of the act and the intimate company of a nonspouse over any other good. The adulterer leaves God, His laws, the lawful spouse, children, and friends out of account. In the act, the sinner prizes affective and physical pleasure and intimacy with a nonspouse as the ultimate good. We can *see* that the adulterer measures things this way in what *follows* the act. After the act, the adulterer has a choice: whether or not to repent. To repent means to *detest* the sin and to decide never to commit it again. That means to reject the former decision. One must reject the standard of measurement that prized pleasure to be the greatest good. Repentance requires a *change of measurement.* If one does not repent, one retains that measurement in one's heart. Failure to repent is impenitence. Impenitence is a hardening of the heart. Not only did one sin in weakness, but one now refuses to come clean about it. Impenitence grows and grows until it anticipates the very state of the damned: the terminally hardened heart.

Failure to repent proves itself in deeds. Consider the adulterer. Some evening, his children are nagging and calling for his attention. What does he do? The adulterer still has affections for his children and so has some desire for their good. But can he truly will their ultimate good, their eternal salvation? When teaching the catechism to his children, what does he tell them about the sixth commandment? Can he honestly say that adultery is evil yet refuse to repent of his wicked deed? Let us say that, in a few days, his sexual desire is boiling over again; his wife is being annoying; and his lover texts from a nearby hotel, awaiting with her pleasant ways. Does he endure the burden of desire and the annoyance of his wife's present bitterness? To what end? For the sake of a true marriage, ordered to God? But that will require him to repent of his secret lust. For the sake of keeping the lust secret so as to maintain human respect? But that is no virtue; it is but the vice of deception, ordered to his own gratification, which he will pursue when the moment is right, covered by the façade of human respect, which he hopes to preserve. The adulterer who does not repent *remains* an evil man. He wills to remain an evil man. As impenitence hardens into an inveterate vice, he makes himself fit for the eternal fires of Hell. We have already anticipated the next reason.

Third, the doctrine of Hell wakes us up to the truth that there is a link between free acts, habits, and character. By our free acts, we form habits. Long-standing habits determine character. The farther down the road we go in certain ways of life, the harder it is to reverse course. This observation is evident to everyone. Those who regularly do good works build up virtue. They are reliable. When we have good friends, we can lean on them. They do not regularly disappoint us, even if they are imperfect. But bad characters are untrustworthy and unstable because they shift and change. We cannot rely on them. We can rely only on their lack of reliability. Can they repent? Yes. Should we trust them now? No. Not for a while. These are obvious truths. However, we have been lulled to sleep about them. Our culture does not want us to judge anyone's character—ever. We have been wooed into a pathetic dream-state by sentimental Christianity.[198] We imagine that we can constantly remold ourselves at any moment. That is a bald-faced lie. Ask any physician whether someone who cuts off a finger can just grow it back. What about those who think mutilating themselves will solve their "identity" confusion? Choices carve out character: good choices leave a good result, and wicked choices leave an evil result. The trajectory of free action is toward a permanent state. If we trace out the limit of these facts, we can conclude that the dogma of everlasting damnation makes sense: there is no repentance in Hell.

Fourth, the doctrine of Hell reminds us of two related things: who God is and what kind of world He designed for us. God has called us to Himself. He made us to be with Him forever. None of us wants to die. We want to live forever. Even suicides only want escape from their problems. Who is this God? He is the Infinite, the Awesome, the Majestic! He is the Good who leans on no other good. He is the Truth that does not deceive

[198] See "Against Candy-Ass Christianity," Edward Feser, November 21, 2019, http://edwardfeser.blogspot.com/2019/11/against-candy-ass-christianity.html.

and looks to no higher authority. He is the Rock upon which everything rests. He is also Life: He is the Father who eternally generates the Son; the Father and the Son eternally breathe forth the Holy Spirit. Our God is an awesome God. And He does not need us. We were created so that God could give Himself to us.

What, then, is our sin? Our sin is a slap in the face of God, who offers us everlasting union with Him. Sin is spiteful and small-minded. The choice of mortal sin makes one unfit for this divine love. Worse, it makes us worthy of punishment. But there is hope. God has pursued us with His redemptive love, shedding blood for us. He has given us countless chances to repent. Those who die in mortal sin have refused the many chances of redemption. They have unrepentantly offended the God of love, and Hell is their fitting abode.

Conclusion

We have disposed of two errors in this chapter. Annihilationism will not work. Our souls are immortal. We have no capacity to cancel ourselves out of existence. Sin is a wound to our character, our way of being, but not the elimination of our very essence. Thus, we can remain in a permanent state of sin and yet not cease to exist. Hell is a real prospect.

Some say that Hell may be empty. Of these, some conveniently ignore the demons. But has the Church ever prayed for poor Lucifer? No. She only rebukes him and casts him out. He is her enemy, a ravenous dragon seeking to devour her children at every moment.

Others, especially Balthasar, commit only to the possibility of a Hell without human beings. Many of their arguments contradict Catholic teaching. They imagine that only one who is entirely evil can go to Hell. They claim that such evil is unlikely, if not impossible. They suggest that a sinner can repent after dying. They suggest that Hell is "infinitely intense" but not infinitely long. They say that God would suffer tragically if but one person were damned. (Never mind that Lucifer is a person.) They degrade Scripture by transforming it into a myth. In all of this, they are opposed to the constant teaching of the Church. St. Augustine's words are apropos: "Our friends who long to get rid of eternal punish-ment should cease to argue against God, and should instead obey God's commandments, while there is still time."[199]

Strangely, some Hell deniers show misgivings. They show a lack of confidence in their hope. How so? They back up their confidence that Hell is or may be empty with a hedge bet on the Lutheran notion of jus-tification. For Luther, even if you commit damnable sins, you can remain justified, provided only that you have faith. In short, if the magic wand cannot make Hell disappear, maybe it can put a cloak on the sinner, so that he might sneak into the kingdom without having to obey the com-mandments. To this, we now turn.

---

[199] St. Augustine, *City of God*, bk. XXI, chap. 23, 1001.

3

Does Faith Alone Justify?

In case Hell might be real, some take shelter in the heresy of justification by faith alone. They hold that God's offer of forgiveness cancels out our need to obey the commandments. They hold that keeping the commandments is not necessary to attain salvation. Sinners are saved by faith alone. This was Luther's error.

Catholics believe, as do Lutherans, that God freely offers to forgive our sins. We cannot merit this forgiveness. Catholics also believe, however, that God's forgiveness comes with power. It is not a mere declaration of innocence. It is not a mere remission of punishment. Rather, God gives a healing power by which we are transformed from children of darkness into children of light, from enemies into friends, from orphans into sons. Because God is good, He offers forgiveness. Because He is powerful, His forgiveness transforms us into friends and enables us to walk toward Him as friends, so that life on Earth is a pilgrimage toward Heaven. The more deeply and faithfully we cooperate with God, the more deeply we drink of God's goodness in the kingdom. This life matters. Finally, if we die in a state of sin, we are judged guilty and cast into the fires of Hell. This is basic Catholicism.

Unfortunately, some Catholics are confused about the Faith. They think that Luther was correct; they think justification is by faith alone. They claim that recent actions and statements of popes justify their position. In this chapter, I will examine the heresy of justification by faith alone. I will expound the teachings of the Catholic Faith that condemn it. Finally, I will address the aforesaid recent actions and statements of popes.

Luther on Justification by Faith Alone

Noble Beginnings That Turn Sour

Martin Luther began with noble aspirations. From his earliest writings, he desired something that many Catholic saints desire: to love God with pure love. He wanted to love God without hope for an *extrinsic* reward. He wanted to love God *just for God's goodness*, not for anything extraneous he might receive from God. Many Catholic saints have expressed this very desire.

Sadly, Luther misconceived even these noble aspirations. He viewed the desire for happiness as being at odds with pure love. So he thought that to love God purely required a renunciation of the desire for happiness: "To love [in the sense of true charity] is to hate oneself, to condemn oneself, and to wish the worst."[200] In short, Luther interpreted the Great Commandment (Matt. 22:35–40) as though it were the demand of a tyrant. He exposes his opinion when he *rejects* the Catholic teaching that the greatest commandment is still a condition for salvation: "[God] requires in addition that you keep the Law in love — not the natural love that you have but a supernatural and divine love that He Himself confers. What is this but to make God a tyrant and a tormentor who demands of us what we cannot produce?"[201] Luther here rejects the Catholic teaching on the law, because he thinks the law is terrible and tyrannical. His misreading of the law echoes the deceit of the Serpent: "Did God say, 'You shall not eat of *any* tree of the garden?'" (Gen. 3:1, my emphasis). Luther's noble

---

[200] Martin Luther, *Lectures on Romans*, ed. Hilton Oswald, trans. Walter Tillmanns and Jacob Preus, vol. 25 of *Luther's Works* (*LW*), ed. Jaroslav Pelikan and Helmut Lehmann (Saint Louis: Concordia Publishing House, 1972), 382.

[201] Martin Luther, *Lectures on Galatians 1535*, trans. and ed. Jaroslav Pelikan, vol. 26 of *Luther's Works*, ed. Jaroslav Pelikan (Saint Louis: Concordia Publishing House, 1963), 129.

aspiration puts him in touch with the desire for holiness. His misreading puts an awful burden on him and paints God as jealous and harsh. The saints, however, embrace both happiness and love. They know that God wants happiness for each person and that true love leads to happiness.

Luther doubled down on this misreading of the law: he broke with the firmly established Catholic tradition that we do *not* necessarily sin just because we act with a less-than-pure love. Say, for example, that we refrain from committing theft simply because of the fear of prison or Hell. The Catholic Church teaches that we do not sin in this case; our fear of Hell is not a love of God, but it does help us avoid sin on this occasion. Similarly, when we seek a reward, we do not necessarily sin. It is only when we place the reward above God that we sin.[202] Sometimes, we have mixed motives: an incipient love of God and a concomitant fear of Hell. A mixed motive does not entail a sin. In short, Catholic tradition does not hold that divine law demands of us a motive of pure love of God in order to escape damnation. Luther rejects the wisdom of this tradition: "Through that entirely false interpretation of the following word, 'God does not demand perfection,' the opinion was spread that no sin is involved if a person does something with less than perfect love." Luther holds that it *is* a sin but that God forgives it (for those who have faith): "God does not demand it because he pardons it, not because he permits it and it is not sin."[203]

Given such a harsh conception of the law, Luther could not but conclude that no one offers God the love that He demands: "Whoever does not do good out of complete and perfect love of God does less than he ought. But every righteous man is that kind of person." Luther explains this inability by pointing to the impulses of the flesh that arise spontaneously and apart from choice: "That we do not love him with all our might, has

---

[202] See, for example, DH 1456, 1489, 1539, 1576, 1581, 1705, 2207, 2212, 2216, 2309, 2310, 2313, 2314, 2315, 2351–2373, 2455, 2460, 2462, and 2625.

[203] Martin Luther, *Heidelberg Disputations*, Explanation to Thesis 6, in *Career of the Reformer I*, ed. Harold Grimm, vol. 31 of *Luther's Works*, ed. Helmut Lehmann, trans. Harold Grimm (Philadelphia: Fortress Press, 1957), 62.

been proven above, for the unwillingness in the flesh and in the members hinders this perfection so that not all members or powers love God. This unwillingness resists the inner will which loves God."[204] Now, a spontaneous inclination toward a free act of sin, an inclination that we do not choose, is aptly called "concupiscence." Luther holds that this inclination itself is a sin. It is a "deeply hidden root"[205] of particular acts of sin, which are like fruit from an evil tree.[206] For Luther, concupiscence is the essence of original sin; it is not only an inability to love God but a faculty of hatred toward God: "Man not only does not love God any longer but flees from Him, hates Him, and desires to be and live without Him."[207] The official Lutheran formularies also identify original sin and concupiscence. They hold concupiscence to be the worst of sins.[208] Luther thinks that he has Paul on his side. He is thinking of Romans 7, wherein Paul describes sin as dwelling within him: "Paul calls that which remains after baptism, sin; the Fathers call it a weakness and imperfection, rather than sin. Here we stand at the parting of the ways. I follow Paul, and you the fathers."[209] We can illustrate the consequence of Luther's definition of concupiscence with a concrete example: if, for Luther, concupiscence is a sin, then, for him, the tendency to sodomy, the homosexual orientation itself, is a sin.

Luther claims that these spontaneous inclinations, which we do not choose, infect our every act. This is true whether or not God has justified us. Thus, there is sin in every work we do, even "good" works: "Plainly

---

[204] Ibid., *LW* 31:61–62; see Luther, *Lectures on Galatians*, *LW* 27:63–65.

[205] Martin Luther, *Against Latomus*, trans. George Lindbeck, from *Career of the Reformer II*, ed. George Forell, vol. 32 of *Luther's Works*, ed. Jelmut Lehmann (Philadelphia: Fortress Press, 1958), 226.

[206] Ibid., 224.

[207] Martin Luther, *Lectures on Genesis*, trans. George Schick, vol. 1 of *Luther's Works*, ed. Jaroslav Pelikan (Saint Louis: Concordia Publishing House, 1958), 165.

[208] *Formula of Concord*, Solid Declaration (SD), I, pars. 5–6, 19, in Robert Kolb and Timothy Wengert, *The Book of Concord: The Confessions of the Evangelical Lutheran Church*, trans. Charles Arand et al. (Minneapolis: Fortress Press, 2000).

[209] Luther, *Against Latomus*, *LW* 32:220.

there is in this life not a single instance of this rule that a good work is without sin."[210] In short, God commands us to do the impossible: "Every saint is obligated to love God as much as he can, indeed more than he can, but no one has or can do that."[211]

Let us summarize. God's demands are harsh and impossible to observe. So we sin in every work. How evil are these sins? For Luther, there are no venial sins. Every sin is mortal. That is, every sin deserves eternal damnation. Every sin is *damnable*:

> Sin is really sin, regardless of whether you commit it before or after you have come to know Christ. And God hates the sin; in fact, so far as the substance of the deed is concerned, every sin is mortal. It is not mortal for the believer; but this is on account of Christ the Propitiator, who expiated it by His death. As for the person who does not believe in Christ, not only are all his sins mortal, but even his good works are sins.[212]

As we see, mixed into Luther's noble desire to love God purely are grave misunderstandings. He divorces happiness and true love. He portrays God as a tyrant who, in His law, demands the impossible. This portrait of a tyrannical God is at the foundation of Luther's problems. It led Luther to despair. He despaired of ever doing enough for God. Try though he may, he could not please God. But Luther invented a solution to this despair, the heresy of justification by faith alone. So much for a robust hope. It is really a theology of despair.

The Chimerical Solution: Justification by Faith Alone
The solution, Luther alleged, is that God freely promises to *consider* or *treat* us as though we are obedient to the law, even though we really

---

[210] Ibid., 235. See also *LW* 32:233, 234, 235, 245, 247; Martin Luther, *The Leipzig Debate*, trans. Harold Grimm, *LW* 31:317; and Luther, *Lectures on Galatians*, *LW* 26:125, 126, and 174.

[211] Martin Luther, *Explanations of the Ninety-Five Theses*, 58th Thesis, trans. Harold Grimm, *LW* 31:213.

[212] Luther, *Lectures on Galatians*, *LW* 27:76.

remain rebellious. God chooses to *declare* us righteous even though we are inwardly unrighteous. God offers us free and unconditional salvation on account of the merits of Christ. God's generous offer to us Luther calls *grace*; he considers grace to be the extrinsic favor of God toward us. For Luther, grace is not a gift that God gives us but the extrinsic favor God has toward us. Now, what good must we do to attain eternal life? Nothing. We must simply receive the promise by *faith alone*.

Faith, Luther argued, is trust in and reception of the benefit of God's promises. When we have faith, we accept God's *declaration* that we are perfectly righteous, all the while acknowledging that we remain sinful inwardly. (And all sin is *damnable*, that for which I can be damned.) Justification is only a change in the way God treats us. How does He treat us differently? In "justifying" us, God simply does not "impute" our sins against us. That is, God does not charge them against us. In itself, justification is not a change in us. So the justified person has sins just as does the unjustified person:

> It is a pernicious error when the sophists distinguish among sins on the basis of the substance of the deed rather than on the basis of the persons. A believer's sin is the same sin and sin just as great as that of the unbeliever. To the believer, however, it is forgiven and not imputed, while to the unbeliever it is retained and imputed. To the former it is venial; to the latter mortal. This is not because of a difference between the sins, as though the believer's sin were smaller and the unbeliever's larger, but because of a difference between the persons. For the believer knows that his sin is forgiven him on account of Christ, who expiated it by His death. Even though he has sin and commits sin, he remains godly. On the other hand, when the unbeliever commits sin, he remains ungodly. This is the wisdom and the comfort of those who are truly godly, that even if they have sins and commit sins, they know that because of their faith in Christ these are not imputed to them.[213]

---

[213] Luther, *Lectures on Galatians*, LW 27:76.

To be more precise, justification involves a twofold legal pronouncement for Luther. On the one hand, God declares us not to be guilty of our sins. As a result, we are shielded from the divine *wrath*, which would otherwise have condemned us to damnation. That is, we are freed from everlasting *punishment*. On the other hand, God declares us to be righteous with the righteousness of Christ Himself. That is, the very righteousness of Christ is legally treated as though it were our righteousness. We do not share in His righteousness internally in such a way as truly to be pleasing in God's sight. Rather, God legally accounts His righteousness, which is extrinsic to us, as though it were ours. Now, Christ's righteousness is perfect; so it cannot grow. Hence, according to Luther, our own justification is perfect. Finally, as a result of being declared righteous, we have the promise of everlasting *happiness* in Heaven. We have and retain this double boon so long as we have and retain *faith*. Our possession of this double boon is not contingent on our obedience to the commandments and our avoidance of mortal sins.

Now, in their understanding of Luther, some Catholics stop here. They say that, for Luther, nothing *ever* changes. They liken Luther's portrait of the justified person to "snow covered dung." The snow is supposed to be God's external favor, and the dung is supposed to be the unchanging sinner. These Catholics complain that Luther did not care about good works at all. This is an erroneous portrait. It fails to do justice to Luther. We don't serve the truth by exaggerating error (just as Luther did not serve God's mercy by magnifying our sin)!

Real but Weak Sanctification

Luther *does* have a doctrine of sanctification, albeit a weak one. The double boon of justification leads immediately to an inward experience of tremendous relief and gratitude. Picture it this way. Pretend your father was a tyrannical person who threatened to beat you at the slightest provocation. Pretend also that you thought he had just cause to do so. Then, suddenly, he told you that he loved you, that he accepted you, no matter what you did. What would your reaction be? Most likely, you would be shaken up inside and want to hug him and do good things for him. This is what Luther counseled his followers to do. He encouraged gratitude and good works. Only, he insisted that one should never treat these deeds as steps on the way to Heaven. Luther refused to see earthly life as a pilgrimage whereby we make our way toward or away from God through the path of charity. Rather, good works should be seen *only* as expressions of the fact that, so long as we retain faith, we already have Heaven in the bank, so to speak.

It is important to get Luther right: he does speak of a transformation (sanctification). At the same time, he radically and constantly divorces the essence of justification from the essence of sanctification. Whereas the Catholic Church holds that the essence of justification is forgiving sanctification, Luther separates forgiveness and sanctification. Moreover, he considers sanctification to be very weak. It is so weak that we can never do a good work that is truly pleasing to God. Even though we begin to be "sanctified," we cannot merit eternal life. The results are devastating. Luther thinks that even the justified person sins in every act. He thinks that every sin is mortal or damnable. He thinks we remain truly wretched. Rather than meriting Heaven with any good work, we merit damnation with every work. But, Luther says, if you have faith, then no sin, even the gravest, will, *in fact*, damn you. The Catholic Church, by contrast, believes that God makes the sinner into a good person, a holy person. The Catholic Church believes that God enables the justified person to fulfill the condition of salvation, obedience to the commandments by which we journey to God. Finally, the Catholic Church believes that not every work is a sin and that not every sin is a mortal sin. But she also believes that any mortal sin will, in fact, damn the sinner, unless he repents. These views are worlds apart. Let us explore the Catholic view in greater depth.

Catholic Teachings on Justification

We can indicate several key Catholic teachings on justification.

1. Baptismal justification is a comprehensive renewal of the inner man, leaving no sin at all: not original sin, not mortal sin, and not venial sin. Trent declares:

In those reborn, God hates nothing because "there is no condemnation" [Rom. 8:1] for those who were "buried with Christ by baptism into death" [Rom. 6:4], "who do not walk according to the flesh" [Rom. 8:1], but who, putting off the old man and putting on the new man, created in accordance with God [cf. Eph. 4:22–24; Col. 3:9–10], innocent, unstained, pure, and guiltless, have become the beloved sons of God ... so that nothing henceforth holds them back from entering into heaven.[214]

This teaching is breathtaking. How awesome is our God. How good and powerful. How lovely! In Baptism, He washes us clean. God is not so impotent as to be unable to heal us. Nor is He so sluggish in generosity as to want to leave us in the misery of damnable sin. To what end would God want to leave us in a state of implicit hatred of Him?[215] How would that benefit us? Sin *is* misery, and God does not will our misery. He sent His Son so that we might have life, and true life is the love of charity and the knowledge of the truth!

2. Following St. Paul and acknowledging the obvious in human experience, the Church has always taught that "concupiscence" remains in the baptized. This concupiscence is a *tendency* to sin that is not freely chosen. Chosen acts of sin are called *actual* sins. These sins contrast with concupiscence and with the inherited state of sin called *original sin*. By contrast to both actual and original sin, there is concupiscence, the simple *tendency* to actual sins. Is this tendency itself a sin? Heavens no! In Romans 7, Paul calls it "sin," but he uses this term in a poetic or *figurative* sense. Trent declares Paul's meaning:

The Catholic Church has never understood that it is called sin [as though] it would be sin in the true and proper sense in those who

---

[214] Trent, Session V, canon 5; DH 1515.

[215] We are presupposing here that God freely loves us. Luther presupposes this too. If we presuppose that God loves us freely, there is no intelligible basis for Him to want to leave us in a state of mortal sin.

have been reborn, but because it comes from sin and inclines to sin. If anyone thinks the contrary, let him be anathema.[216]

This is a condemnation of an error. What is the positive teaching, the Catholic reading of Paul?

There are three aspects to the Catholic reading of Paul: first, the constant Catholic tradition is that sin requires free will. St. Justin and the early Fathers are adamant about this. Sin cannot exist without free will.[217] Second, Catholics point to the light of reason, which is God's gift to every person. This light teaches us that a true act of sin requires responsibility and that responsibility requires the use of free will. Thus, right reason teaches us that sin requires free will. If we contradict right reason, we lose our first principles of thinking. We become madmen. Madness is not what Christ, the Word (or Reason) of God, calls us to. Now, since concupiscence is not chosen, it cannot be a sin. Third, we avoid reading Paul in a *fundamentalist* manner. Recall the principle that Scripture is to be read in a literal way *unless* there is a necessary reason to read it in a poetic or metaphorical way. Here, the Church insists that Paul uses the word "sin" sometimes in poetic ways. In parts of Romans 7, his use of it involves a literary device called *metonymy*. There are various ways in which metonymy works. Through metonymy, a cause can stand for the effect, or vice versa, and the container can stand for the contents, or vice versa. For example, we sometimes say, "Here comes trouble," when the class bully nears. We don't mean that the bully *is* trouble but that he *causes* trouble. Again, a mother tells her child, "Finish your plate." We all know what she means: not "eat all of your plate" but "eat the food on your plate." In Romans 7, Paul calls concupiscence "sin" (1) insofar as it comes from Adam's act of sin and (2) insofar as it can occasion our own acts of sin *if* we freely surrender to it.[218] Paul is no

---

[216] Trent, Session V, canon 5; DH 1515.

[217] See, for example, Justin Martyr, *The First Apology*, chap. 43, and Irenaeus, *Against Heresies*, bk. IV, chap. 37.

[218] It is Catholic dogma that Paul is employing a literary device here. See the same canon cited previously, at DH 1516.

stranger to literary devices. Those who understand him well know that. For instance, in Romans, he speaks of the law of Moses (Rom. 2:12), of the law whose commands are written on the heart (Rom. 2:14–15), of the law that is a general statistical rule (Rom. 7:21), of a law of the mind (Rom. 7:23), of a law of sin (Rom. 7:23), of the law of the Spirit (Rom. 8:2), and so forth. He employs one and the same term in many ways. But the fundamentalist fails to see this. Luther's reading was fundamentalist. The Catholic Church's reading is not.

3. The Church teaches that justification is *not* by faith alone:

> If anyone says that the sinner is justified by faith alone in the sense that nothing else is required by way of cooperation in order to obtain the grace of justification and that it is not at all necessary that he should be prepared and disposed by the movement of his will, let him be anathema.[219]

The gift of divine faith does not justify us by itself. Even though we have true, divine faith, we can still be as lifeless branches on the vine, dead members of the body. In the above canon, Trent indicates the preparation and cooperation requisite to attain justification. In a related passage, Trent indicates that the virtues of hope and charity, gifts from Almighty God, are also necessary: "Faith without hope and charity neither unites a man perfectly with Christ nor makes him a living member of his body."[220] This third point is a reaffirmation of the first point: God's grace is powerfully transformative. He takes our stony hearts and makes them hearts of flesh. He takes our waywardness and turns it homeward. The gift of charity is our share in God's own love of Himself. When we share in that love, we become like Him. Is this our own great deed? No! It is God's great deed in us. When we boast of what God does within us, we do not take credit for the work. We extol God and acknowledge the beauty of His creation. Compare this point with Christ's healing of the paralyzed man. The paralyzed man could not walk. Then Christ healed him. What was

---

[219] Trent, Session VI, canon 9; DH 1559.
[220] Ibid., chap. 7; DH 1531.

the *cause* of this healing? Christ! But what did Christ *do*? What was the *essence* of the healing? It was the paralytic's *being able to walk*! So, too, charity in us is a gift from God: it is our ability to walk home to God. God gives us this ability. He *makes* us His friends and lovers. How sweet and divine! By contrast, Luther's erroneous theory of justification by faith alone rests on despair. Moreover, Luther's is a miserable doctrine. On Luther's reckoning, we are left miserable wretches until the day we die, when, suddenly God finally and instantaneously transforms us. "O Luther," we must ask, "Is God too weak to transform our hearts now? Or is He unwilling to do so? If so, why? Of what benefit is it to us for God to leave us in the perversion of sin?"

4. The Church teaches that there can be true and divine faith without charity. Such faith is true and divine because it is a supernatural gift of God. But, because it is without charity, it remains dead. This is the constant teaching of the Church. Trent dogmatically declares:

> If anyone says that with the loss of grace through sin faith is also always lost or that the faith that remains is not true faith, granted that it is not a living faith [cf. Jas. 2:26], or that the man who has faith without charity is not a Christian, let him be anathema.[221]

Vatican I reaffirmed this dogma: "Faith itself, even when it is not working through love [cf. Gal. 5:6], is in itself a gift of God."[222] Such a faith is a supernatural gift. It is a grace even if it is not living through charity.[223] Most recently, John Paul II, in his masterful *Veritatis splendor*, taught the same: "With every freely committed mortal sin, [man] offends God as the giver of the law and as a result becomes guilty with regard to the entire law (cf. Jas. 2:8–11); even if he perseveres in faith, he loses 'sanctifying grace,' 'charity' and 'eternal happiness'."[224] Thus, the following claim is heretical: true faith cannot exist without charity. To the contrary, even

---

[221] Ibid., canon 28; DH 1578.
[222] *Dei Filius*, chap. 3; DH 3010.
[223] *Dei Filius*, canon 5; DH 3035.
[224] John Paul II, *Veritatis splendor*, art. 68.

though faith without charity is dead, it remains true faith. Can a dead faith help us? Yes, it can. By true faith, we are firmly convinced that God exists and that He rewards those who seek Him and punishes those who reject Him. We believe that He will judge the secrets of all hearts (Heb. 11:6). Thus, faith helps us to evaluate our lives objectively. Faith also disposes us to hope in God because it tells us of His mercy. Though we are sinful, we may hope that God will convert us, so that we may be saved.

5. The "justice" or "righteousness" by which we are justified in God's sight is our *share* in His infinite justice, a share that He pours into our hearts and by which He makes us truly, internally just. This teaching is of monumental importance. Recall Luther's belief that the "grace" of justification is God's extrinsic favor, His eternal attitude toward the sinner; because of this favor, God legally declares Christ's righteousness to be ours. Here, Luther opposes the Catholic appreciation of how God favors, or rather *loves*, the sinner. The Catholic Faith adds the crucial ingredient: *God's love has an effect.* To love includes willing some good to the beloved. So God wills our good. What is our good? Is it to wallow in the misery of sin? Is it merely to escape punishment, even though we remain unbearable? Far from it! Sin and vice make the person miserable to himself and unbearable for others. Only virtue and charity make the person happy and support a good society. The Catholic Faith adds what Luther denies—namely, that because of His favor, God pours justifying grace *into the soul,* and this grace heals and transforms the soul so that it becomes radiant and beautiful in God's sight. By this grace, our souls are cleansed of the stain of mortal sin and partake of the divine nature, like iron heated by fire. Furthermore, the powers of our soul are oriented toward God by the theological virtues of faith, hope, and charity. The core of this transformation is what Trent calls "justifying grace."

Employing Scholastic terminology, Trent declares this justifying grace to be the "formal cause" of justification.[225] This teaching may sound too technical to follow; it is not. Moreover, it is crucial. Oh, for the clarity of years past! What is a formal cause? A formal cause is the *perfection* that an

---

[225] Trent, Session VI, chap. 7; DH 1529.

agent puts into the materials he is working on when he does something constructive. Consider the analogy of a house. A *cause* of the house is any explanation of its being. There are various explanations of the house; so there are various causes of the house. First, there is the agent cause, the one who *makes* the house. Philosophy calls this the "efficient cause." The efficient cause of a house is the carpenter (and others). Then there is the material out of which the agent constructs the house. Philosophy calls this the "material cause." The materials of a house are bricks, lumber, PVC pipe, and so on. Next, there is *the shape* the agent puts into the materials; rather, there is the shape that he constructs out of the materials. This shape is the precise *perfection* that the agent establishes in or with the materials. Philosophy calls this perfection the "formal cause," because form is a certain shape. Finally, there is the reason the agent does the work; philosophy calls this the "final cause" or purpose. Theologians have applied this causal analysis to various theological realities, such as the sacraments and justification. In applying this philosophical analysis to justification, theologians found it necessary to add another cause, the "meritorious cause," which is the cause that procures the payment so that the agent will act.

Now, in the dispute over justification, the formal cause is a pivotal point of divergence between Lutherans and Catholics. How so? Both parties agree that God is the agent (or the efficient cause) who justifies. Both agree that *man* is the one whom (or the material cause) God justifies. Both agree that *salvation* is a reason (or a final cause) for justification. Both agree that *Christ's redemptive work* is the payment (or the meritorious cause) on account of which God justifies.[226] So much agreement! Is there any room left for disagreement? Why all the fuss? In fact, there is a very massive disagreement over the formal cause. This disagreement is about *the very perfection that God gives*. It is a disagreement about *what* God does.

---

[226] God chose to act on account of a just price paid by Christ. He could have redeemed us without that price or sacrifice. But then the human race (through the Savior, Jesus Christ) would not have satisfied the penalty for its sin.

For Lutherans, God's action is but a declaration; the "perfection" given is the extrinsic righteousness of Christ. As a result, the very action of God (His efficient causality) is conceived in a reductively *legal* way. God performs a legal action. Moreover, this legal declaration is *counterfactual*. It is a false declaration because the justified person remains a wretched sinner. (Oh, but God as all-powerful can declare things however He chooses! He can call evil good. Remember, He has tyrannical authority!) The Catholic Faith objects. In contrast to Luther, the Catholic Faith believes that God never lies (Titus 1:2). Further, God is a good lover who brings about a real transformation of the miserable sinner into a holy child of God. So the perfection that God brings about is the justifying grace that He pours into the heart. God's action is more than legal; it is transformative. Thus, the declaration of justification is true and real. The following crucial statement is one locus of this teaching in Trent:

> Finally, the single formal cause is "the justice of God, not [that] by which he himself is just, but [that] by which he makes us just", namely, the justice that we have as a gift from him and by which we are spiritually renewed. Thus, not only are we considered just, but we are truly called just and we are just, each one receiving within himself his own justice, according to the measure that "the Holy Spirit apportions to each one individually as he wills" and according to each one's personal disposition and cooperation.[227]

The single formal cause is *not* the uncreated justice of God (the justice by which He is just). Rather, it is a created gift of grace that God pours into our hearts. By giving us this gift, God makes us to be His holy children and enables us to do holy works and merit Heaven. This grace of justification is properly called ours because it inheres in us. It is also called God's because He is its author or efficient cause.[228] Finally, this same grace is called Christ's because it is given to us on account of Christ's merits. This created gift of grace poured into our hearts, however, is not the righteousness of

---

[227] Trent, Session VI, chap. 7; DH 1529.
[228] Ibid., chap. 16; DH 1547.

Christ: "If anyone says ... *that [men] are formally just by [Christ's] justice itself: let him be anathema.*"[229] Justification is God's divine transformation of the human person. God is able and willing to do this. He really infuses justice or righteousness into us. We are made truly righteous.

6. Those whom He justifies God makes capable of obeying the commandments, "for God does not command the impossible."[230] Thus, it is heresy to deny that those who are just can obey God's commandments: "If anyone says that the commandments of God are impossible to observe even for a man who is justified and established in grace, let him be anathema."[231] The already justified person *is able to obey God's law*. This teaching has immediate practical relevance. We can live life well. We can make this life a pilgrim journey of love toward Love. Of course, we always need divine help. On this journey, we take food for nourishment. Our spiritual food is the Eucharist. God helps His children in countless ways.

The Eucharist as food brings to light the true righteousness God gives. In order to receive the Eucharist rightly, one must be in the state of grace; one must be *just and holy*. Thus, if a Catholic is for the moment "not able" to obey the commandments of God, then he must at the moment *not* be in a state of grace. But if he is not in the state of grace, he may not receive the sacrament of the Eucharist. He must first go to Confession. Now, to receive the sacrament of Confession validly, he must have a *firm purpose of amendment.*[232] Since the justified can obey God's commandments, any person in the state of grace is able to obey them, such as the prohibition against adultery.[233] Thus, anyone who is now unable to obey this commandment must not be in the state of grace. But such a person is therefore not rightly disposed to receive the Eucharist.

---

[229] Ibid., canon 10; DH 1560, emphasis mine.

[230] Ibid., chap. 11; DH 1536.

[231] Ibid., canon 18; DH 1568.

[232] See Trent, Session XIV, chap. 4; DH 1676 and 1678.

[233] Of course, we have to add that obedience to God's commandments requires God's constant help. His help is twofold. First, there is the justifying grace He pours into the soul, which grace inheres in the soul. Second, there are the actual graces of God's manifold help in each moment.

7. We can grow in justifying grace and so be more justified. The reason is that justification is how God *sanctifies* the human person. Because God's holiness is infinite, it cannot increase. The holiness to which He brings any man (that which He infuses into the soul) is finite; so it can increase. Its increase is qualitative, not quantitative. Created holiness is a participation in the divine nature (2 Pet. 1:4). Just as an iron can grow hotter the longer you leave it in the fire, so can a man grow holier the more God infuses grace into him and the more the man cooperates with God. Although there comes a point at which iron melts, because fire is not in every way good for iron, we have no melting point when we participate in God. Participation in God does not damage us or threaten us. It only ennobles us. Thus, there is no intrinsic limit to how deeply a creature can participate in the infinite perfection of God. Created holiness can always be more perfect than it is. So justifying holiness is not to be considered "perfect" in the sense of being incapable of increase. It can increase throughout our earthly pilgrimage, provided we do not sin mortally but cooperate with God. Consequently, Trent declares: "When 'faith is active along with works,' [the justified] increase in the very justice they have received through the grace of Christ and are further justified."[234] Therefore, it is heresy to deny that justifying grace can increase. Correlatively, it is heresy to hold that such works testify only to a justification already received: "If anyone says that the justice received is not preserved and even increased before God through good works, but that such works are merely the fruits and the signs of the justification obtained and not also the cause of its increase, let him be anathema."[235]

8. Eternal salvation is *conditional* upon obedience to the commandments.[236] As we have seen, God enables us lovingly to cooperate with His design, so that we can at last attain salvation. His design comes to

---

[234] Trent, Session VI, chap. 10; DH 1535.

[235] Ibid., canon 24; DH 1574.

[236] Of course, we are speaking about those with the use of free will. Baptized infants, who do not have the use of free will, go straight to Heaven if they die.

us in the form of commandments, which indicate the necessary ways we must act and the ways in which we must necessarily not act. The commandments are God's way of bringing us home. They are not arbitrary, tyrannical precepts. They indicate the paths of justice, consideration, and truth. They indicate the notes of friendship. Thus, they forever bind us. So Trent declares: "If anyone says that a justified man, however perfect he may be, is not bound to observe the commandments of God and of the Church but is bound only to believe, as if the Gospel were merely an absolute promise of eternal life, without the condition that the commandments be observed, let him be anathema."[237]

9. By the grace of God, we can *truly merit* eternal life. God so transforms us that we become capable of cooperating with Him in His design for our salvation. He makes us co-workers with Him (1 Cor. 3:9). Of itself, the transformation that He creates or works in us entitles us to eternal inheritance. So we shall receive this, once we have been purified of all venial sins and of any debt of temporal punishment. This is why Paul calls the adopted son of God an "heir" (Rom. 8:17; Gal. 4:7). God makes us heirs by His power. By this same power, He also equips us for works worthy of the kingdom. Adopted by God and engrafted into Christ, we are enabled by God to act as true sons and thus obtain the inheritance. In short, we have a title to inheritance by God's transformative effect in our lives, and we gain a new title to inheritance by cooperating freely with His ongoing help. The title gained by work is called "merit." In short, endowed with grace, we truly merit eternal life by works of charity! Thus, Trent teaches:

> If anyone says that the good works of the justified man are the gifts of God in such a way that they are not also the good merits of the justified man himself; or that by the good works he performs through the grace of God and the merits of Jesus Christ (of whom he is a living member), the justified man does not truly merit an increase of grace, eternal life, and (provided he dies in the state

[237] Trent, Session VI, canon 20; DH 1570.

of grace) the attainment of this eternal life, as well as an increase of glory, let him be anathema.[238]

The teaching is unequivocal: God's grace so transforms and equips the justified person that he *truly merits* eternal life by his good works.[239]

All Catholics, regardless of their rank, are obliged to believe these dogmas. These teachings do not glorify human nature; they glorify God, whose love is powerful and effective. The above dogmas are some of the basic elements of Catholic teaching concerning justification. Luther's views contradict a number of these dogmas. Unfortunately, some Catholics fail to appreciate the radical difference between Luther's teaching and Catholic teaching. Some are confused and think that we are permitted to embrace Luther's doctrine because of recent statements and actions of magisterial figures. To these statements and actions we now turn.

Recent Magisterial Support for Luther?

Two factors might appear to warrant Catholic acceptance of Luther's theory. First, there are recent papal statements and actions. Second, there is the 1999 statement on justification issued jointly by officials from Lutheran communities and the Catholic Church. This document is the Lutheran-Catholic Joint Declaration on the Doctrine of Justification (JDDJ).[240] We will treat each of these in turn.

Papal Statements and Actions

Pope Benedict XVI

In several instances, Pope Benedict XVI used expressions that some have taken as endorsement for Luther.

---

[238] Ibid., canon 32; DH 1582.

[239] See Christian D. Washburn, "Transformative Power of Grace and Condign Merit at the Council of Trent," *Thomist* 79 (2015): 173–212.

[240] The document may be found in *Origins* 28:8 (1998): 120–27. Except where elsewhere noted, I will provide my own translations.

1. To a general audience he said, "Luther's expression 'sola fide' is true if faith is not opposed to charity, to love."[241] What could the pope have meant? At any rate, the Catholic dogma is that the faith that justifies is living faith, not dead faith. Now, faith lives *by* charity. So, justifying faith does not merely not oppose charity; it includes charity. Therefore, it is true to say "faith alone justifies" only if the word "faith" is used as a literary device to mean "faith, hope, and charity." The literary device would be *synecdoche*, whereby the part (faith) stands for the whole (faith, hope, and charity). (Similarly, the captain says to the sailors, "All hands on deck.") St. Paul's doctrine of justification by faith is, in fact, a synecdoche, as 1 Corinthians 13 implies. There, Paul claims that faith, without charity, leaves him an empty nothing. But when Luther declared that "faith alone" justifies, he was rejecting synecdoche. His error forced the Council of Trent to be very clear and explicit.

In order to avoid confusion or watering down the dogma, we should follow the precision of Trent so as to remain faithful to Paul. Lack of precision may at first be consoling to those who have great zeal for reunion. It may help begin a difficult conversation. But sustained lack of precision would make one lose sight of the rigors of truth; it is thus unhelpful for Catholics who want to embrace their whole Faith. As a result, in the long run, lack of precision is unhelpful for genuine ecumenical progress.

2. A week later, Benedict added, "A faith without charity, without this fruit, would not be true faith. It would be dead faith."[242] What did he mean? Perhaps he meant that dead faith does not justify us and will not save us. Still, we must also remember the dogma that true, divine faith *can* exist without charity. Dead faith is still real and true faith. It won't save you, but it is a supernatural virtue and act by which we believe what God reveals.

3. Pope Benedict commented on a passage in James. St. James teaches, "A man is justified by works and not by faith alone" (Jas. 2:24). Benedict commented, "James accentuates the consequential relations between

---

[241] Benedict XVI, General Audience, November 19, 2008.
[242] Benedict XVI, General Audience, November 26, 2008.

faith and works.... Faith that is active in love testifies to the freely given gift of justification in Christ."[243] A question some may ask is whether Pope Benedict considered good works to be *only* fruits and signs of the justification already received rather than a real cause of the increase of justifying grace. At any rate, it is Catholic dogma that our works are *not* mere fruits and signs. God enables us to do good works and so "increase in the very justice they have received" so as to be "further justified."[244] It may be that Benedict was suggesting that good works follow true justification, which is not by faith alone.

4. In the same audience, Benedict stressed "the insignificance of our actions and of our deeds to achieve salvation." Benedict returned to this theme in *Spe salvi*, writing, "We cannot—to use the classical expression—'merit' Heaven through our works."[245] What do these remarks mean? In point of fact, the Catholic dogma is that the justified who do good works "truly merit" eternal life.[246] Since that is true, our works are significant. Yes, their outward appearance is small and trifling, even if heroic. But their inward character is tremendous. Our works matter. Can we do these works on our own? No. We cannot merit salvation on our own without grace. Perhaps that is what Pope Benedict meant. In any case, all Catholics must cling to the clear and precise dogma.

POPE FRANCIS

Some might point to certain statements and actions of Pope Francis as license for adopting Luther's views.

1. Pope Francis has generally praised Luther. For example, under his watch, the Vatican issued a stamp with the figures of both Martin Luther and Philipp Melanchthon on it. In addition, Pope Francis stated, "Nowadays, Lutherans and Catholics, and all Protestants, are in agreement on the doctrine of justification: on this very important point he [Luther] was

---

[243] Ibid.
[244] Trent, Session VI, chap. 10, DH 1535.
[245] Benedict XVI, *Spe salvi*, art. 35.
[246] DH 1546 and 1582.

not mistaken."[247] How should Catholics respond to these things? Well, these gestures and remarks are not papal words, but words of a pope, which are not magisterial. In any case, the dogmas of Trent condemning justification by faith alone may not be denied by any Catholic. We should also note that Luther's doctrine has devastating pastoral ramifications seldom considered. Take, for example, the homosexual orientation. A Catholic cannot embrace the implication of Luther's theory—namely, that the orientation in itself is a damnable sin. No. For Catholicism, a tendency to sin, as such, is not even a venial sin.

2. In *Amoris laetitia*, Pope Francis gave voice to some positions that are pertinent to this topic. In one part, he addressed the situation of those who have been civilly divorced, have not received a declaration of annulment, and yet have "remarried." Regarding such situations, the Church's perennial practice is to presume validity of the first marriage. Now, no one who is married may validly contract another marriage. Any such second "marriage" would be *invalid*. Further, sexual intercourse is morally good only within the context of a presumably valid marriage. Therefore, the sexual intercourse of the second, invalid "marriage" is gravely evil. But God and the Church, out of love, want the good for those who are in this situation. Thus, God and the Church call the members of this invalid "marriage" to end intimate relations since these would be adulterous. If the spouse who is married to another person is prayerfully convinced in conscience that her first marriage was invalid, then she may apply for an annulment. If, after judicial review, the Church declares the first marriage to have been null or invalid from the start, then she may seek to get married to a new partner. Short of such a declaration and a new, valid marriage, those in this invalid marriage must avoid sexual relations. Since living in the same house would be a proximate occasion of grave sin, they should also separate.

Sometimes, matters are complicated by the fact that the children have been born to this invalidly married couple. Of those in such circumstances, Pope Francis writes: "The Church acknowledges situations

[247] Francis, press conference, June 26, 2016.

'where, for serious reasons, such as the children's upbringing, a man and woman cannot satisfy the obligation to separate.'"[248] Here, Francis is quoting another text. He is citing John Paul II's Apostolic Exhortation *Familiaris consortio*, art. 84. Now, in *Familiaris consortio*, John Paul is very clear and fatherly. On the one hand, he acknowledges that, for the sake of their duties to the children they have together, the invalidly married man and woman may discern that they should not or cannot live in separate dwellings. He rightly states that the Church understands their situation. On the other hand, he clearly emphasizes as well the infallible teaching that this couple *may not engage in sexual intimacy* because to do so would constitute adultery. Thus, John Paul II is merciful and truthful: you may live together, but you may not have sexual relations, lest you sin gravely.

In citing this passage, Pope Francis does not deny, but neither does he include, the very clear counsel from John Paul II. Moreover, Francis also adds a citation from *Gaudium et spes*. Now, this passage from *Gaudium et spes*, in the original context, deals with a situation completely different from that to which it is attached in *Amoris laetitia*. The original context in *Gaudium et spes* regards the situation of a *validly* married man and woman who would undergo serious hardship were another child to be conceived.[249] *Gaudium et spes* depicts such a couple as being faithful to the Church's perennial condemnation of contraception. The spouses refuse to contracept, yet they also judge, for serious reasons, that receiving another child would be too burdensome. Now that we have the context, we can appreciate the passage of *Gaudium et spes* in its proper context. The text of the council document reads, "In such situations, many people, knowing and accepting the possibility of living 'as brothers and sisters' which the Church offers them, point out that if certain expressions of

---

[248] Francis, *Amoris laetita*, art. 298.

[249] For example, the husband has no source of income, or one of the spouses has a very serious illness, or the household is already chaotic enough, causing serious anxiety. Many people are in situations such as these. Some uncharitable Catholics scoff at these hardships. Their response to these difficult personal challenges is an *overreaction* to the contraceptive mindset.

intimacy are lacking, 'it often happens that faithfulness is endangered and the good of the children suffers'."[250] Validly married, they are drawn to marital intimacy with each other and are concerned that total abstinence will endanger the lawful goods of their marriage. *Gaudium et spes* then presents the teaching of Pius XI: this *validly* married couple may make use of marital intimacy during infertile periods and abstain during fertile periods. This practice is what is called Natural Family Planning (NFP). There is nothing objectively wrong with the practice, although its use is warranted only by the proper circumstances.

Pope Francis cites that very passage, but he applies it to a different context not envisioned by the ecumenical council. Francis applies it to the situation of a couple that is *not* validly married. *Gaudium et spes* addresses those for whom marital intercourse is morally good, while Francis addresses those for whom sexual intercourse would constitute the grave evil of fornication and even adultery. Some readers consequently have the impression that sexual intimacy can be morally good for such an *invalidly* married couple. But such an impression contradicts the sixth commandment as well as infallible Catholic teaching. Further, the error of this impression serves as an occasion for them to commit grave sin. Now, to give an unwarranted occasion for sin is scandal.

Why mention this statement in a discussion of Lutheranism? There is a practical pastoral connection. For Luther, everything we do is a sin, even a "mortal (i.e., *damnable*)" sin. However, if we have faith, the "mortal (i.e., *damnable*)" sins that we commit are not *damning*. Although worthy of Hell (*damnable*), they will not actually condemn us (are not *damning*). For Luther, we can commit fornication or adultery and still be in the "grace" of God's favor. There is danger that some Catholics, reading *Amoris laetitia*, might come to believe that we can fornicate adulterously and still remain holy. Such an opinion is false, as is Luther's. Thus, practically speaking, there is a significant point of convergence between Luther and the claim that sometimes fornication is not a "mortal (i.e. *damning*)" sin. But Catholics are obliged to follow the infallible teachings.

---

[250] This is a citation of *Gaudium et spes*, art. 51.

3. There is a related point as well. Later in *Amoris laetitia*, Pope Francis states, "[Conscience] can also recognize with sincerity and honesty what for now is the most generous response which can be given to God, and come to see with a certain moral security that it is what God himself is asking amid the concrete complexity of one's limits, while yet not fully the objective ideal."[251] Some Catholics, reading this statement, might come to hold that, for some people, avoiding certain acts that are objectively sinful is impossible. But it is Catholic dogma that the commandments of God are possible of observance for those who are justified.

4. Lastly, in an early homily, Pope Francis preached, "That is what the Apostle means: a faith without works, a faith that does not involve one's [whole] self, that does not lead to witness, is not faith. It is words—and nothing more than words."[252] Hearing this statement, some Catholics might come to hold that a faith without works is not true faith. But, it is Catholic dogma that true faith can exist without good works.

We Catholics must be clear on our Faith. Let us embody the words of the hymn: "Faith of our fathers, holy faith, we will be true to thee till death."

Now, three popes also spoke highly of an important ecumenical document, the JDDJ. To this we turn.

Joint Declaration on the Doctrine of Justification
The JDDJ is a document jointly issued by the Catholic Church, through the Pontifical Council for Promoting Christian Unity (PCPCU), and the Lutheran World Federation. In this section, we will analyze some of the contents of the JDDJ. But first we must ask whether this document is magisterial in the strict sense—that is, whether it is doctrinally binding. The JDDJ is magisterial in some sense, since it was issued by the PCPCU. The PCPCU is not a doctrinal organ of the Church, however. It

---

[251] Francis, *Amoris laetitia*, art. 303.
[252] Francis, homily, February 21, 2014. This citation is only available in archive: https://web.archive.org/web/20140902063849/http://www.news.va/en/news/pope-francis-friday-mass-in-santa-marta.

is not charged with the authority to bind the Catholic faithful in matters of faith and morals. Instead, it is charged with guiding the ecumenical movement toward a fruitful conclusion. Furthermore, the JDDJ was never signed by the pope. Nor was it even signed by the prefect of the Congregation for the Doctrine of Faith, the relevant congregation charged with teaching doctrine.[253] Three popes have praised it as a significant historical achievement. The JDDJ is quite an achievement, but it is not a doctrinally authoritative document. The crucial locus for Catholic teaching on justification is the declaration of the Council of Trent. The teachings of Trent on original sin and justification are infallible dogmas. They are also precise statements that avoid much ambiguity, unlike the JDDJ (as we shall see). Consequently, the teachings of Trent constitute our most certain and authoritative anchor for disputes on this topic. They serve as a perennial foundation by which to determine any other relevant magisterial teaching less certain or precise.

What of the contents of the JDDJ? As noted, the document does have merits. Among these are the following: First, it is a testament to a charitable work of dialogue and cooperation. Second, it has several doctrinal merits. It focuses on the divine initiative in the order of grace. It drives home the point that we are not saved by our natural good qualities, independent virtues, and merely human works. If we were left to ourselves, we would never become pleasing to God. Eventually, we would offend Him seriously. The JDDJ also praises the love of God, which rescues us sinners through the blood of Christ. Finally, the JDDJ discusses sanctification and good works.

These and other strengths notwithstanding, the JDDJ has significant flaws, to some of which we now turn. In the heart of its doctrinal section, the JDDJ is broken down into various topics. Under each topic, there are three paragraphs: a common paragraph, a Catholic paragraph, and a Lutheran paragraph. The distinctly Catholic and Lutheran paragraphs allow for different emphases and orientations, the Lutherans affirming

---

[253] See Christopher J. Malloy, *Engrafted into Christ* (New York: Peter Lang, 2005), 1–8.

one paragraph and the Catholics affirming the other. Still, the entire document is supposed to be acceptable to each party, as the following four points show. (1) The officials of each communion signed with reference to the whole document. (2) The JDDJ asserts the compatibility of the Lutheran and Catholic paragraphs with each other.[254] (3) The JDDJ asserts that these paragraphs are also compatible with the traditional teachings of both communions.[255] (4) The JDDJ claims to have settled every church-dividing issue on the matter of justification.[256] If the JDDJ has settled all church-dividing issues on justification, it is a grand achievement indeed. But did it? I argue that it did not. Here, I wish to point out tensions between Trent and the JDDJ on a number of key points.

1. Some Lutheran paragraphs claim that Christ's righteousness *is* our righteousness. Recall that Trent condemns the claim that the righteousness by which we are righteous (the formal cause of justification) is Christ's righteousness. This foundational divergence is the basis for others. Lutheran paragraph 23 reads:

> When Lutherans stress that the righteousness of Christ is our righteousness, they wish above all to hold firmly that righteousness is given to the sinner before Christ in God through the declaration of forgiveness and that his life is renewed only in union with Christ. When they say that the grace of God is forgiving love (the "favor of God"),[257] they do not thereby deny the Christian's

---

[254] The JDDJ has this intention: "to show that on the basis of their dialogue the subscribing Lutheran churches and the Roman Catholic Church are now able to articulate a common understanding of our justification by God's grace through faith in Christ." JDDJ, par. 5, in *Origins* 28:8, 120.

[255] "The churches neither take the condemnations [of the past] lightly nor do they disavow their own past." JDDJ, par. 7, in *Origins* 28:8, 120.

[256] "It does encompass a consensus on basic truths of the doctrine of justification and shows that the remaining differences in its explication are no longer the occasion for doctrinal condemnations." JDDJ, par. 5, in *Origins* 28:8, 120.

[257] JDDJ quoting *Against Latomus*: WA 8:106; LW 32:227. WA is the standard German edition of Luther's works.

renewal of life, but rather want to make clear that justification remains free from human cooperation and also does not depend on the life-renewing effect of grace.[258]

There are three claims here: (1) Christ's righteousness is the righteousness of those who are justified. (2) To be justified is to be *declared* forgiven and righteous. (3) The grace of God is the divine "favor." Claim 2 presents justification as a declaration of forgiveness. Claim 1 indicates that it is Christ's rightesouness that is declared to be ours. Taken in its natural meaning, this text asserts that justification consists in a legal pronouncement, not in an actual transformation. Accordingly, in justification I am merely *treated* as though Christ's own perfect righteousness were mine. Claim 3 confirms that reading by citing Luther's notion of grace as "favor." The citation in the JDDJ is to Luther's *Antilatomus*. In that text, Luther contends that grace means God's extrinsic favor, whereby God simply treats us differently although we remain interiorly the same. Taken in its natural sense, therefore, the JDDJ endorses Luther's contention that justification is a *counterfactual declaration*. It is a declaration because it is merely God's legal decree. It is counterfactual because we remain inwardly sinners with the same sin. Trent, however, dogmatically declares that justification is "not only the remission of sins but the sanctification and renewal of the inner man," whereby the man becomes just and holy.[259]

Now, someone will point out that the JDDJ *also* refers to the sanctification of sinners. True; it does. Does this observation satisfy the demands of Trent? I contend that it does not. We have already seen that Luther spoke of sanctification as well. But Luther insisted that his inclusion of sanctification in the overall life of the justified person is *irrelevant*. Luther asserted that there is a vast difference between his teaching and that of Catholic tradition.[260] For Luther, as for the JDDJ's Lutheran paragraphs, justification is a legal, counterfactual declaration. The sanctifying effects

---

[258] Unless otherwise noted, translations of the JDDJ are mine.

[259] Trent, Session VI, chap. 7; DH 1528. For a closer analysis, see my *Engrafted into Christ*, 222–235.

[260] Luther, *Against Latomus*, LW 32:236.

that follow are distinct from justification. (We can say that they are "logically" subsequent.) That is likely why paragraph 23 concludes as follows: "Justification remains free from cooperation and also does not depend on the life-renewing effect of grace." Care is needed to interpret this statement. Since the "grace" referred to is God's eternal, uncreated love, the "effect" of this grace is the interior renewal of the human person, which renewal is created or brought about by God. In short, the interior renewal is what Trent calls the "one formal cause of justification." The JDDJ, therefore, insists that justification remains free from what Trent teaches is the formal cause — the very *essence* — of justification! By anal-ogy, the Lutherans are saying something like this: Creation remains free from the existence of the creature. In response, we must say that of course God's own action is not dependent on the creature, but His act *creates* the creature! To talk about His act and not assert the very existence of the creature is absurd. Similarly, for the JDDJ, justification is and remains a *legal declaration*. You are called forgiven but your sin remains. Sancti-fication is always *distinct*. Correlatively, for the Lutherans, justification remains always perfect, whereas, they hold, one can grow in sanctifica-tion: "Righteousness as acceptance by God and as participation in the righteousness of Christ is always perfect."[261] Trent, by contrast, declares that the justice or righteousness of justification can increase. Whereas this paragraph of the JDDJ teaches that the justice by which someone is justified is the very righteousness of Christ, which cannot increase, Trent teaches that the justice by which someone is justified is *not* the very righteousness of Christ but is a gift from Christ that makes the soul pleasing and that can increase.

This first set of weaknesses raises a question. Does the JDDJ portray sanctification in a robust light, even though (in its Lutheran paragraphs) it distinguishes justification and sanctification? That is, do its Lutheran paragraphs present *as* thorough a sanctification of the human person as Catholic dogma demands? Perhaps, that is, the difference is only a matter of words. Perhaps what Catholics call "justification" Lutherans

---

[261] JDDJ, par. 39.

call "justification and sanctification." This question takes us to the next weakness.

2. The JDDJ's Lutheran paragraphs do not measure up to the Catholic teaching on the nature of sanctification. How so? The key paragraph teaches that the justified person *remains a sinner*. A Catholic objector responds, "So what? Isn't that Catholic teaching too? We're all sinners." No, there is a crucial difference between Catholic teaching and what the JDDJ means here. Catholic teaching is that justification removes *all* mortal sin from the sinner; Catholic teaching also insists that concupiscence, which remains after Baptism, is only a *tendency* to sin, not itself a sin. Concupiscence is not even a venial sin. The Lutheran paragraph contradicts all this. Let us read and then analyze it:

> The Christian is "simultaneously righteous person and sinner." He is entirely righteous because God forgives him his sins through Word and Sacrament and grants him the righteousness of Christ, which becomes his in faith, and makes him righteous in Christ before God. But in looking at himself, he recognizes through the law that at the same time he remains entirely a sinner, that sin still lives in him (1 Jn 1:8; Rom 7:17–20), for he trusts again and again in false Gods and does not love God with that undivided love that God demands from him as his maker (Dt 6:5; Mt 22:36–40). This contradiction to God is as such truly sin.[262]

Five observations and remarks are in order. First, the justified is presented as *at once* both righteous and sinner. Once again, this means that God's declaration of righteousness is counterfactual: God's legal declaration is contrary to what is actually the case. He is declaring that the justified person is innocent, when inwardly he remains unjust. But to hold that the justified person remains inwardly unjust is contrary to the Faith.

Second, the JDDJ also presents the justified as being "*entirely* righteous." Catholic dogma, however, teaches that justified persons can suffer from venial sins, which make their righteousness imperfect. Also,

---

[262] JDDJ, par. 29.

Catholic dogma speaks of an increase in righteousness, since it is not all at once perfect. The fundamental reason the Lutheran paragraph makes this assertion is that it holds, implicitly, Christ's own righteousness to be the "formal cause" of justification. We have seen that such a position contradicts Catholic Faith.

Third and conversely, the paragraph states that the justified remains "*entirely* a sinner" because "sin still lives in him." Here, the Lutherans are speaking about the real interior state of the *justified* person. According to the JDDJ, inside the justified person, there is *true sin*. How grave is this sin? It is *damnable*; that is, it is of such gravity that God could justly damn us to Hell for it. On what basis do I make this claim? The following citation is my evidence: "His sin no longer condemns him and *no longer brings him eternal death*."[263] They say it "no longer" brings eternal death. Now, if it once brought him eternal death, it is in itself worthy of damnation. Thus, the sin that remains is intrinsically worthy of damnation. This implication is further demonstrated by the footnote in the text, which refers us to Philipp Melanchthon's *Apology* or "Defense" of the *Augsburg Confession*. In the passage referenced, Melanchthon declares that the remnant sin "is by nature worthy of death where it is not forgiven."[264] The death of which Melanchthon speaks is damnation. Why, according to the Lutherans, does this sin not actually damn the justified? It is not *damning* because of the *declaration* of forgiveness. So, according to the JDDJ, truly *damnable* sin remains in the justified. But Trent dogmatically teaches that damnable sin does not remain.

Fourth, what is the nature of this remnant sin? Is it an actual sin, a free-will act? No, it is not. It can be described as "pre-free-volitional." It is a tendency, not an act of free choice. Sounds familiar: what the Lutherans here call "sin" is what Catholics call "concupiscence." Once again, concupiscence is a *tendency* toward a free and sinful act but is itself not a free act. How do we know that the "sin" mentioned in this

---

[263] JDDJ, par. 29, quoting *Apology*, II:38–45.

[264] Philipp Melanchthon, *Apology of the Augsburg Confession*, II:40, in *The Book of Concord*, 118.

paragraph is not a free act of sin? There are three indications: (1) There is no mention of free acts of sin in this context. (2) The word "sin" is in the singular, indicating a pervading tendency rather than particular acts. (3) The JDDJ references Melanchthon's text, which asserts that Paul's letters "call concupiscence sin."[265] Let us summarize the upshot. Catholic dogma asserts that concupiscence is not even venial sin, but the JDDJ's Lutheran paragraph presents concupiscence as true sin, sin that is damnable.

The fifth and final point is that justified persons are not described as capable of living a life of stable love of God without mortal sin. Instead, they are presented as merely able to "lead a life in righteousness piecemeal."[266] But Catholic dogma holds that the justified person can, with the help of God, obey all of God's commandments, avoiding all mortal sins.

3. The JDDJ endorses the notion of justification by faith alone. Paragraph 26 reads: "According to Lutheran understanding, God justifies the sinner in faith alone (*sola fide*)." Since the Catholic dogma is that justification is not by faith alone, this statement is thus unacceptable. Many of the Lutherans, however, wanted an even more robust statement. They didn't find the preposition "in" sufficient; they wanted the preposition "by." After protesting, they got what they wanted, but the story is complex. Before the final, mutual signing, both parties had various questions about certain phrases in the main document. These difficulties almost put a halt to mutual signing. But the parties got together to draft another document, an annex, that would "show" that the difficulties were only apparent, that they did not undermine the consensus of the JDDJ itself. With regard to the issue at hand, the annex "remedied" the JDDJ decidedly in favor of Lutheranism: "Justification takes place 'by grace alone' (JD, 15 and 16), *by faith alone*, the person is justified 'apart from works' (Rom. 3:28, cf. JD, 25)."[267] Lutherans were thrilled, even delirious. They

---

[265] Ibid. For a closer analysis, see my *Engrafted into Christ*, 275–280.

[266] JDDJ, par. 29.

[267] Annex, 2C, emphasis mine. Translation available in *Origins* 29:6 (1999): 87–88.

could not believe their eyes: as they saw it, the Catholic Church had turned her back on Trent.[268] Catholics, however, must believe Catholic dogmas, and these remain forever.

The foregoing are only some of the weaknesses of the JDDJ. I have treated these and other weaknesses at greater length in various published works.[269] Suffice it to say, the JDDJ does not show that Luther's thought is compatible with the dogmas of Trent.

Conclusion

There are those who would belittle sanctification and merit in order to magnify God. They think that they glorify God by denigrating man. They think honoring God requires exaggerating human sin. St. Athanasius knew long ago that the corruption of man does not honor God![270] To praise God by condemning man is not Catholic. Moreover, it invites the ridicule of atheists.[271] Of course, in the world of Catholic modernism, Luther's acute sense of sin could serve as an antidote to the liberalizing tendency to deny sin. We will get to that tendency in chapters 8 and 9. Still, errors, though opposite, do not correct each other. In fact, both Lutheran exaggeration of sin and modernizing denial of sin succumb to the same root error: despair. Each despairs of God's power and goodness. Neither believes that God truly enables us to walk in His ways so as to gain an eternal inheritance (Rom. 8:12–17). Hence, both sin by presumption in denying that obedience to the law is a condition of salvation. Catholic prelates who accept Lutheranism do so in the name of "development." That is why we can consider the contemporary acceptance of Lutheran doctrines by Catholic prelates as a type of modernism. The Catholic

---

[268] See my *Engrafted into Christ*, 256–257.

[269] For a summary critique, see my "The Nature of Justifying Grace: A Lacuna in the *Joint Declaration*," *Thomist* 65 (2001): 93–120. For a thorough treatment, see my *Engrafted into Christ*.

[270] See his marvelous *On the Incarnation*.

[271] See, for example, Ludwig Feuerbach's *The Essence of Christianity*, first published in 1841.

truth is above the dialectic of modernism and Lutheranism. Catholic truth holds that because God is so good and powerful, His effects can be good and powerful. We know He is a great creator because of the beauty of creation. Creation is not in competition with God; it is the fruit of His love. Similarly, God shows how great a redeemer He is by reaching into the depths of sinful man's evil heart and transforming it, while forgiving all his past sins. This amazing, life-changing transformation testifies to God's power and goodness. May He who works marvels be praised!

Now, Luther coupled his theory of justification by faith alone with a theory of Christ as sinner. In fact, he anchored the former in the latter. To this blasphemy, we now turn.

4

Christ Became a Sinner?

Martin Luther claimed not only that justification is by faith alone but also that Christ became *sin* and a *sinner*. For Luther, this latter event is what grounds the former boon. Christ appropriated our sins as though they were His own so that we could be pronounced free from sin. He thus became guilty so that we might be proclaimed innocent. For Luther, since Christ became guilty, He was also punished. Since we are proclaimed innocent, we are not punished, even if we do not obey the commandments of God. Luther's theory of redemption was eventually dubbed "penal substitution." The redemption is penal because Christ is punished for being guilty. It is dubbed substitution because Christ's obedience substitutes for ours, provided we have faith. We saw the effect of the "substitution" of Christ's obedience in the previous chapter: justification by faith alone entails that obedience to the commandments is not a condition of salvation. We turn now to the penal aspect of Luther's theory. This theory contradicts Catholic teaching; nevertheless, some Catholics are beguiled by it today.

The Catholic teaching is that our Lord did not become sin, since sin is an evil act, while Christ is good, and not a human act. Nor did Christ become a tendency to sin, since no man is a mere tendency. Nor did Christ become a sinner, since He committed no sinful act. Nor did our Lord become guilty, since guilt is the proper mark of a person who has sinned. Instead, our Lord remained perfectly innocent. Consequently, our

Lord was not punished, properly speaking, since punishment is inflicted only for guilt. Instead, our Lord, though innocent, offered Himself as a sacrifice to atone for our sin and take away the punishment that we deserved. We receive this benefit in justification, and we retain it *provided* that we suffer with Him in this life so as to be glorified with Him in the next (Rom. 8:17).

In this chapter, we will investigate and refute Luther's error and the recent Catholic enchantment with it. First, we will present Luther's thought. Second, we will refute it with the Catholic doctrine on the innocence of Christ. Third, we will treat the confusion that some may experience when encountering certain statements and gestures of the current pope.

Luther on Christ as Sinner

St. Paul writes, "For our sake, he [God] made him [Christ] to be sin who knew no sin, so that in him we might become the righteousness of God" (2 Cor. 5:21). Elsewhere, Paul writes, "Christ redeemed us from the curse of the law, having become a curse for us" (Gal. 3:13). For Luther, these passages do not contain metaphors or figures of speech. Rather, they are straightforward. Paul is serious, Luther argues; so we must take Paul at his word. For Luther, our salvation depends on the *nonmetaphorical truth* of these passages.

Thus, Luther held that Christ really became *sin*. Well, not exactly. Luther knew that Christ could not have become an evil *act*, which is what sin is according to its primary (or literal) meaning. Luther knew that Christ could not have become a perverse *tendency*, which is a metaphorical meaning of sin. Instead, Luther held that Christ became a "sinner." Apparently, Luther was open to Paul's speaking at least *somewhat* figuratively. Luther writes:

All the prophets saw this, that Christ was to become the greatest thief, murderer, adulterer, robber, desecrator, blasphemer, etc., there has ever been anywhere in the world. He is not acting in

His own Person now. Now He is not the Son of God, born of the Virgin. But He is a sinner, who has and bears the sin of Paul.[272]

Now, Luther also made another qualification. He clarified that Christ did not actually commit sins. Apparently, then, Christ did not really become a sinner. Luther thus ventures further into a metaphorical reading of Paul:

> In short, He has and bears all the sins of all men in His body—not in the sense that He has committed them but in the sense that He took these sins, committed by us, upon His own body, in order to make satisfaction for them with His own blood.[273]

As Luther elsewhere states, it is *as though* Christ committed our sins:

> Whatever sins I, you, and all of us have committed or may commit in the future, they are as much Christ's own as if He Himself had committed them. In short, our sin must be Christ's own sin, or we shall perish eternally.[274]

Thankfully, Luther did not think that Christ became an *act* of sin. Thankfully, he did not think that Christ became a concupiscent *tendency* to sin. Also thankfully, Luther did not affirm (in this text) that Christ *committed* sins. Rather, he affirmed that Christ assumed our sinfulness. What did Luther mean? He meant that Christ *assumed our guilt*. He "was made guilty of the sins of the entire world."[275] In short, Luther interpreted Paul as using the word "sin" to mean "bearer of guilt." Now, to interpret "sin" to mean "bearer of guilt" is to read Paul as speaking *figuratively*. So, despite his protestations to the contrary, Luther does reject a nonmetaphorical reading of Paul and endorses a figurative reading. Luther is therefore not true to his own premise. At any rate, the first thesis in Luther's theory of the atonement is that Christ became truly guilty. For Luther, this reading takes Paul seriously.

[272] Luther, *Lectures on Galatians*, LW 26:277–278.
[273] Ibid..
[274] Ibid., LW 26:278.
[275] Ibid., LW 26:279.

False Mercy

The above citations are taken from Luther's public remarks. Some allege that in private Luther taught that Christ *committed* grievous sins. The so-called *Table Talk* reports what Luther allegedly said in off-the-cuff remarks. Although not published in his own hand, the *Table Talk* is not gossip; it was drawn up by his disciples. An infamous passage reads, "Christ committed adultery for the first time with the woman at the fountain, of whom John speaks. Didn't people murmur: 'What did He do with her?' Then, with Magdalene, and next, with the adulterous woman whom He so flippantly absolved. Therefore Christ, so pious, also had to fornicate before he died."[276] Thankfully, we can limit ourselves to the remarks that Luther published in his own hand.

Luther's second thesis is that Christ was therefore *punished*. Here, he is interpreting the following statement from Isaiah: "Upon him was the chastisement that made us whole, and with his stripes we are healed" (Isa. 53:5). Luther interpreted this passage non-metaphorically. For him, Christ was really *punished*. Punishment is pain inflicted against the will on account of guilt. Luther wrote, "The Law came and said, 'Let every sinner die! And therefore, Christ, if You want to reply that You are guilty and that You bear the punishment, you must bear the sin and the curse as well."[277] For Luther, Christ really was made guilty and so really was punished.[278] These two theses work hand in hand.

Luther goes on to describe a great battle within the breast of Christ. He alleges that there was a battle between sin and righteousness in the very person of Christ. Righteousness came out victorious. This, according to Luther, is the redemption by which we, in turn, *can* be justified.

As we previously mentioned, Luther's grand theory, as it includes both atonement and justification, has sometimes been called "penal substitution." For Luther this redemption of Christ has its effect in the sinner "by faith *alone*." Faith, and faith alone, is necessary for the sinner to enjoy

---

[276] Martin Luther, *Propos de table* [*Table Talk*], n. 1472; Weimar edition, 2.107; page 235 of Funck-Brentano's book, *Luther* (Paris: Grasset, 1943).
[277] Luther, *Lectures on Galatians*, LW 26:279.
[278] Ibid., LW 26:280.

the application of Christ's redemption to him. If Christ's redemption is applied, the sinner shall certainly be saved. Salvation is therefore not contingent upon obedience to the commandments. Rather, Christ's own obedience *substitutes* for the believer's obedience. God regards Christ's obedience as though it were that of the believer. The title "penal substitution" captures Luther's thought on the redemptive work of Christ and its application to the believer.

Luther also described the application of Christ's redemption to us with the traditional and venerable phrase "joyful exchange." Of course, Luther bent this phrase to his purposes. In the Catholic tradition, the joyful exchange does not involve our giving our sins to Christ, who thereby becomes sin or a sinner or guilty. In the tradition, the joyful exchange means that Christ, though eternally rich, for our sake became poor by His Incarnation, so that, through His poverty, we might become rich with a share in His divinity (2 Cor. 8:9).

Some Catholic ecumenists are misled by Luther's use of the phrase "joyful exchange," as though, for Luther, it implied a real and adequate divinization of the human being, along the lines of the Catholic tradition. For Luther's mature thought, it had no such implication.[279] Luther did say that we give Christ our sins and God gives us Christ's righteousness.[280] As we saw in the last chapter, however, Luther did not mean that God makes us truly and sufficiently righteous. He meant that God only *considers* us to have the righteousness of Christ. God does not eradicate damnable sin from the justified person but *treats* it as though it is nonexistent. Luther writes, "As far as its nature is concerned, sin in no way differs from itself before grace and after grace; but it is indeed different in the way it is treated.... It is treated as non-existent and as expelled. Despite this, it is truly and by nature sin."[281] God *considers* and *treats* us as innocent, although *we remain inwardly sinful and guilty*. Consequently, God does

---

[279] His earlier essay *Freedom of a Christian* does have traces, however, of a deeper sense of sanctification.

[280] See Luther, *Lectures on Galatians*, LW 26:274, 279, 280, 285.

[281] Luther, *Against Latomus*, LW 32:229.

not punish us. We may surmise that, for Luther, Christ becomes guilty not because He does works worthy of guilt but because God *considers* or *treats* Him as guilty. Christ becomes guilty in the way that we become righteous. We become righteous by legal imputation, that is, by God's *treating* us legally as though we are innocent, although we remain guilty internally. Conversely, Christ remains interiorly innocent but becomes guilty by legal imputation. Because we are treated as innocent, we are not punished. Because Christ is treated as guilty, He is punished. This is Luther's theory of penal substitution.

Catholic Doctrine on Christ's Redemptive Act

Christ Remained Innocent

How does the Church understand Paul's teaching that "God made him ... to be sin" (2 Cor. 5:21)? Just as Luther reads Paul figuratively, so does the Church. But there is a crucial difference. The Church also rejects the idea that Christ became *guilty*. Guilt is a blameworthy state of one who has sinned against God. So every guilty person is, by definition, a sinner.[282] In short, guilt is the proper mark of one who has sinned. The sinner, and only the sinner, is guilty. The notion that guilt can be legally transferred from one person to another is absurd. In fact, the very notion is grounded in a tyrannical conception of authority. A tyrant wields authority whimsically, devoid of reference to truth and justice. Only a tyrannical conception of authority can "justify" the transference of guilt from a sinner to an innocent person. Thus, to claim that God transfers guilt from the wicked to the innocent is to depict God as a tyrant whose decrees can be contrary to fact. It is blasphemous to hold that God would count an innocent person guilty by transferring guilt from the sinner to the innocent. Not just sound reason, but the Scriptures, the liturgy, and the Magisterium all oppose the notion of Christ's becoming guilty.

The New Testament testifies to Christ's perfect innocence. Pilate's wife warns Pilate: "Have nothing to do with that righteous man, for I

---

[282] Original sin is an analogous case, which could be treated separately.

have suffered much over him today in a dream" (Matt. 27:19). The good thief contrasts his own just punishment (capital punishment!) with that of Christ, who deserved no punishment (Luke 23:40–41). Therefore, the good thief proclaims that Christ was not justly punished. Since the guilty are justly punished, Christ was not guilty. St. Peter writes, "Christ also died for sins once for all, the righteous for the unrighteous" (1 Pet. 3:18; see also Acts 3:14). Christ was thus righteous, not guilty. The Epistle to the Hebrews declares that our high priest was "holy, blameless, unstained, separated from sinners" (Heb. 7:26). In short, although He was like us in all things (Heb. 2:17), He was without sin (Heb. 4:15). Finally, St. John also teaches, "In him there is no sin" (1 John 3:5).

The liturgy likewise proclaims Christ's innocence. The Preface for Palm Sunday reads, "For, though innocent, he suffered willingly for sinners and accepted unjust condemnation to save the guilty." The Roman Canon describes the sacrificial offering (which is to become Christ's Flesh and Blood) as "this pure victim, this holy victim, this spotless victim."[283] Sin, the guilt of sin, and the debt of punishment, are all stains or blots. Thus, whoever has guilt or a debt of punishment is spotted, not pure. But Christ has no stain; He is pure. Again, over the offerings, in the Masses for the dead, the Church prays, "In this sacrifice, O Lord, your Son, though innocent, was slain for us and took away all the sins of the world."[284]

Finally, the Magisterium itself *condemns* the notion that Christ became guilty. After a synod in Rome, Pope Damasus issued the following teaching in 382: "The Word ... assumed our soul (i.e., a rational and spiritual one) without sin and saved it."[285] Later, Pope Leo the Great declared in his Tome — a letter sent to Flavian, Patriarch of Constantinople — that Christ assumed our nature but not our guilt.[286]

---

[283] *Roman Missal*, 3rd ed. (Washington, DC: United States Conference of Catholic Bishops, 2011), 309.

[284] Ibid., 1397.

[285] DH 159.

[286] DH 294.

False Mercy

We can now recall the heresy or mistake of Pope Honorius. Posthumously condemned at the Third Council of Constantinople for failing to protect the purity of the Faith, Pope Honorius had falsely asserted that Christ had only one will. Right-thinking theologians and successor popes knew that Honorius's expression was not acceptable. But Pope John IV, Honorius's immediate successor, attempted to give a benign interpretation of his predecessor's clumsy claim. We can say that John IV was exercising the hermeneutic of continuity in its exegetical mode. John IV interpreted Honorius to mean that Christ "assumed all that is ours without bearing any guilt of the sin arising from the inheritance of the transgression.... There was no sin at all in him when he was born and lived."[287] John IV read Honorius's denial of "two wills" to be a denial that Christ was internally divided, as though He were indecisive and unable to accept the Father's plan, like someone who is "of two minds." John's statement may or may not be an accurate reading of Honorius. Regardless, his statement does have an authoritative element in it; besides his orthodox affirmation of two wills in Christ, what is authoritative in John's teaching is his *condemnation* of the notion that Christ had sin or guilt in Him. This condemnation remains authoritative. Shortly thereafter, in 680, Pope Agatho officially declared that Christ had *two* wills, definitively rejecting Pope Honorius's error. Agatho also stressed, with John IV and the entire tradition, that Christ was "without any sin."[288] The Third Ecumenical Council of Constantinople entirely endorsed Agatho's teaching[289] and declared that Christ was "like us in all respects except for sin."[290] In his approval of this council, Pope Leo II underscored that Christ became like us in all things except sin.[291]

According to Pope Clement VI in 1343, Christ, "immolated on the altar of the Cross though he was innocent, ... shed not merely a drop of

---

[287] DH 496.
[288] DH 543.
[289] See DH 553.
[290] DH 554.
[291] DH 561.

his blood—although this would have sufficed for the redemption of the whole human race because of the union with the Word—but a copious flood, like a stream."[292] The Decree for the Jacobites at the Council of Florence described Christ as one "who without sin was conceived, born, and died."[293] Thus, Florence teaches that Christ was innocent His entire life. Most recently, the Second Vatican Council declared, "Christ, holy, innocent, and undefiled (Heb. 7:26), knew nothing of sin (cf. 2 Cor. 5:21), ... [and] came to expiate only the sins of the people (cf. Heb. 2:17)."[294] In its decree *Gaudium et spes*, the same council explicitly linked this constant teaching of the Church with a reference to Hebrews 4:15: "Born of the Virgin Mary, [the Son] has truly been made one of us, like us in all things except sin."[295]

The above teachings of Scripture and the Magisterium make it clear that it is a matter of divine and Catholic faith that Christ was entirely innocent, without sin or guilt. One may not doubt or deny this teaching. So, Christ became neither a sinful act nor guilty of a sinful act. Nor did Christ take on a debt of *punishment* for sin. Only the guilty person has a *debt* of punishment.

In consequence of the foregoing, Paul's evocative statement "God made him to be sin" cannot mean that Christ became an act of sin. Nor can it mean that He became guilty of sin. Nor can it mean that He was sentenced to a debt of punishment. What, then, did Paul mean?

Christ: An Offering in Atonement for Sin

Paul meant that Christ was put forth as the *sacrificial offering* by which our debt was discharged. When Paul describes Christ as "sin," he means that Christ became an offering for sin. There is an Old Testament background to Paul's usage. The Greek translation of the Old Testament is called the

---

[292] Clement VI, *Unigenitus Dei Filius*; DH 1025.

[293] DH 1347.

[294] *Lumen gentium*, art. 8; DH 4120.

[295] *Gaudium et spes*, art. 22; DH 4322. Pius XII made this connection earlier in *Divino afflante Spiritu*, art. 37.

"Septuagint," which means "seventy." We symbolize this with the Roman numeral LXX.[296] The LXX is an authoritative witness to the Bible, even though it is not the original Hebrew. How do we know that it is a worthy witness? First, about five out of six New Testament citations of the Old Testament are taken from the LXX and not from the Hebrew text. The New Testament itself thus treats the LXX as a witness to the deposit of faith. Second, the Church Fathers cite the LXX abundantly. Third, the Catholic Magisterium has taught as much.[297] Now, it turns out that the LXX translation of Leviticus 4:21 uses the word "sin" (ἁμαρτία) to refer to the bull which is to be burned outside the camp.[298] Clearly, the LXX translator is using the word "sin" figuratively. He does not mean that the bull is an act of sin, or is guilty, or has a debt of punishment. Rather, he means that the bull will be the *offering* by which sin is atoned. The Catholic argument is that Paul used the term "sin" similarly, to indicate that Christ became a sacrificial offering.

St. Augustine read St. Paul as using "sin" (2 Cor. 5) the same way the LXX employs the term in Lev. 4:21. For Augustine, Christ did not become guilty, nor did he have a debt of punishment. Rather, he offered himself up to pay for the punishment that we deserved. In short, Christ became an offering for sin. In his battle against the Manichaeans, St. Augustine wrote:

> Sin means both a bad action deserving punishment, and death the consequence of sin. Christ has no sin in the sense of deserving death, but He bore for our sakes sin in the sense of death as brought on human nature by sin.[299]

---

[296] The legend was that this translation from the Hebrew to the Greek was done simultaneously by seventy independently working translators.

[297] See Pope Benedict XIV, "Faith, Reason, and the University: Memories and Reflections," September 12, 2006.

[298] See also Leviticus 4:24.

[299] St. Augustine, *Reply to Faustus the Manichaean*, trans. Richard Stothert, *Nicene and Post-Nicene Fathers*, Series 1, vol. 4, ed. Philip Schaff (Peabody, MA: Hendrickson, 1999), 208.

In short, Christ took on not sin itself but the consequence of sin. A few centuries after Augustine, the Spanish bishops, in their splendid declaration of faith, adopted this reading as their own: "He was conceived without sin, he who alone 'was made sin' for our sake, that is, who became sacrifice for our sins."[300]

St. Paul was thus using a literary device here. The device at play is *metonymy*. Here, restitution for the offense of sin can be called "sin" by way of metonymy because an offering for sin pays the debt of punishment that is incurred in sin. The sinful act is a kind of cause of the offering; it is a cause that disposes one to need an offering. Therefore, the offering itself can be called "sin" by metonymy.

The very context of Paul's utterance further supports this reading. Paul writes that God "made him to be sin who knew no sin, so that in him we might become the righteousness of God" (2 Cor. 5:21). The claim that Paul is using metonymy becomes stronger when we look at the closing clause. Paul describes us as becoming "the righteousness of God." Now, the righteousness of God is none other than God Himself, who is infinite and uncreated. We cannot become God's infinite righteousness without exploding. So Paul cannot be speaking "plainly." What, then, can Paul mean? He can mean that God's righteousness is the *cause* of our becoming righteous. Indeed, God's righteousness *is* the cause of ours in various ways. First, God in His righteousness is the very *agent* that makes us righteous.[301] Second, God's righteousness is the supreme *model* of our righteousness, which is made in the likeness of His. Finally, God's righteousness, which is nothing but God Himself, is the very *goal* of our righteousness, since we are called to union with Him. For these reasons, it is utterly fitting to say that we become God's righteousness, since we become that which He lovingly gives us (Rom. 10:3). Theology, making a precise statement of the riches of revelation, interprets Paul as using metonymy in this final clause. Paul does not mean that we become God Himself; that would be our destruction. Paul means that we become holy

---

[300] Eleventh Synod of Toledo (675); DH 539.
[301] See Trent, Session VI, chap. 7; DH 1529.

by the very righteousness that comes from God, imitates God, and leads to God. Since Paul uses metonymy in the second clause, it is fitting that he does so in the first clause as well. This is grammatical balance. Christ did not become sin, but He offered Himself as a sacrifice for us so that we might receive the gift of righteousness.

Before treating recent Catholic enchantment with Luther, we should note an opposite extreme in the Catholic world, that of Karl Rahner, crypto-modernist of the twentieth century. Luther and the Catholic Church agree that Christ's death was an atoning sacrifice that God willed to be the price of our salvation. Both Luther and the Church agree that God's eternal and unchanging love was the cause undergirding Christ's redeeming death. Neither conceives of God as changing because of the death, but both affirm that God willed this death to be the reason or cause that mercy is offered to sinners. Karl Rahner rejects this understanding. He does so by caricaturing it and rejecting the caricature. The Cross, he says, "cannot be the cause of the uncaused salvific will of God.... God is not transformed from a God of anger and justice into a God of mercy and love by the cross."[302] Rahner denies that the Cross is the cause of the offer of grace to sinners, either as an instrumental cause (Thomistic idea) or as a moral cause (Franciscan idea). For him, if the Cross were such a cause, God would be changed. Rahner also rejects the idea that Christ can even represent us in His suffering. For Rahner, if Christ represented us, we would not need to be transformed. Apparently, Rahner is reacting to theories such as Luther's penal substitution, mistaking them for the Catholic theological tradition that he rejects.[303]

In objection to Rahner, Catholics can readily point to many scriptural texts that speak of the Cross as a sacrifice, ransom, expiation, and so forth. Rahner anticipates the objection and "with caution" replies that these

---

[302] Karl Rahner, "The One Christ and the Universality of Salvation," in *Theological Investigations*, vol. 16, trans. David Morland (London: Darton, Longman & Todd 1979) 207.

[303] For his rejection of the causal efficacy of the Cross, whether moral or instrumental causality, see ibid., 212–215. For his rejection of the notion of representation, see ibid., 207–208.

notions "do not reflect the original understanding of the saving significance of the Cross of Jesus for all men; they are legitimate ideas but they
are secondary notions which must be explained in light of the primary
and original data." Rahner relegates these inspired and inerrant teachings
to the status of second-class citizenship and subjugates them to what he
calls the "primary data." If the secondary ideas were useful to Paul, "in
other cultures and historical periods such ideas do not so easily achieve
this goal."[304] Translation: we don't need no expiation. Elsewhere, Rahner
is less evasive: "At [Paul's] time the idea of propitiating the divinity by
means of a sacrifice was a current notion which could be presupposed to
be valid." Today, however, it "offers little help to us."[305]

Rahner's strategy is deceptive. The pattern is this: he depicts the
dogma of tradition with a caricature, rejects the caricature, and substitutes
his own theory, which does not measure up to the dogma. The caricature
is a changing God, an angry God mollified by bloody murder; no competent theologian in the tradition—Athanasius, Augustine, Anselm,
Bonaventure, e.g.—asserted a changing God mollified by bloody murder.
Rahner rejects the caricature but does not affirm the dogma. Instead, he
substitutes his own theory. As a result, readers are led to deny the dogma.
Meanwhile, Rahner protests (too much!) that there is no smoking gun.
We shall see this strategy again.

---

[304] Ibid., 211.

[305] Rahner, *Foundations*, 282. In America, theologian Brian Schmisek
of Loyola University in Chicago joins those such as Rahner who are
"questioning whether such ideas are germane to a twenty-first century
audience." Schmisek proposes a substitute: "Rather than propose a God
who is pleased with blood-sacrifice, or who interferes to stop some cases
of moral evil and natural disaster but not others, a different way of
theologizing about Christ's death may be this. Christ is the enflesh-
ment, the embodiment of God's love in the world. What is the human
response to incarnate divine love? Our response is misunderstanding,
anger, hostility and violence to the point of murder. Ultimately, we kill
it." See Brian Schmisek, *The Apostles' Creed: Articles of Faith for the 21st
Century* (Leesburg, VA: National Catholic Educational Association,
2008), 36–37.

False Mercy

Rahner's own theory is Christ as the "real symbol" of God's love. Christ is the culmination of human acceptance of God's merciful love and divine self-giving. As one scholar describes his thought, "Christ is, in technical (Aristotelian) terms, not the 'efficient' but the 'final cause' of our salvation."[306] Some aspects of this theory have a certain merit, but others are fatally flawed. It is true that Christ is the supreme self-gift of God to man, and it is true that, as man, Christ offers God the most perfect love and adoration. In this important sense, He is the perfect expression or "real symbol" of divine love in human form.

There are crucial errors, however, in the way Rahner understands this. First, he denies that Christ's death is the reason or cause why we receive grace.[307] As Rahner says, His death is "the consequence and not the cause of the self-giving of God to the world in grace."[308] Evasion again! We must agree with Rahner that God's eternal love is the reason Christ came, for Christ is He "whom God put forward as an expiation by his blood" (Rom. 3:25). Yet we still affirm that an expiation is a real reason why forgiving grace is offered to us; Christ's death is the real price, the true sacrifice. His Cross is the meritorious cause of our forgiveness and justification.[309]

---

[306] Karen Kilby, *Karl Rahner: A Brief Introduction* (New York: Crossroad, 2007), 28.

[307] See K.-H. Menke, *Stellvertretung: Schlüsselbegriff christlichen Lebens und theologische Grundkategorie* (Einsiedeln: Johannesverlag, 1991), 358–362. There are two legitimate Catholic traditions on this causality. The Franciscans stress Christ as a moral or praying cause: in dying for us, Christ efficaciously prayed for us. The Dominicans add that Christ was also an instrumental efficient cause: not only did He pray for us in His humanity, but He also served as an instrument through whom God procured our redemption.

[308] Rahner, "One Christ," *Theological Investigations* 16, 211.

[309] See esp. DH 1529, but also DH 261, 1025, 1690, 1692; Leo XIII, *Tametsi futura prospicientibus*, art. 3; Pius XI, *Miserentissimus Redemptor* (1928), art. 8; Pius XII, *Humani generis*, art. 26; and Vatican II, *Gaudium et spes*, art. 22 (DH 4322). For an insightful treatment of Rahner on the Cross, see Guy Mansini, "Rahner and Balthasar on the Efficacy of the Cross," *The Word Has Dwelt among Us* (Ave Maria, FL: Sapientia Press, 2008), 93–113, esp. 95–99. Note that Mansini also treats the errors of von

Rahner's modernism wants to cancel these ideas as outworn monuments of an ignorant and unjust age. But no, they are all too authoritative! Second, Rahner relates the human act of Christ and the divine act as though actions of two distinct persons; he portrays Christ as a "marriage" of God and man.[310] This smacks of Nestorianism, which presents Jesus and the Word of God as two persons (rational hypostases) in relation to each other. Even theologians sympathetic to Rahner's project have warned about this error.[311] Worse, Rahner even portrays Christ as a recipient of God's *redeeming* love: Christ "has been saved by God."[312] Unwittingly or not, this is blasphemy!

Some Remarks of Pope Francis

An earnest desire for ecumenical progress inspires many Catholics today. Ecumenism is a very good thing, provided it is defined correctly and practiced well. At its foundation, it is the movement to restore visible unity among all Christian ecclesial communities. (We shall turn to this topic in the next chapter.) Sadly, the good intention of seeking corporate reunion of the churches can sometimes be accompanied by despair, imprudence, and mistaken claims. An ecumenist can be so consumed with the

---

Balthasar. He rightly depicts Rahner and Balthasar as opposite extremes. The correct aspects of each thinker are at odds with the errors of the other thinker. When we cancel out the errors, we are left with the basic Catholic tradition, plus a little bit of extra insight. What a great deal: buy a bowl of insight like porridge at the price of our redemption!

[310] "Karl Rahner, "Probleme heutiger Mariologie," in G. Söhngen, ed., *Aus der Theologie der Zeit* (Regensburg: Gregorius-Verlag, 1948), 98n102.

[311] See Walter Kasper, *Jesus the Christ*, trans. V. Green (Mahwah: Paulist Press, 1976), 51–52. See also Burke, *Reinterpreting Rahner*, 157 and 274–276. See my essay, "The Withering," in Flannery and Dodaro, *"Faith Once for All Delivered."*

[312] Rahner, *Foundations*, 284. See the following criticism: Leo Scheffczyk, "Mariologie und Anthropologie: Zur Marienlehre Karl Rahners," in D. Berger, ed., *Karl Rahner: Kritische Annäherungen* (Sieburg: Franz Schmitt, 2004), 302.

good goal that he loses sight of the crucial conditions for its attainment. Further, the obstacles to full unity are formidable; they can sometimes occasion despair. For one who despairs, it is tempting to compromise on truth so as to achieve unity. Alas, as much as we yearn for this goal to be realized, we cannot achieve real unity by compromising truth. Now, we have already seen that we cannot affirm Luther's theory. Some who rightly desire to achieve the goal of ecumenism fail to see this. Some allege that they find support in the following statements from Pope Francis.

1. On March 14, 2016, Pope Francis treated the scriptural background to the notion of Christ's becoming sin. In his morning meditation, he called the serpent a "symbol of sin, the serpent that kills. But the serpent that saves: this is the mystery of Christ." Essentially, the pope was touching on Jesus' teaching in John 3. He juxtaposed two diametrically opposed serpents. Pope Francis also added St. Paul's expression that Christ "became sin." Francis was thinking of the passage we have seen: "For our sake he made him to be sin who knew no sin, so that in him we might become the righteousness of God" (2 Cor. 5:21). Pope Francis commented: "The Son of man, who like a serpent 'became sin,' is lifted up in order to save us.... Sin is the work of Satan, and Jesus defeats Satan 'by becoming sin.'"[313]

Just how should we understand these words of Pope Francis? First, they may be papal words, since they were delivered in a morning meditation. They are not off-the-cuff words on an airplane. Second, we can ask what the word "sin" means here. I am not certain. At any rate, we may take the opportunity to plunge more deeply into contemplation of Christ's love for us. Of course, we do not want to hold that Christ became an *act of sin*, the *work of Satan*. Rather, He took on the *consequence* for sin, offering up His terrible suffering and death for us.

2. A year later, Pope Francis returned to this theme. He stated in a homily, "Jesus 'made himself a serpent,' Jesus 'made himself sin.' He took upon himself all the uncleanness of humanity, all the filth of sin." Consequently, "he took upon himself the appearance of the father of

---

[313] Francis, Morning Meditation, March 14, 2016.

sin."[314] How should we interpret these words? I am not certain. They bear some similarity to Isaiah: He "was numbered with the transgressors" (Isa. 53:12). In short, Jesus appeared unclean. But we must not think that Jesus took on the perversion of sin or guilt for sin. Nor should we think that Jesus *appeared* to look like the devil; such an idea has no grounding in the Catholic tradition. But we do hold that He embraced the consequence of sin.

3. Earlier in his pontificate, the pope had treated this theme in connection with the sacrament of Confession. In a homily in 2013, he stated that Jesus "became the sinner." He went on:

> True reconciliation means that God in Christ took on our sins and became [sin (peccato)] for us. When we go to confession, for example, it isn't that we say our sin and God forgives us. We [find] Jesus Christ and [tell him]: 'This is your sin, and I [will once again commit this sin against you].' And Jesus likes that, because it was his mission: to become [sin (peccato)] for us, to liberate us.... [It is God, in fact, who reconciles the world to himself in Christ, not imputing to men their sins and entrusting to us the word of reconciliation....] Christ became sin for me! And my sins are there in his body, in his soul! This—says the Pope—it's crazy, but it's beautiful, it's true! This is the scandal of the Cross![315]

---

[314] Francis, homily, April 4, 2017.

[315] Francis, homily, June 15, 2013. This English translation was from Vatican Radio, but it has been taken down. I have slightly revised and added to the translation as it is cited throughout the English-speaking blogosphere. My edits and additions are in brackets. The Italian reads: "La vera riconciliazione è che Dio in Cristo ha preso i nostri peccati e si è fatto peccato per noi. E quando noi andiamo a confessarci, per esempio, non è che diciamo il peccato e Dio ci perdona. Noi troviamo Gesù Cristo e gli diciamo: questo è tuo e io ti faccio peccato un'altra volta. E a lui piace, perché è stata la sua missione: farsi peccato per noi, per liberarci.... È Dio infatti che riconcilia a sé il mondo in Cristo, non imputando agli uomini le loro colpe e affidando a noi la parola di riconciliazione.... Cristo si è fatto peccato per me e i peccati sono là, nel suo corpo, nel suo

Again, we can ask, what do the pope's words mean? I am not certain. St. Peter did write, "He himself bore our sins in his body" (1 Pet. 2:24). St. Peter was speaking of the consequence of sin or the price of our redemption. What tremendous gratitude each of us owes Christ for touching us filthy sinners with His deified hand. Now, we must remember that we need to have a firm purpose of amendment when going to Confession. Without a firm purpose of amendment, we cannot make a valid confession. Further, we must not think that Christ became an act of sin. We must not think that God simply "does not impute" our sins against us, although we still interiorly cleave to these sins and do not hate them. We must not think that our acts of sin and guilt are in Jesus' body and soul. What, then, may and must we affirm? Jesus bore in His body and soul the anguish and death that He offered for us to atone for our sins. He bore the weight of our sins in His body.

4. In his Angelus address of February 14, 2021, Pope Francis stated:

> In this episode, we can see two intersecting "transgressions": the transgression of the leper who draws near to Jesus, and should not have done so; and Jesus who, moved with compassion, touches him with tenderness, to heal him. He should not have done that. Both of them are transgressors. There are two transgressions.... The second transgression is that of Jesus: even though the Law prohibited touching lepers, He is moved, extends His hand and touches him, to heal him. Someone would have said: He sinned. He did something the law prohibits. He is a transgressor. It is true: He is a transgressor.... In the face of all this, Jesus announces to us that God is not an idea or an abstract doctrine but God is the One who "taints" himself with our wounded humanity and is not afraid to come into contact with our sores. "But, Father, what are you saying? That God taints himself?" I am not saying this,

animo. Questo è da pazzi, ma è bello: è la verità. Questo è lo scandalo della croce." The Italian is found on the Vatican website: http://www.vatican.va/content/francesco/it/cotidie/2013/documents/papa-francesco-cotidie_20130615_fretta-cristiana.html.

Saint Paul said it: he made himself to be sin. He who was not a sinner, who could not sin, made himself to be sin. Look at how God tainted himself to draw near to us, to have compassion and to make us understand his tenderness.[316]

In thinking about Christ's redemption, we must not think that Jesus transgressed the moral law. We know, however, that He is the lawgiver and that the ceremonial and temporary precepts are under His command and changeable by His just will. So we may hold that Jesus appeared, mistakenly to some, to violate the ceremonial and temporary precepts. But if He did so, He did not do so as one under the law and thus culpable of a violation. Rather, He did so as one above the law demonstrating His abolition of this merely temporary precept. We may also acknowledge that Christ suffered the blasphemy of others who considered Him a sinner (a tainted reputation), while He Himself was in no way spiritually or morally tainted. So Christ suffered both the weight of the consequences of our sin and also the false reputation of a sinner. But He Himself did not become a transgressor or sinner.

We must affirm the Catholic teachings and reject errors. This duty is a baptismal obligation. Still, this duty is not a meaningless and arduous task. It connects us with the beauty of truth.

Conclusion

Catholic teaching depicts for us the beauty and splendor of Christ's redemptive act. This beauty is manifold. First, God is wise; He is not arbitrary and whimsical. Things are not good because He extrinsically declares them to be good. Rather, things are good because they come from Him and insofar as they *imitate* His infinite goodness. The idea that God would call evil good and good evil is abhorrent to the rational mind. Moreover, Scripture teaches us that such a judgment is evil: "Woe to those who call evil good and good evil" (Isa. 5:20). Scripture also teaches: "Wisdom is a

[316] Francis, Angelus, February 14, 2021.

kindly spirit and will not free a blasphemer from the guilt of his words" (Wisd. 1:6). This passage does not mean that God does not forgive, for the same book teaches that wisdom corrects sinners so "that they may be freed from wickedness" (12:2). The passage means that God does not judge falsely or contrary to fact, declaring a guilty person to be innocent (unless He makes him so). So the passage continues, "because God is witness of [man's] inmost feelings, and a true observer of his heart, and a hearer of his tongue.... No one who utters unrighteous things will escape notice, and justice, when it punishes, will not pass him by" (Wisd. 1:6, 8). Our God is a God of truth, whose commandments are right. The idea that God would move guilt from the evildoer to an innocent person is thus abhorrent to the rational mind and to Scripture.

Second, the Catholic teaching is that, despite our sin, God the Father offers us forgiveness, having gone to the extreme measure of sending His divine Son to become incarnate so as to suffer and die for us. God could have abandoned us or annihilated us. (God, not man, can annihilate even the soul.) He could have saved us in other ways. He chose the costliest path so as to teach us how much He treasures us. He sent His only begotten Son to take on our flesh, to walk with us, speak with us, touch us, and heal us. In response, we nailed Him to the Cross. In His love for us, God gave us from the side of the pierced Savior the grace that would save the world. When we take to heart the dying Son of God, made flesh so that we might touch Him, our weary hearts are aroused to love. Loving Him, running to Him with great trust and love, we come to bewail our sins and wretchedness, not morosely but with fervent hope. As the Eastern Christians say, "Lord Jesus Christ, Son of God, have mercy on me, a sinner."

Third, as we saw in the last chapter, the Catholic teaching indicates that, through the graces that Christ won for us, we *can indeed walk in the light of Christ and obey the commandments of God.* We are not merely wretches whom God declares innocent, contrary to fact. No. God makes us holy by the washing of regeneration (Titus 3:5). By this baptismal rebirth, we become members of the True Vine (John 15). He shall lead us home in the bosom of His heart. But this journey requires teaching and grace.

Now, Christ entrusted His Gospel of truth and the life-giving sacraments of His grace to His Church. A lover of the human race, He called His disciples to baptize all nations, teaching them to observe His commandments. Despite all the defects of Christians, the Church is the light that God sends forth to the nations. But some Catholics are confused about the identity of this Church. Is the Catholic Church Christ's one true Church? Or is His Church the set of all Christian churches? Or is there no true Church at all?

5

The Catholic Church Is *Not* the One True Church?

Is the Catholic Church the one true Church founded by Jesus Christ? Today, a number of Catholics answer no. They do so for several reasons. Above all, they have goodwill toward members of non-Catholic Christian communities. They also observe that, for all their imperfections, these communities exhibit many good traits or features that Jesus Christ bestowed on His Church, such as Baptism and the Gospel. Finally, they note the many imperfections that they see in themselves and in the Catholic hierarchy. These Catholics conclude that the Catholic Church cannot be the one true Church. They are embarrassed by the claim that their Church is the one true Church; they see such a claim as a matter of pride or arrogance. Some attempt to support their conclusion by appeal to recent magisterial teachings and words of recent popes. Others come to this conclusion because of inadequate formation. Is their conclusion true? It is not, but their reasoning deserves a response.

That the Catholic Church *is* the one true Church of Christ is a matter of infallible teaching. Still, many of the observations and thoughts associated with a denial of this teaching are not to be dismissed out of hand. To evaluate this question comprehensively, we must approach it from two angles. On the one hand, we should take a holistic view, asking about the Church of Christ as a *whole*, as a *single, united,* and *identifiable* society. On the other hand, we should take an itemized view of the *several features* of this society taken individually, such as sacraments, discipleship, authority, biblical texts, doctrines, moral teachings, liturgical practices, and so forth. Together, both views will give us a more comprehensive understanding of the matter. Consideration of both vantage points will enable us both to affirm that the Catholic Church is the one true Church and also to affirm the good elements of truth and sanctification present in non-Catholic communities. These elements serve as a basis for the fulfillment of the goal of genuine Catholic ecumenism, which is the incorporation of all non-Catholic churches into the Catholic Church.

Synopsis of the Two Approaches

The question of the identity of the one true Church demands two approaches: the holistic approach and the itemized approach. Let us begin with the latter. Let us consider the several features of the Church of Christ taken distinctly. Christ left His Church the Gospel truth as the fulfillment of the Old Covenant. He instituted and entrusted to this Church various sacraments. He bestowed on her the requisite juridical authority. Through these essential seeds, the living high priest incorporates the children of Adam into Himself, the true vine, breathing upon them the Holy Spirit, constituting them as one, and leading them homeward. Thus, He calls for living faith and discipleship. He calls for the embodiment of these seeds in concrete practices, especially the liturgy. This embodiment involves our cooperation with God's grace; the liturgy involves, as one aspect of its reality, natural goods ordered to the worship of God. Note that here we are considering the liturgy as an expression of grace. Human culture, under the light of faith, offers its artistry in the form of prayers and melodies, for instance. We know, however, that this artistry is founded more fundamentally on God's creating and redeeming power. So, more fundamentally, the liturgy is the source through which we receive grace. This embodiment or expression involves a marvelous integration of nature and grace. The supernatural gifts coming down from above cleanse and elevate the gifts that spring up from the earth through the right use of reason. Since nature is not totally corrupt, contrary to Luther, and since the Gospel comes with the power to heal and transform, this or that human community can carry out this embodiment of Christ's calling in various, complementary ways. So Christ's disciples can exhibit a great richness in their fidelity to their Master, their King, and their God.

When we look at non-Catholic churches and communities, we find that they enjoy many of these features. Some of these communities have, for example, valid Baptisms and read many of the sacred books of the Bible. The Orthodox churches have valid priesthood and Eucharist. The Orthodox people have a robust appreciation of truth and tradition. Their theology is rich and ancient while also open to development. They boast ancient liturgies that beautifully lift the soul toward God. By contrast, not a few Roman Catholic parishes now offer uninspiring liturgies that feature the insipid music of David Haas. Other parishes pander to the youth with electric guitars, drums, and so on. The members of Protestant communities can have living faith in Jesus Christ, discipling Him and imitating His virtues. By contrast, many Catholics simply go through the motions of their Faith, not taking it to heart. The Lutheran communities recognize human sinfulness and have a spirit of repentance and faith. The Reformed communities have zeal for the glory of God and His sovereignty. They fervently desire to imitate Christ. They trust in Him for mercy. Evangelical business owners—such as the owners of Hobby Lobby—show more boldness in defending moral rectitude than many a Catholic businessman.

Still, their strengths notwithstanding, each of these non-Catholic communities also lacks some of the features essential to the Church of Christ. No Protestant community has valid priestly orders. Therefore, no Protestant community has a valid Eucharist or Confession. Even the Orthodox churches fail to profess truths of the Faith that have been dogmatically defined since their communion with Rome was broken.[317] Of

---

[317] Catholics can certainly admit that many of their coreligionists were at fault in this break. For example, the cardinal who occasioned that break had a big share in the fault. The papal lust for geographical territory

all the ecclesial societies calling themselves Christian, only the Catholic Church has *all* the features of the Church of Christ in their integrity. Even if individual Catholics do not embody and practice these features well, the Catholic Church has *all* the essential features that make up the Church of Christ. Hence, as Vatican II teaches, the Catholic Church has the "fullness" of these features, whereas non-Catholic communities possess fewer of these same features.

The *itemized* approach to the opening question is indispensable for a comprehensive view. Moreover, this approach has ancient roots. St. Augustine rebuked the Donatists, who refused to recognize the Baptisms of lapsed Catholics—namely, those Christians who denied the Faith under threat of persecution. Although lapsed Catholics severed themselves from the one true Church, Augustine argued, the Baptisms they practiced were valid. The Donatists refused to recognize the Baptisms of the lapsed Catholics. The Church sided with Augustine. Further, the Church has always recognized the validity of the priesthood and the Eucharist in the Orthodox churches. The Church has always insisted that, when an Orthodox church becomes Catholic, this church must be allowed to retain its liturgy and specific way of embodying the Faith, provided that any errors are removed. Of course, the Orthodox must also affirm the entire Catholic Faith. In short, this itemized approach is not the invention of Vatican II, although Vatican II helpfully stressed it. While sound and necessary, this approach must be complemented by another, more significant, approach.

The holistic approach asks the opening question precisely: Is the Catholic Church identical with the Church of Christ? As we shall see, the dogmatic Catholic answer is yes. In instituting a Church, Christ did not simply lay out its several distinct features. Rather, He formed *one* visible body, one people or society, with all the features necessary to

---

centuries earlier understandably upset Eastern bishops. This blame notwithstanding, the lack of communion wounds the Orthodox churches, for it deprives them of an infallible teaching authority and of the doctrines it issues.

flourish and to perpetuate itself until His final coming. To this society He entrusted the entire deposit of faith. To this society He entrusted all the sacraments of life. He bestowed upon this society a robust juridical unity that visibly marks it out, a hierarchical communion of bishops in union with the pope, together with all the faithful who are members of it.

Now, this robust juridical unity is complex because the Church is both universal and particular. That is, the one Church, which we can call the "universal Church," consists in many particular churches. Each particular church is ruled by a bishop. An example of a particular church is a local diocese. So the tight visible unity involves the communion of many particular churches, each being a particular church of the universal, or Catholic, Church. All particular churches that confess the full Faith, accept the entire sacramental system, and embrace hierarchical communion with the pope and the church of Rome are particular churches of the Church of Christ. Every such church enjoys the tight juridical unity that Christ bestows on His universal Church. No other local church or community enjoys that tight unity. In other words, all other local churches and communities are *separated* from the society that Christ founded and from the unity that binds it together; they are not part of it or of its unity. As we see, the holistic perspective involves an absolute claim of paramount importance.

We must combine both of these claims to achieve a comprehensive view of things. Sadly, many Catholics today are confused about these matters. Some think that they do not have to believe that the Catholic Church is the one true Church of Christ: they think they need to believe only that the Catholic Church has the "fullness of the truth." They are only half right. Others are even more confused: they think that the various Christian churches and communities are more or less equal, each having its strengths and its weaknesses. Finally, still others stray in an opposite manner: they erroneously think that there are no elements of truth and sanctification in the Orthodox churches and Protestant communities. They may also falsely think — to the scandal of others — that one can be saved only if one is a card-carrying Catholic when one dies. To be sure, there are very few people who stray in this direction. In what follows, we will correct these errors, focusing on the predominate error of our day, the denial of the dogma that the Catholic Church is the one true Church.

Why Some Think the Catholic Church Is
Not the One Church of Christ

There are four factors related to the erroneous claim that the Catholic Church is not the one Church of Christ. Some of these are not real causes of confusion but rather conditions for the confusion.

1. One condition or occasion, mentioned in the introduction, is the sincere goodwill that Catholics bear toward their non-Catholic brothers. Of course, true goodwill cannot itself be the cause of error or confusion. But, when coupled with doctrinal ignorance and a mistaken sense of humility, humanistic goodwill can be an *occasion* of error. Such is the case here. To correct this, I will show below the dogma of the Church's identity. Here, we should simply remind those of goodwill what true love is. Sincere love needs to be ordered to truth and to the real good of souls. If we will what is best for our neighbor, we will the means for his eternal salvation. Now, as even the itemized approach to the Church shows, the full and integral means for salvation are available *only* in the Catholic Church. Therefore, if we truly desire the good of our neighbors, we will want them to be Catholic and to live the Faith well. On the communal or social level, a Catholic will want a non-Catholic church to be incorporated into the Catholic Church. Love does not rest with coexistence but strives for conversion. Catholics who fail to do this fail to love well. Every Catholic should desire the incorporation into the Catholic Church of every human being and every non-Catholic church. The time may not be ripe for the realization of this desire in this case or that case, but true love retains the desire.

2. A second *occasion* of the current confusion is that, for over five decades, the Magisterium has more or less refrained from employing the holistic approach. Instead, the Magisterium has highlighted the itemized approach. Thus, the main message that the Magisterium has communicated is simply that (1) the Catholic Church possesses the "fullness of

truth" and (2) non-Catholic communities share a portion of that truth. This new mode of expression is not false; it is true. It calls our attention to what *is* the case. So it is integral to a full articulation of the Catholic judgment concerning ecumenism. The first approach is helpful for ecumenism because it draws positive attention to the various blessings really present in non-Catholic communities. Anyone skilled in interpersonal communication recognizes that honest attention to the good aspects of one's dialogue partner facilitates fruitful conversation. We don't win souls by being cranks. Jesus did not trumpet other people's faults unless they opposed His offer of mercy. Think of His way of treating the woman at the well (John 4). He met her where she was, conversed with her, and gently called attention to her current, problematic relationships, inviting her to drink deeply of mercy, which entails repentance. In imitation of this positive approach, the Magisterium has taken the first steps of a difficult conversation.

As indicated above, the itemized approach was not the invention of the Second Vatican Council. That council contributed the notions of "partial" and "full" possession of the truth. By these notions, one can express the ancient Catholic conviction. The declaration on the Church *Lumen gentium* affirms the ancient Catholic conviction: "Many elements of sanctification and of truth are found outside of her [the Church's] visible structure."[318] The decree on ecumenism, *Unitatis redintegratio*, builds from this affirmation. It emphasizes the notion of "full communion" and speaks of various degrees of approximation of full communion.[319] Let us consider this analogy of communion more closely.

Recall that the Church is both universal and particular. We speak of the universal Church when we think of the one Church of Christ taken as a whole. A particular church is, for example, a local diocese under a bishop.[320] Clearly, the one Catholic Church comprises many particular

---

[318] *Lumen gentium*, art. 8; DH 4119.

[319] See *Unitatis redintegratio* (1964), art. 3; DH 4188 and 4190.

[320] I bypass in this popular work the distinction between particular (broad term) and local (strict term).

churches. A question we can ask is *whether* a given particular church is a particular church of the *Catholic* Church. It is *if and only if* three conditions are met: (1) its bishop is in hierarchical communion with the pope, (2) its people confess the whole Catholic Faith, and (3) its people accept all the means of sanctification. Now, *no* particular Orthodox church meets all these requirements, because (1) no Orthodox bishop is in hierarchical communion with the pope, and (2) there are numerous infallible teachings of faith that Orthodox believers do not profess. Thus, no particular Orthodox church is a member of the Catholic Church. Much less is any Protestant community a member because every Protestant community has the additional defect of not possessing (3) the fullness of the means of sanctification.

Still, as we noted, these non-Catholic churches and communities, in "varying degrees,"[321] share in the truth and means of sanctification. Because of their real possession of saving truths and means of sanctification, "the Spirit of Christ has not refrained from using them as means of salvation that derive their efficacy from the very fullness of grace and truth entrusted to the Catholic Church."[322] For instance, some infant is baptized in an Orthodox church and then dies. The infant's soul is now in Heaven. Catholics and the Magisterium have always held this conviction. At Vatican II, this conviction was expressed by the integration of such phrases as the "fullness of grace" and the "fullness of truth" with the notions of "degrees" of participation and "elements" of truth and grace. John Paul II employed these phrases abundantly in his pontificate, especially in his encyclical on ecumenism, *Ut unum sint.*[323]

The Magisterium's recent use of the itemized approach is perfectly acceptable. But the itemized approach is insufficient. Its benefits notwithstanding, the itemized approach is not the whole truth. Ironically, it is not the "fullness of the truth." The holistic approach and its theses are also part—a major part—of the "fullness of truth." The Magisterium's recent

---

[321] *Unitatis redintegratio*, art. 3; DH, 4188.
[322] Ibid.; DH 4189.
[323] See John Paul II, *Ut unum sint* (1995), arts. 13–14 and 86–87.

silence on the holistic approach correlates with widespread forgetfulness of the full truth on the part of Catholics. This forgetfulness constitutes the ignorance that, coupled with humanistic goodwill, leads to denial of the dogma that the Catholic Church is the one true Church. What is needed is a fuller statement of the "fullness of truth," a statement that incorporates the holistic approach as well. Catholics need their full catechism. From decades of silence, we have grown ignorant, and ignorance has led many into error.

3. Third, some Catholics have stumbled into error by abusing words attributed to Pope Francis. For example, Eugenio Scalfari alleged that Pope Francis said to him, "I believe in God, not in a Catholic God, there is no Catholic God."[324] What to make of this statement? Most importantly, it is not a papal word. Thus, it has no authority. Moreover, it is not even a "word of a pope." Rather, it is only a *rumored* or *alleged* word of a pope. We have no obligation to accept it.

Further, the statement, while true, is misleading. It invites us to think something false about God. It is true that God is not a Catholic; He is not registered in some parish somewhere, obedient to the pope. But in denying the existence of a "Catholic God," one invites the listener to think that God did not found the Catholic Church. But, to the contrary, through Jesus Christ, God did found the Catholic Church as the one true Church. So, although true, the statement is misleading and scandalous. Catholics must resist Scalfari and remain steadfast in the faith.

4. A fourth reason for the recent confusion is a common *misinterpretation* of a passage from *Lumen gentium*. The council document took up the topic of the identity of the Church that Christ founded. Which Church that we see in the world today, if any, is the Church of Christ? The council declared, "This Church, constituted and organized in the world as a society, *subsists in* the Catholic Church, which is governed by the successor of Peter and by the bishops in communion with him,

---

[324] Eugenio Scalfari, "The Pope: How the Church Will Change," *la Repubblica*, October 1, 2013, https://www.repubblica.it/cultura/2013/10/01/news/pope_s_conversation_with_scalfari_english-67643118/.

although many elements of sanctification and of truth are found out-side of her visible structure."[325] The key phrase here is "subsists in." The text does not say, "The Church of Christ *is* the Catholic Church" but rather, "The Church of Christ *subsists in* the Catholic Church." These two verbs "is" and "subsists in" seem so different on the surface; perhaps understandably, many have taken the phrase to be a *denial* of the identity of the Catholic Church with the Church of Christ. As they argue, if the Church of Christ "subsists in" the Catholic Church, surely the two must not be identical! It is not just the average, edu-cated Catholic who has taken the text this way. Many theologians have taken it this way.

One of the leading English-speaking theologians who promoted this reading was Fr. Francis Sullivan, S.J. He taught at the Gregorian Uni-versity for decades and thus had an enormous influence on priests and bishops throughout the world. In the past four decades, his own students have further propagated his interpretation of the council. I was taught by a professor who embraced Sullivan's thesis. Sullivan's interpretation of the council is erroneous. Thus, many have fallen into error because of his work. Others have committed worse errors.[326] Since Fr. Sullivan offered the most plausible misinterpretation of *Lumen gentium*, however, my rebuttal will focus on his argument. A successful refutation of Sul-livan will make easier the disposal of other theories that are more alien to the dogma.

Fr. Sullivan argued that there is a "nonexclusive identity" between the Catholic Church and the Church of Christ. The phrase is puzzling:

---

[325] *Lumen gentium*, art. 8; DH 4119, emphasis mine.

[326] Peter C. Phan of Georgetown University, for instance, wrote, nearly thirty years ago, "The empirical claim of uniqueness and universality of the church must be abandoned, or at least severely curtailed, in view of this renewed sense of the church's imperfections," citing Karl Rahner, S.J., in support of his claim. See Peter C. Phan, "The Claim of Uniqueness and Universality in Interreligious Dialogue," in *Being Religious Interreligiously: Asian Perspectives on Interfaith Dialogue* (Maryknoll, NY: Orbis Books, 2004), chap. 5.

identical but not exclusively so. On the one hand, he admits that the Catholic Church has everything—all the features—she needs to be the Church of Christ. She has the fullness; other churches do not. We can see Sullivan practice the itemized approach. He concludes that the Catholic Church is "identical" with Christ's Church in this respect. On the other hand, he points out, other churches and communions have *some* of the various features of the Church of Christ. Sullivan concludes that they must therefore be, to that extent, churches and communions *of the Church of Christ*. Of course, these "other" communities are obviously *not* particular churches of the Catholic Church. Hence, he concludes, these non-Catholic communities are particular churches of the Church of Christ but *not* of the Catholic Church. So, for Sullivan, the Catholic Church is not one and the same thing with the Church of Christ.

We see Fr. Sullivan express this opinion in various ways. First, his very thesis of "nonexclusive identity" explicitly denies that the Catholic Church and the Church of Christ are one and the same thing. Second, he implies non-identity when he states that non-Catholic particular churches *participate* in the Church of Christ in one way and participate in the Catholic Church in some *other* way.[327] In short, he differentiates the following two relationships: non-Catholic particular churches as related to the Church of Christ and non-Catholic particular churches as related to the Catholic Church. Third, he implies non-identity when he holds that the Church of Christ extends beyond the Catholic Church. Thus, Fr. Sullivan draws a subtle but real distinction between the Catholic Church and the Church of Christ.

For many reasons, we must reject Fr. Sullivan's thesis. First, he endorses a "hermeneutic of rupture." He portrays Vatican II as *contradicting* the teaching of Pius XII that the Catholic Church and the Mystical Body (or Church) of Christ are identical.[328] Sullivan says that Vatican II "aban-

---

[327] Francis Sullivan, *Salvation Outside the Church? Tracing The History of the Catholic Response* (New York: Paulist Press, 1992), 149.

[328] See Francis Sullivan, *The Church We Believe In: One, Holy, Catholic and Apostolic* (New York: Paulist Press, 1988), 21.

doned or even weakened" the thesis of total identity.[329] For Sullivan, Vatican II *changed* doctrines! Now, a hermeneutic of rupture is *never* a recommendable hermeneutic, even in matters that are not infallible.[330] Second, a real change in noninfallible teachings should include a clear and unambiguous rejection of the past erroneous teaching. Such clarity is pastoral because it dispels needless confusion. But *nowhere* does Vatican II reject the past teaching. So, for argument's sake, if Vatican II *really did* change the teaching, it failed to do so in a *pastoral* manner. Third, and most importantly, if the previous teaching was *infallible*, it can *never* be changed by any authority whatsoever: not by a pope, not by a council. As I shall argue in the next section, the previous teaching is *infallible*. Therefore, it can never be changed. Consequently, we must forever hold that the Catholic Church and the Church of Christ are one and the same thing!

We need to affirm the whole truth of the Catholic Faith, while retaining our goodwill toward non-Catholics and while affirming the goodness and truth present in non-Catholic Christian communities and churches. We can do so by recovering the holistic perspective, a perspective that includes a crucial dogma. To this dogma we now turn.

The Catholic Church *Is* the One Church of Christ

Reminder of the Importance of the Holistic Perspective
Genuine ecumenism involves, on a communal scale, true love of the other. Now, true love wills the other's good. For a Catholic, true love for any neighbor has one ultimate meaning: to will that person's friendship with God. Now, that friendship is most securely fostered *only* in the society that Christ established with the means to heal, sanctify, instruct,

---

[329] Francis Sullivan, "A Response to Karl Becker, S.J., On the Meaning of *Subsistit In*," *Theological Studies* 67 (2006): 397. Sullivan's thesis, broadly construed, continues to have supporters, such as Massimo Faggioli. See Faggioli, *Vatican II*, 100–102.

[330] See Joseph Clifford Fenton, "The *Humani Generis* and the Holy Father's Ordinary Magisterium," in *The Church of Christ*, 110–123.

and guide. So true love of neighbor will also include the desire that one's neighbor become Catholic so as to benefit from all the truth and all the means of salvation that foster union with God. Analogously, true love in the form of genuine Catholic ecumenism wills that every non-Catholic Christian church become incorporated into the Catholic Church, so as to be, really and integrally, a particular church (or set of particular churches) in the Catholic Church.[331]

The holistic perspective trains our eyes on the big picture. Christ's Church is not just a set of juxtaposed features. Rather, she is a really existing mystical body or society with a tight, visible unity. We should not merely stare myopically at the "trees," i.e., at the several features of the Church, which non-Catholic communities possess in varying degrees. Above all, we should look at the forest, i.e., at the coherence of these features in the one and only society founded by Christ.

When we examine the divisions between the Christian communities in this latter light, we come to some stark conclusions. Either the Church of Christ exists, or she does not exist. If she does not exist, Christ's project was a failure. What Christian will admit that? If she does exist, we must ask *where* she exists. *Which* of the Christian societies is the Church that Christ founded? Can she be the set of all or even some of these Christian communities? No, she cannot. These are divided in government and disagree as to the truth, but what Christ founded will last until the end of time, with one Faith and under one authority. She is one real bride. So, if the Church exists, she must be *one* of the many Christian communities that exist. The Catholic Church has long made the claim that she is that community. In another context, we could make an argument from reason in favor of the truth of this claim. In the present context, we are concerned only with communicating to Catholics that this is, in fact, Church teaching, given that many Catholics have become confused about this since 1965.

---

[331] Local churches can be occasions of marvelous diversity *within* the one true Faith. Think, for example, of the beautiful chant and artwork and theology of the Byzantine Catholic churches or of Maronite churches.

The Catholic Church Is the True Church of Christ:
The Magisterial Sources

We can begin in the thirteenth century with a profession of faith prescribed by Pope Innocent III for the Waldensians in 1208. He commanded that the Waldensians profess this faith as a condition for reconciliation with the Church. The profession states, "We believe with our heart and confess with our tongue the one Church, not of heretics, but the holy Roman, catholic, and apostolic [Church] outside of which we believe that no one is saved."[332] Pope Innocent III thus *identifies* the true Church as the Catholic Church and differentiates the true Church from that of heretics. He is clearly employing the holistic approach.

In 1274, the Second Council of Lyons officially received Emperor Michael Palaeologus's profession of faith. The emperor ruled where the Orthodox churches dominated, and there was an ecumenical effort at reunion underway. Pope Clement IV had sent this profession to the emperor in 1267. The confession reads, "We believe that the holy, catholic, and apostolic Church is the one true Church."[333] Here, the phrase "catholic and apostolic Church" signifies what we refer to in English as the "Catholic Church." How do we know this? The context tells us. The phrase "catholic and apostolic Church" signifies the one Church consisting of many local churches in hierarchical communion with Rome.

Now, this teaching and also Pope Innocent III's profession of faith were issued *after* the Great Schism. So, at the time of these teachings, the one Church consisting of local churches in union with Rome constituted what we refer to in English as the Catholic Church (capital Cs), which did not then include the sets of Eastern particular churches not in union with Rome, the Orthodox churches. Lyons II confirms this interpretation in a subsequent passage: "The Holy Roman Church possesses also the highest and full primacy and authority over the universal Catholic

---

[332] DH 792. Here, "Roman" Church signifies what we refer to in English as the "Catholic Church," which has Rome as its head.
[333] DH 854.

Church."[334] Here, the "Roman Church" is the very diocese of Rome. Lyons II teaches that this diocese has the full primacy over the entire Catholic Church. Again, at that time, the Orthodox churches refused hierarchical communion with Rome. They refuse such communion to this day. In this state, the Orthodox churches are *not* churches of the one true Church. Thus, employing the holistic approach, Lyons identifies the Catholic Church with the one true Church.

Later, in the fourteenth century, Clement VI addressed the Armenian churches, which were at the time in schism from Rome. This is effort at Catholic ecumenism. These churches were entertaining a return to unity with the Catholic Church. Their motives were mixed, to be sure. In no small part, they desired to receive papal aid to defend themselves from the sultan. Not an evil motive, but not a heavenly motive either; still, it is a motive that Heaven can use. Pope Clement commanded the Armenians to profess the following:

> All those who in baptism have received the same Catholic faith
> and afterward have withdrawn and will withdraw in the future
> from the communion of this same Roman Church, which one is
> the one, sole Catholic, are schismatic and heretical if they remain
> obstinately separated from the faith of this Roman Church.[335]

In this teaching, Pope Clement VI identifies the "one sole Catholic" Church with the "Roman Church." So, in his statement, "Roman Church" stands for the entire set of churches — united as one universal Church — that are in hierarchical communion with the particular church of Rome led by the pope as bishop.[336] Pope Clement VI differentiates such particular churches (Catholic ones) from all others. Thus, he teaches that the one Catholic Church consists solely in particular churches in communion with Rome. There is for him no Church of Christ other than the Catholic Church.

---

[334] DH 861.

[335] DH 1050.

[336] To be even more precise, it stands for that set *taken as a whole*, not as a federated group of independent churches that "agree to recognize" Rome.

As we have seen from the foregoing, at times the phrase "Roman Church" indicates the diocese of Rome. At other times, it indicates the Catholic Church. The latter use is employed because the Catholic Church consists in all those particular churches that are in communion with Rome. We should, however, recall that "Roman" does *not* mean that the Catholic Church consists simply in the Roman rite. The Catholic Church, the Roman Church (taken in this sense), refers to the entire Church of Christ, which consists in Roman-rite Catholic churches and many Catholic churches of the various Eastern rites.

In the fifteenth-century decree concerning the Copts and Ethiopians, the Council of Florence declared that the Holy Roman Church "firmly believes, professes, and preaches that 'none of those who are outside of the Catholic Church, not only pagans,' but also Jews, heretics, and schismatics, can become sharers of eternal life."[337] The council was treating the necessity of the Catholic Church for salvation, and it taught that Jews, heretics, and schismatics exist outside the Catholic Church. Schismatics and heretics are members of various Christian communities and churches, but their objective situation is such that they are outside the one Church that is necessary for salvation. Therefore, they are not members of the one true Church. Only Catholics are members of the true Church. Since Catholics are members precisely of the *Catholic* Church, the Catholic Church is the only true Church of Christ.

At this point, some might wonder about the salvation of those outside the Church. Above, I am merely showing the identity of the Catholic Church with the Church Jesus founded. This dogma does *not* mean that only those who die as *actual* members of the Church can be saved. Great theologians such as Bellarmine have taught that this objective situation of Jews, heretics, and schismatics does not mean that they cannot be saved unless they become actual *members* of the Catholic Church. Such persons can have a grace-inspired desire, grounded in faith and emanating from true charity, to obey God's will. If they have this holy desire, they truly,

---

[337] DH 1351.

albeit only implicitly, desire to be members of the Church that Christ instituted. Meanwhile, the grace they have already places them in real communion with the *visible* Catholic Church.

The profession of faith written up shortly after the Council of Trent states, "I acknowledge the holy, catholic, and apostolic Roman Church as the mother and the teacher of all the churches."[338] Here, the "Roman Church" is the Diocese of Rome precisely as the principle of unity of the universal Church. (We could, similarly, read this passage as referring to the one Catholic Church, with Rome as head, as mother of all particular churches.) This one church is *mother* of all other churches. Every Catholic particular church acknowledges this maternity and subjects herself to Rome. Rome's maternal rights extend, however, also to non-Catholic churches, but non-Catholic churches do not acknowledge these rights and do not put themselves in hierarchical communion with the church of Rome. Hence, they stray from their mother. While in this state of alienation, none of these straying churches factors in the constitution of the Church of Christ. They block themselves off from their mother.

On the eve of the first ecumenical council held at the Vatican, Pope Pius IX reached out to non-Catholic Christian churches and communities. He did so as a loving father, longing for the return of these churches and communities to the Catholic fold. As part of his invitation, he pointed out the difficult truth that no non-Catholic church or community is part of the Church of Christ:

> One who carefully considers and reflects on the condition in which the diverse and mutually disagreeing religious societies that are separated from the Catholic Church find themselves ... should be able very easily to convince himself that no particular one of those societies or even all of them joined together in any way constitute and are that one and catholic Church that Christ the Lord established, constituted, and willed to exist, nor can they

[338] DH 1868.

in any way be said to be a member or part of the same Church, because they are visibly separated from Catholic unity.[339]

Here, Pius IX had his eye trained on the holistic truth concerning the one true Church. The sobering fact of division *separates* Protestants and Orthodox from that one true Church. The pope was very aware that these communities confess many of the same truths and that some celebrate many of the sacraments validly. Nonetheless, he declared that they are "separated from Catholic unity" and that they are "not part of Catholic unity."[340] Clearly, he was taking the holistic approach, for he used the notion "Catholic unity" as an absolute concept, a concept of tight and complete unity. This Catholic unity *does not admit of degrees*! To have communion with the Catholic Church in this sense is to be in what Vatican II describes as *"full* communion." Now, a church either is or is not in *full communion*. A particular Catholic church, such as the Diocese of Dallas, *is* in communion in this way. No Anglican community is in communion in this way; no Orthodox church is in communion in this way. As Vatican II says, "Our separated brethren, whether considered as individuals or as Communities and Churches, are not blessed with that unity."[341] As a result, the latter are *not* part of the Church of Christ. On Sullivan's reading, however, the Church of Christ is a society that embraces, in varying degrees, the Catholic Church and other churches, which are really divided from one another. As it were anticipating Sullivan's error, Pius IX rejected it long ago. Leo XIII repeated this condemnation: "Christ did not, in point of fact, institute a Church to embrace several communities similar in nature, but in themselves distinct, and lacking those bonds that render the Church unique and indivisible."[342]

From the foregoing, we see that it is a dogma of faith that the Catholic Church *is* the Church of Christ. Since it is a dogma, all Catholics must confess it. Therefore, no Catholic has any objective excuse to hold any

---

[339] Pius IX, *Iam vos omnes* (1868); DH 2998.
[340] Ibid.; DH 2999.
[341] *Unitatis redintegratio*, art. 3; DH 4190.
[342] Leo XIII, *Satis cognitum* (1896), art. 4; DH 3303.

thesis that waters down, alters, or denies this dogma of strict identity. Sullivan's reading of Vatican II contradicts not just Pius XII's more recent statements but infallible Catholic teaching.

There is a crucial ecumenical consequence of this teaching. As all admit, the goal of ecumenism is union of every non-Catholic particular church with and in the true Church of Christ. But since the Catholic Church *is* that Church, the goal of ecumenism is that every non-Catholic community and church be incorporated into the Catholic Church and thereby become Catholic. For its part, Sullivan's thesis issues in incoherent implications for ecumenism.

Consequence: Genuine Catholic Ecumenism

Some say that Catholics entered the ecumenical movement only in 1965. That is false. As already indicated in passing, the Catholic Church has practiced genuine Catholic ecumenism for centuries.

What is genuine Catholic ecumenism? It is the effort to incorporate non-Catholic churches into the Catholic Church. Understandably, non-Catholic churches conceive of the ecumenical movement differently. The Catholic profession of faith requires a Catholic to hold that the ultimate goal of genuine ecumenism is the incorporation of non-Catholic churches into the Catholic Church. Incidentally, this is the case whether or not we employ the holistic approach. Without question, it is the case for the holistic approach because only the Catholic Church is the true Church of Christ.[343] It is also the case for the itemized approach, for in this approach, we confess that only the Catholic Church has the fullness of these

---

[343] See Pope Pius XI, *Mortalium animos* (1928), art. 10. Pius XI calls for the "return" of non-Catholic communities to the Catholic Church. I put "return" in quotation marks because many individuals were raised from their infancy in non-Catholic churches. So they are not returning to the Church that they personally left. Notwithstanding, they are called to return to that which their forefathers left. Every saving truth and means of grace that any non-Catholic church presently enjoys was taken from the Church to whom Christ entrusts all His truth and means of salvation, the Catholic Church. See *Lumen gentium*, art. 8.

elements and that these elements are properly hers.[344] Therefore, for any particular church to have this fullness—in the way a particular church can—is precisely for her to be a particular Catholic church. So, if next year, a particular church that, not Catholic today, gains that fullness, she will have been incorporated into the Catholic Church.

In the first few centuries after the Great Schism, there were two major attempts at genuine Catholic ecumenism, the Second Council of Lyons and the Council of Florence. Although neither of them enjoyed long-term success, the goal they set out was the genuine Catholic goal. Non-Catholic churches were invited to subscribe to the full confession of the Catholic Faith. Genuine ecclesial unity requires nothing less; we strive for unity in truth.

The foregoing notwithstanding, incorporation into Catholic unity does not require annihilation or dilution of genuine diversity. Non-Catholic churches are permitted, encouraged, and even required to retain their authentic traditions, which are often quite different in appearance (in expression or embodiment) than Latin traditions proper to the Roman Rite. We see here the complementarity of the two approaches. The truth of the holistic approach clearly demands a return to the Catholic Church, and the truth of the several-elements approach clearly celebrates and preserves legitimate differences. Pope Benedict XIV in 1755 expressed both these aspects of Catholic ecumenism: "The Church does not require schismatics to abandon their rites when they return to Catholic unity, but only that they forswear and detest heresy. Its great desire is for the preservation, not the destruction, of different peoples—in short, that all may be Catholic rather than all become Latin."[345] Salutary words.

Gregory XVI stressed numerous times the goal of bringing all non-Catholic Christians into the Catholic Church. Similarly, the Second Vatican Council teaches that the practice of assisting individuals to convert to Catholicism, while distinct from ecumenism, is to be approved.

---

[344] *Unitatis redintegratio*, art. 4.

[345] Benedict XIV, *Allatae sunt* (1755), art. 48, Papal Encyclicals, https://www.papalencyclicals.net/ben14/b14allat.htm.

It is perfectly harmonious with ecumenism.[346] For his part, Gregory XVI, following Benedict XIV, discouraged mixed marriages with utmost rigor. A mixed marriage is a marriage between a Catholic and a non-Catholic Christian. Such marriages, Gregory XVI stressed, have many problematic aspects. Among them is the danger that the Catholic spouse will leave the Catholic Faith. Another is that the Catholic spouse will fail to raise the offspring in the Catholic religion. Sometimes, such marriages were tolerated. Still, Gregory reminded his reader, grave obligations always remain. He spelled these out:

> The Catholic party realized an obligation to work for the conversion of the other party; the Catholic party also realized that all offspring from such marriages be educated only in the sanctity of the Catholic religion. Such precautions are surely founded on divine law, against which, without any doubt, one seriously sins who rashly exposes himself or herself and future offspring to the danger of perversion.[347]

It is an obligation of *divine law* that a Catholic in a mixed marriage not only remain in the Faith but labor to bring the non-Catholic spouse into the Catholic Faith.

We can recall also Pope Pius IX's letter of concern to non-Catholics at the start of the First Vatican Council. His sobering declaration that non-Catholic churches are not part of the Church of Christ formed only the first part of the letter. The second part was an invitation, rooted in love, to these communities to enter Catholic communion: "Wherefore all those who are not part of Catholic unity . . . should seek to free themselves from a situation in which they cannot be certain about their own salvation."[348]

At about that time in the nineteenth century, a movement to restore Christian unity arose in England. It was entitled Association for the

---

[346] See *Unitatis redintegratio*, art. 4.

[347] Gregory XVI, *Quas vestro* (1841), art. 1, Papal Encyclicals, https://www.papalencyclicals.net/greg16/g16quasv.htm.

[348] Pius IX, *Iam vos omnes*; DH 2999.

Promotion of the Unity of Christendom. It was not a Catholic movement, but it admitted Catholics as members. Although much goodwill
inspired this movement, the Catholic Faith finds its vision to be faulty,
albeit understandably so. The movement did not define the union of
all Christians in a Catholic manner. So the Catholic Church needed
to respond to this new movement. The English bishops were slow in
condemning it, perhaps because of the good intentions of the participants. Rome, however, was swifter. In 1864, the Holy Office declared
the following:

> The foundation on which this society rests is such that it com-
> pletely overturns the divine constitution of the Church. For, it is
> wholly in this: that it supposes the true Church of Jesus Christ to
> be composed partly of the Roman Church scattered and propa-
> gated throughout the whole world, partly, indeed, of the schism
> of Photius, and of the Anglican heresy.[349]

The Holy Office was pointing out that the foundation of this movement
contradicts the fundamental dogma of Catholic ecclesiology, that the
Church Jesus founded is the Catholic (aka Roman) Church.

Later that century, Leo XIII addressed the people of Scotland, im-
ploring them to return to the Catholic Faith, which their ancestors had
abandoned. He wrote:

> The ardent charity which renders Us solicitous of Our separated
> brethren, in nowise permits Us to cease Our efforts to bring back
> to the embrace of the Good Shepherd those whom manifold error
> causes to stand aloof from the one Fold of Christ. Day after day We
> deplore more deeply the unhappy lot of those who are deprived
> of the fullness of the Christian Faith.[350]

---

[349] DH 2886. Photius was a very important Greek patriarch and theologian
prior to the Great Schism to whose writings the Orthodox later appealed
in their rejection both of the *Filioque* and of the papacy.
[350] Leo XIII, *Caritatis studium* (1898), art. 1.

Leo XIII also directly invited all non-Catholic churches to return to the Catholic Church:

> Suffer that We should invite you to the Unity which has ever existed in the Catholic Church and can never fail; suffer that We should lovingly hold out Our hand to you. The Church, as the common mother of all, has long been calling you back to her; the Catholics of the world await you with brotherly love.[351]

For his part, Pope Pius XI composed an Act of Consecration of the Human Race to the Sacred Heart of Jesus. It is a lovely prayer that expresses the fullness of the Catholic Faith. After the initial prayers for all, he prays to Christ for various distinct groups. He prays first for Catholics, both practicing and lapsed:

> Be Thou King, O Lord,
> not only of the faithful who have never forsaken Thee,
> but also of the prodigal children who have abandoned Thee,
> grant that they may quickly return to their Father's house,
> lest they die of wretchedness and hunger.

He prays, second, for the return of non-Catholic Christians to the Catholic Church:

> Be Thou King of those who are deceived by erroneous opinions,
> or whom discord keeps aloof
> and call them back to the harbor of truth and unity of faith,
> so that soon there may be but one flock and one shepherd.

This important devotion bespeaks the Faith of the Church.

The ancient liturgy of the Roman Rite (the Extraordinary Form) also gives voice to this indelible doctrine. On Good Friday, the Church prays for distinct groups in the entire world. These prayers exhibit a clear and pressing conviction that all who are outside the Holy Roman and

---

[351] Leo XIII, *Praeclara gratulationis publicae* (1894), Papal Encyclicals, https://www.papalencyclicals.net/reunionofchristendom.

Apostolic Catholic Church are in a situation of peril. The Church prays that these either return to this Church or enter her for the first time. The prayer falls into a threefold sequence. I will cite the first sequence in this chapter and the next two sequences in chapter 7. In the first, the Church prays for non-Catholic Christians as follows:

> Let us pray also for heretics and schismatics: That our Lord God would rescue them from all their errors, and recall them to their holy Mother, the Catholic and Apostolic Church.... Almighty and everlasting God, who savest all and wouldst that none should perish: turn Thy gaze to souls deceived and led astray by the devil; may they cast off the evil of their heresy and in true repentance of their errors return to the unity of Thy truth.

A powerful prayer indeed. This is an authentic, fully articulated prayer, utterly harmonious with Catholic ecumenism. The goal of Catholic ecumenism remains the same through the centuries.

Incipient and scattered movements such as the Association for the Promotion of the Reunion of Christendom became one unified global movement in the early twentieth century. Again, participants had goodwill, but with respect to the Catholic Faith the foundation of the movement was flawed. So Pius XI intervened in order to articulate principles of genuine Catholic ecumenism. Pius XI laid out these fundamental and perennial principles in his marvelous encyclical *Mortalium animos* in 1928. He both invited non-Catholics to return to the Church and took the opportunity to warn about false ecumenism. False ecumenism downplays the Faith and the requirements for true unity. Given that many Catholics have forgotten the holistic approach, this invitation with its warning is prophetically urgent for us today:

> Venerable Brethren, it is clear why this Apostolic See has never allowed its subjects to take part in the assemblies of non-Catholics: for the union of Christians can only be promoted by promoting the return to the one true Church of Christ of those who are separated from it, for in the past they have unhappily left it. To

the one true Church of Christ, we say, which is visible to all, and which is to remain, according to the will of its Author, exactly the same as He instituted it.... For since the mystical body of Christ, in the same manner as His physical body, is one, compacted and fitly joined together it were foolish and out of place to say that the mystical body is made up of members which are disunited and scattered abroad: whosoever therefore is not united with the body is no member of it, neither is he in communion with Christ its head.[352]

Pius XI herein simply articulates the constant teaching of the Church. He asserts, first, that Catholic churches alone are member churches of the Catholic Church. Second, he teaches that the goal of genuine ecumenism is that every non-Catholic church and community would become Catholic.

A reader may be wondering, "What about Vatican II? Didn't the council change all this?" To this we now turn.

What about Vatican II?

As we have seen, Pius XII's teaching that the Mystical Body of Christ and the Catholic Church are one and the same thing was by no means an isolated magisterial utterance.[353] Instead, the teaching has been repeated for centuries by the ordinary and universal Magisterium. Further, the teaching has been issued by the extraordinary Magisterium. Finally, in both cases, the teaching is presented as a matter of divine faith. Thus, the teaching has the highest rank possible; it is a matter of defined Catholic and divine faith. Hence, no Catholic has any just cause to reject this infallible dogma of the Faith. According to the preservative mode of the hermeneutic of continuity, we must reject theological positions that

---

[352] *Mortalium animos*, art. 10.

[353] See Pius XII, *Mystici corporis Christi* (1943), art. 13. Pius XII affirmed the identity of the Church of Jesus Christ with the Catholic Church. He reaffirmed this teaching in *Humani generis*, art. 27.

would lead us to reject this dogma. Now, what did the Second Vatican Council teach?

We may begin this section by acknowledging that many have been confused by the phrasing that the Church of Christ "subsists in" the Catholic Church. Now, confusion paralyzes the mind; therefore, confusion is to be regretted. Confusion about truth that is revealed inhibits communion with God and right action in the world. We must therefore strive to resolve the confusion. In point of fact, the interpretations of the council that put it at odds with the infallible dogma are mistaken. We can show this with several arguments.

1. The Latin phrase *subsistit in* was not introduced by a modernist theologian. For decades, the identity of the person who suggested it was a mystery to scholars. Still, some took generic guesses. Sullivan used to opine that the phrase must have originated with what *he* would style a "reformer." But Karl J. Becker, S.J., recently discovered who it was. It was not a modernist; rather, it was the very man who served as ghostwriter for Pius XII in the document in which he taught the strict identity![354] It was Sebastian Tromp, a stalwart defender of the Faith.[355] Perhaps unsurprisingly, in a twist of irony, Sullivan and others responded to Becker's discovery by claiming that the ideas of the original proponent are irrelevant to a proper interpretation of the text.

2. Vatican II repeated the infallible dogma of identity in a decree on the Eastern Catholic Churches: "*The holy Catholic Church, which is the Mystical Body of Christ*, is made up of the faithful who are organically united in the Holy Spirit by the same faith, the same sacraments and the same government."[356] Here we see a simple identity between the Catholic Church and the Mystical Body of Christ. As proponents of Sullivan's the-

---

[354] See Christopher J. Malloy, "'Subsistit in': Non-exclusive Identity or Full Identity?" *Thomist* 72 (2008): 19–20.

[355] Karl J. Becker, "The Church and Vatican II's *Subsistit in* Terminology," *Origins* 35, no. 31 (2006): 514–522.

[356] *Orientalium ecclesiarum* (1964), art. 2, emphasis mine. Note again: Hünermann does not include this passage.

ory would agree, the Mystical Body of Christ is identical with the Church of Christ. Thus, this text simply identifies the Catholic Church with the Church of Christ. This text received conciliar approval the same day as *Lumen gentium*, which contained the *subsistit in* clause. Thus, Vatican II did not deny but reaffirmed the identity. Fr. Sullivan ignored this passage.

3. At the council, during the process of consideration, a bishop asked for a clear statement in *Lumen gentium* that the Catholic Church and the Church of Christ are identical. He was given the following answer: "What is asked here is sufficiently borne out in the entire text."[357] This response shows us that those responsible for drafting the text did not reject, but accepted, the dogma of full identity. Moreover, they thought the text sufficiently clear already. We can say, in hindsight, that they would have done well to make it explicitly clear.

4. For the past five decades, the Congregation for the Doctrine of the Faith (CDF) has issued various clarifications concerning the phrase *subsistit in*. In these documents, the CDF has consistently defended the continuity of the council with the past teaching, rejecting interpretations that stray from the past teachings. The CDF clarifications do two things for us today. On the one hand, they show us that clarification was needed; clearly, an explicit clarification would have proved highly beneficial in avoiding confusion. On the other hand, the clarifications assure us that the Magisterium has never endorsed a change in prior teaching! The latest document should have removed all doubt from those who wanted to reject the past infallible teaching. It reads, "The Second Vatican Council neither changed nor intended to change this doctrine; rather it developed, deepened, and more fully explained it."[358] Again, it states, "The use of the terms [i.e., *subsistit in*], by preserving the full identity (*plenam identitatem*) of the Church of Christ and the

---

[357] See *Acta synodalia sacrosancti concilii oecumenici Vaticani II*, vol. 3.7, 15.
[358] Congregation for the Doctrine of the Faith, *Responses to Some Questions regarding Certain Aspects of the Doctrine on the Church* (June 29, 2007), response to the first question, trans. in *Origins* 37 (2007): 135.

Catholic Church, does not change the doctrine on the Church."[359] Unsurprisingly, Fr. Sullivan rejected all these clarifications. For him, they represented a rerupture: the CDF was an unfortunate rupturing away from Vatican II, which itself was a glorious rupture from the be-nighted, antiquated tradition.[360] Sullivan was mistaken. It is time to clean up the mess.

A number of reputable theologians wish that the "subsists in" terminol-ogy had not been employed. For them, it is not a matter of the novelty of the expression. The council's comparison of the Church to a sacrament is also novel, but it is a clear teaching that easily bears fruit, whereas the phrase "subsists in" has caused forgetfulness of a doctrine already clearly taught. Other reputable theologians have attempted to find something helpful in the phrase. In either case, all orthodox Catholics must agree that no one may abandon the prior teaching, which is infallible. The Catholic Church is the one Church of Christ. The holistic approach is indispensable.[361]

---

[359] The original Latin response to the third question of the CDF document reads: "Usus vocabuli retinentis plenam identitatem Ecclesiae Christi et Ecclesiae Catholicae doctrinam de Ecclesia non immutat" (English translation is mine), http://www.vatican.va/roman_curia/congregations /cfaith/documents/rc_con_cfaith_doc_20070629_responsa-quaestio-nes_lt.html.

[360] Francis Sullivan, "A Response to Karl Becker, S.J., on the Meaning of *Subsistit In*," *Theological Studies* 67 (2006): 408.

[361] I recommend two articles to readers who would like to explore this mat-ter in greater detail. See my essay "Subsistit in': Non-exclusive Identity or Full Identity?" See also a related article that addresses one remaining question. Sullivan and others hold that unless you hold a *nonexclusive* identity, you cannot be open to ecumenism. Now, the Catholic Magis-terium has repeatedly called for genuine ecumenism. It is not optional. So, if Sullivan were correct, it would argue in favor of his nonexclusive-identity thesis. I argue that you *can* be fully engaged ecumenically with an exclusive-identity thesis. See my "Is Exclusive Identity Compatible with Ecumenism as a *Mutual* Exchange of Gifts?" in *Josephinum Journal of Theology* 22 (2015): 176–202.

Conclusion

The Catholic Church is fully identical with the Church that Christ founded. There is no distinction to be found, unless we call to mind the three *states* of the Church. This entire chapter has dealt with the state of the Church on Earth, the Church Militant. We can also recall that the Church exists in Purgatory as the Church Suffering and in Heaven as the Church Triumphant. Now, the juridical and sacramental structures and actions of the Catholic Church are not at operative in Purgatory and Heaven, although the Church on earth can affect things in Purgatory. So we can differentiate features of the Catholic Church on Earth from those of the Church in Heaven and in Purgatory. However, we can never say a distinction exists between what Christ founded on Earth and the Catholic Church.

This Church has a manifold and marvelous beauty, despite the weaknesses of individual Catholics. Recall that within the Catholic Church there are many particular churches. This multitude of particular churches, each nested in a set of similar sister churches, is one major source of legitimate diversity. Such diversity expresses itself, for instance, in legitimate liturgical differences. The Maronite liturgy looks very different from the Byzantine liturgy, which, in turn, is very different from the Roman liturgy. The unfolding of history has opened up these riches for the Catholic Church. As the Church successfully evangelizes new cultures and brings the people of these cultures into her fold, the particular churches that are instituted will incorporate the legitimate goods of the local patrimony, nature, and custom that can be incorporated into the *way* of being Catholic in that place (subject to approval by the Church's authority). Thus, the Catholic Church is rich and manifold. (She will also purify local customs that contradict human dignity or the Gospel. Through faithful shepherds, for instance, she has defended private property against Marxists and monogamy against polygamists and polyamorists. She has defended the rights of workers against usurers and tyrants.) Marvelously, with all of this diversity, she remains one, a single society governed by one united hierarchy with one Faith and one sacramental system.

False Mercy

The desire of the Catholic Church is for each individual human being to be united with Christ on Earth and abide in Him eternally in Heaven. Since the surest means to this union is the Catholic Church, the Church desires that each person become Catholic. There is no other church appointed by God by which we are to be saved. We might add, as well, that any sanctified person already mystically partakes in the very Catholic Church herself; thus, the Church's desire—which is not always identical with the desire of this or that prelate, who might be attracted by finances, human respect, and numbers—is not to add another figure to the parish registry but to incorporate a child of God into the communion of love.

Analogously, the goal of genuine Catholic ecumenism is that every non-Catholic church and community become Catholic. Thus, genuine ecumenism is not at odds with the truth of the Catholic Church's identity with the Church of Christ. These truths are harmonious. Moreover, achieving the goal of Catholic ecumenism benefits both the non-Catholic church *and* the Catholic Church. The former gains the fullness of truth *and* incorporation into the Church of Christ. The latter, the Catholic Church, gains as well. This may surprise some Catholics who rightly prize the Catholic tradition and Faith. But it is true. The Catholic Church gains all the authentic cultural richness of this newly incorporated church, because this richness is, ultimately, able to be taken up into the liturgy and life of that *formerly* non-Catholic church, to the praise of God the Father.

Let us spell this out concretely. Think of how dismal the celebration of Mass is at some Catholic parishes. No doubt, Jesus is really present. The Real Presence is absolutely a blessing; it is the central blessing. And the real Catholic Church is present. But the music, the gestures, the way of praying, the artistic work, and so forth sometimes leave much to be desired. By contrast, the Orthodox faithful know how to do liturgy, and they do it very well. They also have a marvelous way of doing theology. If what they lack is supplied and what they distort made straight, they can help Catholics better express and embody the things that Christ has committed to His Church. With its practice of the itemized approach,

Vatican II and the recent Magisterium help us cultivate appreciation for the gifts non-Catholic communities have to offer.

For these helps to achieve fruitful completion, we must always remember the holistic approach and recall the tradition. In that way, development will be authentic growth in which truth adds to truth, not the modernistic evolution of dogma, according to which new insights replace older, worn-out dogmas. But the modernists want to do just the opposite. They do not want us to complete Vatican II by recalling the teachings of the past, which, in service of beginning conversations with non-Catholics, have been left unexpressed for some time. The modernists want us to forget that past; they want us to complete Vatican II by marching forward without that past, as though the incompleteness of Vatican II was a signal to cancel the dogmatic past, which is only so much ballast keeping the hot-air balloon of Vatican II from reaching its intended heights.[362] For the modernists, silence is cancellation of the past, patience with error is inclusion, ambiguity is obfuscation, new insights are substantial changes, and so forth.

We must reject such the rebellion of the modernists. True ecumenism seeks to spread truth, not mutations and contagions. True ecumenism seeks to unite in genuine good, not in shallow compromise. Even though the journey is painful, we must not let desire for union dissipate into compromise consisting of banal platitudes. There are moments in ecumenism that are painful. These are moments of the cross. At such times, we must love the truth through the difficulty. Holy accompaniment does not follow the wayward toward the edge of the cliff so as to watch them plunge into the abyss. Holy accompaniment strives to pull straying friends out of the muck of error rather than letting them to wallow in it. Holy accompaniment searches for the right time, the right words, and the right gestures for fruitful advice, while always keeping the goal in mind. It avoids the extremes of passivity and of aggression, of apathy and pressure. Holy accompaniment presents the full truth judiciously, gently, clearly, and in due season. We must follow the path of holy accompaniment. We

[362] See Faggioli, *Vatican II*, 118–138 and also 106–117.

must not withhold gifts from our brothers in the Faith. These gifts are not ours to hoard, as though we were embarrassed Pelagians; they are God's to share. God intends the Catholic religion for everyone. If we are truly working to serve God, we will not refrain from offering our brothers the full truth. We must use tact, of course, but never deception.

We have seen that Catholics who reject the dogma of full identity of the Catholic Church with the Church of Christ cannot claim support in Vatican II. They have no valid excuse to deny the dogma. If they will but yoke their goodwill to the truth, their love for non-Catholic churches and communities will become fruitful.

Before turning to our next topic, one final word is in order about an even more egregious error concerning the Church. It is Karl Rahner's notion of the Church, which rests on his at once brilliant and evasive theory of grace. We can diagnose the nature of his error readily if we but consider his thought on the sacraments and on the Church. All truly pious Catholics believe the dogma of Holy Mother Church that the sacraments of the New Law both "contain and communicate" grace, unlike those of the Old Law, which "did not cause grace."[363] The sacraments of the New Law both contain and confer grace.[364] Rahner does not directly contradict this dogma. Instead, he depicts a caricature of the dogma, rejects the caricature, and then substitutes his own theory, which fails to convey that dogma. The reader will recall this pattern from the previous chapter. First, he rejects a caricature of dogma: "Man does not enter a temple, a [shrine] which encloses the holy and cuts it off from a godless and secular world which remains outside."[365] Note how Rahner caricatures the traditional view as purporting that the world is godless except for the sacred institutions of the Church. This is an absurd cari-

---

[363] DH 1310. For other relevant teachings, such as that on the increase of grace through sacramental participation, see DH 1322, 1515, 1606, 1865, 3315; and CCC 1392.

[364] See DH 1606.

[365] Karl Rahner, "Considerations on the Active Role of the Person in the Sacramental Event," in *Theological Investigations* 14:169.

cature. The tradition affirmed that God is not bound by the sacraments and that grace is offered apart from them. The tradition was, however, sober about the sinfulness of man and unspeakably grateful for the sacraments as true means of grace.

By dismissing the caricature, Rahner implicitly dismisses the teaching that grace comes to us *through* the sacraments. In his own theory, he even inverts this relationship. He describes his theory as a Copernican Revolution: we used to think that *sacraments* bring grace to us, either as instruments of grace or as "moral causes" of grace.[366] Instead, he alleges, *we* bring the grace to the sacraments. That is, the grace (which we used to think is about to come into us) is, in fact, already in us.[367] So why do we even need the sacraments? Not to obtain grace but to embody and express, in a social and ritualistic way, the grace that is already there.[368]

Suffice it to say, this Copernican Revolution is unacceptable. Of course, recipients of the sacraments do receive graces outside of the sacraments. As Rahner rightly notes, they would not otherwise come to the sacraments. But the sacraments are real channels of grace; they confer grace; this much is dogma. Rahner caricatures the dogma, rejects the caricature, and substitutes his own theory, which fails to reaffirm the dogma. So, readers are led to deny the very dogma.

How does Rahner's view of the sacraments connect with his understanding of the Church? For Rahner, the Church is not the community through which grace comes to us by means of her sacred actions (sacraments). Rather, the Church is simply the "historical and social

---

[366] There is legitimate theological disagreement as to how the sacraments communicate grace. Thomists and the majority of theologians hold that they are instrumental causes of grace; the Franciscans hold that they are moral causes of grace. Rahner rejects both schools of thought. See Rahner, "One Christ," *Theological Investigations* 16, 212. On this issue, see my essay, "The Withering."

[367] Rahner, "Considerations," *Theological Investigations* 14, 162–169.

[368] See Karl Rahner, "Baptism and the Renewal of Baptism," in *Theological Investigations*, vol. 23, trans. Joseph Donceel and Hugh M. Riley (New York: Crossroad, 1992), 197.

manifestation of the fact that all persons are called by God."[369] We used to think of the Church as the saving community through whose sacred actions we are saved. Rahner bids us rethink this. Instead, the Church is the result of God's saving work. And here is where pinning down Rahner's error is tricky. It is true that the Church *is* the result of God's saving work. She is also, however, the community that *brings* us saving grace by way of her sacred actions. The Church is not merely the historical and social manifestation of God's grace. She is necessary as an indispensable *means* of salvation. Rahner reduces her to an inevitable result of divine action; she is that, but she is far more than that. Through her actions, God saves the world.

On Rahner's reading of the Church and the sacraments, a pandemic that obstructs access to sacraments should not really present much difficulty for the faithful. They can to some extent express the grace that is within them via Zoom. Not ideal, but not a really big deal. Tell that to those struggling with mortal sins, who are longing to hear the words of absolution. Tell that to weary pilgrims who want to receive our Lord in the flesh. Readers should beware of Rahner and his disciples. They are legion.[370] Moreover, many parish educators and catechists unwittingly imbibe his opinions by way of the texts written by his disciples.

Our conclusion turns us toward a related issue. Christ entrusted to His Church a pattern of life. At the apex of this life is worship of God. That worship includes, in our fallen world, the proper sacrifice offered to God as propitiation for our sins, as a plea for God's graces for all our needs, and as thanksgiving and adoration. Now, these activities are precisely religion. So Jesus left His Church a *religion*. If He founded only one true Church, then the religion that is proper to that Church must be the *one true religion*. To this issue we now turn!

---

[369] Rahner, "Baptism," *Theological Investigations* 23, 201.

[370] In America, one of his disciples on the sacraments was Joseph Martos, author of *Doors to the Sacred: A Historical Introduction to Sacraments in the Catholic Church*, 2nd ed. (Ligouri, MO: Liguori Publications, 2001). For two of my works on Rahner, see "Rahner: The Withering of Faith" and "Rahner's Supernatural Existential."

6

The Catholic Religion Is *Not* the One True Religion?

Is there one true religion appointed by God for the salvation of the world? Or, rather, does God will a plurality of religions?

Nowadays, many Catholics do not know that their Church teaches that the Catholic religion is the one true religion, the fulfillment of ancient Judaism, just as few know that the Catholic Church is the one Church of Christ.[371] These days, many Catholics appreciate the presence of religious truth and reasonably helpful practices found in non-Christian religions, just as they appreciate the sundry features of Christ's Church in non-Catholic Christian churches. This much is good. Unfortunately, some of these Catholics tend to think that such appreciation requires that they affirm that God wills a diversity of religions.

The convictions that some Catholics have about non-Christian religions have a mixture of truth and error in them. We can diagnose the convictions most precisely when we approach the question about the true

---

[371] When used precisely, the terms "religion" and "church" are distinct: "religion" signifying ultimately the act of worship especially in its highest form and "church" signifying the society that offers that worship. The "Catholic Church" is the society headed by the pope in Rome. The "Catholic religion" is, at its height, the eucharistic sacrifice. This sacrifice is licitly offered only by the Catholic Church, which is the one divine society founded by Jesus Christ. So, the claims of "one true religion" and "one true Church of Christ" go hand in hand.

religion—is there one true religion?—in two ways, as we did last chapter with the Church. On the one hand, we can employ the itemized approach. We can train our eye on the various religious truths and acts that are good and fitting, whether grounded in the order of nature or proper to ancient Judaism or Christ's religion. On the other hand, we can take the holistic approach to the initial question, asking what and where *is* the one true religion that Christ left the world. This chapter will first briefly present these two approaches. Then it will consider and address various causes of confusion on this issue. Finally, it will demonstrate the dogmatic character of the claim that the Catholic religion is the one true religion.

The Two Approaches to the Issue

When examined according to its several contents, every religion (Satanism aside) has truths and good practices in it, to varying degrees. Some of the reasons for this are as follows. (1) Human nature is not totally corrupted. So men can arrive at the knowledge of God and some of the broad features of natural law. Aquinas believed that Aristotle arrived at some knowledge of the *real* God, even though Aristotle also affirmed of God things unbefitting Him: "Aristotle's conclusion is that there is one ruler of the whole universe, the first mover, and one first intelligible object, and one first good, whom above he called God, who is blessed for ever and ever. Amen."[372] Likewise, Augustine judged that the Platonists had arrived at knowledge of God. Now, natural reason is operative, with varying degrees of accuracy, in the world religions. So, it makes sense that monotheism is, to some extent, discoverable in various religions. (2) Further, men can recognize the obligations imposed on them by nature and, in response, attempt to develop religious practices. (3) In their cultures, there may well be remnants, albeit disfigured, of the original revelation given to Adam and developed up through Noah. (4) Some religions are influenced by ancient Judaism and Christianity.

[372] Thomas Aquinas, *Commentary on Aristotle's* Metaphysics, trans. John P. Rowan (Notre Dame, IN: Dumb Ox Books, 1995), par. 2663.

Muslims, for instance, give periodic worship to God throughout the day, week, and year, embodying a dictate of natural reason that also imitates the practices of revealed religion. Compared with the laziness of many Christians, there is something truly admirable about these practices. If only Catholics could be half as disciplined! (5) Moreover, some religions, even polytheistic ones, have a deep sense of human wrongdoing and of the need to offer atonement for it. St. John Henry Newman found this acknowledgment of guilt and attempts at expiation to be points of depar-ture for conversation with open-minded pagans.[373] Conversely, he found the liberal Protestant rejection of the notions of sin and expiation — in which we are now drowning — to be acquired dispositions alien to human nature and foreign to Christianity. No surprise that liberal Protestants should completely reinterpret Christianity. Liberal Protestantism has its sister in Catholic modernism. In short, non-Christian religions appreciate *some* religious truths. Still, only the Catholic religion has *all* the saving truths of religion. Just as the Catholic Church is rightly said to have the "fullness of truth" in comparison with non-Catholic churches, so the Catholic religion has the "fullness of religious truth" and the "fullness of religious worship" in comparison with other religions. (6) The concrete development of these things takes place under the care of God, who wills the salvation of all and accordingly works on their minds and hearts with His graces. Nevertheless, we must remember that original sin affects the entire human race. No religious practices invented by men are instituted by God or effective as sacraments. In fact, insofar as these practices are connected with error, they are obstacles to salvation.[374]

Consequently, when a Catholic missionary journeys to a new land, he encounters people who have some preparation for the good news. In every case, God loves the people of these religions for the sake of Christ. The approach we have been summarily unfolding examines the variety of religions through consideration of their possession or nonpossession of this or that religious truth or practice. This examination can thus appreciate

---

[373] See Newman, *An Essay in Aid of a Grammar of Assent*, chap. 10.
[374] CDF, *Dominus Iesus*, art. 21.

how various religions can affirm similar truths. This approach is indispensable for a comprehensive view of the diversity of religions and serves as a good beginning for dialogue. Still, it needs to be complemented by another, more significant approach, necessary for completion of authentic dialogue.

The holistic examination asks about the religion as a whole. Did God establish one religion, appointing a legitimate founder of it, and willing everyone to enter its practice? The Catholic answer is, "Yes, and it is the Catholic religion, entrusted to the Catholic Church." In establishing the New Covenant, which contains the Old Covenant in the state of fulfillment, God appointed this religion for all men. He did so through His divine Son made man, Jesus Christ, a true prophet and the *final* one.

John Henry Newman encourages the holistic perspective. He teaches that the Catholic religion presents itself as a package, something that comes as a whole, has a definite and identifiable message, and has God as its author. It does not present itself as a set of isolable assertions, with which one is at liberty to agree or disagree.[375] Now, if Catholicism were simply a set of truths and religious practices, we could content ourselves with saying that the Catholic set is "full," whereas non-Catholic sets are only "partially full." If, however, Christ left the world not only a set of truths but also a Church and a complete religion with a way of worship and life, we must say more. If Christ gave the Church to the world as a divinely appointed society with a divinely appointed religion, then this Church and religion are to be taken as a whole, not as sets of mere sums of things.

A major reason the message comes as a whole is that it is supernatural. Although it contains some truths that man can in principle arrive at by natural reason, the bulk of it, and certainly its heart and soul, is beyond the reach of natural reason. Although nature tells right reason to worship the Creator periodically, only the supernatural religion rightly specifies that worship. Our religion is truly *supernatural*. God communicates the content of this Faith in a special way, through special messengers. In the early history of mankind, God spoke directly to Adam and Eve and to Noah. Then God spoke through various prophets and messengers to the Jews, with

---

[375] See Newman, chap. 10 in *Grammar of Assent*, 248–316.

whom He inaugurated a supernatural religion, that of the Old Covenant. At last, He sent His own Son to give us the new and definitive message of salvation (Heb. 1:1–2). When we accept the words of Jesus, we do not accept them merely one by one, because this or that one sounds right or beautiful. We accept them because we accept *Him*. We follow *Him*; He is the messenger whom we trust. In fact, He is the God in whom we believe.

The faith we put in Jesus the Incarnate Word is *divine* faith. We believe what He says because He is trustworthy and all-knowing. By faith, we hold that whatever He says is true. Thus, our faith in Jesus leads us to accept *everything* He says *simply because* He says it. In the words of the First Vatican Council: "We believe that what he has revealed is true, not because the intrinsic truth of things is recognized by the natural light of reason, but because of the authority of God who reveals."[376] Consequently, if we did not accept everything revealed by God, we would not have true and divine faith. Rather, we would merely *agree* with God to some extent. Since faith leads us to accept *everything* God reveals, the Catholic Faith hangs together as a whole. We either believe it in its entirety, or we merely agree with parts of it. But if we accept what God says only when we "agree" with Him, we have no true faith at all. We show that we do not accept what He says simply because He says it. There is no such thing as having faith in "half" of the Catholic truth. We must accept it whole and entire.

The Church herself teaches this absolute character of faith. The Council of Florence, in its Decree for the Armenians, laid out the creed called Quicumque (the so-called Athanasian Creed) as a rule of faith for their return to the Catholic communion. This creed declares, "Whoever wills to be saved, before all things it is necessary that he holds the catholic faith. Unless a person keeps this faith whole and undefiled, without doubt he shall perish eternally."[377] Pius IV issued the Tridentine Profession of faith, which declares:

---

[376] *Dei Filius*, chap. 3; DH 3008.
[377] From Tanner, *Decrees of the Ecumenical Councils*, 551. For the reference to this passage in Denzinger, see the editorial remarks prior to DH 1328.

> I ... with firm faith believe and profess each and every article contained in the profession of faith that the Holy Roman Church uses.... This true Catholic faith, outside of which no one can be saved, which of my own accord I now profess and truly hold, I ... do promise, vow, and swear that, with the help of God, I shall most faithfully keep and confess entire and inviolate, to my last breath.[378]

Leo XIII declared that every Catholic must hold each and every dogma of the Faith. If someone rejects but one dogma, he loses faith entirely: "If then it be certain that anything is revealed by God, and this is not believed, then nothing whatever is believed by divine Faith."[379] More recently, Pope Benedict XV declared, "Such is the nature of Catholicism that it does not admit of more or less, but must be held as a whole or as a whole rejected."[380]

No one may distinguish dogmas into those that are fundamental and necessary and those that are peripheral and not necessary. Although some dogmas depend on other dogmas, every dogma must be believed, as Pope Pius XI taught:

> In connection with things which must be believed, it is nowise licit to use that distinction which some have seen fit to introduce between those articles of faith which are fundamental and those which are not fundamental, as they say, as if the former are to be accepted by all, while the latter may be left to the free assent of the faithful: for the supernatural virtue of faith has a formal cause, namely the authority of God revealing, and this is patient of no such distinction.[381]

Pius XII gives us a concrete example of the implication of this teaching. The implication is that infidelity regarding one dogma entirely disqualifies our faith. After declaring infallibly Mary's Assumption into Heaven, he warns, "Hence, if anyone, which God forbid, should dare willfully to

---

[378] DH 1862 and 1870.
[379] Leo XIII, *Satis cognitum*, art. 9.
[380] Benedict XV, *Ad beatissimi apostolorum* (1914); DH 3625.
[381] Pius XI, *Mortalium animos*, art. 9.

deny or to call into doubt that which We have defined, let him know that he has fallen away completely from the divine and Catholic Faith."[382]

Now, *how* does God reveal these things to us? Recall the first chapter. The sources of revelation are Sacred Scripture and Sacred Tradition. Thus, we take these as the Word of God, accepting in advance, by the virtue of faith, whatever they really assert.[383] Since, however, it can at times be difficult to discern the meaning of God's Word, Christ left His disciples the teaching authority of the Church. When the Church clarifies infallibly that X is contained in the deposit of faith, Catholics are bound to give the assent of divine faith to that teaching.

In short, true religion comes as a "package," with God as its Author. We are called to accept God's word whole and entire. True religion is not like a "cafeteria line" from which we order à la carte. Catholics understand that Jesus Christ has instituted a religion and a society; so Catholic discipleship has a necessary relation to the Catholic Church. The holistic examination indicates that Christ founded only one religion and only one Church. Only this religion is the true one. Judaism was the divinely appointed religion to prepare the way for the Christian religion. It was thus the true religion then; the time for anticipating the Messiah, however, has past. The various branches of Christianity retain various divinely appointed elements of the true religion, even its eucharistic heart. Their practice of this religion is blemished, however, in this or that respect. All other religions, those without a divine foundation, are false, even if they have numerous elements of truth in them. As we see, this holistic perspective involves an absolute claim of paramount importance.

When combined, these two perspectives will help us navigate through the difficult waters of confusion, so harmful to souls and wounding to psychic and social health. We will begin with the sources of confusion. In each case, we will summarily indicate a correction. Then in the next section, we will offer the remedy, the healing balm of the infallible teaching of the Church: the Catholic religion is the one true religion.

---

[382] DH 3904.
[383] See *Dei verbum*, art. 10; DH 4213.

False Mercy

False Claim: There Is Not One True Religion

There are several occasions of confusion on this topic.

1. Once again, one occasion is rooted in the goodwill that Catholics bear toward non-Christians. If this goodwill is coupled with the zeal of charity and faith, it grounds friendships that can convince others of the one true religion. But Catholics who do not prioritize their faith and charity are embarrassed by echoes of the claim to be part of the "one true religion." Again, it seems to them to be an arrogant claim. (Of course, it would be arrogant if it were not true. But, if it is true, it is a *gift* of God, not something Catholics have created and can take credit for.) They ask themselves, "How could my friend or co-worker, who is so considerate and generous, be part of a 'false' religion?"

It is important not to underestimate this sentiment. It affects many people, especially contemporary Americans, for whom niceness or politeness is a paramount virtue. It is an error to treat niceness as supreme. Still, there is a good at stake with this trait. The classical virtue here is amiability or friendliness. Thomas Aquinas, following Aristotle, praises this virtue.[384] It is part of the natural law that we recognize the importance of being amiable; that is, we must not be arrogant and rude, disregarding "the rest of men" as so many lost heathen (see Luke 18:11).

Why is amiability a virtue? It is *part* of a good relationship toward neighbor; it is a necessary feature of a life of charity. If we were simply cranky, we would never develop friendships; prudence would direct non-Christians to avoid contact with us. Thus, their human prudence would keep them from means of salvation—and the fault would be ours. Being proud and dismissive is no way to lead people to Christ. But treating others with dignity and respect, especially when such respect is founded on true charity, can help open them up to the higher goods toward which we would like to point them. Recall Jesus with the woman at the well.

So, amiability is indeed part of a good relationship, but it is not all. Charity is the ultimate virtue because it is the supernatural love whereby

---

[384] Thomas Aquinas, *Commentary on the Ethics*, bk. IV, lect. 14.

we love God above all things as an intimate Beatific Friend. Consequently, we love our neighbor as ourselves. Now, in love we will good to the one whom we love. What is the ultimate good we will for ourselves? The society of beatific friendship with God. So, the ultimate good we should will for our neighbor is also the society of beatific friendship with God. Amiability is ordered to this higher good.

Amiability is good, but when we make niceness the ultimate virtue, the high good of charity is eclipsed from our minds. We just want to get along. Claims about a "true religion" become embarrassing and, we mistakenly think, harmfully divisive. Today, amiability divorced from truth reigns. That is, politeness reigns.[385] Catholics are often embarrassed to share their Faith, to stick out. They are easily worried that sharing their Faith in all its depth, contour, and rigor will make them seem "holier than thou" to their peers. It may make them seem judgmental and indifferent to the plight of someone living a sinful lifestyle. Of these Catholics, some *rightly* want to accompany their sinful friend toward the good way. Still, they find it difficult to carry this out in practice. In conversations, they consistently steer clear of tough doctrines. As a result, they muffle the clarion message of Christ: "Repent, for the kingdom of God is at hand!" (see Matt. 3:2). These Catholics are also motivated by the recognition that they, too, are sinners and often make mistakes. Furthermore, they do not want to seem to take credit for more than they can achieve. The Catholic Faith is something they greatly esteem. It is so tremendous that they can at times find themselves embarrassed by its grandeur when in the company of others. Why? Perhaps they conflate its objective grandeur with *their* participation in the religion. They mistakenly think that if they claim the Catholic religion is the only true religion, then they are being like Pelagians who brag about their own accomplishments and talents. They correctly recognize that, apart from Christ, they have nothing to offer and that bragging about oneself is sinful and erroneous. Sadly, the foregoing ingredients—mistaken goodwill, embarrassment, false worry about ownership of the truth, and so forth—mix together and form

---

[385] Look into the first commandment of MTD, moralistic therapeutic deism.

the harmful poison of relativism. But relativism and truth are opposed. We must wed goodwill to truth.

2. A second occasion of the current confusion is the recent practice of avoiding the holistic approach to this question. There has been a notable silence. To the best of my knowledge, for the past sixty years, there have been only a couple of magisterial pronouncements on the Catholic religion as the one true religion.[386] If I am mistaken on this point, I am happy to be corrected; I believe that any exceptions will only prove the recent rule. Suffice it to say: we do not hear the teaching all that often. Unsurprisingly, the recent silence correlates with an eclipse of this truth from many a Catholic mind. This truth has been forgotten. Consequently, we now witness wholesale abandonment of the holistic approach to the diversity of religions. We no longer ask the crucial question: What religion is the true religion appointed by God for the salvation of the world? We no longer think of all other religions as *false*.

3. The Magisterium has recently stressed the positive in non-Christian religions, approaching the question from the itemized viewpoint, highlighting the several features that go to make up religion. So the Magisterium speaks of the Catholic Faith as having the "fullness of truth" and of other religions as having various "shares" in that fullness. The Second Vatican Council teaches:

> The Catholic Church rejects nothing that is true and holy in these religions. She regards with sincere reverence those ways of conduct and of life, those precepts and teachings that, though differing in many aspects from the ones she holds and sets forth, nonetheless often reflect a ray of that Truth which enlightens all men. Indeed, she proclaims, and ever must proclaim, Christ "the way, the truth, and the life", in whom men may find the fullness of religious life.[387]

---

[386] See *Dignitatis humanae*, art. 1, and CDF, *Dominus Iesus*, art. 23. Once again, note that the Denzinger edition edited by Peter Hünermann omits both passages.

[387] *Nostra aetate* (1965), art. 2; DH 4196.

The first and last sentences are salient: (1) there are elements of truth in these other religions and (2) only in Christ is the fullness of truth found. These claims are true. We saw a similar approach with the question of the Church of Christ last chapter. Just as the Catholic Church and non-Catholic Christian communities are said to enjoy, respectively, the "fullness of the truth" and various "participations" in it, so only the Catholic Church practices the fullness of true religion, whereas non-Christian religions enjoy "participations" in features of that religion. John Paul II took up this approach in interreligious dialogue.[388]

The council also reports the claims of various religions, attempting to do so without a negative judgment, in the spirit of friendly conversation. For example, it claims that "Buddhism ... teaches a way by which men, in a devout and confident spirit, may be able either to acquire the state of perfect liberation or to attain, by their own efforts or through higher help, supreme illumination."[389] No Christian in his right mind would ever claim to achieve supreme illumination while on Earth, much less by his own efforts. Were he to do so, he would be at once guilty of pride and Pelagianism. So we cannot read this quote as a simple assertion of the truth of the claim; it appears rather to be a report about the Hindu claim. If we read the passage as a report about what Buddhists claim, we avoid the just noted problems. Of course, the Church's magisterial competence extends to the deposit of faith, not to Buddhist doctrines; so we would do well also to consult competent experts on Buddhism.

Another example is the council's treatment of Muslims: "They adore the one God, living and subsisting in himself; merciful and all-powerful, the Creator of heaven and earth, who has spoken to men; they take pains to submit wholeheartedly to even his inscrutable decrees, just as Abraham, with whom the faith of Islam takes pleasure in linking itself, submitted to God."[390] To be sure, Muslims profess to adore the Creator who has spoken

---

[388] See John Paul II, *Redemptoris missio* (1990), arts. 55f. See also *Nostra aetate*, art. 2; DH 4196.

[389] *Nostra aetate*, art. 2; DH 4196.

[390] *Nostra aetate*, art. 3; DH 4197.

to men. (This statement is simply descriptive, not evaluative.) It is a difficult question to determine whether they worship the same God that we Christians worship. We proclaim that God is three Persons; they proclaim that God is not three Persons. Because of this contradiction, some hold that we do not at all worship the same God. The actual matter is subtler.

Muslims can describe the God whom they worship as the Creator who is one and personal. Now, we worship the Creator God who is one and personal. In this respect, the target of our worship is the same as that of theirs. Similarly, the God of Abraham revealed Himself as one and personal to Abraham and Moses. We Christians still accept that revelation. Further, as Pius XII taught, human reason can demonstrate the existence of God, one and personal.[391] But the object of such a demonstration would not be some *other* God. Right reason can affirm only some aspects of God; genuine revelation does not deny these aspects but simply adds more. Concretely speaking, of course, reason often goes astray and adds false aspects. So, concretely speaking, revelation has to correct these errors. Furthermore, the rejection of the Trinity by Muslims and Jews is entirely false. Whereas right reason does not know that God is triune, it cannot know that He is not triune. Whereas the Old Testament does not know that God is triune, it cannot and does not teach that He is not triune. Catholics can in no way accept the Jewish and Islamic rejection of their Faith.

Notwithstanding the above, it is possible to divide the Islamic and Jewish claim about God into two parts, the true and the erroneous.[392] The erroneous part should be clear enough from the above. The true part would be the simple affirmations that a Creator exists, that He is one God, and that He is personal, living, and so on. As we can see from the above citation, Vatican II highlights this true part. By way of this division, we indicate a path for dialogue on this particular issue. We must also avoid the implicit tritheism of recent Catholic thinkers who so stress the distinction

---

[391] See DH 3892.

[392] For a closer study, see Christopher J. Malloy, "The 'I-Thou' Argument for the Trinity: Wherefore Art Thou?" *Nova et Vetera* 15 (2017): 113–159.

of persons that they divide God into three beings. Hans Urs von Balthasar comes to mind. Such implicit tritheism must horrify Muslims who want to be true to the rational inference that God is Pure Act, simple and perfect.

In summary, we see that Vatican II reports the claims of key religions of world history and highlights some truths of their claims. Catholic readers must exercise care in reading these documents in the context of Catholic tradition, keeping the truths of the Catholic Faith as a matter of paramount importance. We also see that Vatican II takes the itemized approach. This new mode of expression has merit. It helps us appreciate reality. It is well suited to begin a difficult conversation. It does not, however, offer a complete picture; it cannot finish the conversation. (Much less should we take it as the first stage of the demolition of the past!) The holistic approach has been left in silence. We must remember not to fall into forgetfulness of truth, forgetfulness of doctrine. For instance, in discussing what Catholics and Muslims have in common, we must not neglect the holistic approach as well. We must ask whether a prophet is true or not. Christian faith is categorical: Jesus was the final true Prophet, and He was divine as well. All men after Christ who claim to bear a public revelation are false prophets.

4. Some have abused a well-intentioned but misleading gesture of John Paul II so as to defend their errors. In 1986, Pope John Paul II, wanting to affirm the religious impulse in the human heart, invited leaders of the various world religions to pray in Assisi. The event was called Meeting of Prayer for Peace. Reportedly, during the period of the event, pagan statues were brought into several Catholic churches to be worshipped. A statue of a Buddha was even placed above a tabernacle.[393] Also, reportedly, sacrileges were committed upon holy altars. Some who witnessed this event, whether firsthand or through media reports, were confused. They seemed to ask themselves, "Are we now supposed to celebrate non-Christian religions? Does God will a diversity of religions?"

---

[393] That is, the worship connected with such statues was offered. Not all idolatry needs to be understood as the crass worship of the physical symbol. Nonetheless, idolatry it remains, since it is worship given to false gods.

False Mercy

Since nothing happens without God somehow willing it, we must say that God somehow wills a diversity of religions. But theologians distinguish between what God *positively* wills and what He permits. God permits evil to exist, but He does not will it to exist as a thing desirable in itself (i.e., as a good). Rather, He permits evil to exist for the sake of the good that He can draw into the universe because of it. God positively wills what is desirable in itself (i.e., what is simply good). For example, health is desirable in itself; so God wills His creatures to be healthy. It may be, however, that a sinner stricken by physical illness abandons a sinful lifestyle and embarks on the road of virtue. So God can permit the illness for the sake of virtue. Similarly, God can permit an act of persecution for the sake of the good of holy martyrdom, by which His mercy and power shine forth and convert hardened hearts. God wills the holy zeal of martyrdom and permits the evil of murder. Similarly, error is an evil in the intellect. Error is not desirable in itself. Still, God permits error because of the good that He can draw from it. For example, from the errors of heresy, God can draw forth the great good of genuine dogmatic development. Thus, God wills the good of dogmatic development and permits the evil of heresy.

Now, false religions have errors in them, and God does not will error. Moreover, God did not appoint the founders of or institute the claims and practices of these religions. So God does not positively will the existence of false religions. Rather, He allows them to exist so as to bring good into the universe because of them. On the one hand, he allows them because of their positive elements, which we have noted. These aspects of those religions can help awaken a desire for God within the human breast. That very desire can lead to a search for truth, for the true religion. But why allow the negative? Perhaps the question needs to be reframed. Above all, let us remember original sin. The human race fell in Adam. Since then God has been rescuing men for Himself. But His plan has included groups, not just individuals. So, in founding His religion, God has been working to *rescue* the human race from that Fall. Meanwhile, men have invented their own religions according to their own lights, the remnants of true religion, and superstitions, and so forth. Practitioners of false religions, when they hear the truth spoken with power, can repent and leave behind old ways, heroically following God over their own families. The very same dynamism is at work when God calls a Christian to a way of life that confronts the worldliness of his age: fellow Christians often resist and persecute God's chosen one. The heroism of victory over worldliness and false religions is another good that God can bring out of human sinfulness and false religions. Some practitioners of false religions may even bring about the glory of martyrs. God allows persecution to glorify His holy ones (Ps. 116), not in a triumphalistic way but in a way that reveals the depths of divine love and forgiveness, even for persecutors. Hence, the centurion was moved to pity and conversion at the sight of the Jesus whom he crucified (Matt. 27:54).

Why didn't God just make us all confirmed in holiness to begin with? We do not know. We cannot fathom God's will. Still, we can observe, with Augustine, that we often take for granted things that come easy. We often greatly esteem treasures that cost us dearly. Perhaps God allowed us to fall in our negligence so that He could inculcate sincere gratitude and devout discipline in us.

We must return to the question at hand. Does God positively will false religions? The question requires the holistic approach. The religion that God wills is a united whole, a package deal. God reveals the truths central to the religion, institutes the proper actions, and appoints the proper authorities. One either accepts this religion in its entirety, or one does not. Some theologians abuse the Assisi event as justification for holding the false opinion that God positively wills a diversity of religions. For his part, Pope John Paul II explained to the Roman Curia that the event was by no means intended to inculcate such relativism. He rejected the idea that God positively wills a diversity of religions.[394] At least this address was clear.

5. Some theologians may hope to use remarks of Pope Francis as reason to hold that God positively wills the diversity of religions. In 2019, Pope Francis and Imam Ahmad Al-Tayyeb jointly issued A Document on Human Fraternity for World Peace and Living Together. Therein, they state, "The pluralism and the diversity of religions, colour, sex, race and

---

[394] See John Paul II, speech to the Roman Curia, December 22, 1986.

language are willed by God in His wisdom, through which He created human beings."[395] How should we respond? This is not a magisterial document identifying and interpreting the deposit of faith. Catholics must take as their supernatural authority magisterial documents that identify and interpret the deposit of faith.

As for its contents, the passage cited lists various categories of diversity. Now, the varieties of color, language, and race, and the distinction of sex into male and female — the only legitimate categories of sexuality — are desirable in themselves; they are simply good. The multiplicity of these goods enriches the world. Hence, these varieties and distinctions are *positively* willed by God. Now, the list includes one more item, namely, "diversity of religions." As astute readers have noted, since "diversity of religions" is included within a list of things that are simply good, a reader can naturally take the document to present religious diversity as also willed by God *positively*, as something desirable in itself or simply good. The Catholic truth, however, is that religious diversity involves error, which is an evil that God allows or permits. Thus, we need to distinguish error from truth. A pastoral sensibility, leading people to the truth that liberates, calls for a clear distinction. God does not positively will error, and God has appointed only one true religion.

6. We must never underestimate the influence of Karl Rahner, S.J., whose theory of religion can embolden one to embrace the notion that God positively wills "false" religions.[396] Recall that, for Rahner, God's grace is ubiquitous, already transcendentally present at the heart of all human subjectivity. Through this grace, God becomes present. For Rahner, God's presence is not like that of *an object* among other objects that we see out there. His presence is more like the very power of eyesight itself; since it is nestled in the power of eyesight itself, you see other things but not God's presence. Now, the constancy of this presence raised questions:

[395] Pope Francis and Imam Ahmad Al-Tayyeb, "A Document on Human Fraternity for World Peace and Living Together." The Italian and French would seem to read, "are the one wise divine will." The German reads, "correspond to the wise, divine will."

[396] On this, see my essay "The Withering."

if God is part of our very subjectivity, how can we ever sin? To be sure, Rahner often qualified this presence as being "in the mode of offer," so as not to deny absolutely the possibility of committing mortal sin. (Indeed, we could critique his moral theory of the so-called fundamental option on another occasion; it makes mortal sin a rare possibility.) Still, Rahner claimed that this transcendental presence of God through His grace, at least as offer, is engaged in each and every concrete act regarding concrete objects. When I take a drink or discuss something or make a decision, this transcendental presence of God through His grace is engaged. So concrete objects have a role to play. None of them is God, but I respond to God—to His grace of self-gift—only by way of my thoughts and actions regarding concrete objects. Any such objects, Rahner held, can mediate God to man, because God, as the silent horizon, "is present as such in every assertion, in all knowledge, and in every action."[397]

We can see why, in light of this theory, Rahner by no means stressed the necessity of the Church for salvation. The grace is already there. The Church and missionaries do not bring God's grace and presence to the people. They announce its presence.

But the narrative plot here is thick. Rahner added that this ever-present grace instills a drive toward *thematic* expression in every person and culture. That is, the human race makes progress in history trying to express this grace better and better: this culture and that culture develop objects and words that try to capture the *religious* nature of human thought and action. In short, the human race develops religious languages and actions. These words and actions are "thematically" religious, even though *any* concrete object—however secular—can and does serve as vehicle of engagement of grace for man. Some religious objects and claims are thematically correct, and some are thematically incorrect. To be sure, Rahner claimed that only Christianity has thematic expressions that are simply correct. Still, he held that any concrete object can serve as an object of engagement for grace. Unsurprisingly, he concluded, "It is absolutely possible to conceive of a religion before Christianity even apart from the Old Covenant—a

[397] Rahner, *Foundations*, 77.

religion quite legitimate in the eyes of the saving providence of God, i.e., positively willed by providence even though it might inseparably contain certain elements not willed by God."[398]

We must explore this matter a bit more. One of Rahner's perpetual struggles was squaring his theory with *any* major world religion that claims to be the true religion uniquely appointed by God. Every such religion "declares phenomena existing within our experience as definite and exclusive objectifications and manifestations of God"; other religions are therefore false. Recall Elijah threatening the false prophets of Baal (1 Kings 18:21). But Rahner remained distressed that any such notion of religion "seems incompatible with [my] transcendental starting point."[399] Given Rahner's basic analysis of man as an always-transcending subject, it is "not clear why and to what extent this kind of mediation should belong to one particular categorical existent rather than to another."[400] Why this religion versus that religion? Rahner struggled with this question.

Rahner suggested that the connatural trajectory of man's natural inclination to transcendence — perhaps even when under the influence of grace — is to express itself in "devotion to the world." Rahner even surmised that "one person would worship nature as divine."[401] (So much for Aristotle and Plato and Thecla and Plotinus rising above the religions of their day to an awe for the God above all!) Thankfully, Rahner did not leave the matter here, but neither does he satisfy pious Catholic ears.

Rahner always rightly insisted on the infinity of God. He rightly noted that no finite object can be infinite. But he then worried that all expressions of truth and all actions, being finite, fail to put us in touch with God as a real object or interlocutor, as a real "Thou," we might say. Why? Because, being finite, they fall infinitely short of God. Now, Rahner was making a crucial point: God is infinite. Thus, He cannot be

---

[398] Karl Rahner, "History of the World and Salvation-History," in *Theological Investigations*, vol. 5, trans. Karl-H. Kruger (New York: Seabury Press, 1966), 106..

[399] Rahner, *Foundations*, 82.

[400] Ibid., 84.

[401] Ibid., 85.

contained by a building or a tabernacle. Whatever we *picture* God to be, we must know that God transcends the picture. Hence, Jesus told Mary Magdalene not to grab hold of Him (John 20:17). Here, we see Rahner's connection with the mystical tradition of the Church. Lamentably, this connection melted under the steel glare of Rahner's modernism. He neglected the concrete, the historical, the tangible, the incarnational.

Against Rahner's modernism, we cannot forget that God became man! Thus, "He who sees me sees him who sent me" (John 12:45). And the disciples saw and touched the Eternal Life (1 John 1:1–4). Further, God Himself directly addressed Moses (Exod. 3:3–6). And the psalmist sought God's face (Ps. 27:8). Likewise, Catholics have thought the sacred actions of Christ's Church were instituted by Christ so as to be the very ways in which they can encounter God. They have thought that God *comes* to them through or on account of these sacraments. They have thought that grace is *newly* communicated to those who receive and participate in the sacraments, so that they receive an abundance of grace that they would not otherwise have received.[402] Yes, God is there among the pagans, offering grace. But they struggle in darkness and despair; they yearn for the breath of the Spirit, like swimmers gasping for air while struggling in turbulent waters. Catholics have thought that missionary preaching enlightens the minds of those who were once in darkness. They have thought missionaries bring their hearers into God's presence in a unique way, by offering them truth claims crucial to salvation and a right way of life and by offering them the substantial presence of the Word made flesh, sacrificed for their salvation. Rahner implied that none of these concrete and categorical *Catholic* objects and words really do what Catholics have always thought they do. For Rahner, "There can be a 'presence' of God ... only insofar as the representation of this presence of God (in human word, in sacrament, in a church, in a revelation, in a scripture, and so on) can essentially be nothing other than something

---

[402] Even those in prison long for the sacraments, and their desire for the sacraments is not incidental to their receiving grace despite the lack of the availability of the sacraments.

categorical which points to the transcendental presence of God."[403] Isn't that what, according to Rahner, any object, religious or secular, can also do? Recall that, for Rahner, God's grace is already ubiquitously present. The sacraments do not bring about the presence of grace, do not newly communicate grace, do not put us in touch with God as with someone whom we encounter. Rather, they are simply the self-expressions of the grace that we already have. Similarly, the Church is simply the historical manifestation of the fact that the human race is the People of God.

To all this, we must ask, is that it? Is that all a missionary brings to the table? When Christians say that the Eucharist is the Real Presence of the God-Man, are they really saying that the Eucharist only points them away from itself and toward their inner transcendental experience? When they claim that they would renounce bodily life and self for the sake of the Holy Sacrament, are they failing to get the real meaning of the sacraments as simply signs of the grace within? Worse, when truly pious Catholics bow down before the Eucharist, are they bowing down merely before a categorical object, as though in idolatry? Nonsense!

Unsurprisingly, we might add, Rahner's low estimation of what Christianity offers the world was echoed in his deprecation of Judaism: "It is not the concrete content of this history before Christ in the old covenant which makes it the history of revelation, for nothing really happens in the realm of the categorical which does not also happen in the history of every other people."[404] If neither Christianity nor Judaism is all that special, it is also no surprise that Rahner celebrated the anthropocentrism in the theology of his day: "The tendency today to talk not about God, but about one's neighbor, to preach not about the love of God, but about the love of neighbor, and to use not the term 'God,' but 'world' and 'responsibility for the world' … has an absolutely solid foundation."[405]

7. There is a certain excessive focus on man of late. As we have just seen, Rahner approved of such anthropomorphism. He conflated the

---

[403] Rahner, *Foundations*, 85.
[404] Ibid., 167.
[405] Ibid., 64.

psalmist's search for the face of God with the injunction that we are to accept ourselves radically.[406] To be sure, he was not calling for worship of man, but his theology stressed man to the point of obsession and thus obscured the quest for God. Other factors contribute to an insufficient focus on God. There is the commonplace liturgical practice, in much of today's Roman Rite, of the people and the priest facing each other, rather than both facing God, as they do in the *ad orientem* practice. Joseph Ratzinger was emphatic that the *ad orientem* practice should be reinstituted for the eucharistic prayers. In the current practice, with the focus on the priest, "less and less is God in the center."[407]

Some recent magisterial documents also focus on the human. In itself this can be a good way to highlight God's marvelous works and to communicate with contemporaries. Perhaps such a stress was even lacking before. By now, however, balance and precision are needed, even if this may seem tedious. A crucial passage of Vatican II did not distinguish the second commandment from the first. Our Lord distinguishes these: the love of God is "the great and first commandment" (Matt. 22:38). The Vulgate describes it as the "greatest [*maximum*] and the first." Jesus describes the love of neighbor as *like* the first and *second* to it (Matt. 22:39). *Gaudium et Spes*, however, left the two commandments undistinguished: "Love for God and neighbor is the first and greatest commandment."[408] Of course this is not a disavowal of our Lord's doctrine. We may read the statement as synecdoche, whereby the part stands for the whole. The phrase "first and greatest" would mean "the two greatest" and thus refer to both commandments. There is precedent for this. Paul spoke this way, describing love of neighbor as fulfillment of the "whole law" (Gal. 5:14). More recently, Pope Francis in *Evangelii Gaudium* identified "the first and the greatest of

---

[406] See Karl Rahner, "On the Theology of the Incarnation," *Theological Investigations* 4:108, 119; *Theological Investigations* 14:290; and *Foundations*, 228 and 401.

[407] Joseph Ratzinger, *The Spirit of the Liturgy*, 2nd ed., trans. John Saward (San Francisco: Ignatius Press, 2014), 80. See all of chapter 3 of this work.

[408] *Gaudium et spes*, art. 24, DH 4324.

the commandments" with love of neighbor.[409] Of course, we can decide to read this statement as regarding the second table: of all the commandments regarding our neighbor, love is the first and the greatest. Moreover, unless we love our neighbor, we do not also love God. So we can know that we fail to love God when we fail to love neighbor. Nonetheless, the fact is that the love of God ranks supreme and is not identical with love of neighbor. Our love of our fellow man is nothing unless it is rooted in the love of God. It is high time we imitate our Lord's own words precisely. It is high time we focus on God. As Leo XIII said, "The world has heard enough of the so-called 'rights of man.' Let it hear something of the rights of God."[410]

Now, if (as Rahner said) nature worship is only "thematically" erroneous, while nonetheless effective as a mediation of grace, and if (as Rahner implied) no historical religion can really do what pious Catholics think Catholicism does, and if we should focus on the love of neighbor more than on the love of God, would it not make sense for those who embrace Rahner's theology to welcome, court, and even revere a false religion that worships false gods?

8. More recently, in October 2019, a group of pagans was invited to worship their earth-goddess idol, Pachamama, within the sacred halls of Catholic churches. It was almost as though Karl Rahner's notion of revelation and religion came to concrete expression.[411] A heroic man valiantly hurled several of the Pachamama idols into the Tiber River, evoking memories at once of St. Benedict and St. Boniface. Alas, the idols were (allegedly) retrieved. Afterward, they were brought into St. Peter's Basilica to be worshipped *yet again*. The event made it seem as though we should repent, not of the sin of idolatry, but of the righteous act by which the idols were cast away. The worship of the idols was a grave abomination. Many of the faithful had a deep sadness that Christ had been betrayed. Some of the faithful feared that they had witnessed

---

[409] Francis, *Evangelii gaudium* (2013), art. 160.

[410] Leo XIII, *Tametsi futura prospicientibus* (1900), art. 13.

[411] In a twist of irony, the Pachamama fiasco becomes the "real symbol" of Rahner's errant theology.

a partial fulfillment of the prophetic words of Christ: "When you see the desolating sacrilege spoken of by the prophet Daniel, standing in the holy place …" (Matt. 24:15). As we know from Scripture, apostasy and idolatry deserve punishment. The Scriptures prophesy that punishment follows grave acts that contravene the first commandment.

Furthermore, the Fathers of the Church tell us that the antichrist will be permitted by God to punish us for sins against the Faith and practice of our religion. John Henry Newman wrote an essay in four parts concerning the patristic idea of the antichrist. As he noted, following Paul, a rebellion or apostasy must come first, before the antichrist, the "man of lawlessness" (2 Thess. 2:3), is revealed. Today, some are skeptical of the idea of an antichrist. They think of the antichrist either as a remote figure of the past, such as Nero, or as some tyrant to come only in the remote future. They don't think that the Scriptures concerning him can be relevant at all times, even now. Newman offered us a better perspective. He had a subtler reading of the text. He showed that Paul's letter—in conjunction with passages from Daniel 7 and 11, 1 John, and Revelation 12 and 13—describes in outline the vague features of a terrifying figure. He reminded us that the fulfillment of prophecy is what guides its best interpretation. He suggested that the "type" of the antichrist has been partially realized in various ways throughout history. Each actual but partial fulfillment helps us read the prophecy more accurately. By these partial fulfillments, we get a more and more detailed description—of course, still a general one—of the man of sin yet to come.

For Newman, Antiochus IV was the first partial fulfillment. He outlawed the Jewish religion and desecrated the Temple. According to Newman, this persecution followed the religious negligence of the people of God (1 Macc. 1:11–15) as a just punishment. Julian the Apostate was another figure by whom God punished the Church for the heresy of Arianism, into which both lay and hierarchical members had fallen. According to Newman, a "false prophet" and "impostor"[412] from Arabia

---

[412] Newman, "The Patristical Idea of Antichrist: I. The Times of Antichrist," in *Discussions and Arguments*, 55, 58.

assembled a new and heretical creed from the Christological heresies from the fifth through the sixth centuries.

Newman's reading of Scripture helps us to be ready at all times for the coming of the antichrist. For his part, Newman was worried that the liberalism in his day — e.g., the divorce of man from God, the creation of secular education divorced from religion, and the divorce of the civil authority from religion — forebode the coming of the antichrist. But the liberalism of Newman's day pales in comparison to the godlessness of ours, which exchanges the truth of God for a lie and wars against nature herself (Rom. 1), invoking the wrath of Heaven.

If Newman was right, diverse antichrists follow in the train of diverse apostasies. Given the recent abominations, should we be surprised if a chastisement is or has been sent among us, to call us back to our heavenly Faith?[413] Or should we cower in fear, attributing disease and calamities to the false goddess Mother Earth? In coming back to our senses, we should recall that our heavenly Faith has, at its center, the deepest conviction that the religion Christ left His Church is the only true religion.

The Catholic Religion Is the Only True Religion

Jesus handed on to the Church the religion of the New Covenant. He instructed us on the ways to worship God and to receive His grace. Jesus established the new and definitive covenant in His blood, the eucharistic sacrifice, which is the center of the religion He gave us. The Catholic Church guards the religion that Christ entrusted to her. This religion is the only one appointed by God. Hence, it is the only true one.

Scripture teaches us that the religion Christ instituted is the New and everlasting Covenant. Christ fulfilled the Old Law (Matt. 5:17–18). This means that the things of the Old Law are now found in the New Law and in the mode of the New Law. Consequently, those things that had their place *only* as preparatory have no place in the New Law. They

---

[413] On reading these prophecies, consult Newman, "The Patristical Idea of Antichrist."

are abrogated. Those things that were not simply preparatory can carry over. The Ten Commandments are not preparatory, even though they may be augmented, but the ceremonies were preparatory. So the Ten Commandments carry over into the New Law, but the ceremonies do not. As the Letter to the Hebrews states, "In speaking of a new covenant [God] treats the first as obsolete" (Heb. 8:13). As we know, Jesus gave us this New Covenant the night before He died (Luke 22:19–20). Now, the Magisterium teaches that the Catholic religion is the one true religion in two ways, directly and indirectly. We will consider the latter first.

Indirect Approach

The claim that the Catholic Church is or practices the "one true religion" follows from the dogma that the Catholic Church is the one true Church of Christ. Jesus did not institute His Church simply to be a storage house for the deposit of faith. He instituted His Church to live and to promulgate a way of life, one that culminates in duly appointed worship of God. Nor did He enjoin just any form of worship. Rather, He commanded us to perpetuate His New and Eternal Covenant, the eucharistic worship. Since the Redeemer accomplished His mission, this is the one form of worship that God positively wills. It is the one true religion. All religions devoid of the divine appointment are false. Ancient Judaism was a preparation for the true religion, and various forms of Christian worship approximate the true religion according to the divinely appointed relics of it that they retain. This true religion alone leads to eternal salvation. Hence, the Church declares, "She firmly believes, professes, and preaches that 'none of those who are outside of the Catholic Church, not only pagans,' but also Jews, heretics, and schismatics, can become sharers of eternal life."[414]

Since God does not positively will error and evil, He merely permits false religions to exist. A civil authority ordered in an ideal way can imitate God's patience and permit certain evils, including false religions, provided the common good warrants it. Accordingly, Pope Leo XIII teaches, "God Himself in His providence, though infinitely good and

---

[414] DH 1351.

powerful, permits evil to exist in the world, partly that greater good may not be impeded, and partly that greater evil may not ensue."[415] Furthermore, this eucharistic worship is an act, the primary act, of Christ's Church. Only within this Church, in the unity with which He established her, is eucharistic worship undertaken *as* our Lord commands. The Eucharist is validly but not perfectly practiced without the bishop, and the bishop has no jurisdiction without communion with the Roman see. Bishops that are in communion with Rome are Catholic bishops serving the Catholic religion. So, the one true religion is rightly called the Catholic religion.

Direct Approach

The direct approach can be expounded in two ways. The Church's teachings concerning Judaism imply this truth, and the Church explicitly teaches this truth.

First, in her teachings concerning Judaism, the Church directly implies that she alone practices the one true religion. The Church infallibly teaches that ancient Judaism has been fulfilled in the Catholic religion and is therefore, in its state *as* independent from the Catholic Church, no longer appointed by God. Now, it is a matter of the constant Christian tradition that ancient Judaism is the one existing religion, besides the Christian one, that has been divinely appointed. Other existing religions indeed have elements of truth in them, but none has ever been appointed by God. As stated above, these true elements may be grounded in both nature and the original revelation given to Adam and passed on through Noah. These seeds prepare for the Gospel. In their current state in the various world religions, however, these remnants of truth are disfigured in various ways. None of the world religions except ancient Judaism and Christianity was ever appointed by God. Ancient Judaism was appointed by God during the time of the Old Covenant. That covenant has been fulfilled in the New Covenant and thus continues to have validity only in its fulfilled state. It no longer has validity in the state of nonfulfillment.

---

[415] Leo XIII, *Libertas* (1888), art. 33.

Since Judaism has been fulfilled in Catholicism, there is now only one divine religion: the Catholic religion.

Where is it taught that ancient Judaism is fulfilled in the Catholic religion? Hebrews declares, "In speaking of a new covenant he treats the first as obsolete. And what is becoming obsolete and growing old is ready to vanish away" (Heb. 8:13). Of course, God's covenantal commitment to the Jewish people remains throughout history, for the gifts of God are without repentance (Rom. 11:29). Now that the fullness of time has come, however, everything anticipatory in the Old Covenant gives way to its fulfillment in the New Covenant. The ceremonies must be set aside (Col. 2:14–17; Eph. 2:11–16), while the law is amplified (Matt. 5:17–48).

There was a brief period in which the early Christians continued to practice some of the Hebrew ceremonies, but this was a period of transition and dispensation. Gradually, the apostles were instructed in ways that showed the end of old ways (Acts 10:13; Gal. 6:12–15). The destruction of the Temple in AD 70 marked a dramatic end Christian converts from Judaism practicing the old religion. Thenceforth, those who clung to Jewish practices exhibited lack of faith in Christ.

In the eighth century, the Second Council of Nicaea commanded Catholic converts from Judaism to discontinue their Hebrew practices. Warning that those not willing to cease these practices should not be baptized, it adds:

> If one of them makes his conversion with a sincere faith and heart, and pronounces his confession wholeheartedly, disclosing their practices and objects in the hope that others may be refuted and corrected, such a person should be welcomed and baptized along with his children, and care should be taken that they abandon Hebrew practices. However, if they are not of this sort, they should certainly not be welcomed.[416]

---

[416] See Nicaea II, chap. 8, in Tanner, *Decrees of the Ecumenical Councils*, 145–146.

In the Council of Florence, in its Decree for the Jacobites, the Church taught that the ceremonies of the Old Law have been abrogated:

> [The Church] firmly believes, professes, and teaches that the legal prescriptions of the Old Testament or the Mosaic law, which are divided into ceremonies, holy sacrifices, and sacraments, because they were instituted to signify something in the future, although they were adequate to the divine cult of that age, once our Lord Jesus Christ who was signified by them had come, came to an end and the sacraments of the New Testament had their beginning.[417]

Florence elsewhere declared, "These rites [i.e., those of the Old Covenant] lost their efficacy with the coming of the Gospel."[418] The Copts and Ethiopians had to formally confess these teachings in order to return to union with the Catholic Church. Thus, these teachings are of high rank. In 1756, Benedict XIV taught that the Jewish rites were abrogated by Christ.[419] More recently, Pius XII reiterated this teaching:

> By the death of our Redeemer, the New Testament took the place of the Old Law which had been abolished; then the Law of Christ together with its mysteries, enactments, institutions, and sacred rites was ratified for the whole world in the blood of Jesus Christ. For, while our Divine Savior was preaching in a restricted area—He was not sent but to the sheep that were lost of the House of Israel—the Law and the Gospel were together in force; but on the gibbet of His death Jesus made void the Law with its decrees, fastened the handwriting of the Old Testament to the Cross, establishing the New Testament in His blood shed for the whole human race.[420]

These teachings simply reiterate the constant conviction of Christians that is rooted in Scripture.

---

[417] Florence, *Cantate Domino*; DH 1348.
[418] DH 1350.
[419] See Benedict XIV, *Ex quo*, art. 61.
[420] Pius XII, *Mystici corporis*, art. 29.

As we have seen, it is Catholic teaching that ancient Judaism came to an end; that is, its divine appointment as an independent religion came to an end. Judaism continues as divinely appointed only *in* its fulfilled state within the Catholic religion, which is the eucharistic religion.

As stated above, God's love for the descendants of His people remains. They remain His chosen people, and it is His plan that one day they be converted to the true Faith and accept Christ as their Savior.[421] Note also that whereas Gentile converts are grafted onto the original stock of the people of God, Jewish converts return to their roots. So the promises to them are still on offer, even though the mode of religion as an expectation of the Christ who has not yet come is no longer valid.

God's love for the Jews should inspire Catholic love for the Jews. It is true, though utterly detestable, that some Catholics have treated Jewish persons horribly over the course of centuries. Such treatment has always been foreign to Catholic teaching and foreign to the Gospel. Long ago, Pope Gregory the Great denounced Catholics who used to interrupt or outlaw Jewish ceremonies in Southern Italy. He admonished them to show gentleness and persuasion, not force and severity: "By being encouraged more by reason and gentleness, they [the Jews] are to wish to follow, not flee from, us, so that by showing them what we affirm from their Scriptures, we may be able, with God's help, to convert them to the bosom of Mother Church."[422] In short, as Pope Alexander II later put it, the zeal to convert Jews is noble, but this zeal must be ordered, prudent, and animated by charity. It is absolutely necessary to respect the freedom of choice of others when recalling them from error, just as Jesus did.[423] Alas, Pope Innocent III had to repeat these admonishments: no one may harm any Jewish person nor disturb Jewish worship.[424] In short, Catholics are called to *love* their Jewish brothers and sisters. Such love

---

[421] See Rom. 11:26 and CCC 674.

[422] DH 480.

[423] See DH 698.

[424] See DH 773. For more on this topic, see Edmund J. Mazza, *The Scholastics and the Jews: Coexistence, Conversion, and the Medieval Origins of Tolerance* (Kettering, OH: Angelico Press, 2017).

demands both a minimum of benevolent respect, understanding patience, and also magnanimity of hope. Hopeful love calls Catholics to will the conversion of their Jewish friends.

Out of these convictions, for well over a millennium, the Church on Good Friday has beseeched God for the conversion of the Jews and all pagans. St. Bernard in an epistle made reference to this prayer. Pope Benedict XIV, in his encyclical *A quo primum*, cites Bernard: "Surely it is not in vain that the Church has established the universal prayer which is offered up for the faithless Jews from the rising of the sun to its setting, that the Lord God may remove the veil from their hearts, that they may be rescued from their darkness into the light of truth."[425]

Similarly, the second stanza of Pope Pius XI's Consecration of the Human Race to the Sacred Heart expresses the Church's desire that both Jews and Muslims become Catholic:

> Be Thou King of those who are still involved in the darkness of idolatry or of Islam, refuse not to draw them all into the light and Kingdom of God. Turn Thine eyes of mercy toward the children of that race, once Thy chosen people. Of old they called down upon themselves the Blood of the Savior; May it now descend upon them a laver of redemption and of life.

This is a bold and loving prayer. From this prayer, we see that non-Christian religions are not true religions. Although many have natural religious truths and the remnants of an original revelation, and although contemporary Judaism has a rich and divinely revealed legacy, the people practicing these religions must still be called to the supernatural light of Christ. The holistic perspective is of paramount importance.

More recently, Paul VI, in his encyclical *Ecclesiam suam*, undertook a dialogue consisting of various circles of conversation according to various degrees of proximity to the Catholic Faith. He addressed all of mankind first, then all who worship one God. He affirmed the monotheism of all

---

[425] Benedict XIV, *A quo primum* (1751), Papal Encyclicals, https://www. papalencyclicals.net/ben14/b14aquo.htm.

who worship one God, including Jews and Muslims. He then confidently declared, "The Christian religion is the one and only true religion."[426] By implication, Judaism, as anticipatory of it, is no longer the true religion. Now, if Judaism — which actually had a divine appointment and real prophets — is not now the true religion, much less are Islam and any other monotheistic religion except Christianity.

The foregoing teaching clearly shows that Christianity is the fulfillment of Judaism, which, in its separated and unfulfilled state, is therefore no longer divinely appointed. But what about other Christian churches and communities? Don't they also have and practice this true religion? Clearly, they have more of the elements of the one true religion than do Jewish communities. Still, some Christian communities do not have the eucharistic sacrifice, which is the heart of our religious worship. The Eucharist is not celebrated by all Christians. Only those Christian churches with a valid priesthood celebrate the Eucharist. No Protestant community has valid priestly orders. Therefore, no Protestant community whatsoever offers the central act of the one true religion. The worship offered in Protestant communions lacks crucial elements and also includes positive errors.

What about the Orthodox? They celebrate a valid Eucharist, but they lack that interior reference to the pope in Rome by which their churches would render worship in the manner that God enjoins. They practice the one true religion *insofar* as they are Catholic. Paul VI in *Ecclesiam suam*, after encouraging true ecumenism, pointed out that the Catholic Church is the one house of God. His final circle of dialogue was, in fact, the "Catholic huddle," i.e., addressed to Catholics. He wrote, "We address Ourself finally to the sons of God's house, the one, holy, Catholic, and apostolic Church of which the Roman Church is 'mother and head.'"[427] We see here another witness to the Catholic Church being the one true Church of Christ. Now, Paul VI taught the Christian religion is the "one

---

[426] Paul VI, *Ecclesiam suam* (1964), art. 107. Note that this encyclical was released before 1965, so that it is not another exception to the rule even though it is exceptional.

[427] Ibid., art. 113.

and only true religion."[428] Paul VI thus invited us to hold that only in the Catholic Church do we find the pure practice of the one true religion.

In *Evangelii nuntiandi*, Paul VI declared, "Our religion effectively establishes with God an authentic and living relationship which the other religions do not succeed in doing, even though they have, as it were, their arms stretched out towards heaven."[429] He here does link the one true Christian religion precisely with that of the Catholic Church, which has a mission to evangelize to the ends of the earth. In summary, the holistic perspective teaches us that the one true religion is practiced only in the Catholic Church.

Second, the Church has explicitly taught that the Catholic religion is the true religion. The Fifth Lateran Council charged Thomas of Esztergom to bring back the Bohemian heretics "to the light and harmony of the true faith." He was to dialogue with them so that they would recognize their errors and "be led back, with God's guidance, to the true practice of religion and into the bosom of holy mother church."[430]

In 1791, Pius VI declared the Catholic religion to be "the one true religion which both confers eternal life and makes safe and thriving civil societies."[431] In *Mirari vos*, Gregory XVI condemned religious indifferentism, which holds that one can be saved through any religion. In this very context, he taught, citing the creed Quicumque, that unless one holds the Catholic faith whole and entire, one cannot be saved.[432] The same pope celebrated Catholic missionaries who rescued pagans from error and led them into the Catholic religion: "They search out those who sit in darkness and the shadow of death to summon them to the light and life of the Catholic Religion."[433]

---

[428] Ibid., art. 107.

[429] Paul VI, *Evangelii nuntiandi* (1975), art. 53.

[430] Fifth Lateran Council, Session VIII, December 19, 1513, in Tanner, *Decrees of the Ecumenical Councils*, 608.

[431] Pius VI, *Charitas* (1791), art. 32, Papal Encyclicals, https://www.papalencyclicals.net/pius06/p6charit.htm.

[432] See Gregory XVI, *Mirari vos*, art. 13. It is understood that he is speaking of the objective necessity of the Church and her religion for salvation.

[433] Gregory XVI, *Probe nostis* (1840), art. 6, Papal Encyclicals, https://www.papalencyclicals.net/greg16/g16probe.htm.

Pius IX formally condemned the following proposition: "The Church does not have the power of defining dogmatically that the religion of the Catholic Church is the only true religion."[434] But the Church has no power to define dogma erroneously. Therefore, the Catholic religion is the only true religion.

The First Vatican Council distinguished Catholic truth from false religions in a binary manner. It declared, "The condition of those who by the heavenly gift of faith have embraced the Catholic truth and of those who led by human opinions follow a false religion is by no means the same."[435] Accordingly, there is no middle between the Catholic religion and a false religion.

Leo XIII repeated this teaching in many places. In his treatment of naturalism, he declared: "This manner of reasoning [religious indifferentism] is calculated to bring about the ruin of all forms of religion, and especially of the Catholic religion, which, as it is the only one that is true, cannot, without great injustice, be regarded as merely equal to other religions."[436] In his treatment of citizenship, he returned to this teaching: "The enemies of the Church have for their object—and they hesitate not to proclaim it, and many among them boast of it—to destroy outright, if possible, the Catholic religion, which alone is the true religion."[437] In his treatment of ecclesiology, he wrote, "The Church alone offers to the human race that religion—that state of absolute perfection—which He wished, as it were, to be incorporated in it. And it alone supplies those means of salvation which accord with the ordinary counsels of Providence."[438]

In his treatment of Church and state in *Immortale Dei*, Leo XIII proclaimed this teaching many times. First, he referred to "the religion which God enjoins, and which certain and most clear marks show to be the only one true religion."[439] After noting the various signs of the Catholic

---

[434] DH 2921.
[435] *Dei Filius*, chap. 3; DH 3014.
[436] Leo XIII, *Humanum genus*, art. 16.
[437] Leo XIII, *Sapientiae Christianae* (1890), art. 34.
[438] Leo XIII, *Satis cognitum*, art. 9.
[439] Leo XIII, *Immortale Dei* (1885), art. 6.

religion, he commented, "From all these it is evident that the only true religion is the one established by Jesus Christ Himself, and which He committed to His Church to protect and to propagate."[440] Leo thus reminded rulers of the duty "to inquire which of the very many religions is the only one true."[441] He warned that it is "unlawful to place the various forms of divine worship on the same footing as the true religion."[442] In his treatment of freedom, he declared:

> And if it be asked which of the many conflicting religions it is necessary to adopt, reason and the natural law unhesitatingly tell us to practice that one which God enjoins, and which men can easily recognize by certain exterior notes, whereby Divine Providence has willed that it should be distinguished, because, in a matter of such moment, the most terrible loss would be the consequence of error.[443]

In each case, he is speaking about the Catholic religion. Leo repeated the claim again: "Since, then, the profession of one religion is necessary in the State, that religion must be professed which alone is true, and which can be recognized without difficulty, especially in Catholic States, because the marks of truth are, as it were, engraved upon it."[444]

Following his predecessors Pius X and Pius XI, Pope John XXIII also taught this doctrine. In his encyclical *Ad Petri cathedram*, he denounced religious relativism, declaring:

> This mistaken sort of action leads directly to that absurd proposition: one religion is just as good as another, for there is no distinction here between truth and falsehood. 'This attitude,' to quote Pope Leo again, 'is directed to the destruction of all religions, but particularly the Catholic faith, which cannot be placed on a level with other

[440] Ibid., art. 7.
[441] Ibid., art. 25.
[442] Ibid., art. 36.
[443] Leo XIII, *Libertas*, art. 20.
[444] Ibid., art. 21.

religions without serious injustice, since it alone is true.' Moreover, to contend that there is nothing to choose between contradictories and among contraries can lead only to this fatal conclusion: a reluctance to accept any religion either in theory or practice.[445]

Clearly, it is the constant teaching of the Church that the one true religion is the Catholic religion belonging to the Catholic Church. Since it is a constant teaching, it is infallible.

What about the Second Vatican Council? Since the prior teaching is infallible, the recent council did not have the authority to reject it. Nor did Vatican II reject this teaching. To the contrary, the council reaffirmed it: "We believe that this one true religion subsists in the Catholic and Apostolic Church, to which the Lord Jesus entrusted the office to spread it to all men."[446] A few observations are in order:

1. The council expresses faith in the one true religion.

2. It does so even though it tries to emphasize the positive in non-Catholic religions and to address a worldwide audience.

3. The phrase "subsists in" calls to mind the previous chapter on the Church. The phrase should *not* be taken to indicate that the true religion happens to exist in the Catholic Church but may also exist elsewhere. We have already disposed of that reading of "*subsistit in*" concerning the Catholic Church. Since we are dealing with the essence of the one true religion and not an itemized listing of its features, the same findings apply here. To repeat, the true religion is a whole; it is an integral reality; as such, it really exists *only* in its integrity and as a whole. We see once again the importance of the holistic approach, without denying the itemized approach. The true religion exists only in its integrity; it is the Catholic religion.

4. To be sure, the Second Vatican Council did not express this teaching as clearly as Pope Leo XIII did. Nor did the council explicitly teach that all

---

[445] John XXIII, *Ad Petri cathedram* (1959), art. 17. See also, in context, Pius XI, *Mortalium animos*, art. 6. Pius X rebukes the modernists for *reducing* the Catholic claim to being merely that the Catholic religion has more truth in it (*Pascendi*, art. 14).

[446] *Dignitatis humanae*, art. 1, my translation.

other religions are false. Generally, it refrained from the holistic perspective. We must nevertheless forever remember these Catholic doctrines.

5. The traditional, long-standing teaching of the Church did come to brief expression in the council: "It [the council] leaves untouched the traditional Catholic doctrine on the moral duty of men and societies with respect to the true religion and the one Church of Christ."[447] A passing phrase, but significant nonetheless. The new *Catechism* and the CDF's *Dominus Iesus* repeat this teaching.[448]

Conclusion

There are crucial consequences to this teaching. Since the Catholic religion is the one true religion, we Catholics should go out and spread this Faith as widely as possible. If God wills that every human being become Catholic and practice the Catholic religion, then we who love God and our neighbor should undertake this task with joy, confidence, humility, and respect. In short, we should evangelize. This task can begin with friendship and dialogue. We leave judgment up to God. We listen to our hearer. All the while, we never withhold the food of truth from those ready to eat.

Catholics must evangelize *precisely* to assist non-Christians toward salvation. In the evangelizing work, Catholics can follow St. Paul and see the truths and useful practices of their audience as preparation for the Gospel (Acts 17). So the missionary will both appreciate these elements of religion and also retain the divine faith that God wills the Catholic Church to be the instrument of salvation for *all* humanity.[449] But some today think that evangelization is nonsense and a sin. To that issue we now turn.

---

[447] *Dignitatis humanae*, art. 1, my translation.
[448] See CCC 2105; CDF, *Dominus Iesus*, art. 23.
[449] See CDF, *Dominus Iesus*, art. 22.

7

Is Evangelization a Sin?

Another error afflicting us today is the erroneous claim that evangelization is a sin. Some subscribe to this claim in the form of a *distaste* for evangelization. They do not support the practice of Catholic missionaries laboring to win the hearts and minds of non-Catholics for Christ. They contend that preaching one's Faith is a form of "colonization," an "imposition" of one's personal views on innocent natives who should be left alone in the utopia of human nature. Apparently, according to these critics, original sin spreads only through Christian preaching! For them, missionary activity is a form of violence, rooted in pride and selfishness. They claim that a missionary wants only to make others like himself. Of course, the use of violence or financial or social pressure to coerce others into one's religion or irreligion is unacceptable. But the distaste some Catholics have for evangelization is mistaken. The Church has a permanent missionary mandate from Jesus Christ Himself, whose command it is that we preach the Gospel to every last human being and who desires that all men willingly and joyfully enter and remain in the Church.

There are three "occasional causes" for the current confusion about evangelization. First, there are extreme positions integral to the "political correctness" movement, which forbids anyone to claim to have a truth that objectively obliges others. Second, there is a widespread discomfort with self-love and love of one's own community, be it family, neighborhood, nation, or church. Third, some want to use the words of

False Mercy

Pope Francis as an excuse to jettison the Church's missionary mandate. We will discuss each cause in turn. For each, we will present the error, diagnose it, and prescribe a remedy. Then we will present the magisterial teaching on the Church's permanent missionary mandate.

Correcting PC Distaste for Evangelization

The political correctness (PC) movement is erroneous in substance and direction. Still, it rests in part on a foundation of truth. This foundation does not belong to PC in particular; it belongs to God's creation. This foundation attracts some who are misguided but seek to have goodwill. These people accomplish some good, but they also defend and advance the PC agenda on account of the attractive features of this true foundation, which (to repeat) belongs to God and not to PC. But more importantly, major players in the PC movement wield this foundation with duplicity so as to employ in their service unwitting helpers. Thus, we must disentangle the lie from the truth. As we proceed, we will distinguish the malicious iteration of PC from the seriously misguided but quasi-benign iteration.

What is the truth that serves as partial foundation for PC? Every human person in his or her uniqueness is a gift to others. (Indeed, believers know that every person is a gift from God.) There is something to be treasured in each person. Maybe it is buried under vice or indigence, but it is there to be discovered, nourished, and cultivated. The PC movement gets its energy from this and like truths. It is a movement with a moral root. For this reason, it galvanizes much labor to its ends without cost. We underestimate PC's power if we fail to see this.

Think of the power the PC movement wields. Certainly, some of this power results from the cash of hidden or not-so-hidden agitators. Still, it would not be possible for PC so quickly to gain strong legal footholds the way it has unless there were some genuine moral claim associated with its foundations. This foundation is the dignity of the human person. The dignity of the human person is discoverable by human reason and is also a doctrine promulgated to the world through the Old and New Covenants. If human reason easily forgets this doctrine in various ways at various times and in various cultures, the Christian *fact*—the phenomenon of Christianity—ever reminds the world of this truth.

Following the dignity of the human person comes an obligation on our part. We must respect the freedom and "space" of the individual. We must allow the exercise of freedom. To be sure, different people in different situations have different responsibilities. Catholics have obligations that non-Catholics do not.[450] Adults have the use of freedom. Very young children, the severely retarded, and others do not have the use of freedom, although they do have dignity. At any rate, respect for the freedom of non-Christians should steer us clear of using obnoxious billboards and bullhorns and pressuring non-Christians to convert. Rather, we must appeal to the reason of the person with whom we are speaking. These and other truths associated with PC can be affirmed.

Notwithstanding, there are grave errors in the movement in both its forms. Among the weaknesses of the quasi-noble iteration are the following. Above all, the movement conflates the dignity of the individual with moral excellence. The movement claims—in its "noble" iteration—that the very uniqueness of the person as an individual *is* that person's moral excellence. So everything about me as an individual is considered morally "good." Let's say I have some odd tick or feature or desire: that tick or desire is itself considered morally good. Say I am born with a limp. Just because I have a limp, people should affirm the limp as good. Of course, this already goes against common sense and right reason. No one of sound judgment wants a limp. A limp puts a cramp in the ability to walk and run. Even if someone makes the best of it and becomes a better person because of it, the limp itself is a debility.

So far, we have not indicated behavioral oddities and debilities. Let us say, however, that I like cuddling with poodles for hours at a time. This is a strange, immature, and disordered behavior. But according to PC, just because I like to do this, my desire is supposed to be good. In this "noble but seriously misguided" version, the PC movement claims to celebrate "diversity" as though celebrating the richness of God's creation. (That is, it does so *if*

---

[450] See DH 3036.

the PC preacher admits that God exists. If the PC preacher does not admit that God exists, he is working from the scattered bits of Christianity that still remain in the culture.) In fact, however, the PC movement is *not* celebrating God's riches but confusing the peculiar traits of individuals, some of which are natural and some of which are disordered, with moral excellence.

This confusion is common to both the quasi-noble and the malicious forms of PC. The confusion itself constitutes an error and leads to aberrant cultural practices. The "benign" form of the error (according to the "noble" iteration of PC) leads to participation trophies. Every last kid on every last soccer team gets a trophy. If these awards are mildly tolerable for four- to six-year-olds, they are pampering and condescending for the twelve-year-olds. This and like practices waste money, tax the environment, take time and energy, and mislead children.

The truth is that some kids have capacity, and some do not; some have practiced well, while some have not; some teams win, and some do not. The participation trophy, which is taken home to be displayed, bids us to deny the obvious or to pay no attention to it. Why not just celebrate as a team with cupcakes after the season is over? At any rate, while you may think your child is being affirmed rightly through these programs, your neighbor may be trying to get his child into the elite soccer league by hiring a private coach. The participation trophy is in concert with other efforts to ignore all claims to merit based on performance. We create a dream world for children and push that world as far as we can. The bubble has got to burst at some point (application for a job, entrance requirements into college or medical school). This dream also runs contrary to a deep human desire for excellence. So even this "benign" practice is in grave error. It has a dumbing-down effect on performance in the workplace. Those of us who have had phone conversations with many an incompetent quality-control person suffer from this rotten practice. Things are falling apart. Are we surprised that some of these children, pampered and spoiled with false narratives, are now Marxist agitators, looting and burning down cities, as the unwitting slaves of hidden power brokers who control the corporate media and other institutions? We have come to the malicious form of the confusion.

The *malicious* form of PC opposes sound morals. Instead of the (odd) desire to cuddle poodles, this malicious form might highlight the perverse desire for unnatural sex acts. It says: "Just because *I* like to act in perverse ways, my desire is good. Just because *I* act in perverse ways, these ways are good." Thus, PC champions all sorts of moral turpitude, and it does so *on putatively moral grounds*. Hence, it goes to the lawmakers and demands legislation punishing "hate crimes." Whoever disagrees with the championing of moral sickness is labeled a "hater" and a "bigot." The malicious form of PC gives the *lie* to the "open-minded" moralism with which the movement began.

The lie is that the movement refuses to celebrate anyone with the *peculiar oddity* of "loving the truth." Those who love the truth are not prized and cherished.[451] Rather, they are marginalized, vilified, and "canceled." If trends continue, truth lovers will one day be put in jail or even put to death. Why are they so maltreated? Quite simply: conscience is bothering those who prop up immoral ways of living with ideology. In the end, the PC movement is not a movement of love; it is not sympathy for those who sin out of weakness. Rather, it is distaste for God and man. It thus religiously attempts to enshrine its perversions into law. The movement hates especially those who once embraced sinful lifestyles but now live in repentance. Since conscience cries out against such perversions, proponents of malicious PC are internally conflicted. Their own consciences rebuke them (Rom. 2). But they fight this internal rebuke every step of the way, attempting to banish the universal laws of truth from their hearts. Like bright lights in the eyes of those who crave darkness, those who pursue truth and even *attempt* to live righteous lives remind the perverse of the laws they are trying to efface from memory. The righteous stand in the way of the lie. Therefore, they must be taken out of the way. Think of John the Baptist: Herodias, attempting to justify her sin, wanted to be rid of him. She stopped at nothing short of murder.

---

[451] I am, of course, presuming that the Catholic Faith and its teaching on natural law are true; on another occasion, the point could be argued out. Such an argument is not the task of this work.

False Mercy

Proponents of malicious PC, imitating the wicked of old, have begun the soft persecutions. They lie in ambush on Facebook and Twitter and Instagram. Some of their number have even uttered violent thoughts. The thinking of such relativists is well expressed in Scripture: "Let us lie in wait for the righteous man, because he is inconvenient to us and opposes our actions.... Let us test him with insult and torture, that we may find out how gentle he is" (Wisd. 2:12, 19).

In virtue of its yoking perversion to a moral foundation, the malicious iteration of PC secures zealots that spread its faith far and wide. Some of these zealots are what the Marxists call "useful idiots"; they aim to espouse the "benign" form of PC, whereas they build the engines for malicious PC. Of course, there are also some bleeding hearts who are less than prudent. At any rate, those who lead the show—with political, economic, educational, and media power—are proponents of malicious PC. Hence, we must stop treating PC as a really and concretely benign theory with which merely to dialogue. We must recognize the poisonous aberration that it has become, even while holding on to our teaching concerning human dignity and the evils of racism and hatred. And, of course, we may always tap into the depths of the PC proponent, showing him that we agree with that deep longing for respect of the individual.

We must not only resist; we must replace. We must replace PC with the truth of human dignity. Human dignity is twofold. First, there is the dignity of *being* an individual human, a person; this is our ontological uniqueness. Second, there is the dignity of being a *good* human being. The latter, being a good human being, is acting virtuously; it is achievement or fruition. Similarly, we distinguish the simple existence of an orange tree from its existence in the state of producing delicious fruit. We must ever distinguish these two dignities of human persons. The first offers the *possibility* for the second, but the first does not always come with the second.

Each person is unrepeatable. This uniqueness is in itself a gift for others. We love and treasure the infant. When the individual comes to maturity, this original giftedness must correspond to the possibilities of freedom. For those who have the use of freedom, the original giftedness is not sufficient; virtue must be developed. The promise of each person must be cultivated and developed. If virtue is not developed, vice certainly will be. The child who grows up in body only to be rude and obnoxious is not good in the truest and simplest sense. Moreover, even our individual uniqueness is not given all at once; it is not "static." Rather, the uniqueness with which I am born is a promise of greatness. If I follow the will of God, I enter more and more on the unique path He sets for me. I become more and more "unrepeatable." Not just in my looks and bodily disposition, but, more importantly, in my character and in the set of talents I develop.

This is true not only on the natural plane but, above all, on the plane of grace. No two saints are identical. Each of us is called to be a saint, and every saint is great and unique. Here we find the truest excellence, being "fully alive." Notice that this kind of achievement (rooted in the gift of grace but inclusive of our cooperation) involves purpose, dedication, and labor. When I use my freedom rightly, I develop this excellence. Conversely, when I use my freedom for ill, the promise degenerates; I become evil. The one who habitually lies etches this vice into his character. The proud man isolates himself on his pretended mountain. Because of repeated sins, the initial promise of my uniqueness grows fetid and rots. In the end, an evil life is suited only for the dunghill. Ontological uniqueness is a gift *and* a task. It is a project that must be accomplished. Our personhood must develop.

Because personhood must develop, it is gravely harmful to affirm someone simply in his own ontological uniqueness without helping him grow toward perfection. If we simply affirm anyone in his uniqueness while letting him wander on his errant way, we are like those who sear their own eyes with scalding irons and then reach out blind hands to help others, saying yes to whatever the person is doing right now. What if the person is a sinner, alienated from God, floundering near a high cliff, about to fall? Are we to say yes to someone as he denies a Catholic truth? Does accompaniment mean that we walk with a straying sheep toward a cliff and watch it plunge into the abyss? What good would any of this contribute to the person we say we love? We would only confirm sinners in their malice, which portends Hell. False mercy destroys.

The PC movement, by its confusion of the ontological uniqueness of the person with the maturity of moral achievement *emasculates* true love.

False Mercy

True love is ordered to the good of the person. If I love someone in truth, I not only want to be with him but also want his real good. If my love is sincere and not empty, I help him achieve it insofar as I am able. Thus, if he is a sinner, I direct him—gently and with respect—away from sin and misery and toward virtue and true happiness. Notice how the PC movement hates this. It does not allow us to "hate the sin but love the sinner," for it insists that the two are one. But they are not one! The PC movement is also self-contradictory. We gather this from its brutal hatred of everyone who does distinguish between ontological uniqueness and moral achievement. It calls such persons "fascists" and cruelly gathers its mobs to beat the pulp out of the difference. In denying the difference, however, PC stifles the life within us that wants to come to maturity. Instead of giving in to this aberrant form of "love," which starves humans of their noblest dignity—holiness and moral excellence—let us lead hungry souls to real food. Let thirsty hearts slake their drought with the fountain of life. *We* are not this drink. *The Holy Spirit* is. So let us spread the good news that God's eternal Word has become flesh, poured out His life, and now nourishes souls through the Sacrament of His Body and Blood, rightly celebrated in the Catholic Church. Let us evangelize.

Correcting the Hatred for Self-Love

The second occasion of distaste for evangelization is a deep sense of unease about self-love. Our culture wants us to worry about those who show confidence and a sense of self-worth. The contemporary allergy to all self-love, as though no good self-love were possible, is born of an *aberrant* reading of Christ's command to die to self. Christ *is* demanding; He bids us to subject our lower appetites to our higher appetite and to direct our higher appetite to God. We are to focus on God, not on self. Still, it is a perversion to consider this other-centered focus to be inimical to all self-love, and vice versa.

The deepest element of self-love is the desire for happiness, for true fruition. Note that this fruition and happiness are the *perfection* of human individuality. It is in happiness that we say we have reached our end, our purpose. Genuine self-love wants the true good. What is that true good?

Friendship with God and neighbor. The true good is *being in a dynamic friendship with God as our ultimate end.*

Mistakenly, some claim that a true friendship demands that we never think of ourselves but only of the "other." They think, further, that to want to draw any happiness or delight from being with our friend runs against the character of true friendship. So they want happiness and delight to take a backseat, if they don't want them to die and disappear altogether. Is this a good way of being a friend? Imagine saying to your friend, "I'm not too fond of you, but I choose to display charity toward you as toward an anonymous 'other' whom I am supposed to love." Imagine a husband saying to his wife, "Dear, I'm not excited to be with you, but I choose to live with and serve you for magnanimous reasons that do not delight me." Rather, imagine the consequences for the husband! And what about us? Would *we* take it as real love if our "friend" said something similar to us? The proposition that all self-love is opposed to genuine love is ugly.

There is such a thing as genuine self-love—namely, love of one's *true* good. Now, one's true good is not one's own narrow and private good, such as wealth, or honor, or the delights of the palate. These are means to one's true good; they have their place provided they are ordered justly. One's true good is knowing the true, loving the good, and being with others in friendship. Genuine self-love takes us out of our narrow, individualistic focus. It leads us to become *friends*, to enter into communion with others. The human person is not an isolated unit, an island, all perfect within itself. Rather, the person is *ordered* to others; the person is, potentially, part of a greater whole. Hence, a person attains a greater good in communion with others than in individualistic activity. The union of two in marriage is *more* than the sum of the two individuals. Their very fellowship is a *common* good, a good they can have only by being together. As the distinguished scholar Russell Hittinger once wrote, if the man leaves the marriage, he cannot take half the marriage with him. Instead, the very common good that is the marriage vanishes.[452]

---

[452] Of course, the marriage bond does not vanish. So, if the man shacks up with another woman, he is committing adultery. When I say the marriage

It is similar with a musical band. When the instruments come together and harmoniously unite in the performance of a certain piece of music, they constitute something greater than the sum of the instruments taken separately. The friendship of two is greater than the two taken separately but added together. Thus, entering into a union of friendship grounded in virtue is good for the self. Failing to enter into a friendship with another is failure to be human. Above all, failure to enter into friendship with God through charity is a failure to live well.

Interestingly, it is precisely here that we again encounter PC's erroneous reading of the truth that is its partial foundation. The foundational truth of PC is human dignity. But genuine dignity is *ordered* to communion with others, to friendship with others. Human dignity as mere existence (being a human) is not to be prized as an isolated good. Every Sunday, Catholics confess that the ultimate community of love on earth is the Catholic Church. (Given the scandals and confusions that are besieging us these days, it takes faith to affirm this truth. But the Church has been through very rough times before.) Thus, for Catholics, true self-love should, when followed out under God's grace and true guidance, lead one to remain in the Church, not begrudgingly but gratefully. Finally, if Catholics truly love others, they should gracefully lead their friends toward this society of love.

Where did the contemporary hatred for self-love come from? At least in part, from the Protestant Reformation. Recall from chapter 3 that, for Martin Luther, love of self is sinful. For Luther, God demands absolutely perfect love of Himself without any admixture of love of self. But Luther recognized that self-love is inescapable for us now. As he saw it, such self-love *infects* everything we do. Hence, he concluded, each one of us is a great sinner in all that we do. Luther thought that we can escape this

---

vanishes, I mean the activity of being together. Since the bond remains, the husband can be called back by God's mercy to rekindle the activity of marriage. I have seen this happen. There is hope. God is more powerful than human weakness. Let us not despair of God's power, so as to have recourse to erroneous solutions of accompaniment that takes the form of throwing wandering sheep off the cliff into the abyss.

selfishness only if God decides to accept us in advance and entirely, *no matter how sinfully we continue to live*. As Luther alleged, we only need to trust His love, and we are saved. This thought process is one origin of his thesis, "faith alone justifies." Once we trust that we will not be damned but will be saved no matter what we do, we recognize that we do not need to do anything for our salvation. Salvation is in the bank. With the remaining time we have left on earth, we can do "random acts of kindness" without any thought for reward. This was the way that Luther thought God gets us to love Him freely. There are some noble sentiments here. It is noble to want to love God without ulterior motive. But there are a number of profound errors as well. Having exposed some in chapter 3, we can now expose a contradiction at the heart of Luther's enterprise.

Let us ask Luther a question: Why is the Gospel *good* news? It is good news because it promises deliverance from eternal damnation. Why do we want that? Because we love ourselves, we want to avoid Hell and attain Heaven. Thus, self-love is a major reason that we find the Gospel to be good news. For Catholicism, this conclusion is not a problem. The Catholic Church teaches that the fear of Hell and the love of happiness are *good* things, even though they will not get us to Heaven by themselves.[453] Luther, by contrast, considers the fear of Hell a sin because it is rooted in self-love.

Luther must therefore answer a question: Is the Gospel good news or not? If being saved from Hell is not good news, then deliverance from damnation by faith alone should not be a reason to rejoice either. Luther clearly will not want to surrender the goodness of the Gospel news. Therefore, he must come to admit that there is a good self-love. If there is a good self-love, then we are not totally corrupt; there remains in our wills an orientation to the good. Consequently, on the basis of that orientation, God can transform our stony hearts, which are not as yet cemented in malice, into hearts of flesh by which we can worship Him rightly and love our neighbor as ourselves (Deut. 30:6; Ezek. 36:25–27;

---

[453] Recall the references from chapter 3: DH 1456, 1489, 1539, 1576, 1581, 1705, 2207, 2212, 2216, 2309, 2310, 2313, 2314, 2315, 2351–73, 2455, 2460, 2462, and 2625.

Rom. 8:3). If that is the case, then justification does not need to be "by faith alone." Luther has to take his pick right here: either retain his condemnation of self-love as evil and thus reject the idea of the Gospel as *good* news, or embrace the Gospel as *good* news and thus reject the blanket condemnation of all self-love and the pseudosolution of "faith alone."

At any rate, Luther unwittingly embraced this and other contradictions, such as the absurd claim that we are "simultaneously justified and righteous." After the Protestant Reformation, unease with self-love continued to haunt Protestant Christianity. One calls to mind the 1987 Danish film *Babette's Feast*. In the movie, Protestant villagers have distaste for good food, as though it were against Christian duty ever to eat well. Babette, a French lady who, although not pious, represents a Catholic sensibility, invites them to another, more appreciative way of approaching food. I will avoid spoilers and simply recommend the movie to readers.[454] The dour attitude that haunts Christianity has roots in Protestantism.

The negative status of self-love was also taken up and secularized in the moral theory of Immanuel Kant. The desire for happiness, for Kant, is a merely animal affair devoid of positive ethical significance. The only ethical thing that is unconditionally good is a good will, and he defines this as a will that acts only on the principle of "duty" or law. Desire for happiness is not relevant. In the twentieth century, Lutheran theologian Anders Nygren taught that true "agape" toward God must be devoid of all "eros" for happiness. Agape is the love that only gives; it is "disinterested." It does not want to be with the other but only that the other have his good.

How on earth does all this relate to evangelization as a sin? By a sick and twisted path! The preceding narrative shows how unnatural the hatred of self-love is. So, when Christianity is (mistakenly) identified with this kind of unnaturalness, commonsense people want nothing to do with Christianity. Thus, Friedrich Nietzsche found Christianity to be a sick and sickening religion. Nietzsche was raised Protestant. As he

---

[454] I have one theological correction of the movie's thesis. The important final speech by the military officer overlooks the importance of human cooperation with the divine. Our spiritual well-being depends on it.

saw it, Christianity was *anti* everything natural and robust in man. In response, Nietzsche rejected Christianity. But he added an interesting critique. Knowing that, in reality and no matter how much we pretend otherwise, everyone always seeks happiness, he argued that Christians, *too*, seek "happiness."[455] They do so, he charged, in an indirect and twisted way: they love infecting other people with their own sickness. They do this by making healthy, happy people feel guilty about their own excellence. Christianity (and before it, Judaism) makes strong, robust, healthy, successful, and excellent people feel guilty about these noble traits. Christians torture the strong and the healthy; they delight in the agony of conscience that they inject into others. Thus, they (weak Christians) score a victory over their opponents (erstwhile strong and healthy pagans). For Nietzsche, Christians who do this are playing a power game. So all their talk about the virtue of humility is empty; they are only trying to get the upper hand in a twisted way. Nietzsche calls their bluff and "unmasks" their secret desire for power and their sick delight.

Nietzsche's atheistic and relativistic fans have carried on his project after him. They now write books that attempt to unmask Catholic saints as closet masochists and imperial tyrants who want to take over society through their twisted, ascetical ways. One would think that Christians might respond by distinguishing perverse hatred of self-love from true Christian discipleship. Some do that. Alas, others take Nietzsche's unmasking project as a call to renounce even more vehemently the pulverized remnants of self-love within their breast. In short, Nietzsche's project of unmasking is now fueling the self-hatred rooted in aberrant Christian guilt. The very Christians who hate self-love take Nietzsche's critique to be a call to double down. Rather than abandoning their visceral and twisted

---

[455] To be sure, Nietzsche's philosophy is itself twisted. He claims that at the core, we all have a "will to power." At first glance, this may sound diametrically opposed to Christ. On closer inspection, we find him fumbling his way toward an affirmation of exuberance and life. In short, he *wants* to affirm a desire for happiness. This is the reading I give him in my attempt to find good in his critique of a sickening portrait of Christianity. On this topic, see, especially, his *Genealogy of Morals*.

hatred of self-love, they flagellate themselves all the more for what they see to be their own sinful desire for power. They launch Nietzsche's unmasking project against their very desire for truth, goodness, and beauty! They concede, "Nietzsche is right: when we say we love truth, we are really only after power and a sick hatred of others." It is as though they have found their very love of truth, goodness, and beauty to be from Satan. In reaction, they no longer defend truth, because defending truth means being assertive and powerful. They no longer seek goodness and beauty, because seeking such things is only selfish, elitist, and sinful. Finally, they no longer seek to share the good news of Christ with others. To do so would be to impose on someone else. Missionary work, they think, is an act of imperial colonization. Nietzsche's critique should have gotten them to see that genuine self-love is good and healthy. (That is not to say that Nietzsche should be consulted as an authority on self-love. He should not. His books are bad and dangerous. Give them to your teenage son at your own peril. This is to say that Nietzsche was rightly indignant about the stupidity of Luther's notion of sinfulness.) Rather than benefiting from Nietzsche, many Christians have become even sicker.

One more factor must be countenanced. Anti-Christians are aware of this Christian disease. They use it to paralyze Christian action in the world. If a Christian rises to defend truth or cling to the good and denounce evil, they claim victim status and express shock at the "hypocrisy" of a proud and self-righteous Christian. Christians who accept such criticism beat their breasts, apologize, and renounce the truth and their own rights. Some priests, for instance, in lame sermons admit a generic guilt, acquiesce in it, and then fail to encourage the congregation toward holiness. Meanwhile, the anti-Christian forces advance against nature, against the Church, and against God and His Christ. They advance, laughing hysterically in their secret corners. For their part, the Marxists exploit this misguided guilt so as to incorporate former Christians into their mindless Borg. Others, such as violent Islamists who hate the West, exploit this guilt so as to make Christians effete.

The solution is not that complicated. The answer is that there is a genuine self-love deep in human nature. Noble aspirations for the true, the good, and the beautiful are to be celebrated. The desire for happiness is a fundamental root of human morality. Therefore, defending the truth and human nature, loving the good, affirming beauty, are harmonious with and necessary for a Christian life. To be sure, we must love the *true* good, the *higher* good. We often set our sights too low. When we try to find happiness in pleasures and honors or money, we find ourselves ultimately disappointed. Further, immoderate love of such things leads to hoarding, and hoarding leads to conflict, and conflict bursts forth in riots and war (James 4:2). In pursuit of our true heart's desire, we must leave these behind. When we shift from seeking worldly goods to seeking spiritual and heavenly goods, it is not that we are "hating ourselves." Rather, we are hating the narrowness of sin, which sets its sights too low. In undergoing the pain of conversion, we are opening up to our truer potential, to the real happiness that fulfills, to God and neighbor.

In this journey, we need Christ. Because we need Christ, we need the Church. But for those who are not in the Church, who will lead them to her? Who will give them the words of Christ so that they can be fed with the sacraments at the proper time? *Those who bring good tidings.* Blessed are the feet of those who evangelize.

Words of a Pope

There is another occasion for today's distaste for the missions. Some renegades want to use statements attributed to or uttered by Pope Francis as reason to hold that the Church now condemns evangelization. But, as we shall see, the Church cannot renounce her permanent missionary mandate. We will consider a few examples.

1. First, Eugenio Scalfari alleged that the pope said to him personally, "Proselytism is solemn nonsense, it makes no sense. We need to get to know each other, listen to each other and improve our knowledge of the world around us."[456] Prior to this interview with Scalfari, Pope Francis

---

[456] Words attributed to Pope Francis by Eugenio Scalfari with regard to his October 1, 2013, interview later published in *la Repubblica*.

issued the following video message to the world: "Am I going to go out to convince someone to become a Catholic? No, no, no! You are going to meet with him, he is your brother! That's enough!"[457] What are we to make of these statements?

Several remarks are in order.

A. Consider the meaning of "proselytism." The word classically referred to the efforts associated with inviting a person of another faith tradition to become a member of one's own. Such efforts can include simple expositions of one's faith, arguments in favor of it, responses to objections, indications that aspirations of another religion can find fulfillment only in one's own religion, and arguments against the errors of another religion. It can also include the acts of preaching—that is, presenting the message in the mode of an announcement from God. In short, "proselytism" was a generic word for *evangelization*. "Evangelization" is a Christian word referencing the good news of the Gospel. What is unacceptable about all this? Nothing. Sadly, however, the word "proselytism" has come to be used, especially in English-speaking Catholic circles, in pejorative fashion. Thus, it now bears connotations of bullying or pressuring the hearer. Of course, it is unacceptable to bully or pressure one's hearer to spread one's religion.[458] The baptized, on the other hand, do have obligations to fulfill. Incidentally, the Church solemnly teaches that she has the authority to punish the baptized who neglect to fulfill their obligations. Such punishments are not merely exclusion from the sacraments:

> If anyone says that when the little children thus baptized have grown up, they are to be asked whether they wish to ratify what their sponsors promised in their name when they were baptized; and if they answer that they are unwilling, they are to be left to their own judgment

---

[457] Pope Francis, "Pope Francis's Message for the Feast of Saint Cajetan," Zenit, August 7, 2013, https://zenit.org/articles/pope-francis-message-for-the-feast-of-saint-cajetan/.

[458] That some Catholics have used pressure and violence to spread Catholicism in the past is true. And the Church rightly rebukes them for such actions, because these actions contradict Catholic belief.

and are not, in the meantime, to be compelled to a Christian life by any penalty other than the exclusion from receiving the Eucharist and the other sacraments until they repent, let him be anathema.[459]

Alas, Rahner relegated this constant and solemn teaching to the dustbin of history. He remarked that the Church *used to* conclude "that she had the right to use compulsion against baptized people, a right which, as she understands herself, she did not have with regard to the non-baptized. But the Church no longer draws such a conclusion, because she admits that both the baptized and the non-baptized enjoy the same freedom of conscience."[460] How does Rahner's teaching square with the dogma? Further, the Church has officially taught that states that recognize the one true religion can have the authority to protect and defend Catholicism.[461] Who on earth is even aware of these teachings anymore? Oh, the forgetfulness of doctrine! Most importantly, there is the solemn command, from Jesus Christ our Lord, to go out to all the ends of the earth and preach the good news.

B. Pope Francis did not present his message to the world in the mode of doctrinal authority. Rather, he issued it as a word of advice. For this reason, it is not a papal word but only a word of a pope. What might be a good concern in the message? Perhaps the pope was trying to point out that when one "prays and labors so that the fullness of the whole world may enter into the People of God," as the Second Vatican Council bids us do, one should do so respectfully.[462] As we know, respect, charity, and prudence are always called for. Still, the task of evangelization is mandatory; it must be carried out with great love.

---

[459] DH 1627. See also DH 945 and 2605. See Pius IX, *Quanta cura*, art. 5, and Leo XIII, *Libertas*, art. 40. See also the 1917 *Code of Canon Law*, canon 2298, and the 1983 *Code of Canon Law*, canons 1311 and 1312. Baptism places obligations on the faithful, whereas the unbaptized do not have these obligations: see DH 1621 and 1671. See the various fine articles by Thomas Pink on this topic.

[460] Karl Rahner, "Baptism," *Theological Investigations* 23, 201.

[461] See IV Lateran, chapter 3; Pius IX, *Quanta cura*, art. 3; Leo XIII, *Diuturnum*, art. 25; and 1917 *Code of Canon Law*, canons 2198, 2259, and 2267.

[462] *Lumen gentium*, art. 17, my translation. See DH 4141.

False Mercy

C. As for the statement from the Scalfari interview, this is not even a word of a pope; it is only an *alleged* word of a pope. As such, it has no authority. Moreover, Pope Francis sometimes distinguishes between evangelization and proselytization.[463] Accordingly, he uses the word "proselytization" to refer to that manner of evangelizing that offends human dignity in one way or another. Defined this way, proselytization is *bad* evangelization, and of course that is to be rejected. Here we call to mind the Latin dictum *abusus non tollit usum*, which means "abuse does not take away use." Our saying in English is, "Don't throw the baby out with the bathwater." In other words, don't let the evil use of something good take away its proper use. In the matter at hand, the advice is this: when you throw away the bathwater of high-pressure proselytism, don't throw out the soul of the pagan baby as well. Rather, lovingly bring the pagan *to* the waters of Baptism. Evangelization remains a good. Pope Francis has indicated the good of evangelization. Such indications are in continuity with the doctrine on the *permanent* missionary mandate of the Church, which is to be expounded below.

2. Pope Francis has several times explicitly denounced proselytism among Christians. For instance, the Pope asks:

> But what should I do with a friend, neighbour, an Orthodox person? Be open, be a friend. "But should I make efforts to convert him or her?" There is a very grave sin against ecumenism: proselytism. We should never proselytise the Orthodox! They are our brothers and sisters, disciples of Jesus Christ.... Do not condemn. No. I must not do this. Friendship, walking together, praying for one another. Praying and carrying out works of charity together, when this is possible. This is ecumenism. But never condemn a brother or a sister, never refrain from greeting an Orthodox brother or sister because they are Orthodox.[464]

---

[463] Pope Francis, homily, May 8, 2013.
[464] Pope Francis, Apostolic Journey to Georgia, October 1, 2016.

Again, Pope Francis stated, "All proselytism among Christians is sinful. The Church never grows by proselytism but 'by attraction', as Benedict XVI said. So, proselytism among Christians is a grave sin in itself."[465]

What can we say about these remarks? First, as noted above, if we define "proselytism" as bad evangelization, we must reject proselytism. Second, absolutely, Catholics must not condemn but respect the Orthodox as brothers and sisters. They already believe in Christ and are baptized and celebrate the Eucharist with a valid priesthood and episcopate. "Evangelization" primarily refers to work with the nonbaptized; still, at times the term is used in an extended way for any announcement of the Gospel or call to conversion or completion, even to Catholics, as in the "New Evangelization." Third, evangelization must be done with prudence, at the right time, and with the right words. With some people, it may even require years of patience, lived in friendship, before the good news can be fully shared. A delay would not be celebrated but lamented, even though the friend would be loved in earnest through the delay. We must not only condemn proselytism but affirm every effort by which non-Catholics are lovingly and patiently invited to become Catholic. Fourth, the call to conversion is not a condemnation of the one we are calling. When God called Abram, He was not condemning him. When Jesus called Paul, He was not condemning him. When He called the woman at the well, He was not condemning her. When the glorious popes of times past urged all non-Catholic Christians to return to their Mother, the Holy Catholic and Roman Church, they were not sinning. When we offer the goods of Christ to non-Christians, we are not condemning them. We are not sinning. We are not failing to be brotherly. In fact, we would be starving them, abandoning them, abusing them — yes, even condemning them — if we did not preach to them. As St. Paul declared, "Woe to me if I do not preach the gospel!" (1 Cor. 9:16). Should we work to convert our non-Catholic neighbor? Most certainly — *if* we love him.

---

[465] Stefania Falasca, "Papa Francesco: non svendo la dottrina, seguo il Concilio," *Avvenire*, November 18, 2016, https://www.avvenire.it/papa/pagine/giubileo-ecumenismo-concilio-intervista-esclusiva-del-papa-ad-avvenire.

Respectful evangelization is not solemn nonsense; it is solemn teaching, as I shall now demonstrate.

Catholic Doctrine on Evangelization

The Catholic Church is called to reach to the ends of the earth in order to incorporate all human beings into her unity. In expounding this teaching, we can use terms in their strict sense to convey crucial distinctions. In this respect, we distinguish both ecumenism and evangelization from the effort to bring individual non-Catholic Christians into the Church. Strictly speaking, these activities are distinct enterprises. Nonetheless, they are related tasks. As we have seen, the goal of Catholic ecumenism is the full incorporation of all Christian communities and churches into the Catholic Church. The ecumenical goal has to do with communities and churches, not just individuals. Thus, the ecumenical task is distinct from the effort of Catholics to help their non-Catholic Christian friends become Catholic. Nonetheless, as Vatican II teaches, "there is no opposition between the two" tasks[466] because the goal of both is incorporation into the Catholic Church. The difference is that ecumenism regards churches and communities, whereas invitations to friends are extended to individual non-Catholic Christians. Precisely love of the other guides Catholics to this common goal in both cases.

Now, if the first two efforts have incorporation into the Catholic Church as their goal, so does evangelization. Evangelization, strictly so-called, regards bringing the Gospel to non-Christian individuals. Just as Catholics work in the first two ways to incorporate non-Catholic Christian individuals and churches into the Catholic Church, so they pray and labor so that non-Christians become Catholic. In what follows, we can see that the Church has never ceased to have this major, indispensable goal.

Pius IX warned against the error being proposed in his day that salvation is possible outside the Catholic Church. He reiterated the dogma

---

[466] *Unitatis redintegratio*, art. 4.

that salvation outside the Church is not possible. This dogma raises questions and calls for considerable care and precision.

The Church is necessary in various ways. She is necessary both by a necessity of precept and by a necessity of "means," as the theologians say. Our Lord commands that all human persons enter the Catholic Church; thus, the Church is necessary by a necessity of precept. Leo XIII writes, "If those about to come back to their most loving Mother (not yet fully known, or culpably abandoned) should perceive that their return involves, not indeed the shedding of their blood (at which price nevertheless the Church was bought by Jesus Christ), but some lesser trouble and labour, let them clearly understand that this burden has been laid on them not by the will of man but by the will and command of God."[467] The Church is also necessary by a necessity of *means*. She is necessary by a necessary means in two ways: both intrinsically and instrumentally. The Church is necessary instrumentally as having the fullness of the means of salvation: "For it is only through Christ's Catholic Church, which is 'the all-embracing means of salvation', that the fullness of the means of salvation can be attained."[468] The way that leads to life is hard, and few even find it. Practically speaking, salvation is extremely difficult without the regular use of the sacraments and without a clear, unambiguous, and complete presentation of the Catholic Faith. Serious Catholics will attest to this. But only in the Church can we find the fullness of these means. So the Church is necessary as having the very instruments by which one can attain salvation. Finally, the Church is also intrinsically necessary. This means that *absolutely no one* can be saved outside the Catholic Church. We see this teaching in various documents, especially in the Decree for the Jacobites from the Council of Florence: "She firmly believes, professes, and preaches that 'none of those who are outside of the Catholic Church, not only pagans,' but also Jews, heretics, and schismatics, can become sharers of eternal life, but they will go into the eternal life 'that was prepared

[467] Leo XIII, *Satis cognitum*, art. 1.
[468] Second Vatican Council, *Unitatis redintegratio*; DH 4190.

for the devil and his angels' [Matt. 25:41] unless, before the end of their life, they are joined to her."[469] Being in the Church is *constitutive* to sanctity and salvation; it is part of what it *is* to be justified, to be in a sanctifying relationship with God, the end of which is eternal life (Rom. 6:22). As Boniface VIII solemnly declares, "That there is only one, holy, catholic, and apostolic Church we are compelled by faith's urging to believe and hold, and we firmly believe in her and sincerely confess her outside of whom there is neither salvation nor remission of sins."[470] In short, there is a threefold necessity to the Church.

An anxious and understandable question arises: are all those who fail to die as members of the Catholic Church damned? The short answer is no. God wills the salvation of all, and He therefore gives the grace sufficient for this effect to all who have the use of freedom. By this grace, it is possible for a non-Catholic to come to believe that God exists and that He rewards those who love Him (Heb. 11:6). Having this faith and the help of God's sufficient grace, it is possible for this person also to come to hope in and love God with charity. In this state one is sanctified, and everyone in this state wills to do the will of God, whatever that may be. This is an actual desire to obey God. In this actual desire, there lies an *implicit* desire to do the concrete things that God wills. God wills that all be baptized and enter the Catholic Church. So everyone who is sanctified has an actual desire to do God's will and at least an implicit desire to be baptized and become Catholic. In virtue of this holy desire, such persons can obtain those fruits of the sacraments without which no one can be saved. Thus, salvation is possible for non-Catholics. Salvation is not easy for them; indeed, it is much more difficult for them than it is for Catholics. The perils of worldly allurements and the pride of life all too often ensnare the souls of non-Catholics. But unrepentant Catholic sinners will be the more severely judged! (Luke 12:47).

Does this mean that the "necessity" of the Church is softened? No, it does not. We can now parcel out how the salvation of non-Catholics

[469] DH 1351.
[470] DH 870.

connects to the three kinds of necessity. First, the necessity of precept binds only those who are responsible to know the precept. The ones to whom the precept was adequately promulgated are responsible. It is possible for someone to be innocently ignorant of the precept. The technical expression is "invincibly ignorant." Membership in the Church is necessary by a necessity of precept; hence, a non-Catholic who is invincibly ignorant of this necessity can still be saved.[471] Second, the necessity of instrumental means is indeed a serious necessity but not an absolute and intrinsic necessity. God is all-powerful; thus, He can and certainly does give many of the effects of the sacraments outside of the sacraments. As we saw from the previous paragraph, those non-Catholics who are sanctified receive these effects apart from the sacraments *but not without a real, at least implicit, desire for the sacraments.* Hence, they, too, are oriented to the reception of the sacraments and to membership. Third, as St. Robert Bellarmine argues, every sanctified person is *mystically* inside the one *visible* Church. That is, every sanctified person already drinks from the grace and truth entrusted to the Catholic Church. The Church is a *visible* society. So *membership* in it involves *visible* indicators (Baptism, the profession of the faith, and hierarchical communion). There is no invisible Church. Thus, non-Catholics are not *members* of the Church. Still, non-Catholics can, as Bellarmine teaches, mystically partake of the grace of the Church.[472]

Pius IX presents the perennial notes of balance. He affirms the absolute necessity of the Church for all who desire salvation. And he affirms the possibility that nonmembers can be saved *if* they are living the commandments by the power of sanctifying grace, even though they are invincibly ignorant of Christ's command. Pius IX thus gives us precise and helpful advice; he does not say that it is enough for us simply to

---

[471] Still, as Fr. Philip Wolfe, FSSP, rightly says, ignorance does not save. Invincible ignorance only means that one is not culpable for nonfulfillment of a precept. We are not saved by ignorance but by grace. The Church is necessary with regard to grace as well, as is clear from what follows above.

[472] See Robert Bellarmine, *On the Church*, bk. III, chap. 6. He is treating the excommunicated, but his thesis is analogically applicable to other situations.

welcome our non-Catholic Christian as a brother. We should welcome our brother, but this is not enough. If we love him, we must not leave the brother ill equipped for salvation. We *are* our brother's keeper. We must remember the unspeakable helps of the sacraments and of the teaching of the Holy Catholic Church. (Or do we no longer believe that grace comes through the sacraments?) Further, if our brother is already participating mystically in the Church by being in the state of grace, his heart is even better prepared to recognize and welcome the truth of Christ's Catholic Church when it is confidently, clearly, completely, and lovingly presented to him. But how can he believe this if no one preaches it to him (Rom. 10:14)?

The balance that Pius IX set forth is not a static balance. It is dynamic. Pius did *not* promote static "coexistence." The erroneous idea of coexistence paralyzes action. In fact, the "coexistence" theory wars against all religions. What Muslim in his right mind could affirm static and perpetual coexistence? Not a one. Lamentably, there are many Christian "useful idiots" who promote coexistence because they believe Christianity is no better than any other religion. Thus, they cede ground to people who know the situation well and take advantage of it. Western relativists and militant Islamists have struck a pact not to bother each other—for the time being—as they together make naïve Christians surrender their strongholds and defenses. The hypocrisy of the relativists and the Islamists will be unveiled in two stages. The first stage is underway: they are colluding in the as yet soft but real persecution of truth-loving Christians. This persecution will ripen to the issuance of fines and termination of employment. Finally, it will end in imprisonment and possibly death. The second stage will follow, when, after the Christians are in the camps, the Islamists and relativists draw swords against one another. Contrary to the coexistence error, we Christians must *love non-Christians toward the true and the good, calling them out of the shadows of darkness* into the marvelous light of God's kingdom.

Nor should we make a confusing mess of things. Rather, we should act truly; Christianity matters. Pius IX did just this: he entered the fray dynamically, urging the Catholic faithful to labor fruitfully so as to bring straying Christians back to the Church, *always* in a respectful and charitable manner. Let us read from his important teaching on the necessity of the Church for salvation, on the possibility of invincible ignorance, on the need to be friendly to non-Catholics, and on the need to evangelize:

> Here, too, our beloved sons and venerable brothers, it is again necessary to mention and censure a very grave error entrapping some Catholics who believe that it is possible to arrive at eternal salvation although living in error and alienated from the true faith and Catholic unity. Such belief is certainly opposed to Catholic teaching. There are, of course, those who are struggling with invincible ignorance about our most holy religion. Sincerely observing the natural law and its precepts inscribed by God on all hearts and ready to obey God, they live honest lives and are able to attain eternal life by the efficacious virtue of divine light and grace. . . .
>
> God forbid that the children of the Catholic Church should even in any way be unfriendly to those who are not at all united to us by the same bonds of faith and love. . . . First of all, let them rescue them from the darkness of the errors into which they have unhappily fallen and strive to guide them back to Catholic truth and to their most loving Mother who is ever holding out her maternal arms to receive them lovingly back into her fold.[473]

Christians who find themselves outside the Catholic Church are to be guided back to her, always with the gentleness of friendship. This is good and true advice given by a loving pastor. As we saw earlier, Pius IX himself undertook this very task just before the First Vatican Council, inviting all non-Catholics to become Catholic.

And as we saw in chapter 5, Leo XIII issued the same call in his Consecration of the Human Race to the Sacred Heart. This prayer reaches out to everyone and calls each person, whatever his religion, to the full

---

[473] Pius IX, *Quanto conficiamur moeror* (1863), art. 9, Papal Encyclicals, https://www.papalencyclicals.net/Pius09/p9quanto.htm.

and sanctifying practice of the Catholic religion. Leo's prayer reflects the ancient practice of the Church to pray for all on Good Friday. We saw in chapter 5 that the Church prays that all non-Catholic Christians would return to the harbor of truth. The Church thereafter prays for the evangelization of all non-Christians, exhibiting the task of evangelization in the strict sense of the term. This evangelizing prayer is twofold. First, the Church prays for the Jews. In the Extraordinary Form of the Roman Rite, the prayer runs thus:

> Let us pray also for the Jews: that our God and Lord may illuminate their hearts: so that they may acknowledge Jesus Christ, the Saviour of all Mankind.

Lastly, she prays for all others who are bereft of all divinely instituted ways of worship — namely, the pagans:

> Let us pray also for pagans: that almighty God would remove iniquity from their hearts: that, putting aside their idols, they may be converted to the true and living God and His only Son, Jesus Christ our God and Lord.... Almighty and everlasting God, deliver them from the worship of idols: and join them to Thy holy Church for the praise and glory of Thy Name.

These prayers from the Extraordinary Form of the Roman Rite exhibit the fullness of Catholic truth. When the liturgy expresses the fullness of truth, we have a better hope that Catholics will remember it.

Pius XI likewise encouraged all men to submit themselves to the sweet yoke of Christ. He wrote, "Thus the empire of our Redeemer embraces all men.... Nor is there any difference in this matter between the individual and the family or the State; for all men, whether collectively or individually, are under the dominion of Christ. In him is the salvation of the individual, in him is the salvation of society."[474]

Pius XII echoed this call in his important encyclical *Mystici corporis*, inviting every single person to become Catholic:

---

[474] Pius XI, *Quas primas* (1925), art. 18.

We ask each and every [non-Catholic] to correspond to the interior movements of grace, and to seek to withdraw from that state in which they cannot be sure of their salvation. For even though by an unconscious desire and longing they have a certain relationship with the Mystical Body of the Redeemer, they still remain deprived of those many heavenly gifts and helps which can only be enjoyed in the Catholic Church. Therefore may they enter into Catholic unity and, joined with Us in the one, organic Body of Jesus Christ, may they together with us run on to the one Head in the Society of glorious love.[475]

Of course, Pius XII recognized that salvation is possible for one who does not die a Catholic. Salvation is difficult enough, however, even for those who have all the means of salvation and the fullness of truth. Indeed, practicing Catholics who are deprived of the sacraments during a plague are driven to sadness; they must make acts of trust to buoy their hope. How much more difficult for those without such saving truth and means of sanctification. Thus, Pius XII issued this invitation out of deep love.

More recently, Vatican II repeated this call of the Lord. Salvation is possible for those not visibly incorporated into the Catholic Church, but the missionary mandate remains utterly urgent. Vatican II gave several reasons why it remains urgent. First, although salvation is possible for non-Catholics, "Often men, deceived by the Evil One, have become vain in their reasonings and have exchanged the truth of God for a lie, serving the creature rather than the Creator."[476] Thus, the salvation of many hangs in the balance. Second, "It is only through Christ's Catholic Church, which is 'the all-embracing means of salvation,' that the fullness of the means of salvation can be attained."[477] Third, God wills that Catholics not sit idly by while their neighbors languish in error and sin. Rather, He wills that Catholics go out of doors and spread the invitation

---

[475] Pius XII, *Mystici corporis*, 101.
[476] *Lumen gentium*, art. 16; DH 4140.
[477] *Unitatis redintegratio*, art. 3; DH 4190.

far and wide: "To promote the glory of God and procure the salvation of all of these, and mindful of the command of the Lord, 'Preach the gospel to every creature' [Mark 16:16], the Church fosters the missions with care and attention."[478] There is no restriction on this mandate: "The Church prays and works so that the fullness of the entire world might pass into the People of God, the body of the Lord and the Temple of the Holy Spirit."[479] Fourth, charity, which is absolutely necessary for salvation, objectively orients every person to the society of love, which is the Catholic Church. As the great theologian Joseph Clifford Fenton argues, following Bellarmine, the non-Catholic who has charity is by that charity mystically in communion with the Catholic Church; while not becoming a member of the Church, such a person is *in* the Church invisibly in such a way as to be able to be saved.[480] Nor does this thesis dodge or water down the dogma of the Church. Charity objectively orders its bearer to membership in the Church. Preaching to those who are sanctified will yield abundant fruit.

John Paul II stressed the Church's permanent missionary mandate. This mandate is not optional. John Paul II clearly teaches that missionary service "is the primary service which the Church can render to every individual and to all humanity in the modern world."[481] The Church is not primarily a social justice institution, worried about plastics and face masks. Her primary end is not resolving youth unemployment, climate change, and loneliness. Her primary end is the salvation of souls.

John Paul II was alarmed at the status of missionary work early in his pontificate. He lamented:

> Missionary activity specifically directed "to the nations" (*ad gentes*) appears to be waning, and this tendency is certainly not in line with the directives of the Council and of subsequent statements of the Magisterium. Difficulties both internal and external have

---

[478] *Lumen gentium*, art. 16; DH 4140.

[479] Ibid., art. 17, my translation.

[480] See Fenton, "The Theological Proof for the Necessity of the Catholic Church," in *The Church of Christ*, 141–202.

[481] John Paul II, *Redemptoris missio*, art. 2.

weakened the Church's missionary thrust toward non-Christians, a fact which must arouse concern among all who believe in Christ. For in the Church's history, missionary drive has always been a sign of vitality, just as its lessening is a sign of a crisis of faith.[482]

If he was worried then, what would he say now? John Paul II went on to exhort all Catholics to this effort. He proclaimed:

> God is opening before the Church the horizons of a humanity more fully prepared for the sowing of the Gospel. I sense that the moment has come to commit all of the Church's energies to a new evangelization and to the mission *ad gentes*. No believer in Christ, no institution of the Church can avoid this supreme duty: to proclaim Christ to all peoples.[483]

Most recently, Pope Francis exhorts, "Let us go forth, then, let us go forth to offer everyone the life of Jesus Christ."[484] Evangelization is not solemn nonsense; it is solemn teaching.

Conclusion

Although it is clear that the Church's teaching has not changed, we must still lament the current state of affairs. We seldom hear about the one true religion. Even some of those who remind us of the need to evangelize seem unduly anxious to stress only the positives in other religions. As a result, we normally hear only half the truth, while the difficult parts of Catholic doctrine are passed over in silence. The fruits of this silence and ambiguity are obvious. A Consolata Catholic missionary expressed pride in being part of a mission in South America in which not one indigenous person has been baptized for over fifty years.[485] This is soul

---

[482] Ibid., art. 2.

[483] Ibid., art. 11.

[484] Pope Francis, *Evangelii gaudium*, art. 49.

[485] On the mission associated with the Consolatas, see Luis Miguel Modino, "Los indígenas pueden ayadar a la Iglesia a limpiarse," *Religión*, December

desecration. Let us remember that in the United States, the Catholic Church loses 6.5 adults for every adult that she gains. We have not been evangelizing effectively.

We need to wed the strengths of recent pastoral strategies to the full Catholic picture. Listening and dialoguing are important but not enough. Our ultimate goal should be to offer the full truth to our neighbor when the time is right, with gentleness and confidence. We must come to non-Christians not only treasuring their dignity as human persons *but also* longing for their completion in Christ.

In our everyday living, we should remember death and the gravity of human life. We seem to think that human life is a temporary state of momentary delights, to be surpassed in the next world by an eternal state of unending delight. We no longer see our life as a pilgrimage in a foreign land, with the *overriding* task of journeying to our real fatherland. Our salvation is possible only if we enter a dynamic relationship with God through faith, hope, and charity, dying to our lower appetites by ordering them to our higher appetite and ordering our higher appetite to God for His own sake. But we begin in the state of original sin.

Perhaps nowhere is our failure to convert cultures to Christ more evident than in the moral realm. Western societies are afflicted by moral rot. Having exchanged the truth of God for a lie, having fallen down before idols, having abandoned Christ's call to preach to the nations, former Christians are now committing all sorts of moral evils. Many of these evils pertain to sins of the flesh. As Our Lady of Fátima said, most people go to Hell for sins of the flesh. Unbridled desire for sexual pleasure ranks foremost among these. This unbridled desire had a beginning stage but is now reaching the nadir. It began with the denial that procreation is the end of the marital act and marriage. It is coming to fruition in the celebration of sodomy. We will treat the former denial in chapter 8 and sodomy in chapter 9.

20, 2018, https://www.periodistadigital.com/cultura/religion/america/20181220/corrado-dalmonego-indigenas-ayudar-iglesia-limpiarse-noticia-689400013477/.

8

Are Marriage and Sex *Not* Ordered to Procreation?

As is widely known, there are a number of erroneous opinions entertained and fostered these days concerning marriage and the sexual act.
Some of these errors depend logically on others. A principal reason for
many of these errors is the loss of belief in the infallible doctrine that
marriage — and the sexual or marital act — is essentially ordered to the
procreation and education of offspring.[486] That marriage is so ordered is
the constant teaching of the ordinary and universal Magisterium. It is
therefore infallible. Unfortunately, this truth of natural law has been cast
aside by modern secular culture. Worse, more and more Catholics have
been rejecting this divine teaching. Renegade theologians claim, for
instance, that contraception, which violates the procreative end of the
marital act, is not intrinsically evil and that it is, therefore, acceptable
in some circumstances.[487] Although the Church has for two millennia

[486] This means that marriage is, by its very essence, ordered to the procreation
and education of offspring.

[487] See Karl Rahner, "On the Encyclical *Humanae Vitae*," *Catholic Mind* 66
(1968): 2–4. For the document of the dissenters, prepared by Charles
Curran, see Daniel Callahan, *The Catholic Case for Contraception* (London: Macmillan, 1969): 67–70. Other dissidents included Hans Küng,
Bernard Häring, Richard McCormick, and Lisa Sowle Cahill. More recently, Stephen Pope and Richard Gaillardetz of Boston College described
the Church's teaching on contraception as not infallible and therefore
reversible. See their article "Doctrine Air: Room to Breathe on Church

been clear on her teaching, some have found themselves confused by recent remarks of Pope Francis. As its chief aim, this chapter will treat this infallible teaching and the recent confusion concerning it; however, the telling of this story requires one more ingredient.

The Church has *also* taught for some time that procreation is the *primary* end of marriage. The Church recognizes that there are other, secondary, ends of marriage as well, especially the mutual assistance or friendship and personal good of the spouses. As we shall see, comprehensive treatment of this second end requires care and nuance, for this end also pertains to the very essence of marriage. The third end is the "remedy for concupiscence"; this end pertains to marriage in our fallen state. This means that marriage provides for the legitimate use of the sexual urge in such a way as to foster continual growth in virtue and a corresponding lessening of unruly concupiscence over time.[488]

Teaching," *Commonweal* (July 21, 2016), https://www.commonweal-magazine.org/doctrine-air. Gaillardetz had earlier come to the defense of Sr. Margaret Farley with regard to her work *Just Love: A Framework for Christian Sexual Ethics* (New York: Continuum, 2006). In this work, Farley rejects the Church's teachings regarding the intrinsic evil of masturbation, homoerotic acts, homosexual unions, and so forth. Contraception as an intrinsic evil isn't even on the table for her. The Vatican issued an excellent notification condemning these and other errors in her work. See CDF, "Notification Regarding the Book *Just Love*," March 30, 2012. For Gaillardetz's defense of Farley, see "Magisterium and the Faithful," *America*, September, 2012, https://www.americamagazine.org/issue/5151/article/road-ahead.

[488] People on both sides err regarding this end, treating it as an excuse for wantonness in marriage. Some affirm this reading as good, and some reject it. But this end is not to be read as an excuse for wantonness. It means, instead, that marriage serves as the ultimate context of virtue within which one may engage in the marital act. Motivations for this act are not always aligned with perfect virtue, but that someone has submitted to the marital state already indicates the priority of higher ends over lower goods. Thus, even if one chooses the act with a lower good foremost in mind, one's habitual inclination to the higher goods of marriage remains in place unless one deliberately excludes them. The theological tradition—Bonaventure, Aquinas, et alia—regards such a

Now, the language of an order of ends was discontinued with the Second Vatican Council. As a result, some theologians—even good ones not intent on a revolution of morals—came to think that the Church overturned this tradition. In the course of presenting the Church's infallible teaching on the ends of marriage and the marital act, this chapter will *also* explain this long-standing teaching on the primary end. It will not defend this latter teaching as infallible. Instead, it will simply demonstrate that this age-old teaching has never been overturned but even confirmed in different words.

This secondary narrative also enables us to appreciate a legitimate development of doctrine concerning the ends and essence of marriage. It helps us defend both a preservative and an exegetical exercise of the hermeneutic of continuity. These two narratives will be woven together, but the claims are distinct. It is infallible that procreation is an essential end of marriage and the marital act. It is long-standing teaching, never overturned, that this end is primary. According to both teachings, contraception is intrinsically and gravely evil and, therefore, never morally good.

This chapter intends to accomplish three aims. First, it presents the Church's teaching, both in overview and through a documentary sketch. Second, it argues that the change in magisterial expression represents a legitimate development of doctrine that does not contradict the prior teaching. Third, it confutes those who attempt to defend their revolutionary desires with some words of Pope Francis.

Overview of the Church's Teaching

Because marriage is ordered to the procreation and education of offspring, several conclusions follow. Before unfolding these, we must note that marriage is not just a sacrament but also a reality in the order of nature. Thus, we can spell these conclusions out with respect to two orders: the order of nature and the order of grace. Further, since marriage is a

---

decision as venially sinful. This habitual inclination and one's state in life consequently serve as gentle correctives and calls toward virtue.

natural reality, even *right reason* can reflect on its properties. Nevertheless, the Church soberly recognizes that because of sin and its effects,
human reason in its current condition cannot offer a guaranteed and
detailed depiction of marriage even as a natural reality.[489] Thus, human reason requires the illumination of revelation to have an accurate
and detailed depiction of marriage even as something natural. So this
overview, which is addressed to committed Catholics, is taken from the
Church's own teaching.

Let us first consider the conclusions that follow for any marriage in
the order of nature. As we will see, some conclusions are absolute, and
some are highly fitting. First, because human procreation requires sexual
complementarity, marriage must absolutely be a heterosexual union of a
man and a woman. No other arrangement can in any way be called marriage. Second, integral to entrance into this union is the mutual offering
and acceptance of persons by way of a mutual offering and acceptance of
spousal rights over the body. That is, marriage is a union that a man and
woman enter when each offers the other his or her very self by way of the
right to the marital act and accepts the other's offer. Hence, the very union
itself has a proper act, the sexual or marital act. Third, polyandry — one
woman's taking several husbands — is absolutely incompatible with the
end of marriage. The reason is that one woman is not made more fruitful
by several men than by one man. Fourth, polygamy — one man's taking
several wives — chafes seriously against several aspects of marriage. The
very union and the marital act involve a radical offering of self to another

---

[489] The wider aspect of this teaching is that we cannot know the natural law
in its full parameters and with surety without revelation. See Leo XIII,
Humanum genus, arts. 21 and 24; Leo XIII, *Arcanum* (1880), art. 27; Leo
XIII, *Libertas*, arts. 17–18; Pius XI, *Casti connubii* (1930), art. 102; and
Pius XII, *Summi pontificatus* (1939), art. 30. Hence, we need the Catholic
Church. Catholic organizations that strictly insist, in some of their events,
on not mentioning Christ and His Church so as to address a secular and
even non-Catholic audience, are mistaken on a fundamentally crucial
point. Once again, it is time to evangelize, not merely to attempt natural
law arguments!

in the most vulnerable way. Such an offering takes study, dedication, and a totality of energy. A man who fulfills this commitment has exhausted his resources. Thus, the union calls for exclusivity, namely, monogamy. Further, such exclusivity provides the best context in which children may thrive. For their part, women who experience polygamy frequently engage in competition with each other, vying for the position of favorite wife. The defects of polygamy point, as it were asymptotically, to monogamy as the proper way of marriage. Still, polygamy is not absolutely incompatible with the procreative end.[490] Hence, we are here speaking of a high degree of fittingness. Fifth, because the proper formation of children requires many years, the union should be lasting. Indeed, since the parental and filial relationships remain, the union should remain. Aquinas held that God permitted divorce not because the act could be good but only to avoid a greater evil—namely, wife murder. Aquinas notes that divorce was not a sin in such cases but that it was always inordinate. It was neither virtuous nor punishable.[491] Moreover, the very nature of the union and the mutual offering and acceptance of spousal rights calls for totality and permanence. Further, since children thrive best in the context of a total commitment between their parents, the good of society itself calls out for permanence.

With respect to natural marriage, the Church reveals some aspects of her teaching concerning the state and civil society. Marriage is a *natural* institution. That is, God is its author.[492] Because of God's authorship, the essence and properties of marriage are not subject to human law. Marriage is therefore *anterior* to the state and civil society. Hence, the state

---

[490] The asymmetry between polygamy and polyandry reveals the primacy of the procreative end. Both polyandry and polygamy strain the unitive side of marriage, yet polygamy has been permitted on rare occasions according to divine authority, whereas polyandry is intrinsically evil and therefore never permissible. See Thomas Aquinas, *Supplement of the Summa theologiae*, q. 65, arts. 1–2.

[491] See Aquinas, *Supplement of the Summa theologiae*, q. 67, arts. 1–3.

[492] Trent, Session XXIV; DH 1797; Leo XIII, *Arcanum*, art. 19; Pius XI, *Casti connubii*, art. 5.

has no power to define and establish marriage and its properties; rather, the state must acquiesce to the divinely instituted properties of marriage as a natural institution. The state must *recognize* the essence of marriage and the anteriority of its claims, legislating accordingly. The state may legislate only concerning the benefits and responsibilities that follow from marriage. Were a state to presume to define marriage, the very act itself would be null and void in its very form, because states have competence only to operate out of a true apprehension of the essence of marriage.

Now, marriage and family are bedrock to all society; so it is in the interest of states to have a true apprehension of what marriage is in virtue of the laws of God, who instituted marriage in both the natural and supernatural orders. If, however, a state were to issue materially false laws concerning marriage, these laws would not only be formally null and void but the state would thereby become a snare and an occasion of grave sin because laws direct action and form opinion. We think that what is legal is good. This is why the Church has historically favored a close cooperation between church and state in which the state defended in law essential institutions such as marriage that strengthen public morality and social welfare. The severing of this union by modern liberalism has led to the secularization of public life. Catholics who favor this new political arrangement are not following long-standing Catholic teaching on the proper relationship between church and state.[493]

---

[493] For the divine institution of marriage and the consequent incapacity of states to legislate about what it is and its properties, see Leo XIII, *Arcanum*, arts. 5–8 and 19; *Humanum genus*, art. 21; and Pius XI, *Casti connubii*, arts. 5 and 123–126. For the need of states to recognize the Catholic Church as bearer of the one true religion, see Pius IX, *Quanta cura*, art. 4; Pius IX, *Syllabus of Errors*, art. 55; Leo XIII, *Libertas*, arts. 17–18, 21; Leo XIII, *Humanum genus*, art. 13; Leo XIII, *Sapientiae*, arts. 20, 31; Leo XIII, *Tametsi*, art. 12; Leo XIII, *Immortale Dei*, arts. 6–7; Pius X, *Vehementer nos*, art. 3; Benedict XV, *Ad beatissimi*, art. 5; Pius XI, *Quas Primas*, arts. 1, 18, and 24; Pius XI, *Casti connubii*, arts. 123–124; and Pius XI, *Ubi arcano Dei consilio*, arts. 47–48. Good articles on this topic include the following: Joseph Clifford Fenton, "Principles Underlying Traditional Church-State Doctrine," in *The Church of Christ*, 288–301,

The Catholic tradition recognizes the distinction in marriage—as a merely natural institution—between absolutely essential properties and highly fitting properties. Since Jesus Christ has made determinations about the latter properties, prohibiting polygamy and annulling the permission of divorce, for example, we see the great utility in a state's recognizing the one true Church. Before Jesus made these determinations, we might say that God tolerated some of what was unfitting. So this distinction helps us understand some exceptions found in the Old Testament. For instance, there are cases of polygamy. Most cases of polygamy are by no means celebrated as ideal; still, they are not condemned as intrinsically evil.[494] Further, by God's authority, Moses permitted divorce. In no case do we see polyandry accepted. But as we indicated, Jesus Christ the King abolished the permission for divorce and the tolerance of polygamy, not just for the sacrament of marriage, which He instituted, but also for natural marriages.[495]

In the order of grace, marriage is a sacrament. That is, when both spouses are baptized and validly married, their marriage is necessarily also sacramental. As the Church teaches, this is the case whether or not the spouses are aware of or affirm the sacramentality of marriage. As a sacrament, marriage provides graces to the spouses whereby they can fulfill their marital duties and thereby grow in virtue and holiness. Further, the sacramental union of husband and wife reflects the union of Christ and His Church. Marriage reminds us that Christ loved us to the end, dying for us. He will love us to the end of our lives. This faith can give us great hope in the midst of our sinfulness, difficulties, and trials. It is a wonderful joy and a great responsibility to enter the married state, to signify the union of Christ and His Church.

---

and Thomas Pink, "The Interpretation of *Dignitiatis Humanae*: A Reply to Martin Rhonheimer," *Nova et Vetera* 11 (2013): 77–121.

[494] Solomon is a case of absurd proportions that does not factor into this comment and that also involved the grave danger of exposure to false religions.

[495] See Leo XIII, *Arcanum*, art. 8; Pius XI, *Casti connubii*, art. 34.

False Mercy

Now, the essential truths concerning natural marriage are true also in sacramental marriage: it is a heterosexual union, and it involves the mutual offering and acceptance of spousal rights. A sign of Christ's choice of and fidelity to His Church, sacramental marriage adds an absolute character to both exclusivity and indissolubility. As in natural marriage, the bond of a sacramental marriage is intrinsically indissoluble; that is, the spouses may not break the bond. Moreover, a valid and consummated sacramental marriage may not be broken even by the power of the pope.[496]

Now, exclusivity and indissolubility — which are properties of both natural and sacramental marriage — connect with the nature of the marital act and its proper end, procreation. If we consider the order of nature globally, we clearly see that the sexual act is the means by which sexual beings reproduce their kind. All living things replicate, but they accomplish this *either* sexually or asexually. Therefore, "sexual" specifies the mode of reproduction for living kinds that are sexual. Living kinds that are sexual are divided into *male* and *female*. Thus, the sexual act is essentially between a male and a female and ordered to reproduction.

What is generically true of all sexual reproduction is also true of human reproduction. Yet, unlike reproduction among the beasts, the marital act is a *human act*. Thus, one must engage in this act with the dignity of human rationality and affectivity. We can examine these aspects both with respect to the reproductive end of the act and with respect to the act as the love of two persons. With regard to the former, the act involves freedom and cooperation with the intention of the Creator. So the sexual act is not merely reproductive but *procreative*. The act is not ordered simply to the production of offspring as a numerical goal; it is not mere breeding. Rather, the marital act is ordered to the procreation of human persons, who are in the image of God and called to beatific union with God. Thus, we say in a fuller expression that the act is

---

[496] On this topic and against the rebellion of the modernists, see the important book *Remaining in the Truth of Christ: Marriage and Communion in the Catholic Church*, ed. Robert Dodaro (San Francisco: Ignatius Press, 2014).

ordered to the *procreation and education* of offspring. "Education" points not merely to intellectual formation but to personal, moral, religious, and spiritual formation.

Further reflection on the marital act helps us see that it should occur in the context of marriage as a heterosexual union that is lifelong (indissoluble) and exclusive (monogamous). The sexual act involves a total bodily giving of one person to another. This is a wonderful act that demands totality. Hence, the marital act should be engaged in only between two persons who have already consented to and contracted a marital bond. The totality of the act calls for the bond to be monogamous and lifelong. Moreover, procreation as the end of the act also entails a monogamous and lifelong bond because the goals of human formation and flourishing require as much. So marriage is an exclusive and indissoluble bond between a man and a woman, who offer and accept spousal rights, ordered to the procreation and education of children.

Now, when the objective end of marriage as procreation is not appreciated, one risks conceiving of marriage simply in terms of the other goods associated with marriage. Among these goods are the sexual friendship of the spouses and the delights—physical, emotional, and rational—of intimacy. These features, when not ordered to the good of offspring, become unmoored and disfigured. Suddenly, the rationale for marriage is reduced to a contract for affectionate sexual union. Already, the very union itself is disordered, i.e., severed from its proper end. Furthermore, this affectionate sexual union quickly devolves into a focus on the subjective experience of genital pleasure. This devolution logically opens the door for unnatural sexual unions because subjective genital pleasure has been sundered from its order to procreation and to the sexual complementarity that thoroughly defines the essence of all the affectivity—not merely the climactic act itself—in the relationship. Thus, marriage is deformed from a society of male and female that is ordered to the procreation of children into a society of male and female ordered simply to each other and to their genital pleasure. From this point, there is no conceivable limit as to what characteristics may or may not be ascribed to marriage: polyandrous, homosexual, transsexual, nonsexual, and so forth.

False Mercy

Documentary Sketch of the Church's Teaching

Scripture, Theology, and Magisterial Teachings before Vatican II

The opening chapter of Genesis celebrates a major activity of every bodily thing that lives—namely, to produce another of its kind. This celebration begins on day 3. It continues on day 5 and reaches a climax on day 6, with the command issued to the human race: "Be fruitful and multiply." This beautiful hymn thus portrays the rhythm of the heartbeat of physical life. As Plato insightfully observed, procreation is a physical thing's way of imitating the eternity of God. The division of male and female is ordered to procreation. Accordingly, the early chapters of Genesis go on to condemn the perversions of homosexual intercourse (Gen. 19) and contraceptive sex (Gen. 38:9–10).[497] Moreover, on the night of his wedding, Tobit spoke to the Lord, "You know that I do not take my sister for the sake of pleasure but solely for the love of posterity" (Tob. 8:9 in the Vulgate). The Bible clearly envisions that sexual intercourse belongs only in marriage and has procreation as its end.

For their part, most of the Fathers of the Church taught that the *only* permissible motivation for intercourse was procreation; and, of course, all Fathers taught that the act is reserved for marriage.[498] Other Fathers more

---

[497] Although the Fathers and the Church's Magisterium have consistently interpreted Onan's death as punishment for his act of *coitus interruptus*, some biblical scholars have recently claimed that Onan was punished for breaking the Levirite law according to which a brother is to marry his elder brother's widow if she was left childless. Christian Washburn has shown that this interpretation does not avail, because other people violated the Levirite law but were not killed. Only Onan was killed. See Christian Washburn, "Fruitful Married Love: The Catholic Church's Teaching on Marriage, Abortion, and Contraception" (National Catholic and Evangelical Dialogue, 2021 [forthcoming]).

[498] I refer the reader to the study of the dissenter John Noonan. See John T. Noonan, *Contraception: A History of Its Treatment by the Catholic Theologians and Canonists* (Cambridge, MA: Harvard University Press, 1966), 57–58. Noonan's treatment of the history shows that the Church has consistently rejected contraception. His own animus against this teaching simmers throughout this treatment. He juxtaposes love (affection) and

reasonably insisted that other motivations were acceptable; they insisted only that the marital act never be unnatural—that is, that it always be open to life—regardless of the couple's intentions. While the former set of Fathers are too strict in eliminating other possible, subordinate ends, they give clear witness to the long-standing Catholic tradition on the primary end, as does the second set of Fathers. In fact, we might ask whether we have a consensus of the Fathers on the primary end; if we have such a consensus, then the teaching would be infallible.

The Magisterium does not appear to teach on the ends of the marital act and of marriage until the fifteenth century. Earlier theological labor had prepared for this teaching. Against certain rigorists who promoted virginity and considered marriage essentially tainted by sin, St. Augustine and other Fathers defended the goodness of marriage. Focusing on sacramental marriage, Augustine highlighted three goods of marriage: faith (or the fidelity between spouses), offspring, and sacrament.[499] Later, St. Isidore of Seville (d. 636) highlighted three *causes* or reasons one may have for getting married. These are the three "ends" listed above.[500] As Isidore laid them out, the second of Augustine's goods, offspring, is the first cause or end. Peter Lombard (d. 1160) expressly ranked offspring as the primary reason for entering marriage: "Therefore, the chief (*principalis*) reason (*finalis causa*) for contracting marriage is the procreation of offspring."[501] The theological tradition followed Lombard on this point, but it also added numerous other considerations from various points of view.[502] Thus, the theological tradition offers a rich set of reflections on this not so easy topic.

---

nature (procreation) as two separable goods. In short, his own worldview is badly in need of the vision of John Paul II. Notwithstanding, his historical treatment shows that the patristic and theological traditions are unanimous in condemning contraception.

[499] Augustine, *De nuptiis et concupiscentia*, I, chap. 11, no. 13.

[500] See Isidore, *Etymologies*, IX, 9.27.

[501] Peter Lombard, *Sententiae in IV Libris Distinctae*, IV, d. 30, chap. 3:7–8 (Rome: Grattaferrata, 1981), vol. 2, 441, my translation.

[502] See, for example, St. Bonaventure, *Liber IV Sententiarum*, d. 31, q. 2 (Florence: Quaracchi, 1949), 703–704.

St. Thomas Aquinas's analysis is profound. Our exposition of it will accomplish three things: (1) affirm the infallible teaching on procreation as the essential end of marriage, (2) affirm the long-standing teaching on procreation as the *primary* end, and (3) demonstrate that the teaching on the primary end is a complex matter and that the order of matrimonial goods can be appreciated in different lights.

St. Thomas takes up Augustine's goods—faith, offspring, and sacrament—and considers their hierarchal ordering. (Note that Thomas is here considering sacramental marriage.) A hierarchy of goods, he notes, may be viewed from different vantage points. One may look at what is most excellent or at what is most essential (nearest to what a thing *is*). Salvation is most excellent, but our human nature is most essential. Aquinas applies this distinction as follows. The most excellent good of marriage is sacrament, since it pertains to the order of grace. In the order of what is most essential, Aquinas again offers distinct viewpoints. Marriage consists in a union of man and woman who offer and receive spousal rights. Every valid sacramental marriage is a real marriage, whether or not the spouses make use of these rights or bear fruit from that use. So, once again, the *sacrament* or bond of the two is most essential when we consider the marriage *itself*. (If the marriage is valid, there always is a sacrament, whether or not there are children.)

If, however, we consider the nature of the institution to which the engaged partners are about to consent, then another ordering of goods comes to light. When consenting to the marriage, the man and woman consent to enter a society that is ordered to procreation. It is ordered to procreation because it is a society marked by the mutual offering and acceptance of spousal rights. Thus, those who enter marriage intend to enter a society of this description. That consent points to the act proper to marriage, the marital act. Now, this act has its *telos* or end, offspring. Thus, that to which the contracting parties ultimately give consent is an orientation to offspring. Aquinas asserts that, according to this analysis, offspring is the most essential good in marriage.[503] The reader will readily

---

[503] See Thomas Aquinas, *Supplement of the Summa theologiae*, q. 49, art. 3.

see that this analysis is rather complex. It should come as no surprise, then, that the order of ends admits of nuance. One thing it does not admit: *a denial that procreation is an essential end of marriage and the marital act.*

The Council of Florence, in its Decree for the Armenians, offers what may be the first magisterial teaching on the ends of marriage. It takes up Augustine's three goods but puts them in a precise order, highlighting offspring as the first good: "A triple good is found in matrimony. The first is the begetting of children and their education to the worship of God."[504] This same council also links the *purpose* of sacramental marriage—that to which it is ordered—not to the good of the married couple but to the good of the increase of the Church. As it states, whereas five of the seven sacraments are ordered to the perfection of the recipients, holy orders (priesthood) and matrimony are ordered (*ordinata sunt*) to "the governance and the increase of the whole Church."[505] We see here, without the precise language, the beginnings of the magisterial affirmation of the primary end. By no means does this suggest that the sheer existence of a human being, a natural good, is of greater excellence than a human being with grace. The sacrament involves a good greater than sheer existence. Nonetheless, grace exists only *as* a perfection of an existing human being. So the council is teaching that marriage is ordered to procreation as the ultimate good *proper* to marriage. Further, even the very good of procreation, a natural good, is itself ordered to the state of grace. Thus, the Council of Florence shows us that the procreative end of marriage itself pertains to the supernatural order as well.

The *Roman Catechism*, issued after the Council of Trent, gives us an important official indication of the mind of the Church. The document declares, "The words of the Lord, 'Increase and multiply' ... declare the purpose of the institution of marriage."[506] Once again, we see an implicit affirmation of the primary end. We also learn from this catechism that the Church's view of marriage is complex and rich. It specifies the

---

[504] DH 1327.
[505] DH 1311.
[506] *Catechism of the Council of Trent*, pt. III, chap. on Matrimony, 343.

various aims that a young man and woman may have in mind when proposing to enter marriage, listing them in the following order: (1) an instinct to enter a sexual friendship with the hope also of thereby bearing life more easily, (2) the desire for a family, and (3) a remedy for concupiscence.[507] So long as the man and woman propose to achieve some one of these ends and do not contradict the other ends, they may enter a valid marriage.

As we see from this catechism, the centrality of procreation as end does not mean that a young man and woman must choose procreation as the chief reason for marrying. Quite naturally, a young lady may find being with a young man, full of strength and virtue, to be the most attractive reason for marriage. Conversely, a young man may find being with a young woman of beauty and virtue to be what most attracts him. Often enough, their first interest is simply to join together in holy matrimony. That is, they first think about the very *form or essence* of marriage as a lifelong, indissoluble union. What the Church teaches, and what nature and cultural history attest, is that this union is itself ordered to a good outside of this immediate bond and that that good is offspring. The reason is that marriage has the marital act as its proper act, the act for which it is uniquely suited and the act uniquely suited to it. So the form of marriage is by nature ordered to the end of procreation. Young couples are led to that end by way of their attraction to the form and its proper act. This is only natural. God's ways are good.

Beginning as early as Leo XIII in 1880, we see explicit stress on procreation as the *primary* end of marriage. Leo teaches on the hierarchy of ends in his encyclical on marriage, *Arcanum*. Although he teaches that marriage is a natural institution, he stresses that only sacramental marriage will bring about the cultural healing so necessary for our times. Leo then notes two ends of marriage: procreation and love. He presents them precisely in this order, and he does so by extolling the transposition of those ends onto a higher plane by sacramental grace: "First, there has been vouchsafed to the marriage union a higher and nobler purpose than

---

[507] See ibid., 343–345.

was ever previously given to it. By the command of Christ, it not only looks to the propagation of the human race, but to the bringing forth of children for the Church."[508] In short, Leo here teaches the natural end of marriage by implication. He points out the transformation of the primary end of marriage on the natural plane that occurs by sacramental grace. Whereas nature's end is offspring come to a state of natural virtue, the end of the sacrament is children reared for the kingdom of God. Leo repeats twice more in *Arcanum* that marriage was instituted for the purpose of procreation.[509] In *Rerum novarum*, Leo further declares, "No human law can abolish the natural and original right of marriage, nor in any way limit the chief and principal purpose of marriage ordained by God's authority from the beginning: 'Increase and multiply.'"[510]

The 1917 *Code of Canon Law* repeats this teaching: "The primary end of marriage is the procreation and education of children" (canon 1013 §7). Later, on December 8, 1938, Pius XI issued a *motu proprio* stating: "Because Christian matrimony aims not merely at spiritual union and the temporal good but chiefly (*praecipue*) was divinely ordered for the generation of offspring, so that the human race, according to God's command, 'might increase and fill the earth,' therefore may it be the only and true seedbed for both the Church and society."[511] Here, we see the chief end of matrimony is the generation of offspring, not simply insofar as children, conceived and educated unto maturity, fulfill the natural order but also insofar as they are ordered to a supernatural end and the increase of the Church. This teaching thus echoes that of Florence.

Pius XI most clearly expounds this teaching in his marvelous encyclical *Casti connubii*. First, he follows Florence's ordering of the goods: "Amongst the blessings of marriage, the child holds the first place."[512] He then cites the *Code of Canon Law* in article 17. Then, in his own voice, he explicitly teaches that the primary end of the marital act is procreation:

---

[508] Leo XIII, *Arcanum*, art. 10.
[509] Ibid., arts. 26 and 35.
[510] Leo XIII, *Rerum novarum* (1891), art. 12.
[511] Pius XI, "*Qua cura*," AAS 30 (1938), 410.
[512] Pius XI, *Casti connubii*, art. 11.

"Since, therefore, the conjugal act is destined primarily by nature for the begetting of children, those who in exercising it deliberately frustrate its natural power and purpose sin against nature and commit a deed which is shameful and intrinsically vicious."[513]

Crucial results follow, whether we simply consider procreation as an essential end or whether we focus on procreation as the primary end. *Any* intervention against this end in the exercise of the sexual act is gravely sinful: "Any use whatsoever of matrimony exercised in such a way that the act is deliberately frustrated in its natural power to generate life is an offense against the law of God and of nature, and those who indulge in such are branded with the guilt of a grave sin."[514] Pius XI recognizes the presence of secondary ends of the matrimonial act, but he teaches that these must be subordinated to the primary end. The secondary ends can justify Natural Family Planning: under certain conditions, one may make use of the marital act even when it is not possible to conceive. Nevertheless, one must at least subordinate one's love of the marital act to the objectively primary end of procreation.[515] This subordination occurs when the marital act is performed according to nature, for it is gravely sinful for spouses to choose that it not terminate in the proper manner. One must never deliberately act against the primary end, as happens in contraceptive intercourse:

> For in matrimony as well as in the use of the matrimonial rights there are also secondary ends, such as mutual aid, the cultivating of mutual love, and the quieting of concupiscence which husband and wife are not forbidden to consider so long as they are subordinated to the primary end and so long as the intrinsic nature of the act is preserved.[516]

---

[513] Ibid., art. 54.
[514] Ibid., art. 56.
[515] A perverse rejection of procreation can constitute a "contraceptive mindset."
[516] Pius XI, *Casti connubii*, art. 59.

Pius XI clearly teaches that procreation is the primary end of marriage and the marital act. Importantly, like Leo XIII, Pius XI is also critical of the error of naturalism, which reduces marriage to a mere means for the production of offspring. Such a reduction treats women like baby machines. Such a reduction is abhorrent to the Church. Moreover, Pius XI appreciates the *Roman Catechism's* insight regarding various ways of conceiving marriage and its goods. Specifically, he highlights the beauty of marital fidelity and friendship. These can be foremost in the minds of an engaged couple:

> This mutual molding of husband and wife, this determined effort to perfect each other, can in a very real sense, as the *Roman Catechism* teaches, be said to be the chief reason and purpose of matrimony, provided matrimony be looked at not in the restricted sense as instituted for the proper conception and education of the child, but more widely as the blending of life as a whole and the mutual interchange and sharing thereof.[517]

Pius XI retains his teaching on the primary end but brings to bear other considerations as well.

Pius XII repeatedly confirmed the prior teaching on the primary end. He did so in the face of opposition from theologians who proposed dropping the hierarchy of ends. Some theologians were clamoring that there is no single primary end of marriage but that there are two equally primary ends.[518] Others boldly claimed that procreation is only a secondary end or, worse, that it is not an essential end.[519] Pius XII unequivocally rejected these suggestions on numerous occasions. At the same time, he

---

[517] Ibid., art. 24.

[518] See Herbert Doms, *The Meaning of Marriage*, trans. George Sayer (New York: Sheed & Ward, 1939).

[519] Bernhardin Krempel, who released an important document regarding attestation of a human being damned in Hell, rejected procreation as an integral end in his *Die Zweckfrage der Ehe in Neuer Beleuchtung* (Zürich: Verlagsanstalt Benziger, 1941).

rejected the false notion that procreation is the only end. On October 3, 1941, he declared:

> In this question, as delicate as it is difficult, two tendencies must be avoided: the one which in examining the constitutive elements of the act of generation gives weight only to the *primary purpose* of marriage, as if the *secondary purpose* did not exist or at least were not the *finis operis* established by the very Orderer of nature; and that which considers the secondary purpose as equally *principal*, loosing it from its essential subordination to the primary purpose, which by logical necessity would lead to deadly consequences. If in other words truth stands in the middle, two extremes are to be avoided: on the one hand, the practical denial or excessive denigration of the secondary purpose of marriage and of the generative act; on the other, dissolving or separating beyond measure the conjugal act from the primary purpose to which according to its whole internal structure it is primarily and principally ordered.[520]

A year later, Pius XII reiterated the teaching: "God has established that the father and mother cooperate in the *essential and primary purpose* of the conjugal bond, which is the *generation of children*."[521]

An official agent of doctrinal teaching, the Holy Office also confirmed this teaching on the hierarchy of ends with regard to marriage as a natural institution during the reign of Pius XII. In fact, the Holy Office declared twice on this matter. Each time, the Holy Office taught that the primary end is procreation.[522]

Still later, in a lengthy allocution on October 29, 1951, Pius XII returned to this theme:

---

[520] Preparatory Document for Vatican II, *Dogmatic Constitution on Chastity, Marriage, the Family, and Virginity*, pt. II, art. 11, no. 21, trans. Joseph Komonchak, available at Catholic eBooks Project, https://catholicebooks. wordpress.com/2017/10/11/online-texts-the-original-schemas-drafts-of-vatican-ii/, hereafter *DCM*.
[521] Pius XII, speech, March 18, 1942, in *DCM*.
[522] See CDF declarations of March 29 and April 1, 1944.

> The truth is that marriage, as a *natural institution*, in virtue of *the will of the Creator*, does not have as its primary and intimate purpose the personal perfecting of the spouses, but *the procreation and education of new life.*[523]

He went on to say, "The other ends, inasmuch as they are intended by nature, are not equally primary, much less superior to the primary end, but are essentially subordinated to it."[524]

As if those speeches were not enough, Pius XII repeated himself again on May 19, 1956. Pius XII chose his language carefully; he was a precise theologian. He is not contradicting Aquinas's assertion, and that of the theological tradition, that existence in grace is a loftier good than merely natural existence. Rather, he is claiming that marriage as a natural institution has procreation as its primary end. This end is retained in the sacramental order, but a more excellent good is made available — namely, grace. Still, this good of sacramental grace is *premised* on the natural constitution of marriage as a society ordered to procreation that is inseparable from the definition of marriage. For that very reason, there is no marriage in Heaven, although grace abounds (Luke 20:35–36). And, of course, the very children that are the fruit of the marriage are ordered to the acquisition of grace and glory. That is to say, the procreative end is not simply surpassed by grace; it, too, has grace in its scope.

After Pius, Pope John XXIII held a synod in Rome in 1960. This synod reiterated the perennial teaching: "The primary (*primarius*) end of matrimony is the procreation and education of children (see canon 1013 §1). The other ends, including the betterment of the person, are essentially subordinated to this principal end."[525]

---

[523] Pius XII, allocution on October 29, 1951, in *DCM*.

[524] This translation is widely available online but not on the Vatican website. See Pius XII, "Address to Midwives on the Nature of Their Profession" (1951), Papal Encyclicals, https://www.papalencyclicals.net/Pius12/P12midwives.htm.

[525] *Prima Romana Synodus* (Typis Polyglottis Vaticannis, 1960), 191.

False Mercy

As indicated in this chapter's introduction, the explicit language of primary and secondary ends was discontinued at the Second Vatican Council. The brief history above shows that the language of primary and secondary ends had been in use for at least eighty years. The Council of Florence did not expressly use this language but certainly situated procreation as the primary good. As a result of these considerations, we can say that the doctrine of procreation as the primary end of marriage is at the very least long-standing.

Vatican II and Recent Teaching

Some, however, claim that this doctrine was abrogated at the Second Vatican Council. They argue as follows: First, they point out that Vatican II did not employ this language in *Gaudium et spes*. They contrast this text with that of the preparatory schema, which retained the language of primary end.[526] Thus, they rehash the tired mantra: "We used to believe X; now we believe Y." Second, they cite the following statement of Paul VI in *Humanae vitae*: "This particular doctrine, often expounded by the magisterium of the Church, is based on the inseparable connection, established by God, which man on his own initiative may not break, between the unitive significance and the procreative significance which are both inherent to the marriage act."[527] Paul VI refers to "two meanings" of the marital act but not to primary and secondary ends. Consequently, some theologians began to speak of two equal ends. Third, they showcase the pontificate of John Paul II, who frequently cited this very passage from Paul VI.

Five comments are in order. First, the most important takeaway from the prior tradition is that procreation is the end of marriage and the marital act. Second, from this infallible teaching, we know that contraceptive intercourse and any other exercise of the sexual act divorced from its natural order to procreation are always gravely evil. Third, in what follows, we will see that the new language does not contradict the teaching on the primary end. Fourth, in fact, recent documents reaffirm

---

[526] See *DCM*, art. 11.
[527] Paul IV, *Humanae vitae* (1968), art. 12.

the teaching on the primary end, albeit in different language. Fifth, these recent documents also draw out the implications of the complexity concerning these issues, a complexity already abundantly attested to in the tradition. Concerning this last point, we see a true development of doctrine. Unfortunately, there were bishops and cardinals at the council who pushed for a rejection of procreation as the primary end.[528] Even more rebellious at the time of the council were those who rejected the absolute prohibition of contraceptive intercourse.[529]

Gaudium et spes, the relevant document of Vatican II, reaffirms the perennial tradition, albeit in different words. It declares:

> For God himself is the author of marriage and has endowed it with various benefits and with various ends in view.... By its very nature the institution of marriage and married love is ordered to the procreation and education of the offspring and it is in them that it finds its crowning glory.[530]

Here, the council speaks of "various ends" of marriage but does not use the expression "primary end." Silence, however, is not denial of past doctrine. Moreover, the council clearly states that both marriage itself and conjugal love *are ordered* to procreation and education of children as to their *crowning* culmination. Now, that to which something is ordered is an end. Thus, Vatican II presents procreation as the *end* of conjugal love. This means that procreation is higher as a proper end of this institution. This point is confirmed by the description of procreation as a *crowning* culmination. Procreation is a primary and controlling end. Thus, Vatican II teaches the prior tradition, albeit in different language, repeating this expression later.[531]

---

[528] Some examples include Cardinal Léger of Montreal, Cardinal Alfrink of Utrecht, and Patriarch Maximos IV of Antioch. See Noonan, *Contraception*, 502.

[529] These include Thomas Roberts, S.J., Gregory Baum, Louis Dupré, and Michael Novak. See Noonan, *Contraception*, 512–513.

[530] *Gaudium et spes*, art. 48.

[531] Ibid., art. 50.

Paul VI uses a similar expression: "And if each of these essential qualities, the unitive and the procreative, is preserved, the use of marriage fully
retains its sense of true mutual love and its ordination to the supreme
responsibility of parenthood to which man is called."[532] As he teaches,
both aspects are crucial, the dimension of love and that of procreation.
Still, the act has an ordination to its *supreme* service in paternity or procreation. Once again, this is the ancient teaching put in different words.

John Paul II taught the same for much of his priestly career. Before
becoming pope and taking the name John Paul II, Karol Wojtyla defended the Church's teaching on the primary end at least as late as 1960:
"The proper end of the [sexual] urge, the end *per se*, is something supra-
personal, the existence of the species *Homo*, the constant prolongation
of its existence."[533] Because we are animals, this end is fixed by human
nature. Importantly, however, we are not merely animal but also rational. Hence, we need love. So, the very *manner* in which we fulfill that
urge requires love and personal affection and an orientation of genuine
love. The act is one of complete dedication of oneself to the other; it
signifies a relationship of mutual self-giving. The "personalists" appreciated Wojtyla's stress on this aspect, and rightly so. However, *some* of the
personalists misunderstood that emphasis to mean that the love between
spouses is an end equal to or higher than that of procreation. Wojtyla
rejected that thesis. Marital love lived rationally should color the entire
way the sexual urge is experienced and exercised. However, procreation
remains the end of that urge:

> On no account then is it to be supposed that the sexual urge,
> which has its own predetermined purpose in man independent
> of his will and self determination, is something inferior to the
> person and inferior to love. The proper end of the sexual urge is
> the existence of the species *Homo*, its continuation (*procreatio*),
> and love between persons, between man and woman, is shaped,

---

[532] Paul VI, *Humanae vitae*, art. 12.
[533] See Karol Wojtyla, *Love and Responsibility*, trans. H.T. Willetts (San
Francisco: Ignatius Press, 1981), 51.

channeled one might say, by that purpose and formed from the material it provides.[534]

Wojtyla never retracted that thesis.

As John Paul II, he delivered messages on the Theology of the Body. In these, he reaffirmed that sexuality "is ordered to an end."[535] He specified that the new language of the Magisterium does not alter the traditional ends of marriage or their ordering; instead, it adds the depth that we will explore further in the next section:

> Although, in approaching the issue, neither the conciliar constitution nor the encyclical use the traditional language (defining the hierarchy of ends: "procreation," "mutual aid," and "remedy of concupiscence"), they nevertheless speak about that to which the traditional expressions refer.... In this renewed orientation [or formulation], the traditional teaching on the ends of marriage (and on their hierarchy) is confirmed and at the same time deepened from the point of view of the interior life of the spouses, of conjugal and familial spirituality.[536]

In *Familiaris consortio*, he repeated the substance of this teaching although in different words: "According to the plan of God, marriage is the foundation of the wider community of the family, since the very institution of marriage and conjugal love are ordained to the procreation and education of children, in whom they find their crowning."[537] This is an echo of *Gaudium et spes*. Without using the words "primary end," John Paul effectively conveyed the same meaning. We see here continuity, not rupture.

Finally, the recent *Catechism* notes that a child is the "supreme gift" of marriage.[538] The choice of wording—gift—is apt. It is obvious that a

---

[534] Ibid., 52–53.

[535] John Paul II, *Man and Woman He Created Them: A Theology of the Body*, trans. Michael Waldstein (Boston: Pauline Books and Media, 2006), 184.

[536] Ibid., 642–643.

[537] John Paul II, *Familiaris consortio* (1981), art. 14.

[538] CCC 2378.

couple can be lawfully and happily married and yet not be blessed with the gift of children. As Thomas noted, children do not constitute the essence but the end of marriage. Notwithstanding, this society of love has children as its primary end. So, to undertake to enter that society without appreciation of its objective orientation to procreation is absurd. Still, fruitfulness remains a gift that cannot be demanded but only welcomed. Those who demand it, by way of in vitro fertilization, for example, sin against the sixth commandment. And what if, after a devastating war, an unrighteous nation were to treat young adults as breeding machines, divorced from the society of marriage? The primary purpose of sexual intercourse does not mean that bare reproduction is a good to be pursued in itself and at all costs.

Those who reject the teaching on the *primary* end and cite recent magisterial teachings as support are practicing a hermeneutic of rupture. Their interpretation is not supported by the evidence. As we have seen, the Magisterium has never rejected this precise teaching. Rather, it has confirmed it in different words. Why the change in approach? I argue that there has been a legitimate development of doctrine, which is already anticipated in the tradition.

A Legitimate Development of Doctrine

We may interpret the recent magisterial expressions as part of a legitimate development of doctrine. As some theologians have noted, the new term being employed is "meaning" or "significance" (*significatio*). This term is not the same as "end" (*finis*). In a sense, "meaning" is less descriptive because it is less precise. In another sense, it is potentially richer because it is open to more concerns. We might take the term to mean something like "good aspect" or "integral aspect." Read in this way, the marital act has two good, integral, and inseparable aspects — procreation and union (i.e., the sexual union of two in lifelong friendship).

A question remains: How can we relate this new approach to the previous approach? St. Thomas Aquinas's reflections — not to mention St. Bonaventure's — invite an answer, as does the *Roman Catechism*. Representative of a compelling solution, Ramón García de Haro presents an analysis that accords with Aquinas's invitation. De Haro argues that the "two meanings" of which *Gaudium et spes*, Paul VI, and John Paul II speak consist in the formal cause and the final cause of marriage and the marital act. The final cause is an "end" or purpose, while the formal cause is really the *essence* or "what it is" of something. Take a car, for instance. The final cause of the car is expeditious arrival at some destination. This is the purpose or reason we have cars. However, this reason is not identical to the very essence of the car. The essence of the car is that it is a motor vehicle for passengers. Again, we might say that the end of a sports team is victory or at least athletic excellence, but its very essence is an ordered group of players undertaking an athletic action in common. When we want to appreciate something, we should take into account not only its end but also its essence. Both aspects help us gain an understanding of it. The same is true with marriage.

De Haro contends that while the primary end of marriage is procreation, the essence of marriage is an indissoluble sexual bond of man and woman. His comment aligns well with Aquinas's analysis. If we take de Haro's insight and read it in light of theology and canon law, we should distinguish two aspects of this sexual bond. On the one hand, there is the essence of the bond itself. The bond is authored by God and remains in place until the death of one of the spouses. This fact is the foundation of marriage in canon law. This bond exists whether or not the spouses remain faithful and become the better for their marriage. Still, this contractual bond does have a purpose or a point. When lived rightly, the bond issues in a deep and sincere *friendship*. This beautiful implication is what *should* take place. If such friendship fails to develop, it remains a valid marriage, even though marked by tragedy. It is not a "failed marriage" that needs to be annulled. No. It is a wounded marriage that must be healed. As de Haro argues, the recent Magisterium has stressed the essence of marriage as the sexual bond of man and woman, a bond oriented toward a life of fruitful communion. Recent magisterial statements, therefore, do not pit the marital bond against the primary end of fruitful communion, as though these were rival ends. There is no rupture. The prior tradition remains true and yet the new focus on the sexual bond highlights hitherto known but not stressed aspects of marriage. I think de Haro's observation on this point is accurate.[539]

Current Confusion on Contraception

Opponents of the Church's condemnation of contraception use statements from Pope Francis to defend their position. Two statements come to mind. Before treating these difficulties, we should note that these rebels do not cite Pope Francis's clear teachings in support of real family and procreation. For example, in Manila, Francis said, "The family is also threatened by growing efforts on the part of some to redefine the very institution of marriage, by relativism, by the culture of the ephemeral, by a lack of openness to life."[540]

1. Of the statements that renegades may use, most memorably, there was what some call "Rabbitgate." In an interview on an airplane leaving the Philippines, Pope Francis said, "Some think that—excuse the word—that in order to be good Catholics we have to be like rabbits." In response to this proposition, he retorted, "No."[541]

What should we think of this comment? Most importantly, it is not a papal word; it is a nonauthoritative remark. As for its content, we can make two remarks. On the one hand, some have taken it as an insult. They don't feel built up by these words; they feel torn down. On the other hand, there is a point to be made here, which could have been made tactfully. Just as we are called to be tactful toward non-Catholics, we can be tactful toward Catholics. Now, what is this legitimate point? Catholics should not be pressured into having so many children that their households become extremely disordered, chaotic, and unmanageable.

---

[539] See Ramón García de Haro, *Marriage and the Family in the Documents of the Magisterium* (San Francisco: Ignatius Press, 1989), 234–256.

[540] Pope Francis, Meeting with Families (January 16, 2015).

[541] See Joshua J. McElwee, "Francis Lambasts International Aid, Suggests Catholics Should Limit Children," *National Catholic Reporter*, January 19, 2015, https://www.ncronline.org/news/francis-lambasts-international-aid-suggests-catholics-should-limit-children.

They should not feel guilty for spacing out their children with the licit use of Natural Family Planning (NFP). People in such circumstances should recognize that the primary end of marriage involves more than one responsibility. The primary end is the "procreation *and education*" of offspring. As a husband, I am not called to produce as many children with my wife as is physically possible. I am called to be generous in procreating children *so as to raise them up well as citizens of Heaven.* If I cannot manage the children I have, then, in seeking more and more of them, I risk doing injustice to those that I already have. The Christian life is orderly and measured; we are not called to make a mess of things. Still, in our culture, few couples struggle with the prospect of too many children. Most couples struggle with selfishness, with not wanting a second or third child to interrupt or cramp their lifestyle of vacations and leisure or of excessive ambition. There is a balanced and middle way, and to communicate that path may have been the pope's intent.

The pope went on to tell a story. He mentioned a woman whom he had recently met; she had had seven cesarean sections and was at the time pregnant with her eighth child. He commented, "That is an irresponsibility!" It is not clear to me whether he said this to the woman herself. At any rate, some comments are in order. A pastoral way of dealing with the woman's situation would be to affirm what is most important first and to offer advice second. Since the woman was already pregnant, it would have been good first to affirm the new life and the woman's heroism, even if imprudent. Despite the medical obstacles she faced, she was generously open to new life. If counsel toward moderation and the use of NFP were warranted, this would be fruitfully added second as regards possible future situations. In a meeting with families in Santiago, Pope Francis took this latter approach and said, "A child is a hope."[542]

2. A year later, Francis made a remark about contraception and the Zika virus. On February 17, 2016, he conducted an airplane interview on his way home from Mexico. A journalist asked him whether a woman with the Zika virus could abort her child if she became pregnant or at

---

[542] Pope Francis, Meeting with Families, September 22, 2015.

least use contraception to avoid conceiving a deformed child in the first place.[543] Pope Francis responded as follows:

> Abortion is not a "lesser evil". It is a crime. It is wiping out one to save another. That is what the mafia does. It is a crime, it is absolutely evil. Regarding a "lesser evil": preventing pregnancy is one thing—we are speaking in terms of the conflict between the 5th and 6th Commandments. The great Paul VI, in a difficult situation in Africa, allowed nuns to use a form of artificial contraception amid the violence. It is important not to confuse the evil of preventing pregnancy, in itself, with abortion. Abortion is not a theological issue: it is a human issue, it is a medical issue. One person is killed in order to save another—in the best case scenario—or in order to live comfortably. It is against the Hippocratic Oath that physicians take. It is an evil in and of itself. It is not a "religious" evil, to start with, no, it is a human evil. Evidently, as it is a human evil—like all killing—it is condemned. On the other hand, preventing pregnancy is not an absolute evil, and in certain cases, such as the one I mentioned of Bl. Paul VI, it was clear.[544]

What should we think of this statement? Again, it is not a papal word; it is a word of a pope aired publicly. Words of a pope are not magisterial.

We should also examine the contents of the statement. The question that was asked concerned a woman who *freely* engages in sexual intercourse. It was asked whether abortion and contraception are permissible for her. Some might interpret the cited remarks to include the

---

[543] The concern is that a woman infected with Zika might give birth to an infant with microcephaly, i.e., a shrunken brain. See Catholic News Agency, "Full text of Pope Francis' in-flight interview from Mexico to Rome," February 18, 2016, https://www.catholicnewsagency.com/news/full-text-of-pope-francis-in-flight-interview-from-mexico-to-rome-85821.

[544] "In-Flight Press Conference of His Holiness Pope Francis from Mexico to Rome," February 17, 2016, http://www.vatican.va/content/francesco/en/speeches/2016/february/documents/papa-francesco_20160217_messico-conferenza-stampa.html.

following five assertions: (1) Abortion is an "absolute evil," which in no case is permissible. (2) That abortion is an evil is a matter not of special religious teaching but of the natural law, which is knowable by natural reason. (3) By contrast, contraceptive sexual intercourse, while evil in some sense, is not an absolute evil. (4) Hence, a ban on contraceptive sexual intercourse admits of exceptions. In such cases the contraceptive method is good. Finally, (5) some may take the remarks to imply that knowledge that contraceptive sexual intercourse is generally evil is not a matter of natural law but of special religious teaching.

As I have formulated them, theses 4 and 5 contradict Catholic teaching. Let us return to these formulations after analyzing statement 3. Statement 3 and statement 1 mention "absolute evil." What does "absolute evil" mean? Two possible answers suggest themselves: absolute evil is (a) evil itself existing or (b) an intrinsically evil act. Which of these two is the meaning of the original remark? Does the remark present absolute evil as (a), evil itself existing? Well, the assertion that there exists an "absolute evil" contradicts the Catholic teaching that everything that exists, insofar as it exists and is of some nature, is good. The Council of Florence declares:

> The Holy Roman Church most firmly believes, professes, and preaches that the one true God ... is the creator of all things, visible and invisible.... They are good since they were made by him who is the highest good, but they are mutable because they were made out of nothing. She asserts that there is no such thing as a nature of evil, because all nature, as nature, is good.[545]

The council goes on to declare that the Church "firmly believes, professes, and preaches that every creature of God is good."[546] If the remark does

---

[545] DH 1333.

[546] DH 1350. To be sure, this teaching does not mean that everyone goes to Heaven or that no one can be truly morally wicked. It just means, for example, that the devil, insofar as he has an angelic nature and exists, is good. But this existence is quite loathsome to him, for he hates everything about himself and about God, and it is loathsome to every other person. Truly, he is tortured, just as all unrepentant sinners are tortured.

not present absolute evil as (a), evil itself existing, perhaps it presents absolute evil as (b), an intrinsically evil act. Now, an intrinsically evil act is an act that is inherently evil. Because it is fundamentally evil by nature, it is never a morally good thing to choose, no matter one's intention and no matter the circumstances. Intrinsically evil acts are always and everywhere prohibited by what we call a "negative moral norm." Negative moral norms apply always and everywhere, since they absolutely forbid this or that action.[547] Now, the remarks present what is "absolutely evil" as never permitted. By contrast, they present what is not "absolutely evil" as permissible in certain circumstances. Further, they present what is absolutely evil as that which is evil "in and of itself." Therefore, the remarks seem to present absolute evil as (b), an intrinsically evil act. But this raises a difficulty. How? Claim 3, that contraceptive intercourse is not absolutely evil, would then mean that contraceptive intercourse is not an intrinsic evil. Further, it would entail (4) that contraceptive intercourse is at times permissible. Now, these two claims contradict the constant and infallible teaching of the Church. But no one may deny infallible teaching. So, according to the preservative mode of the hermeneutic of continuity, no one may use this Zika statement as an excuse to claim that contraceptive intercourse is not intrinsically evil.

Pope Francis presents two arguments in defense of the claim. In the first, he presents a woman with the Zika virus who *freely* wants to engage in sexual intercourse as being trapped in a moral *dilemma*. A dilemma is a situation in which there is no morally good option available: no matter what you do, you will violate right living. Now, the woman is depicted as being in a situation in which she is able to obey only one of two commandments, either the fifth commandment or the sixth commandment, not both. Allegedly, she must violate one of these commandments. We are not told how or why this is the case. Commentators have taken the comment

---

[547] By contrast, we cannot always and in all circumstances fulfill a positive norm. For example, the commandment to "love the Lord above all things" cannot be fulfilled in sleep. Neither, of course, is it violated in sleep (contrary to Luther's heresy).

to mean the following: contracepting will violate the sixth commandment, which prohibits adultery, whereas taking the risk of conceiving a child with the birth defect of microcephaly will violate the fifth commandment, which prohibits killing, maiming, and so on. Thus, allegedly, the woman is in a moral dilemma. Now, on this reading, major problems arise.

From the Catholic doctrinal vantage point, moral dilemmas are pure figments of the imagination. The notion of a dilemma contradicts Catholic teaching. In any situation, a possible course of action is always not to act. Rather than betray *either* this person *or* that person to the Marxist usurpers, one may simply not act. In so doing, one fulfills one's obligation to the negative moral norm. True, one has not achieved the result one wishes, to save both, but neither has one done evil. We are not consequentialists. Now, we need God's strength to live rightly. He offers us this strength. As we have seen, it is solemn Catholic teaching that God's laws are possible to obey for the justified: "If anyone says that the commandments of God are impossible to observe even for a man who is justified and established in grace, let him be anathema."[548] Accordingly, the justified person may always obey the commandments of God.[549] The as yet unjustified can always pray for the grace of justification. A true moral dilemma is thus impossible. Pius XI of most happy memory applied this dogma to a husband and wife struggling with hopelessness in a difficult situation. He counseled them not to despair: "No difficulty can arise that justifies the putting aside of the law of God which forbids all acts intrinsically evil. There is no possible circumstance in which husband and wife cannot, strengthened by the grace of God, fulfill faithfully their duties and preserve in wedlock their chastity unspotted."[550] There is no such thing as a moral dilemma. Difficulties, yes; dilemmas, no.

For his part, Pius XI stressed that a couple who rightly judge that conceiving another child would be too great a burden may refrain

---

[548] Trent, Session VI, canon 18; DH 1568.
[549] As for sinners, they are called to repent. God offers them the grace of repentance.
[550] Pius XI, *Casti connubii*, art. 61.

from the marital act or at least not use the marital act during times of fertility. The spouses *have the strength* to do this; they can refrain because grace is available. Because they can refrain from acting, they are not stuck in a moral dilemma. We can apply Pius XI's authoritative teaching to the woman Francis was considering. How can the woman avoid conceiving a child deformed with microcephaly? She can do so by freely choosing *not* to engage in sexual intercourse, or at least not to engage in it during a fertile period. Does she have strength to do this? Yes, because Christ can help her, just as He will support her husband so that he might show appropriate tender affection for his bride. There is no doubt that such a situation can be a severe trial. A severe trial is not a dilemma, except for those who do not believe in Christ or who despair of His grace.

Another comment about this chimerical "dilemma." When I first considered the allusion to a conflict between the fifth and sixth commandments, I interpreted it in a different way, contrary to the commentators. I earlier thought that, by alluding to a violation of the fifth commandment, the story implied that the woman would very likely *die* if she were to become pregnant. Now, *even* if that were the case, the woman would not be in a dilemma; she and her husband would be able to refrain from the marital act. Further, even if they, in a moment of vulnerability, engaged in the act during a time of fertility, they would most certainly *not* violate the fifth commandment. They would be engaged in a naturally good act. They would not be acting immorally. They would be performing a good act, which might have an *accidental, unintended, and indeed tragic* side effect. Since Catholic moral reasoning is not consequentialist, Catholic moral theology would not condemn their action even if it happened to result in the tragic death of the woman. Her death would be a side effect of an act that is good in itself, an act proper to marriage.

But let us leave aside this reading. The commentators more reasonably read the remark as regarding the conception of a deformed baby. According to this reading, the remark *alleges* that the fifth commandment would be violated because of a potential birth defect. Now, the suggestion of a violation of the fifth commandment here is erroneous. One does not violate the fifth commandment by conceiving a child, *even* if that child is likely to have a birth defect. A child is a child. The defect would be a heavy cross, to be sure. The child would bear that cross as would the parents. But such a birth defect would not be an evil that the parents inflict on their child. It would be the accidental and unintended result of a good marital act.

In a second defense of the claim, Pope Francis references a popular story of Paul VI granting permission to certain nuns to use artificial contraception.[551] We can ask why such permission would be morally licit. Nuns in such a situation could expect with moral certainty to be *raped*. As such, they would be merely passive victims of the rape; they would not be free partners in a sexual act. Hence, they would bear no moral responsibility to consent to the natural end of this act: fertilization of the egg by the sperm. Now, according to medical knowledge at the time, the pill would simply prevent ovulation. But a nonfertilized egg and a solitary sperm have no moral status; they are not human beings. So, they have no "right" to unite. Consequently, it was permissible for these nuns to take the pill so as to make their bodies indisposed to pregnancy should they be raped. (At that time, we did not know that the pill also occasionally has an abortifacient effect. Moralists must now weigh this issue in light of the new knowledge, which does not necessarily demand an opposite conclusion; it is a difficult matter to think through.) In short, the nuns were *not* permitted to engage in contraceptive intercourse.

The Church's condemnation of artificial contraception is not directed at physical things but rather against the use of those things for inappropriate acts — namely, contraceptive intercourse. Problematically, the appeal to the story of the nuns gives the *appearance* that *contraceptive* intercourse can be permitted at least in some circumstances. But this proposition contradicts perennial and infallible Church teaching. The nuns were never permitted to engage in contraceptive intercourse; they

---

[551] According to anecdotes, the nuns in the Congo were using anovulant pills to avoid pregnancy in case of possible rape, beginning in the year 1960. It should be noted that Paul VI was not pope until 1963.

were protecting themselves from the consequences of rape.[552] Contraceptive intercourse is always intrinsically evil and therefore never permissible under any circumstance.[553]

[552] They would never be able to procure an abortion, for to do that would be to commit murder.

[553] We should also warn the reader about a new movement in moral theology, called the New Natural Law (NNL). Many proponents of this theory espouse a seriously faulty notion of the moral object of an act. To be sure, proponents of the NNL wish to uphold the Church's moral teaching, and they have nobly fought in defense of Church teaching against dissenters and consequentialists. They are good Catholics and orthodox theologians. Still, little *o* orthodoxy does not mean correct. Their thought is problematic. In a nutshell, they think that one's intention has much more power to determine the nature of an act than do traditional moralists. Traditional moralists hold that when one intelligently chooses to perform some act, X, that one necessarily chooses also those effects that are *per se* connected to the act. For example, crushing a baby's skull (craniotomy) has a *per se* effect: it kills the baby. Everyone knows this. Now, every baby is innocent. But to choose to take the life of an innocent person is murder. Therefore, traditional moralists hold that whoever chooses to crush a baby's skull chooses to commit murder. The culprit may plead with us that he "only wanted to save the mother," but, in fact, he has saved the mother *by* killing the baby. Many of the proponents of the NNL hold, to the contrary, that one may rightly perform a craniotomy on a baby. They argue that one's intention determines the act. They hold that someone may choose this act not as a first and murderous step—crushing an infant's skull—to a woman's health but as a single act, the "reshaping" of the baby's skull so as to fit it through the birth canal. They say that the "side effect" of the skull reshaping is the baby's death. People of sound prudence and good moralists reject this. They hold that we may never do evil so that good may come. Consequently, they hold that we may never undertake the crushing of an infant's skull, even if both baby and mother were to die. To perform the craniotomy would be to commit murder. Why? Because the *per se* effect of skull crushing is the death of the infant. When I choose skull crushing, I choose the baby's death, even though I "wish" that the baby would not die. We see a similar contrast on sperm collection. Good moralists hold that no one may commit the sin of masturbation so as to procure a sperm sample for medical use. It would be doing an evil so that good may result. But NNL logic would hold that one's intention changes the act. Instead of masturbating, one

Conclusion

The Magisterium of the Church teaches that the end of the marital act and of marriage is the procreation and education of offspring. This teaching is infallible. The Church has also long taught that this end is the primary end. This latter teaching has never been overturned, and the recent Magisterium has reaffirmed it in different words.

The recent Magisterium has also approached marriage and the marital act from a different perspective, according to which we can speak of two meanings of the marital act and hence of two fundamental aspects of marriage. This new approach has roots in none other than the Angelic Doctor and the *Roman Catechism*. It is by no means a deviation from the deposit of faith. Rather, it is a legitimate development of doctrine.

The consequences of this basic teaching are crucial. Marriage is a society whose proper act is the sexual act. Thus, the tradition speaks of the marital act and of its use. Since the sexual act is ordered to procreation, it is essentially an act of two persons of the opposite sex. Therefore, marriage requires, and is defined or characterized by, the exchange of consent to enter a society which includes the right to intercourse, which will, of course, be heterosexual. So sexual intercourse is morally good only if three conditions are met: (1) The act is engaged in between two of the opposite sex. (2) These two are joined in real marriage. (3) The act terminates in a manner proper to procreation. In this chapter, we have dealt with various confusions that either violate condition 3 or deny that procreation is the end of the marital act. In the next chapter, we deal with the sin of sodomy, which violates all three conditions.

---

is merely "procuring sperm." This is absurd. We can see that the NNL theory is highly problematic. For more in-depth treatment of NNL and the moral act, see Steven Long, *The Teleological Grammar of the Moral Act* (Washington, DC: Catholic University of American Press, 2008).

9

Is Sodomy Now Permitted?

As we saw from the previous chapter, the Church teaches infallibly that the sexual act is good only if it meets three conditions: (1) It is engaged in by a man and a woman. (2) The man and woman are married to each other. (3) The act terminates in a manner that is *per se* open to procreation. A sexual act that fails to meet any of these conditions is intrinsically and gravely evil. Fornication, adultery, contraceptive intercourse, and sodomy all violate one or more of these conditions. Having already addressed the sin of contraception in the last chapter, we now proceed with a discussion of the sin of sodomy. What *is* sodomy?

The great Doctor of the Church, St. Peter Cardinal Damian, devoted much attention to this particular vice in a book he wrote for Pope Leo IX titled *Liber Gomorrhianus* (*The Book of Gomorrah*). In it he defines sodomy broadly to include four forms: "Some pollute themselves, others are soiled by fondling each other's male parts, others fornicate between the thighs or in the rear, and these ascend by grades, such that each one is worse than the previous."[554] Peter Damien's definitions in modern translation include solitary and mutual male masturbation (the first two forms) as well as what is typically understood today to mean sodomy or

---

[554] St. Peter Damian, *The Book of Gomorrah and St. Peter Damian's Struggle against Ecclesiastical Corruption*, trans. Matthew Cullinan Hoffman (New Braunfels, TX: Ite ad Thomam Books and Media, 2015), 83.

anal intercourse (the fourth form). Each of these acts fails to terminate in a manner that is open to conception. St. Peter's descriptions can be understood to include female sodomy by analogy. Finally, because sodomy is by nature infertile, some of his definitions have implications also for heterosexual sodomy and, even more broadly, contraceptive intercourse. All these actions are both intrinsically and gravely evil, the fourth form being the gravest.

All human persons have dignity and deserve respect and love. This is true whether or not they are attractive, enjoyable to converse with, virtuous, or struggling with difficulties. So, too, it is true with those who are tempted by the sins of sodomy, with those who, out of weakness, occasionally engage in such sins, and with those who embrace a lifestyle centered on such sins. Jesus Christ calls His disciples to love everyone. Thus, Jesus calls us to love all such persons. He, the Truth, teaches that love must be true, since truth sets one genuinely free. Now, sodomy is a sin against human nature. It therefore damages the person who commits it. Genuine love does not withhold truth; it communicates it. Thus, genuine love wills the sinner's conversion from the sin of sodomy.

This chapter, first, draws some relevant distinctions rooted in Catholic moral thought. Second, it presents the Church's teachings on sodomy. Third, it treats remarks and gestures of Pope Francis that some have found confusing.

Distinctions

A proper treatment of this topic requires some crucial distinctions. We distinguish the sin itself from the tendency to be attracted by the sin. We also address the question of a homosexual identity, separating a deep-seated from a transitory tendency. Finally, we differentiate between sins of weakness (which are still gravely evil) and the embrace of a sinful lifestyle or impenitence.

1. Acts of sodomy in any of the above forms are both intrinsically evil and gravely evil. As intrinsically evil, they are never good. As gravely evil, they are such as to destroy the life of sanctity in the soul. These acts

are the result of a series of actions that prepare the way. Now, because the climactic action is sinful, the free acts that are preparatory to it are sinful in the measure that they partake of the disorder of the act. This is the case for any sin. For instance, to buy pornographic material so as to masturbate is already disordered. Similarly, for a married man to give a gift to a woman other than his wife so as to awaken her romantic interest is already sinful. So, to court a relationship with a view to the second, third, or forth acts of sodomy is sinful. Taking the path to sin so as to sin is harmful to the soul.

2. What about the sheer *tendency* to acts of sodomy? Some people at times feel a spontaneous, unwanted attraction to sodomy or the affections ordered toward it, or both. Such spontaneous, unwilled attractions are not sinful. They are a certain form of concupiscence that the Church describes as "an objective disorder."[555] As the Church teaches, it is a "disordered sexual inclination which is essentially self-indulgent."[556] So we distinguish acts of sodomy from unwelcomed desires for such acts.[557]

3. What about a so-called homosexual identity? This question requires some reflection. Following Scripture, the Church teaches that sexual identity regards one's physical makeup as either male or female.[558] In extremely rare cases, due to genetic deformity or organic deformities, it may be difficult to determine whether a given person is male or female. However, *that* each person is either male or female is a revealed datum of the faith. Now, this sexual identity has a natural order toward complementarity. The masculinity of the male is ordered to the femininity of the female, and vice versa. This mutual ordering is the basis for the joy of marriage (Gen. 2:23), which has its crowning in the joy of fecundity (Ps. 139:13–16).

---

[555] CDF, *Letter to the Bishops of the Catholic Church on the Pastoral Care of Homosexual Persons* (1986), art. 3.

[556] Ibid., art. 7.

[557] On the pastoral care of persons struggling with this disorder, see *Living the Truth in Love: Pastoral Approaches to Same-Sex Attraction*, ed. Janet Smith and Paul Check (San Francisco: Ignatius Press, 2015).

[558] See Gen. 1; John Paul II, *Man and Woman*, 166; and CCC 2331–2336.

Consequently, by nature we are ordered to this complementarity. Each person has a *natural* sexual inclination toward the complementarity of male and female and toward fecundity.[559] Normally, this natural inclination is experienced in an ordered way. Such an experience represents a natural development of a natural inclination. Some people, however, experience transitory — not deep-seated — impulses of sexual attraction to persons of the same sex. If these experiences are transitory, the person should not think of himself or herself as "homosexual." Further, such experiences do not represent a natural development of a natural inclination; rather, they represent a disordered development. People mistakenly speak of such inclinations as "natural" because they are *inclinations*. That is, the person suffering them does *incline* to the act. We must say in response that an inclination is natural only if it corresponds to the good of the nature. Since the sexual organs have procreation as their end and since sodomy thwarts that end, neither sodomy nor the inclination to it is natural. As indicated in point 2 above, there is not necessarily any moral culpability for having such an inclination.

For other persons, however, these experiences are deep-seated and long-lasting. Once again, there is not necessarily any moral culpability in this case either. (As with other sins, there can be culpability if sinful habits have been built up — e.g., self-indulgence and narcissism — on account of which any disordered tendency can become more vehement.)[560] Should these people be called "homosexuals"? It depends on the use of the term. Certainly, they have an enduring and difficult cross to bear. They deserve compassion. Children of God loved from eternity, they are called to resist the temptation to act on the tendency.[561] Other people bear other crosses. For example, the angry man must learn to keep his cool, and the busybody must resist the temptation to pry into another's business. Still, we do not and should not define any man by his anger.

---

[559] See Thomas Aquinas, *Summa theologiae*, Ia-IIae, q. 94, art. 2.
[560] See Gerard J. M. Van den Aardweg, *The Battle for Normality* (San Francisco: Ignatius Press, 1997).
[561] CDF, *Pastoral Care of Homosexual Persons*, art. 12.

Even an "alcoholic" should not have this label as his first identity. We should not categorize people by their vices, disorders, or struggles.

Each person is first and most importantly a child of God, called to virtue. But the spirit of the world—what Augustine called the City of Man—rebels against God's order and refuses to worship Him. The City of Man wants to swallow confused and troubled souls. It wants everyone who has even transitory impulses toward sexual affection for members of the same sex to claim "homosexual" as his or her core identity. Not only that, but the City of Man woos such victims to live out its gospel of darkness, seducing the young to adopt sinful lifestyles.

If we use the label "homosexual" to indicate a person struggling with homosexual attraction, then we should differentiate someone who is simply "homosexual" from two other kinds of people. First, we differentiate someone who is simply homosexual from one engages in sodomy in moments of weakness. Second, we differentiate someone who is simply homosexual from a person who embraces a sodomitical lifestyle, to be treated next. If we do not draw these distinctions, we will end up making mistakes. Either we will cast moral blame where none should be found, or we will exonerate sinful acts as though they were good. Worse, we will celebrate a destructive lifestyle.

4. Finally, we must discuss the "gay lifestyle." Some people describe themselves as "gay" or "lesbian," meaning not merely that they have deep-seated tendencies but that they embrace a way of life in accordance with them. They are committed to celebrating acts of sodomy. St. Paul teaches that commitment to *any* sinful lifestyle represents impenitence, a refusal to repent. About impenitence, he warns: "Do you not know that God's kindness is meant to lead you to repentance? But by your hard and impenitent heart you are storing up wrath for yourself on the day of wrath" (Rom. 2:4–5). Impenitence is far worse than committing a sin of weakness out of passion.

In summary, we should keep the following matters distinct: (1) the sinful act of sodomy, (2) the attraction itself not as freely willed, (3) a deep-seated or long-lasting presence of such an attraction, and (4) an impenitent way of life. The very effort to blur the distinction between the tendency and "being gay" (as a "lifestyle") is a strategy inimical to human dignity. It is a strategy of the City of Man, which collectively lusts to absorb unsuspecting victims into its decadent subculture.

A Christian must love everyone, regardless of his or her tendencies, actions, and lifestyle. Thus, those who struggle with this tendency deserve to be loved. Those who commit sodomy deserve our love. Those who embrace the lifestyle deserve our love. We owe love to all because God first loved us, and each of us is a sinner. Now, love is ordered to the truth. So, true love necessarily calls one's friend toward the true good and away from what is sinful and harmful. Therefore, we who love must will that our friend *not* commit acts of sodomy and *not* pursue those things (e.g., relationships) that are ordered to such acts. We want our friend's salvation in virtue, not his damnation in vice. Further, on a very practical level that appeals to the legitimate self-love of each person, we can and should point out the serious health issues associated with gay sex.[562] Above all, we must also point out the sinfulness of these actions. To accept the person is *not* to call a disorder natural, nor to embrace sodomy as good, nor to welcome a sinful lifestyle as praiseworthy. Parish programs should reflect these points. The CDF has clear instructions for pastors:

> No authentic pastoral program will include organizations in which homosexual persons associate with each other without clearly stating that homosexual activity is immoral. A truly pastoral approach will appreciate the need for homosexual persons to avoid the near occasions of sin.[563]

Alas, the simple, clear, infallible teaching of the Church has been obscured by modernists, using remarks of magisterial figures so as to mislead the sheep. We shall tackle this obfuscation in a moment. First, let us consider the Church's teaching more deeply.

---

[562] See, for example, John R. Diggs, M.D., "The Health Risks of Gay Sex," https://www.catholiceducation.org/en/marriage-and-family/sexuality/the-health-risks-of-gay-sex.html.

[563] CDF, *Some Considerations Concerning the Response to Legislative Proposals on the Non-Discrimination of Homosexual Persons* (1992), art. 15.

Catholic Teaching on Sodomy

The Big Picture

The Church has always held, and infallibly taught, that the four forms of sodomy noted at the beginning of this chapter are intrinsically and gravely evil. Consequently, all acts that are ordered to sodomy, including "courtship" and the acquisition of pornography, are sinful in the measure in which they are ordered to sodomy. No one should take any road that leads to ruin.

Why is sodomy sinful? Answering this controversial question requires a big-picture perspective. An aerial view will remind us that everyone needs to repent and to receive forgiveness. None of us is perfect. This does not mean that sin is not sin or that God does not care how we act. God does care, and He has the power and the goodness to forgive us and heal us. Let us consider, then, the big picture.

Although perfectly happy in Himself, God freely created the world. Further, He freely invited the human race to *immediate* union with Him in eternity. That is, He opened up human minds and hearts so that the human person would not merely be united with God indirectly, by way of philosophical discovery and inference, but also immediately, as truly and objectively as one can see the moon or be with a friend, only more so, since we can bear the very oceans within our heart's desire. Union with God is more than touch. Since such an immediate union is above the capacity of human nature, God grants us the graces by which we can achieve this end.

Mortal sin destroys these graces. Further, the act of mortal sin is a direct offense against God and thus deserves everlasting abandonment. Any act of mortal sin has this effect *unless and until* the sinner repents. The first humans committed personal mortal sins by their defiance of God; in the same act, our first father lost for all his posterity the grace of divine fellowship. Consequently, you and I are prone to temptations even from within. Further, by our own mortal sins, we personally enter that original defiance. Each mortal sin that I commit objectively merits my damnation for eternity and fosters in me a habit of vice. The opening chapter on Hell is very much to the point here. Damnation is a terrifying thought, one that is very difficult even to entertain these days, since our culture treats it with such levity. We seem to float free of any moorings, free even from our human animality. In a frivolous age like ours, we drift and float away even from human nature, living life only virtually, and thus become confused about sex.

Thanks be to God, however, who sent His Son among us to become man, to model for us the way to live, to be for us the source of life, to leave us the institutions of salvation, and to offer Himself in sacrifice so that God might be praised and that we might not be damned. Even so, we remain weak and fragile creatures who suffer the effects of Adam's defiance. At the same time, we are invited concretely to return to God, to repent and amend our lives, and to come to Jesus, meek and tender of heart (Matt. 11:28–30), and to lean on the countless means of grace inaugurated by Him. He bears us in His wounded heart and wishes that we, we great sinners, may dwell with Him in the bosom of the Father (John 1:18). The Catholic Church is the saving institution by which God the Father wants to bring us, in the Holy Spirit, through Jesus Christ, to eternal union with Him. The Catholic Church has the road map by which we can discover our true purpose in life and the right way to real Life. The Catholic Church has the resources necessary for us to remedy *any* difficulty we find ourselves in, whether it is our fault, someone else's, or no one's. Salvation is concretely possible because God entered the muck of our lives, dwelt among us, instructed us, instituted for us the saving sacraments, redeemed us by His excruciating Passion and death, gave us the promise of eternal life by His Resurrection, and intercedes now for us.

We must not construct moralities of presumption based on despair. Despair says that I can never change my ways or that I can never become lovely for God, having defiled myself so many times already. Despair says that even God cannot help me, who am so cruel and wrongheaded. Moralities of presumption err in two ways. One form is that, if I only have faith, God does not judge me for my works. If I have faith, I do not need to obey the commandments to be saved. This is Luther's heresy of justification by faith alone. The other form is to say that sin is not sin. I claim that I am "just made that way; I cannot control myself." This second form claims that the sinner is not adversely affected by sin, not made spiritually dead by sin. This presumption suggests that beneath all mortal sin is a shining piece of immaculate gold, the human person himself.

In fact, this form of presumption can get worse. It can come to claim that sin *is good*. This abysmal result is similar to the error noted in chapter 7, according to which the very being of the person is considered to be the telos or end of the person (i.e., being a person and being virtuous or reaching one's end are not distinguished). The confusion in chapter 7 regarded the conflation of being and virtue. The confusion treated in this chapter rests on a denial of nature. But to deny nature is to deny any natural end and thus to affirm any act whatsoever, so long as it is acceptable to those directly affected by it. Hence, this presumption claims that I with my choices should be received and welcomed, now and for eternity, just because I am the way I am. This ideology is contrary to common sense and is deadly. By mortal sin I destroy the spiritual life of my soul; I *embrace* hostile ways; I transform myself into an enemy of God. Henceforth, I cannot have charity toward anyone in the entire world — *unless and until* I repent. After committing mortal sin, I am locked into my selfishness, *until* I repent. Even my *apparent* virtues — such as attractive speech, a handsome appearance, an orderly household, good gardening, a warm smile, culinary skill, musicality, and professional success — are not true virtues, because they fail to achieve the true end of virtue. Although these talents are good in their own way, they do not make me virtuous. They can even be tools for my malice, if I use them to seduce others. Granted, when I garden well, I am not necessarily sinning. Even if I am in a state of mortal sin, not all that I do is a sin (contrary to Luther's error). Still, nothing I do is a true act of virtue *until* I repent.

We can see how this is the case concretely. After I commit a mortal sin, I face a choice: follow God on the path of life by way of repentance or continue on the path of death by way of love of my idol (pleasure, money, honor, and so on). The results that face me are clear: either I obtain eternal life with God by way of repentance, embracing His mercy in the blood of Christ, or I condemn myself to everlasting boredom in

Hell, clinging to my sin. Everyone is faced with this choice. What will we choose? Those who have embraced the lifestyles of sodomy in any of its forms face the same choice as the rest of us who have sinned mortally.

As the Catholic Church teaches, sodomy violates various aspects of the sexual act. As stated above, every sexual act must be (1) between a man and a woman, (2) open to the procreative end, and (3) engaged in the context of true, heterosexual marriage. Sodomy strikes against each of these principles. First, it is always a sexual act committed outside of true marriage. Second, it is, by its very essence, devoid of reference to fecundity; it is against nature. As a result, the whole demeanor and way of being ordered to this lifestyle is against nature. The person who embraces this lifestyle fails to develop a mature sexual identity. Sexual affectivity that should be oriented to the opposite sex is embraced as oriented either to oneself (masturbatory sodomy) or to a member of the same sex (homosexual sodomy). Just as we mitigate concupiscence by virtuous action, so we exacerbate it by sinful action. We wound ourselves deeply when we embrace sinful action. Lastly, both masturbation and homosexual sodomy violate the first aspect of a good sexual act, its sexual complementarity. Contraceptive intercourse violates the second aspect, and adultery and fornication violate the third aspect.[564] So, sodomy of all kinds is even more objectively grave and deadly. These are some of the reasons that sodomy is sinful. We can now briefly trace the history of revelation and doctrine concerning sodomy.

Scripture
The early chapters of Genesis already speak of sodomy as a great sin in the account of Sodom and Gomorrah (Gen. 19:1–11). Some modernists claim that the sin of these men was simply inhospitality, not sodomy. The men of Sodom were indeed inhospitable, but the Church has always read this chapter as also condemning the sin of sodomy. We are speaking chiefly of male homosexual sodomy in its fourth form. The CDF teaches:

---

[564] Adultery adds the malice of injustice against a valid marriage.

In Genesis 19:1–11, the deterioration due to sin continues in the story of the men of Sodom. There can be no doubt of the moral judgment made there against homosexual relations. In Leviticus 18:22 and 20:13, in the course of describing the conditions necessary for belonging to the Chosen People, the author excludes from the People of God those who behave in a homosexual fashion.[565]

The Church also notes that sodomy is one of the four sins in the Bible that "cry out to heaven for vengeance," referencing Genesis 18:20 and 19:13.[566] The Old Testament clearly teaches that sodomy is intrinsically and gravely sinful.

The New Testament is likewise clear. In his Epistle to the Romans, Paul teaches the sinfulness of sodomy:

For this reason God gave them up to dishonorable passions. Their women exchanged natural relations for unnatural, and the men likewise gave up natural relations with women and were consumed with passion for one another, men committing shameless acts with men and receiving in their own persons the due penalty for their error. (Rom. 1:26–27)

Alas, once again, some modernists twist Paul's words so as to find him condoning sin. Therefore, we should cite the Church's interpretation of Paul's message. The CDF teaches:

In Rom. 1:18–32, still building on the moral traditions of his forebears, but in the new context of the confrontation between Christianity and the pagan society of his day, Paul uses homosexual behavior as an example of the blindness which has overcome humankind. Instead of the original harmony between Creator and creatures, the acute distortion of idolatry has led to all kinds of moral excess. Paul is at a loss to find a clearer example of this

---

[565] CDF, *Pastoral Care of Homosexual Persons*, art. 6.
[566] See CCC 1867.

disharmony than homosexual relations. Finally, 1 Tim. 1, in full continuity with the biblical position, singles out those who spread wrong doctrine and in v. 10 explicitly names as sinners those who engage in homosexual acts.[567]

As Paul proclaims, sodomy is a low point in the spiraling devolution of morals in society. Sin begins with ingratitude toward God and devolves into idolatry. From there, it leads to sexual deviance, which has its nadir in sodomy.

Paul also condemns sodomy elsewhere. For example, in 1 Corinthians 6:9–10, he lists various intrinsically evil acts that exclude one from the kingdom of God. We don't quite see Paul's teaching concerning sodomy in most English translations. The RSVCE reads, "Do not be deceived; neither the immoral, nor idolaters, nor adulterers, *nor homosexuals*, nor thieves, nor the greedy, nor drunkards, nor revilers, nor robbers will inherit the kingdom of God" (emphasis mine). Significantly, there are two Greek expressions at play for the one word "homosexuals," μαλακοί (*malakoi*) and ἀρσενοκοῖται (*arsenokoitai*). The Vulgate translates the Greek words with *molles* and *masculorum concubitores*, which have the same meaning as the Greek. These words refer, respectively, to the vice of being soft or effeminate or passive and to the vice of active sodomy. Conjointly, these words display the two aspects of male sodomy: the effeminate or passive aspect of allowing oneself to be violated and the active aspect of violating another.[568] Paul's teaching has analogous implications for females. It goes without saying that Paul is not calling the sheer tendency to sin a sin; nor is he saying that those who have the tendency will be excluded from Heaven. The sinful act excludes from Heaven, unless one repents before death.

---

[567] CDF, *Pastoral Care of Homosexual Persons*, art. 6.

[568] Although the text immediately describes male homosexuals, it implies female homosexuality as well. This implication is really necessitated by the text, not just vaguely present. The text from Romans 1:18–32 bears out the implication explicitly.

The Magisterium

In terms of the Magisterium itself, the CDF's recent teaching against sodomy, cited above, has a long history. First, this teaching is implicit in the Church's teaching on the purpose of sexual intercourse. Every species of sodomy is *per se* closed off to procreation. Thus, every species of sodomy is disordered. Now, violations of the primary end of sex are always *gravely* evil. Second, the condemnation of sodomy is implicit in the Church's constant and infallible condemnation of contraception. If contraception is morally evil although it only violates the procreative (and thereby the unitive) aspect of the sexual act, sodomy is morally evil because it directly violates the other aspects as well. As we have seen, "Any use whatsoever of matrimony exercised in such a way that the act is deliberately frustrated in its natural power to generate life is an offense against the law of God and of nature, and those who indulge in such are branded with the guilt of a grave sin."[569] This teaching includes in its scope contraceptive intercourse, masturbatory sodomy, and homosexual sodomy. Each of these is intrinsically and gravely evil.

Because of the importance of true teaching on sexual morals in a confused world, Pope Pius XI immediately warned priests to be very clear in their teaching:

> We admonish, therefore, priests who hear confessions and others who have the care of souls, in virtue of Our supreme authority and in Our solicitude for the salvation of souls, not to allow the faithful entrusted to them to err regarding this most grave law of God; much more, that they keep themselves immune from such false opinions, in no way conniving in them. If any confessor or pastor of souls, which may God forbid, lead the faithful entrusted to him into these errors or should at least confirm them by approval or by guilty silence, let him be mindful of the fact that he must render a strict account to God, the Supreme Judge, for the betrayal of his sacred trust, and let him take to himself the words

[569] Pius XI, *Casti connubii*, art. 56.

of Christ: "They are blind and leaders of the blind: and if the blind lead the blind, both fall into the pit."[570]

This is such a salutary warning for us today. May our priests be good shepherds who lead their sheep on the way of truth. May they not be wolves in sheep's clothing, wanting our approval of them more than our eternal welfare and the glory of God. May they not so greatly relish sharing a meal or an opera with us sinners that they fail to call us to conversion.

Moreover, not one of the Fathers of the Church condones sodomy. Whenever any treats it, he condemns it as evil. Now, when the Church Fathers have such unanimity, they infallibly guide us in the Faith.[571] So this teaching is infallible by the consensus of the Fathers.

Finally, the Church has explicitly taught that sodomy is gravely evil. Let us note, first, the witness of the Council of Trent. The Council cites that important passage from 1 Corinthians 6:9–10 and interprets this passage as listing mortal sins that exclude one from salvation:

> Thus is defended the teaching of divine law that excludes from the kingdom of God not only unbelievers, but also the faithful who are immoral, adulterers, [the effeminate,] sodomites, thieves, greedy, drunkards, revilers, robbers, and all others who commit mortal sins that they can avoid with the help of divine grace and that separate them from the grace of Christ.[572]

The English translation of this passage offers only the one English word "sodomite," whereas, in the Latin, we have two words for the two aspects of sodomy discussed above. With great authority, the Council of Trent teaches that sodomy is a mortal sin.

The *Catechism of the Council of Trent*, issued by order of the pope, explicitly teaches that the sixth commandment forbids not simply adultery but every act of unchastity: "Every species of immodesty and impurity

---

[570] Ibid., art. 57.
[571] DH 3007.
[572] See Trent, Session VI, chap. 15; DH 1544.

are included in this prohibition of adultery."[573] It goes on to note, with St. Paul, that both the effeminate and the active sodomites are included in the prohibition.[574]

More recently, in 1916, under Benedict XV, the Apostolic Penitentiary condemned sodomy between any lawfully married man and woman. The teaching was occasioned by a question about what a woman should do who is married to a man who insists on using a condom or birth control device. Is his wife permitted to consent to the sexual act while rejecting his use of the contraceptive device? The Apostolic Penitentiary answered in the affirmative. On her side, she would not be cooperating with the evil of her husband. Obviously, she should strive to encourage her husband to change his ways. Even if she does not achieve that goal, however, the act is natural on her side and thus good, because she took no action to prevent conception. However, the Apostolic Penitentiary then addressed the question of sodomy between husband and wife (the fourth form of sodomy, but with male and female). The Apostolic Penitentiary unequivocally condemned such a practice:

> If, however, the husband wishes to commit the crime of the Sodomites with her, since sodomitic intercourse is against nature on the part of both spouses who are united in this way and, in the judgment of all the learned teachers, is gravely evil, there is clearly no motive, not even to avoid death, that would permit the wife legitimately to carry out such a shameless act with her husband.[575]

As we see here, the condemnation of contraceptive heterosexual intercourse, which is at least good and natural in its generic description (if we abstract the contraception), stands *a fortiori* as a condemnation of sodomy even in a heterosexual relationship. So, according to Catholic teaching, all the more grave is homosexual sodomy, wherein there is even greater deviation from God's order. The greater deviation is this:

---

[573] *The Catechism of the Council of Trent*, The Sixth Commandment, 432.
[574] Ibid., 433.
[575] DH 3634.

sexual affectivity is naturally directed to one of the opposite sex, but in homosexual sodomy it is directed toward the same sex.

More recently, in 1975, the CDF issued a declaration on homosexual sodomy entitled *Persona humana*. A lengthy citation is in order:

> At the present time there are those who, basing themselves on observations in the psychological order, have begun to judge indulgently, and even to excuse completely, homosexual relations between certain people. This they do in opposition to the constant teaching of the Magisterium and to the moral sense of the Christian people....
>
> In the pastoral field, these homosexuals must certainly be treated with understanding and sustained in the hope of overcoming their personal difficulties and their inability to fit into society. Their culpability will be judged with prudence. But no pastoral method can be employed which would give moral justification to these acts on the grounds that they would be consonant with the condition of such people. For according to the objective moral order, homosexual relations are acts which lack an essential and indispensable finality. In Sacred Scripture they are condemned as a serious depravity and even presented as the sad consequence of rejecting God. This judgment of Scripture does not of course permit us to conclude that all those who suffer from this anomaly are personally responsible for it, but it does attest to the fact that homosexual acts are intrinsically disordered and can in no case be approved of.[576]

The Church's teaching does not change and has not changed.

For his part, John Paul II cited 1 Corinthians 6:9–10 as issuing a list of intrinsically evil acts that are grave. In fact, he referenced Trent in the process. The English translation of John Paul II's text fails to capture all of the Latin. John Paul follows Paul's Greek and the Vulgate, including

---

[576] CDF, *Persona humana*, art. 8.

both aspects of homosexual sodomy. I amend the citation to reflect the authoritative Latin:

> Saint Paul declares that "the immoral, idolaters, adulterers, [the effeminate, sodomites,] thieves, the greedy, drunkards, revilers, robbers" are excluded from the Kingdom of God (cf. 1 Cor. 6:9–10). This condemnation—repeated by the Council of Trent—lists as "mortal sins" or "immoral practices" certain specific kinds of behavior the willful acceptance of which prevents believers from sharing in the inheritance promised to them.[577]

Most recently, the *Catechism of the Catholic Church* declares:

> Basing itself on Sacred Scripture, which presents homosexual acts as acts of grave depravity (cf. Gen. 19:1–29; Rom. 1:24–27; 1 Cor. 6:10; 1 Tim. 1:10), tradition has always declared that "homosexual acts are intrinsically disordered." They are contrary to the natural law. They close the sexual act to the gift of life. They do not proceed from a genuine affective and sexual complementarity. Under no circumstances can they be approved.[578]

As we can see, the Church's teaching remains constant.

Ecclesiastical Penalties for Sodomy
We might briefly note, as well, that the Church for many centuries deemed it prudent to legislate ecclesiastical penalties for those who committed the fourth form of sodomy. We can mention some examples. The Council of Ancyra in 314 issued penalties for the fourth form of sodomy. In the eleventh century, St. Peter Cardinal Damian presented his *Book of Gomorrah* to Pope Leo IX, who received it approvingly. Damian called for penalties against those who committed sodomy. Pope Leo IX agreed that penalties should be meted out: "Those who are polluted by impurity of any of the four kinds mentioned are expelled from all the grades of the

---

[577] John Paul II, *Veritatis splendor*, art. 49.
[578] CCC 2357, quoting CDF, *Persona humana*, art. 8.

immaculate Church."[579] Leo IX did, however, lighten the penalties called for by Damian. Pope Leo held out hope of return to ministry for those who had fallen into one of the first three forms of sodomy, *provided* that the sin was not long-lived. However, he held out no hope of return to ministry for prelates who engaged in the fourth and most extreme form of sodomy.[580] The conversion of sinners is always possible while they breathe. Of course, Pope Leo IX hoped for their repentance before death since he loved them. He merely deemed it prudent to exclude them from any future ministry.

In 1179, the ecumenical council Lateran III issued canonical penalties for the fourth form of sodomy:

> Let all who are found guilty of that unnatural vice for which the wrath of God came down upon the sons of disobedience and destroyed the five cities with fire, if they are clerics be expelled from the clergy or confined in monasteries to do penance; if they are laymen they are to incur excommunication and be completely separated from the society of the faithful.[581]

The Church's aim in this penalty was to underscore the sinfulness and infectious character of the sinful act. Excommunication has always come with the hope that the punished person repents, does penance, confesses his sins, and returns to fellowship with the faithful. For the Church, even when such hope was not realized, however, the penalty achieved its end as redress of the wrong and as protection for the wider community. The Fifth Lateran Council issued similar penalties.

Shortly after the Council of Trent, Pope St. Pius V declared, "That horrible crime, for which corrupt and obscene cities were destroyed by fire through divine condemnation, causes us most bitter sorrow and shocks our mind, impelling us to repress such a crime with the greatest possible

---

[579] DH 687.

[580] DH 688.

[581] Lateran III, canon 11, in Tanner, *Decrees of the Ecumenical Councils*, vol. 1, 217.

zeal."[582] The policy decision the pope encouraged, whatever one thinks considering it, expresses the Church's infallible teaching that sodomy is a grave sin.

Reasons for Confusion

Reasons for confusion are legion. In the United States, infamous priests celebrate "Pride" parades and laud those who embrace the homosexual lifestyle, which orients itself around sodomy. They disguise their support of sin by claiming to celebrate an identity. But they never call sin "sin," and they refuse to acknowledge that the tendency to sodomy is intrinsically disordered. They lament it when the Church reaffirms her teaching that no sodomitical "union" can be blessed. These priests are ruining human lives and laying waste to immortal souls. They do this, moreover, with ecclesiastical impunity. Some bishops have acted likewise. No wonder Catholics are confused and non-Catholics scandalized. Still, we should consult the actual teachings of the Church in order to avoid being scandalized.

Remarks and Gestures of Pope Francis
Some who seek to overturn infallible teaching abuse, in vain, various remarks and gestures of Pope Francis. We will mention five cases and comment on each in turn.

1. Most famously, there was Pope Francis's remark early in his papacy: "Who am I to judge?" The remark came in the context of an airplane interview. A journalist prompted the pope to speak of a so-called gay lobby in the Church and also about allegations that Bishop Ricca, of the Vatican bank, had committed homosexual acts. The pope replied:

> I believe that when you are dealing with such a person, you must distinguish between the fact of a person being gay and the fact of

[582] See "Horrendum illud scelus," The Josias, August 30, 2018, https://the-josias.com/2018/08/30/horrendum-illud-scelus/.

someone forming a lobby, because not all lobbies are good. This one is not good. If someone is gay and is searching for the Lord and has good will, then who am I to judge him?[583]

How should we react? This statement is not a papal word but only a word of a pope. Thus, it is not magisterial. Regarding its contents, there are a few points to make. First, it is true that we must not judge the soul of another. Second, it is not clear what he means by "being gay." He distinguishes being gay from "forming a lobby"; this distinction makes sense in light of the question, but it leaves unresolved what "being gay" means in this context. Third, each of us should distinguish the tendency *qua* tendency (not as embraced and lived) from the sinful acts and the lifestyle. Perhaps the pope wanted to draw attention to these factors. Fourth, the media portrayed the comment as making light of the Church's perennial teaching, as though the Church is now "okay" with sodomy. Significantly, *Time* magazine named Pope Francis the person of the year in 2013, citing his "Who am I to judge" statement as one reason. By contrast, some Christians who believe in traditional morality reacted negatively. Lutheran Satire referenced this episode in one of its animated cartoons.[584]

2. Others point to an interview conducted by Jesuit Fr. Antonio Spadaro, titled "A Big Heart Open to God." In the interview, Pope Francis brought up his famous "Who am I to judge" remark and made the following comment:

By saying this, I said what the catechism says. Religion has the right to express its opinion in the service of the people, but God in creation has set us free: it is not possible to interfere spiritually in the life of a person. A person once asked me, in a provocative manner, if I approved of homosexuality. I replied with another question: "Tell me: when God looks at a gay person, does he

---

[583] Francis, press conference, July 28, 2013.
[584] Lutheran Satire, "Frank the Hippie Pope," YouTube video, 4:24, October 20, 2013, https://www.youtube.com/watch?v=WEchg1KhmTY.

endorse the existence of this person with love, or reject and condemn this person?"[585]

A few comments are in order. First, these are only words of a pope, not papal words. They have no authority. Second, there are good things in the rest of the interview, such as Pope Francis's insistence that true mercy must be neither too rigorous nor too lax. Third, Pope Francis does not here indicate that homosexual actions are sinful. He notes that the Church has moral teachings and that he is a son of the Church. This is perhaps an implicit reference to the sinfulness of sodomy. It could have been of great help if the pope explicitly reminded the audience of what the Church teaches. Fourth, Francis speaks of a religion having a "right to express its *opinion*." This is true, yet we must say even more. The Catholic Church has dogmatic teachings concerning God's truth. These are more than mere opinions, since opinions may be false. Fifth, it would be good to bring up the distinction between the acts and the tendency. Sixth, it would be good to distinguish between the tendency and the lifestyle. Finally, when the Jesuits broadcasted this interview around the world, they did not charitably clarify Church teaching on the sinfulness of sodomy. Today, many people remain lost and confused. Immortal souls and human lives are going to ruin. For its part, society itself is crumbling.

3. In January 2015, Pope Francis received at the Vatican a transgender person going by the name of Diego Neria Lejarraga. Diego was born female. However, she had surgery and hormone treatments in an attempt to acquire traces of some masculine characteristics. The pope received both Diego and Diego's "fiancée" in an audience. How should we treat this episode? Above all, this event was a gesture, not a vehicle for doctrinal teaching. Now, "Diego" deserves love, for God loves each human being, even though each of us is a sinner. True love is ordered to the true good. A sinful lifestyle is opposed to the true good. So a full expression of love should include a call to repentance from a sinful lifestyle. Since

[585] Antonio Spadaro, "A Big Heart Open to God: An Interview with Pope Francis," *America*, September 30, 2013, https://www.americamagazine.org/faith/2013/09/30/big-heart-open-god-interview-pope-francis.

"Diego" is a female, any sexual acts with her female "fiancée" constitute homosexual acts. Moreover, the acts of transitioning involve mutilation of the body and its natural processes. Mutilation is a violation of the fifth commandment. It is a pollution of God's beautiful creation. It is a sin against human ecology.[586] A female who "transitions" to male and engages in intercourse with another female is committing homosexual acts all the same. In her meeting with the pope, did "Diego" experience a call to conversion? Did "Diego" come to repent of a confused and sinful lifestyle? According to the media reports, "Diego" took the meeting to be confirmation of her lifestyle choice. She still wanders by the edge of high cliffs that tower over an infernal abyss, confused and abandoned, like a sheep longing for a shepherd's hand.

4. Later that year, in August 2015, Pope Francis issued a letter of response to a woman named Francesca Pardi. This woman is famous for promoting sodomitical lifestyles. She had written to the pope, sending him her newly published book *Piccolo Uovo* (*The Little Egg*) and a letter of complaint about criticisms of the book. The book depicts a little egg that encounters animal "families" of various stripes, including male homosexual penguins rearing a little penguin and female homosexual cats rearing a kitten. The letter of response, penned by Vatican official Peter B. Wells, states: "His holiness is grateful for the thoughtful gesture and for the feelings which it evoked, hoping for an always more fruitful activity in the service of young generations and the spread of genuine human and Christian values."[587]

How should we treat this episode? Once again, the letter is neither a papal word nor a word of a pope. It is only a report about a word of a pope. It has no magisterial authority. We should also note how misleading this episode has been. The *Guardian* published the above-cited portion of

---

[586] See CCC 2297 and also "16 Facts on Gender Confusion," Family Watch International, https://fwipetitions.org/fwi/16-facts-on-gender-confusion/.
[587] Rosie Scammell, "Pope Francis Sends Letter Praising Gay Children's Book," *Guardian* (UK), August 28, 2015, https://www.theguardian.com/world/2015/aug/28/pope-francis-sends-letter-praising-gay-childrens-book.

the Vatican's letter. Consequently, many interpreted the letter as though it were a papal endorsement of a pro-sodomy book. As far as the public knows, the letter contains no fraternal correction or teaching about the sinfulness of sodomy. Thankfully, the Vatican did indicate that the letter, with its final blessing, was offered simply to the author and did not constitute an endorsement of sodomy. Still, the damage of scandal has been done. By "scandal" I do not mean what is "shocking." I mean something that needlessly occasions sin. As far as I can tell, Francesca Pardi has expressed no change of heart, and her book sales have not been impeded. As it seems, then, she, too, wallows in her approval of these sinful ways of life, like a sheep longing for a shepherd. Since she not only approves them but also promotes them, thousands have been negatively affected.

5. On another occasion, the *Guardian* claimed in 2018 that Pope Francis met with a homosexual man and told him, "God made you like this." The man, Juan Carlos Cruz, had earlier in his life been the object of homosexual predation by clergy. We must, first of all, deplore the predation perpetrated by those priests. We must also love this man, and our love must be ordered to the truth. Unfortunately, celebrity priests regularly cite this statement before their audiences, describing the attraction to sodomy as a gift, not as a disorder. In this way they lure confused souls into celebrating Pride Month. They are instruments of the City of Man, victimizing souls, enticing them into sinful ways of life.

How should we treat this report? Again, the remark is only a word of a pope; it has no authority. Further, we must offer a few comments. God creates each of us and grants us a deep and natural inclination to the good. We cannot remove this deep inclination. However, there can be obstacles to the normal development of this inclination on the level of experience. For instance, we may have a somatic constitution (bodily makeup) that makes us quick to anger, or more easily aroused sexually, or slow to respond, and so forth. We all suffer various obstacles because of original sin, which exposes us to *concupiscence*.

The inclination to sodomy is in the broad category of concupiscence. It has, however, its own place in that category. Some sinful tendencies draw us to acts that are *generically* good. For example, excessive sexual desire has as its object an act that is good within the proper context, sexual intercourse between male and female. The tendency is sinful insofar as the desire is excessive or adds some defect. Other tendencies are toward acts *generically* evil. The homosexual inclination is an example. Whereas a sexual act between male and female *may* be good, no sexual act between two males or two females is ever good. Now, despite the deep tendency each of us has to the good, we struggle with obstacles that deviate from this deep tendency. We must struggle against such deviations, and we do so by acting virtuously. When we act repeatedly for the good (by God's grace), we develop a love for, and a spontaneous inclination toward, the good. Those who act chastely develop a spontaneous inclination to chaste acting. This spontaneous inclination quiets, tames, and orders spontaneous tendencies. Thus, what formerly was concupiscence is less and less active. Concupiscence will remain until death, but its movements become less violent and more manageable. One has become virtuous, and the virtuous experience peace of heart, a treasure of inestimable value.

Moreover, through prayer, virtuous action, and therapy, some people have recovered from sinful habits of pornography and masturbation. Others have been cured of the homosexual disorder and been empowered to embrace their sexual identity (as male or female) fully so as to enter and remain in healthy heterosexual marriages. Prudent pastoral and psychological counseling can help those who become anxious about the tendency itself, even though they are not acting on it. Should anyone who desires complete healing from the disorder be convinced that healing can and will come before death? I do not think so; I do not think our faith demands that we say yes, even though many can indeed be healed. Some heroic men have made their way out of this destructive lifestyle and are now dedicating much time to helping others achieve liberation from the sin and from the inclination. This is truly noble; may their work prosper and many be healed. Still, we live in a fallen world, and no one should put a burden on himself greater than he can bear. Some are healed of the disorder, and some are not. Professionals firmly committed to correct teaching on the natural law are the best guides on this topic. God gives grace, however, so that we can avoid mortal sins.

6. Some people also point to personnel decisions that favor a change of Catholic teaching or attitude concerning sodomy. They point to a number of disappointing episcopal appointments. Some bishops appointed within the last eight years are urging or signaling change in Catholic doctrine that undermines Church teaching and is unworthy of sacred ministers.

7. Another scandal occurred at the October 2020 release of *Francesco*, a documentary film about the current pope. The movie juxtaposed two remarks of Pope Francis taken from distinct occasions. In the first, Francis said that homosexuals have a right to be part of the family. In the original context, he meant that a child with these tendencies has the right to be kept in the family. In the second remark from the movie, Francis spoke of practicing homosexuals who live together. He suggested that they should be given the legal protection of a civil union. The editor spliced these two statements. Their juxtaposition transformed the original remarks of the pope so that it implied the following: a homosexual couple has a *right* to form a civil union and to adopt children.

How should we respond to this episode? First, taken individually, these are words of a pope, not papal words. Second, in their juxtaposition together, they are not even alleged words of a pope; they are an invention of the editor. Third, we must offer religious submission of mind and will to actual Church teaching. Now, actual Church teaching rejects civil unions. Following her master, the Church teaches that violence against homosexuals is a crime and a sin. This violence must firmly be condemned. This important teaching notwithstanding,

> the proper reaction to crimes committed against homosexual persons should not be to claim that the homosexual condition is not disordered. When such a claim is made and when homosexual activity is consequently condoned, or when civil legislation is introduced to protect behavior to which no one has any conceivable right, neither the Church nor society at large should be surprised

when other distorted notions and practices gain ground, and irrational and violent reactions increase.[588]

Everyone has human rights, but no one has a right to sinful action. The CDF declares, "There is no right to homosexuality"; therefore, the homosexual orientation "should not form the basis for judicial claims."[589] A moral disorder does not constitute the basis for a civil right. The CDF therefore teaches:

> Including "homosexual orientation" among the considerations on the basis of which it is illegal to discriminate can easily lead to regarding homosexuality as a positive source of human rights, for example, in respect to so-called affirmative action or preferential treatment in hiring practices.[590]

The Church is clear: the homosexual orientation should not be treated as a protected right.

All of these considerations have ramifications for the question of homosexual unions. Pius XI already rejected the civil recognition even of heterosexual unions that are not true marriages: "Legitimately constituted authority has the right and therefore the duty to restrict, to prevent, and to punish those base unions which are opposed to reason and to nature."[591] From teachings such as these, the CDF draws the conclusion that civil unions between homosexual persons are unacceptable. The CDF gives counsel for political action in various situations. Always, Christians must witness to the whole truth, "which is contradicted both by approval of homosexual acts and unjust discrimination against homosexual persons."[592] Various good political actions include:

---

[588] CDF, *Pastoral Care of Homosexual Persons*, art. 10.
[589] Ibid., art. 13.
[590] CDF, *Non-Discrimination of Homosexual Persons*, art. 13.
[591] Pius XI, *Casti connubii*, art. 8.
[592] CDF, *Considerations Regarding Proposals to Give Legal Recognition to Unions between Homosexual Persons* (2003), art. 5.

unmasking the way in which such tolerance might be exploited or used in the service of ideology; stating clearly the immoral nature of these unions; reminding the government of the need to contain the phenomenon within certain limits so as to safeguard public morality and, above all, to avoid exposing young people to erroneous ideas about sexuality and marriage that would deprive them of their necessary defences and contribute to the spread of the phenomenon.[593]

One must distinguish *de facto* toleration of immoral cohabitation from legal acceptance of homosexual unions. Legal acceptance of said unions is never acceptable: "In those situations where homosexual unions have been legally recognized or have been given the legal status and rights belonging to marriage, clear and emphatic opposition is a duty."[594] Furthermore, as the CDF has recently clarified, for cases in which a "law" recognizes such unions, against the order of true justice, the Church may not bless these unions. The reason is that "it is necessary that what is blessed be objectively and positively ordered to receive and express grace." Therefore, "it is not licit to impart a blessing on relationships, or partnerships, even stable, that involve sexual activity outside of marriage (i.e., outside the indissoluble union of a man and a woman open in itself to the transmission of life), as is the case of the unions between persons of the same sex." In short, God "does not and cannot bless sin."[595] These are the guidelines that Catholics, Catholic politicians, priests, and bishops must follow, for they—not the private opinions of magisterial figures, even those that are aired publicly—are authoritative Church teaching.

Private remarks of magisterial figures can have either constructive or destructive cultural effects. Messages that conflict or appear to conflict with the Church's true teaching are destructive. Illinois lawmaker Michael Madigan, for example, appealed to Pope Francis's remark "Who am I to

---

[593] CDF, *Unions between Homosexual Persons*, art. 5.

[594] Ibid.

[595] CDF, "*Responsum* of the Congregation for the Doctrine of the Faith to a *dubium* regarding the blessing of the unions of persons of the same sex" (March 15, 2021).

judge?" when working in 2013 to promote gay marriage. Moreover, some who embrace the gay lifestyle claim inspiration from these remarks. They do not interpret these words and gestures of Francis as a call to conversion but as confirmation of their impenitence. For example, Elton John called Pope Francis "my hero" at an AIDS benefit in New York on October 28, 2014.[596] He has shown no signs of repentance. Remarkably, a few years later, the Vatican invested more than a million dollars to assist the production of the film *Rocketman*, which celebrated the life of Elton John.[597]

For these and other reasons, many have worried or claimed that the Church is on the cusp of rejecting her "policy" against sodomy. Souls are being lost because of this confusion. Others are being scandalized. Still, Catholics who abuse words of magisterial figures in order to embolden impenitence have no excuse. They have a responsibility to know and affirm Catholic teachings. Moreover, they should consult authoritative statements of Pope Francis that accurately convey this teaching and thus lead the flock to living waters. In a lengthy interview in 2018 with Fr. Fernando Prado, Pope Francis unequivocally condemned homosexual acts as sinful.[598] Francis also reiterated the Church's position that men with deep-seated same-sex inclinations are not to be admitted to the priesthood. Decades earlier, Pope John XXIII had issued strict norms concerning the admission of candidates struggling with this issue and with inclinations to other forms of sodomy and sexual incontinence. Had

[596] Jenn Selby, "Elton John Brands Pope Francis 'My Hero': 'He Is a Compassionate, Loving Man Who Wants Everybody to Be Included in the Love of God,'" *Independent* (UK), October 29, 2014, https://www.independent.co.uk/news/people/elton-john-brands-pope-francis-my-hero-he-compassionate-loving-man-who-wants-everybody-be-included-love-god-9825296.html.

[597] Thomas D. Williams, "Vatican Invests $1.1 Million in Steamy Elton John Biopic," Breitbart.com, December 6, 2019, https://www.breitbart.com/faith/2019/12/06/vatican-invests-1-1-million-in-steamy-elton-john-biopic/.

[598] See Pope Francis and Fernando Prado, *The Strength of a Vocation: Consecrated Life Today* (Washington, DC: United States Conference of Catholic Bishops, 2018).

these norms been implemented, they could have borne much fruit.[599] Moreover, Pope Francis has condemned the theory that disassociates gender and sex.[600] On December 16, 2015, he spoke in favor of true marriage, to help the Slovenians defend heterosexual marriage in a referendum. Most recently, he approved the CDF's document declaring that homosexual unions may *not* be blessed. Of course, many experience the overall message these days to be mixed and confusing. Elton John was, understandably, disturbed and hurt by the recent CDF document; it seemed an about-face to him: "How can the Vatican refuse to bless gay marriages because they 'are sin', yet happily make a profit from investing millions in 'Rocketman'—a film which celebrates my finding happiness from my marriage to David?? #hypocrisy."[601]

The office of teacher requires clarity, accuracy, and comprehension. As Vatican II teaches on ecumenism, "It is, of course, essential that the doctrine should be clearly presented in its entirety."[602] Why? Ambiguous, imprecise, and unclear messages lead to error and confusion of one sort or another. Similarly, incomplete presentations lead to confusion and imbalance. When incompleteness of presentations is sustained for a long time, people begin to perceive the silence as denial. Love requires speaking the whole truth clearly.

Conclusion

That sodomy in any of its forms is intrinsically and gravely evil is the constant teaching of the ordinary and universal Magisterium. Thus, the

---

[599] Congregation for Religious, *Religiosorum Institutio* (February 2, 1961), EWTN, https://www.ewtn.com/catholicism/library/religiosorum-institutio-2007

[600] Pope Francis, *Laudato si'* (2015), art. 155.

[601] "Elton John on Vatican Hypocritical for Gay Marriage Blessing Refusal ... You Financed 'Rocketman'!!!," March 15, 2021, TMZ, https://www.tmz.com/2021/03/15/vatican-rejects-gay-marriage-unions-catholic-church-blessing-pope-francis/.

[602] *Unitatis redintegratio*, art. 11.

teaching is infallible. No authority whatsoever can change this. The misguided theologians, priests, and bishops who promote sodomitical lifestyles have no theological basis for their teachings. Although they disguise this promotion by the rhetoric of love of and acceptance of persons, what they mean is acceptance of a sinful lifestyle. The Church asks her pastors, to the contrary, clearly to present the Church teaching on the sinfulness of sodomy.

We must, indeed, love those who struggle with various tendencies to sodomy. We must love those who simply feel confused. We must love those who sometimes engage in sinful acts. We must love those who embrace a sinful lifestyle. This love should leave us always open to them as persons created in the image and likeness of God. We should also remember our own faults, which are many. We should pray for ourselves and for those who struggle with sin.

Now, true love comes from truth and leads back to truth. So our love for ourselves should lead us to hate our sins. Our love for others should lead us to want them to overcome sin, to repent, and to live in the grace of God and arrive at eternal salvation. True love wills nothing less. Let us not listen to the devil and his minions, who tell us that sin is not sin or that a tendency is an identity. Let us not listen to the devil, who masks a sinful lifestyle with a label masquerading as an identity. The devil prowls about, seeking souls to devour. Resist him, steadfast in your faith.

10

More Confusions Addressed In Brief

I have treated a number of heresies and errors in the foregoing chapters. The aim in each one was to exhibit the following in some detail: (1) the reasons for the confusion, (2) the teaching of the Church, (3) the reasons for the teaching, and (4) why the reasons for confusion do not justify rejection of the teaching. To journey from darkness of confusion to the transparent light of truth is not easy. It is my hope that the thought processes common to these chapters show that the journey is possible. It is possible to hold the true and unchanging teachings of the Church, despite the difficulties. It is still possible to be a real Catholic.

As many readers know, however, there are additional teachings being questioned today that require a defense. All of these cannot possibly be treated in the same detail. Earlier chapters show how each case can be treated. By adopting the argument style used in previous chapters, the reader can develop habits of mind so as to tackle new cases with skill and confidence. Of course, important tools are necessary. The reader can recall some of these noted in chapter 1. We need books such as a clear and comprehensive catechism, a good edition of Denzinger, and Ludwig Ott's *Fundamentals of Catholic Dogma*. There are also some manuals of high rank, even though they are dated. I think, for instance, of the multivolume work by Msgr. Joseph Pohle. There is also *Sacrae Theologiae Summa*, a collaborative effort recently translated by Kenneth Baker and published through Keep the Faith. There are also good websites that contain many

Church documents not available on the Vatican's website. Among these is PapalEncyclicals.net.

When informing oneself about the truths of the Faith, one must, however, keep in mind that we are dealing with transcendent myster-ies. This does not mean truth is murky. It means that mysteries demand reverence. We must take off our shoes and walk admiringly through the claims, for we aim to behold a treasure. Even more: we aim to behold our God! So, for instance, when we read that the unity of the Church is perfect, we must not merely think of the juridical unity of the Church. This is part, a crucial part, of the mystery. But we must also gaze upward at the "Jerusalem above"; she is free, and she is our mother (Gal. 4:26). The Holy Trinity, Love Itself, reaches outward to cleanse, forgive, and divinize us in body and soul. May He be praised. May the number of those who look to Him increase and multiply, now and until the Day of Judgment.

This chapter will address in a cursory fashion other errors and heresies. This will help us get a picture of the vast scope of the current crisis. For each error covered below, I will summarily run through the Church's teaching on the topic and then briefly present the current confusion and the remedy for it.

Mere Obedience to Natural Law Saves?

It is solemn Church teaching that no one can be saved without dying in the state of sanctifying grace, which includes faith, hope, and char-ity. Only those who die with faith, hope, and charity will be saved. The Church declares: "Faith without hope and charity neither unites a man perfectly with Christ nor makes him a living member of his body."[603] By contrast, those who die in the state of actual mortal sin or original sin only cannot be saved.[604] The reason is the grandeur of Heaven and the corruption of original sin. Salvation is a supernatural union with God in knowledge and love. Even pure nature, undefiled by sin, is not

---

[603] DH 1531.
[604] DH 1306.

capable of such a friendship with God, for this friendship is founded on sanctifying grace. Moreover, our nature is fallen from its original height. Thus, union with God begins in the justification of the ungodly and is consummated in eternity. Justification is not by faith alone but includes the gifts of sanctifying grace and charity.[605] Justification begins on Earth but is consummated in eternity.

Countering a Confusion

Some, however, have gone astray from this holy Faith. They opine that anyone can be saved simply by "being a good person." By "being a good person" they think merely of obedience to the natural law. Further, they think that anyone can obey the natural law simply by the resources of human nature. This error is, as it were, "in the air." Those who wish to justify this error by theological savvy may add that it is the heresy of Lutheranism and Calvinism to say that nature is corrupt. If they are crafty, they might make appeal to the following passage from Pius IX:

> We know as well as you that those who suffer from invincible ignorance with regard to our most holy religion, by carefully keeping the natural law and its precepts, which have been written by God in the hearts of all, by being disposed to obey God and to lead a virtuous and correct life, can, by the power of divine light and grace, attain eternal life.[606]

The teaching of Pius IX is of high authority. He speaks as pope; he speaks firmly and simply; and he speaks on a matter of faith and morals. So, does Pius IX justify heresy?

No, Pius IX does not justify heresy. First, the (modernist) interpreter's claim that only obedience to the natural law is necessary for salvation contradicts the dogma of the faith. Thus, even if Pius IX meant to teach the contrary, Catholics would be bound to ignore his teaching and obey the prior, ever-authoritative dogma. Second, Pius IX was not making

---

[605] DH 1561.
[606] DH 2866.

a complete statement regarding requirements for salvation. Rather, he was speaking of the real possibility that someone who is not a member of the Catholic Church can nonetheless be saved. He was noting that, if a person is invincibly ignorant of the necessity to be a member of the Catholic Church and thus is not a member, such a person is not judged worthy of damnation on that account. Instead, such a person can live the will of God. Such living of the divine will would be *evidenced* by careful obedience to the natural law but would *consist* chiefly in acts of charity. Third, the pope even refers to the power of divine light and grace in relation to this virtuous obedience of the natural law. Hence, the pope calls to mind that the very way the non-Catholic obeys God's law is *as a child of God, sanctified in the Holy Spirit*. True, the pope does not draw out this implication in depth. Nor should he be required to do so. It is the heretic who uses a pope's truncated expressions as an excuse to deny already established dogma. But if we wish to be good Catholics, we will cling to the dogma and not use truncated expressions as excuses for denial.

On this note, Joseph Ratzinger was rather critical of a key passage in Vatican II's document *Lumen gentium*, article 16. The passage treated the relation of individuals in various circumstances to the People of God, i.e., the Catholic Church. Ratzinger found that *Gaudium et spes* more aptly treated this matter in its article 22, which stressed the agency of the Holy Spirit and the salvific death of Christ. By contrast, he said, *Lumen gentium* "lays too much emphasis on man's activity." It has "extremely unsatisfactory expressions."[607]

Sacred Tradition Has No Content?

The constant teaching of the Church is that the deposit of faith is found both in Sacred Scripture and in Sacred Tradition. Thus, we must believe

---

[607] Joseph Ratzinger, "The Dignity of the Human Person," in *Pastoral Constitution on the Church in the Modern World*, vol. 5 of *Commentary on the Documents of Vatican II*, ed. Herbert Vorgrimler (New York: Herder & Herder, 1969), 162–163.

that revelation is found not only in Scripture but also in Tradition. In this section, we stress that Tradition has real *content* that must be believed.

Trent offered the classical expression of this, referring to the deposit of faith as a truth and a rule: "This truth and rule are contained in the written books and unwritten traditions."[608] Vatican I repeated this teaching and phrasing.[609] Leo XIII asserted that this revelation is contained "both in unwritten traditions and also in the written books."[610] Pius XI declared, "Sacred Tradition is a true fount of divine Revelation."[611] Pius XII taught that Tradition has sacred content: "Each source of divinely revealed doctrine contains so many rich treasures of truths." He referred to "the doctrine contained in Sacred Scripture or in Tradition."[612] Moreover, Vatican II's *Dei verbum* taught that the one Word of God—i.e., the deposit of faith—is expressed *both* in Scripture *and* in Tradition: "The task of authentically interpreting the Word of God, whether written or handed on …"[613] In fact, Vatican II taught that Tradition passes on the Word of God *in its integrity*: "Now, Sacred Tradition transmits wholly (*integre*) the Word of God entrusted by Christ the Lord and the Holy Spirit to the Apostles."[614]

Professions of faith also indicate that Tradition has real content. The profession issued after the Council of Trent states, "I most firmly accept and embrace the apostolic and ecclesiastical traditions."[615] The current profession reads, "With firm faith, I also believe everything contained in the word of God, whether written or handed down in Tradition."[616]

---

[608] DH 1501.

[609] See DH 3006.

[610] Leo XIII, *Providentissimus Deus*, art. 1, my translation.

[611] Pius XI, *Mortalium animos*, art. 9.

[612] Pius XII, *Humani generis*, arts. 21 and 35.

[613] *Dei verbum*, art. 10; DH 4214.

[614] Ibid., art. 9, my translation.

[615] DH 1863.

[616] "Profession of Faith and Oath of Fidelity," https://www.vatican.va/ro-man_curia/congregations/cfaith/documents/rc_con_cfaith_doc_19880701 _professio-fidei_en.html.

Clearly, the Church's teaching that Tradition contains revealed content constitutes a perennial, infallible doctrine. It cannot be contradicted or watered down.

Countering a Confusion
Unfortunately, some modernists decided to adopt a portion of the Protestant error concerning revelation. They opined that Tradition does not have any content. The great Cardinal Joseph Siri pointed out many recent errors and heresies in his book *Gethsemane*. Regarding the denial of Tradition as a source of revelation, he singled out Karl Rahner, S.J., as one example.[617]

More recently, Pope John Paul II penned a sentence that modernists might like to take as support for denying that Tradition has any content. It begins with the following phrase: "The relationship between Sacred Scripture, as the highest authority in matters of faith, and Sacred Tradition, as indispensable to the interpretation of the Word of God ..."[618] Modernists might wish to find three assertions implicit in this phrase: (1) Scripture is an expression of the Word of God; (2) Tradition is not an expression of the Word of God; and (3) Tradition's role is to assist in the interpretation of Scripture. Clearly, proposition 2 contradicts infallible Catholic doctrine. Therefore, we may not hold proposition 2 to be true. What might John Paul II have meant?

Several remarks are in order. The pope does not explicitly state nor necessarily imply proposition 2. So I see no reason to interpolate that proposition into his encyclical. Why, then, did he not clearly affirm that Tradition has revealed content? The context of the remark may provide an answer. The encyclical is *Ut unum sint*, which treats the ecumenical movement. Perhaps John Paul was attempting to *open* a discussion with Protestants, stating only part of the truth—namely, that Scripture expresses the Word of God. If this is the case, he merely omitted the more difficult part of the discussion—namely, that Tradition also expresses the Word of God. If so,

---

[617] See Joseph Cardinal Siri, *Gethsemane: Reflections on the Contemporary Theological Movement* (Franciscan Herald Press, 1981), 33–38.
[618] John Paul II, *Ut unum sint*, art. 79.

we should also note that he was not entirely silent on difficult issues. He did state assertion 3, that we need Tradition to fathom Scripture. In taking this path, he might have been attempting to help Protestants make their way *toward* the fullness of faith. He would have been inviting them to think about the necessity of something other than Scripture. Now, the ultimate burden in genuine ecumenism is to expose the *whole* truth, as John Paul elsewhere notes.[619] A *half* statement is not the whole truth. Protestants are called forward one step by this strategy; for their part, Catholics need to remember not to fall back a step. There is a danger that repetition of only half the truth may be *mistaken* for denial of the other half. We Catholics need to recall our roots: Tradition is a source of revealed truth. We must allow the light of faith to shine, for the truth will set us free.

Original Sin Is Not Inherited?

Original sin is a solemn teaching of the Faith. More precisely, there are several dogmas regarding this teaching. We distinguish, of course, the first act of sin in human history from the state of original sin in which we are conceived. The Council of Trent teaches that the state of original sin involves (1) the death of the soul because of the absence of supernatural holiness and justice, (2) the lack of the preternatural gift of integrity by which gift we had been immune to the wayward inclinations of concupiscence, and (3) consignment to a life of mortality. We come into existence *lacking* the supernatural grace that God bestowed upon Adam and Eve. In short, our soul is dead spiritually because it lacks the life of supernatural grace. As a result, we come into existence bereft of any title to a supernatural fruition, to the glory of Heaven.[620] If we ever achieve the vision of God, it will be because God in His mercy grants us this gift by bestowing His forgiving grace upon us. By losing this grace for

---

[619] Ibid.

[620] By nature, we can have no such title. Adam was gratuitously constituted with that title, but he lost it for himself and for us. Thus, we are cast out from an order and title that by nature we cannot claim.

us, Adam thrust us into a situation of alienation from God, from which we do not recover unless we receive redeeming grace. Granted, we are not compelled to sin; the sins we commit are freely chosen. If we sin, it is our fault. Still, given an extended length of time, we are sure to fall into some mortal sin or other.[621] So, we find it impossible without grace to live a life that is truly just even in the natural sense of the term. A *fortiori*, it is utterly impossible to do anything in the order of grace until God first reaches into our lives and makes us holy and just.

It is the next teaching on which I wish to focus here. Trent teaches, further, that this condition or state in which we are conceived is handed on to us *by propagation* from Adam; it is received by us through *inheritance*. Trent thus issues the following anathema:

> If anyone asserts that this sin of Adam, which is one in origin and is transmitted by propagation, not by imitation, and which is in all men, proper to each, can be taken away by the powers of human nature or by any remedy other than the merits of the one mediator our Lord Jesus Christ ... let him be anathema.[622]

The council asserts that original sin is transmitted by propagation, not picked up by imitation. That is, this state is natively ours, post Adam's fault. We are born into this state because we receive it from Adam by way of generation. The Church is here condemning Pelagianism. The Pelagians held that each of us is born with a human nature that is in the good condition that Adam and Eve enjoyed before their Fall. According to the Pelagians, we are not internally weakened, but we encounter bad examples in our relationships with others, and we sometimes imitate them. We suffer the threat of original sin insofar as we are forced to experience their bad example. We become tainted only if we imitate them. The Church condemned this theory and taught that original sin

---

[621] These two claims may seem like a contradiction, but they are not. The sin that we commit we can avoid. However, our weakness is such that we will at some point freely commit a mortal sin. We need grace. See Thomas Aquinas, *Summa theologiae*, Ia-IIae, q. 109, art. 8.

[622] Trent, Session V, canon 3; DH 1513.

is passed on by propagation. As a result, even infants — who cannot yet freely imitate anyone — need Baptism "so that by regeneration they may be cleansed from what they contracted through generation."[623] The council repeats this point in its Decree on Justification: "Men would not be born unrighteous if they were not born children of Adam's seed, since it is because of their descent from him that in their conception they contract unrighteousness as their own."[624]

Various popes have repeated this teaching. Pius XI declared, "The very natural process of generating life has become the way of death by which original sin is passed on to posterity."[625] Pius XII repeated that original sin is passed on "through generation."[626] Paul VI repeated this again, countering confusion:

> It is human nature so fallen, stripped of the grace that clothed it, injured in its own natural powers and subjected to the dominion of death, that is transmitted to all men, and it is in this sense that every man is born in sin. We therefore hold, with the Council of Trent, that original sin is transmitted with human nature, "not by imitation, but by propagation" and that it is thus "proper to everyone."[627]

That original sin is passed on by way of propagation and inherited is thus a dogma of the Catholic Faith. It is heresy to deny it.

Countering a Confusion

We can point to two possible occasions of confusion here..

1. Only days before he announced his abdication, Pope Benedict XVI took up some reflections on creation, man, grace, and sin. When he turned to original sin, he asked, "What is the meaning of this reality that is not easy to understand?" He seemed to be expressing an anguished human reaction to the doctrine of original sin. Is it fair? Is it intelligible?

---

[623] Ibid., canon 4; DH 1514.
[624] Trent, Session VI, chap. 3; DH 1523.
[625] Pius XI, *Casti connubii*, art. 14; DH 3705.
[626] Pius XII, *Humani generis*, art. 37; DH 3897.
[627] Paul VI, *Solemni hac liturgia* (1968), art. 16.

On the one hand, many of us have struggled with these difficult ques‐ tions. Those who know the work of Benedict XVI (Joseph Ratzinger) know that he wanted to enter the anguish of that question. On the other hand, many of us also look soberly at the world and find original sin to be in tune with common sense. And those who know Ratzinger's work know that he did not ignore sin. Indeed, for all of his appreciation of the Vatican II document *Gaudium et Spes*, Joseph Ratzinger lambasted its treatment of freedom as offering a standpoint that is "quite simply an unreal one." He continued, "The whole text gives scarcely a hint of the discord which runs through man and which is described so dramatically in Rom 7:13–25. It even falls into downright Pelagian terminology."[628]

At any rate, Benedict did not repeat the dogma that original sin is passed on by propagation and received by inheritance; neither did he deny it. Instead, he explained its spread as follows. We become wounded because we enter a world that is distorted by ruptured relationships. As a consequence, we suffer from these relational fractures. This relational fracturing is sin. He writes, "If the relationship structure is disordered from the outset, every human being comes into a world marked by this relational distortion, comes into a world disturbed by sin, by which he or she is marked personally; the initial sin tarnishes and wounds human nature."[629]

Because the pope did not advert to the dogma of the inheritance of original sin by way of propagation, modernists might hope that he denied it or asserted the Pelagian notion of original sin as picked up by way of "imitation." They might think he was suggesting that when we enter this fractured world, we acquire relationally a similar fracturing. The substance of this claim does not encompass the full dogma on original sin, but neither does it contradict the dogma. Now, to have gone further and explicitly claimed that original sin is not spread by propagation would have been to contradict the Faith. It is obviously true that there is such a thing as relational fracturing and that, for most of us, this fracturing

---

[628] Ratzinger, "The Dignity of the Human Person," in *Pastoral Constitution on the Church in the Modern World*, 137–138.
[629] Pope Benedict, General Audience, February 6, 2013.

inhibits the growth of virtue. We know that we cannot be happy except in relationships. In this respect, Pope Benedict was adding another dimension to our appreciation of the depravity of our condition. As the dogma teaches, we receive from Adam by way of generation a human nature *shorn* of supernatural graces. But as we note from experience, we are, often enough, *also* dragged down by situations of sin since we are by nature relational — the classical word is "political" — beings. This negative influence of harmful relationships is important to consider.

This truth notwithstanding, our being is not itself the relationship. Rather, our being is *for* relationships. Our being is not simply a relation. There is something "there" *by which* we are related to others. What is it? It is our essence or substance, our being animal and rational. We have this essence by existing. Good relationships are things that are made possible *by* our having this essence. Original sin is not constituted relationally but with respect to our essence and powers. Original sin is the absence of grace and theological virtues in our soul and spiritual powers. We "receive" this essence of original sin — this *lack* of grace — when we are generated from Adam. We have this absence, this lack or privation, from the moment we are conceived. So we do not suffer original sin because we enter a world that has fractures. Rather, we suffer original sin because when we enter the world, we are bereft of the proper equipment for supernatural friendship with God and others. Thankfully, the pope also points to the *Catechism* and indicates that we are wounded in our nature. These remarks can point in the right direction, the direction of the infallible dogma. Still, the sheep will be well guided by completeness.

Moreover, difficulties arise if we locate original sin in relational fracturing. This problem comes to light when we take into account the analogy of faith. Consider the holiness of Jesus and Mary. We confess that Mary was conceived *immaculate*. But she, too, entered our situation, our fractured world. Now, if we pick up original sin by entering a fractured world, she should have picked up original sin. But if she could exist in a fractured world and yet not suffer original sin, then existing in a fractured world does not constitute the state of original sin. We can think also of Jesus, since He existed in this fractured world, yet He was utterly without any sin. Finally, Baptism supplies another light on this topic. After Baptism we are *no longer in the state of original sin*, even though we continue to exist in a fractured world. Therefore, existing in a fractured world does not constitute having original sin.

Whereas Pope Benedict did not deny the dogma of the inheritance of original sin with his incomplete presentation of it, Karl Rahner invited his readers to do so.[630] How? He depicted a caricature of the dogma, rejected the caricature, and substituted his own theory that does not present the substance of the rejected dogma. He wrote that original sin "in no way means that the moral quality of the actions of the first person or persons is transmitted to us, whether this be through a juridical imputation by God or through some kind of biological heredity, however conceived."[631] This is a rejection of a caricature. Of course, the personal guilt of Adam is not imputed to us. Nor is original sin a genetic defect passed on to us. Rahner rejected strawmen! As the state we inherit, original sin is the condition of not having sanctifying grace and the other gifts of original justice. Rahner did not affirm this dogma. Instead, he opined that original sin is a negative element that radically, albeit not insurmountably, affects human freedom. He called it a "negative existential of freedom."[632] In a nutshell, it amounts to something along the lines of what Pope Benedict described as relational fracturing. Once again, we can affirm a real insight here, but we need to add that original sin is inherited by way of propagation. Rahner's rejection of the caricature of dogma, however, presents an obstacle in our path. Hence, his readers are left to draw the conclusion that contradicts the dogma.

2. More recently, Pope Francis declared in his encyclical *Fratelli tutti*, "Every person is immensely holy and deserves our love."[633] If a modernist were to presume to conclude from this that no human being is conceived

---

[630] On this topic, see my essay "The Withering."
[631] Rahner, *Foundations*, 111.
[632] See ibid., 110–115.
[633] Pope Francis, *Fratelli tutti* (2020), art. 195.

in original sin and thus lacks grace until justification, he would find himself opposed to Catholic dogma. Unbaptized infants are not in the state of grace. Nor are those who have committed mortal sins in the state of grace. We may not deny this.

Properly speaking, the words "holy" and "holiness" signify the state of grace. Therefore, properly speaking, no infant is holy until Baptism, and no adult sinner is holy unless and until he repents. But if we take into mind the providential care of God, we recognize every living human as being at least *potentially* holy. Similarly, Aquinas described some humans (namely, Catholics) as *actual* members of the Body of Christ and all other living humans as *potential* members of the Body of Christ. By analogy, we can say that some humans are actually holy, but every living human being is at least *potentially* holy. God reaches out to all persons so as to convert the unholy and so as to sanctify more deeply the already holy. For our part, we can love each person from the bottom of our hearts. We must reach out in fraternal dialogue, correcting those who err and calling back those who stray. We should reach out to as many people as we can, extending the love of Christ that has been shown to us. We owe a debt to everyone. Now, love is based on truth, for Christ is the Truth that sets us free. So we must proclaim the fullness of the truth and not hide it under a bushel basket. Part of the truth is that all humans are conceived and born in original sin. Baptism is urgent. This is true Catholic brotherhood.

We can add that on a different occasion Pope Francis described original sin as an inherited disease: "Their rejection of God's blessing fatally leads them to a delirium of omnipotence that ruins everything. That is what we call 'original sin'. And we all bear the inheritance of this disease from birth."[634]

Is Capital Punishment *Per Se* Evil?

Following the teaching of Scripture, the Church teaches that capital punishment is not intrinsically evil. It is not a *per se* evil. If it were *per*

---

[634] Pope Francis, General Audience, September 16, 2015.

se or intrinsically evil, capital punishment would never, under any circumstances, be permitted. Its very object—executing a criminal for a capital offense—would always and everywhere be evil.[635] Revelation and the Church teach, however, that capital punishment can be rendered without sin.

This teaching begins early in the history of revelation. In Genesis 9:6, God declares, "Whoever sheds the blood of man, by man shall his blood be shed; for God made man in his own image." God later promulgated penal laws through Moses. These laws include execution as punishment.[636] God permits evil, as noted in previous chapters. God does not, however, command evil (Wisd. 12:15). Therefore, capital punishment is not *per se* evil. To call it so would be to call God wicked and to reject the Old Testament. It would thus be anti-Semitic. What about the New Testament?

St. Paul locates the justice of the death penalty in Almighty God. Rulers have authority from God, and rulers bear the sword as instruments of God. Of course, we should obey rulers above all because of love of the good. However, even if our love falters, we still have motive in fear: "But if you do wrong, be afraid, for he does not bear the sword in vain; he is the servant of God to execute his wrath on the wrongdoer" (Rom. 13:4).

---

[635] The reader may notice circularity in the "definition" of capital punishment: the offense is stipulated as "capital" and the punishment proportionate to such an offense would be "capital." The circularity is inescapable but does not render the statement meaningless. If the act were *per se* evil, one never could identify any offense as "capital." As it is, history has admitted cases in which one can identify an offense as capital. The Church's own canonical legislation accepted capital punishment for heretics as legitimate for more than six centuries, beginning with Boniface VIII's *Liber Sextus*, in 1298. Now, if it were the case that conditions in some culture were such that no crime could be identified as capital, then the definition would have no practical relevance. Nevertheless, that irrelevance would not render the object *per se* evil.

[636] See Edward Feser and Joseph Bessette, *By Man Shall His Blood Be Shed: A Catholic Defense of Capital Punishment* (San Francisco: Ignatius Press, 2017), 99–103.

This and other New Testament passages bear witness to the legitimate use of capital punishment.[637]

Edward Feser and Joseph Bessette show that the patristics read the scriptural witness as teaching that there can be a morally licit use of capital punishment. Even opponents of the death penalty admit as much.[638] Feser and Bessette rightly note that when the Fathers with moral unanimity agree on the interpretation of Scripture, we are to hold this interpretation. Since the Fathers with such unanimity teach this reading of Scripture, they conclude, we are to hold it.[639]

The Magisterium itself teaches that capital punishment can be justly imposed. Pope Innocent I, in 405, assured Catholics that he was not going to overturn the practice of capital punishment, even after the empire became officially Catholic. He noted that it had long been accepted that states have this authority. He wrote:

> About these things we read nothing definitive from the forefathers. For they had remembered that these powers had been granted by God and that for the sake of punishing harm-doers the sword had been allowed; in this way a minister of God, an avenger, has been given. How therefore would they criticize something which they see to have been granted through the authority of God? About these matters therefore, we hold to what has been observed hitherto, lest we may seem either to overturn sound order or to go against the authority of the Lord.[640]

Centuries later, Pope Innocent III mandated that the Waldensians, as condition for their union with the Catholic Church, affirm that capital punishment can be exercised without mortal sin. This condition regarded entry into the Church, a necessary condition for eternal salvation. It is

---

[637] Ibid., 103–111.

[638] See E. Christian Brugger, *Capital Punishment and Roman Catholic Moral Tradition* (Notre Dame, IN: University of Notre Dame Press, 2003), 95.

[639] See Feser and Bessette, 111–117.

[640] Innocent I, *Epistle VI* (to Exsuperium), as quoted in Feser and Bessette, 123, and Brugger, *Capital Punishment*, 89.

therefore a teaching of high rank: "With regard to the secular power, we affirm that it can exercise a judgment of blood without mortal sin provided that in carrying out the punishment it proceeds, not out of hatred, but judiciously, not in a precipitous manner, but with caution."[641] This is to say, capital punishment is not intrinsically evil. How can we draw this conclusion, when the text simply says "without mortal sin"? We are dealing with matter that would be grave were it intrinsically evil. Human life cannot be taken without just cause; to take it without just cause is necessarily gravely evil matter. Since the oath states that capital punishment can be rendered without mortal sin, it necessarily implies that capital punishment is not intrinsically evil.

The *Roman Catechism* states:

The power of life and death is permitted to certain civil magistrates because theirs is the responsibility under law to punish the guilty and protect the innocent. Far from being guilty of breaking this commandment [Thou shall not kill], such an execution of justice is precisely an act of obedience to it. For the purpose of the law is to protect and foster human life. This purpose is fulfilled when the legitimate authority of the State is exercised by taking the guilty lives of those who have taken innocent lives. In the Psalms we find a vindication of this right: "Morning by morning I will destroy all the wicked in the land, cutting off all evildoers from the city of the Lord" (Ps. 101:8).[642]

Pope Leo XIII wrote, "Clearly, divine law, both that which is known by the light of reason and that which is revealed in Sacred Scripture, strictly forbids anyone, outside of public cause, to kill or wound a man unless compelled to do so in self-defense."[643] As Feser and Bessette note, Leo ex-

---

[641] DH 795. He added this clause in 1210.

[642] Translation by Christian Washburn. See *Catechismus Romanus seu Catechismus ex decreto Concilii Tridentini ad Parochos Pii Quinti Pont. Max. iussu editus*, ed. Petrus Rodríguez et al. (Città del Vaticano: Libreria Editrice Vaticana/Ediciones Univ. de Navarra, 1989), 465–466.

[643] Leo XIII, *Pastoralis officii* (1891), art. 2.

empted both the public cause of capital punishment and self-defense from the condemnation of murder. Pius XII affirmed that capital punishment is not intrinsically evil. In an address on September 14, 1952, he taught:

> Even when it is a question of the execution of a condemned man, the State does not dispose of the individual's right to life. In this case it is reserved to the public power to deprive the condemned person of the enjoyment of life in expiation of his crime when, by his crime, he has already dispossessed himself (*il s'est déjà dépossédé*) of his right to live.[644]

For his part, John Paul II was famously critical of the contemporary *use* of the punishment. Still, he defended a *"true right to self-defense,"* which can include and even oblige one to the use of lethal force.[645] In precisely this context, he took up his discussion of capital punishment. Notably, John Paul II refused to condemn capital punishment as intrinsically evil. Moreover, he underscored the contrast between the unconditional illegitimacy of every direct taking of innocent human life from the conditional legitimacy of capital punishment.[646] To be sure, John Paul II added rigor to the conditions for its use, expressing that it is justly used only "when it would not be possible otherwise to defend society."[647] Finally, he opined that today, practically speaking, these conditions are rare if not nonexistent.

We can distinguish three affirmations in John Paul II's teaching. First, he reaffirmed that capital punishment is not intrinsically evil. Second, he stressed that it may be justly employed only if it is the only way society can defend itself. Third, he opined that in practically all cases, today's penal system allows society to defend itself in other ways. Only the first two teachings are magisterial. The third affirmation regards a concrete judgment of such circumstances as are outside the scope of the certainty of magisterial

---

[644] Pius XII, *The Moral Limits of Medical Research and Treatment* (1952), Papal Encyclicals, https://www.papalencyclicals.net/pius12/p12psych. htm. Alternatively, see also AAS 44 (1952): 787.

[645] John Paul II, *Evangelium vitae* (1995), art. 55.

[646] Ibid., art. 57.

[647] Ibid., art. 56.

authority. Rightly, therefore, in a letter to then Theodore Cardinal McCarrick, Joseph Ratzinger clarified that one who disagrees with John Paul II on the application of the death penalty in contemporary circumstances — which is the third affirmation above — may still present himself for the Eucharist. By contrast, those who support abortion may not. Ratzinger wrote:

> Not all moral issues have the same moral weight as abortion and euthanasia. For example, if a Catholic were to be at odds with the Holy Father on the application of capital punishment or on the decision to wage war, he would not for that reason be considered unworthy to present himself to receive Holy Communion.[648]

As for the second affirmation in John Paul's teaching, questions have been raised about it. "Self-defense" is a *preemptive* measure taken against a morally certain act of *future* aggression. Punishment, by contrast, is not preemptive but retributive. Punishment is always executed *after* criminal action. (Concrete, embodied, or expressed plans to carry out criminal activity already count as punishable criminal activity.) How, then, can capital punishment be a "defensive" action? Because of this difficulty, some have suggested that John Paul was referring to a society's defense of its own *common* good. Such a defense would not be narrowly construed as the self-defense against an active aggressor but more broadly as a society's inflicting proportionate punishment for a capital crime already committed. This suggestion may have merit. Still, it raises other questions. If we are supposed to read John Paul in this way, how would improved penal systems restrict the infliction of *punishment* proportionate to a *capital* crime? Such systems are defensive by detaining criminals from possible *future* action. But punishment pertains to an already committed crime.

For his part, Pope Benedict XVI oversaw the publication of the *Compendium of the Catechism of the Catholic Church*. This important document,

---

[648] Cardinal Joseph Ratzinger, "Worthiness to Receive Holy Communion — General Principles," *L'espresso* (June 2004), posted at Catholic Culture, https://www.catholicculture.org/culture/library/view.cfm?id=6041.

relatively clear and concise, also carefully avoids describing capital punishment as intrinsically evil.[649]

As we have seen, the Magisterium has consistently taught for centuries that capital punishment is not an intrinsic evil. Revelation itself indicates that capital punishment is not intrinsically evil. Finally, the Fathers of the Church concur with revelation on the legitimacy of capital punishment. As we have noted elsewhere, such teachings are infallible. Of course, even though capital punishment is not an intrinsic evil, consideration of circumstances is always necessary before one can judge that a concrete application of such a punishment is a morally good act in this or that case. An act is good only if it is good in its object, in its circumstances, and in the intention of the agent. I have shown simply that capital punishment is good in its object.

Countering a Confusion
Today, people are confused about the Church's position on the death penalty. They read the following passage in a newly edited section of the Catholic *Catechism*:

> Recourse to the death penalty on the part of legitimate authority, following a fair trial, was long considered an appropriate response to the gravity of certain crimes and an acceptable, albeit extreme, means of safeguarding the common good.
>
> Today, however, there is an increasing awareness that the dignity of the person is not lost even after the commission of very serious crimes. In addition, a new understanding has emerged of the significance of penal sanctions imposed by the state. Lastly, more effective systems of detention have been developed, which ensure the due protection of citizens but, at the same time, do not definitively deprive the guilty of the possibility of redemption.
>
> Consequently, the Church teaches, in the light of the Gospel, that "the death penalty is inadmissible because it is an attack on

---

[649] See *Compendium of the Catechism*, art. 469.

the inviolability and dignity of the person", and she works with determination for its abolition worldwide.[650]

Some take the final paragraph to mean that the death penalty is intrinsically evil. Why? First, it says that the death penalty is "inadmissible." They argue that what is inadmissible must be always and everywhere evil. But what is always and everywhere evil is precisely an intrinsically evil act. Second, they observe that the explanation for its inadmissibility—what follows the "because"—is that the death penalty is an attack on the inviolability and dignity of the person. If it is an attack on the dignity of the person, then it seems it must be *per se* evil. Are these interpreters correct?

Given the argument laid out above, the Church's prior teaching that the death penalty is *not* intrinsically evil is infallible, and infallible teachings cannot be violated. Accordingly, it is not likely that the new expression proscribes the death penalty as intrinsically evil. Second, the word chosen here is "inadmissible." This is not a normal term in moral theology. The traditional term is *per se* evil or intrinsically evil. An act is either evil in its object or not. If it is evil in its object, it may never be chosen, regardless of the circumstances and intention. If the act is not intrinsically evil, then it is possible that it be the object of a good act, provided the circumstances are fitting and the intention good. So, what might "inadmissible" mean?

In order not to read the latest formulation as a rupture from the prior magisterial teaching, we should not read "inadmissible" as "intrinsically evil." Perhaps we could interpret the passage as indicating that today the conditions of the penal system are such that the death penalty is no longer appropriate. If we were to read it this way, we would find the latest formulation to be both a reaffirmation of John Paul II's formulation on the circumstances necessary for a just use of the penalty and also a conclusive judgment that these circumstances do not exist today. So read, the teaching would be dependent on circumstances. If the circumstances were to change, then the applicability of the teaching would change. (Let's say world powers collapsed and rioters broke out and chaos emerged.

[650] CCC 2267.

Let's say new forms of order and government were to take shape. What kind of temporary penal systems would need to be instituted during a prolonged chaos and meltdown of the public order? No one can foresee all circumstances; hence, no one can judge with certainty concerning all circumstances. Intrinsically evil acts are always and everywhere evil. Other acts are not always and everywhere evil.)

We may also recall John Paul II's judgment concerning concrete circumstances. As it would seem, the actual state of concrete circumstances concerning capital punishment does not fall within the certain judgment of the magisterial office. The Magisterium can authoritatively condemn the direct killing of the innocent as *per se* evil. Magisterial figures can also publicly express personal judgments about clear cases of direct killing of the innocent, such as the bombings of Hiroshima, Dresden, and Nagasaki. It does not seem, however, that magisterial figures can *authoritatively* judge such bombings, even though they are, to many people at least, clear cases. Magisterial figures can prophetically indicate that Hiroshima and Dresden were *instances* of direct killing. Read in this manner, the teaching that the death penalty is inadmissible today would seem to be a prophetic claim that the right circumstances for lawful use of the death penalty no longer exist. Since a prophetic witness is not doctrinally binding, however, could one not remain a good Catholic and yet judge otherwise in a concrete case? Recall Ratzinger's letter to McCarrick.

Yet another reflection may steer us away from reading "inadmissible" as "*per se* evil." Notice the word "consequently" at the beginning of the last paragraph. That word indicates that what follows is known to be true *because* of the prior reflection. The prior reflection includes attention to things such as enhanced penal systems. If the conclusion—the death penalty is inadmissible—depends on those prior reflections, then once again the term "inadmissible" does not mean "intrinsically evil" but simply "not justified in the present context."

It would be tempting to leave it at that, but there is a possible objection to this interpretation. The text *also* claims that the reason the death penalty is "inadmissible" is that it violates personal dignity. Now, if this reason were absolute, then the death penalty could never be a legitimate object of choice. It truly would be intrinsically evil. But if it truly were intrinsically evil, then God commanded evil in the Old Testament, Paul misled us in the New Testament, the Fathers of the Church erred despite their moral unanimity on a matter of faith and morals, and the Church has in her ordinary and universal Magisterium misled us in the past about capital punishment. But it is impossible for a Catholic to hold that God commands evil, that Paul erred, that the Fathers collectively erred, and that Mother Church definitively misled us.

One is left, then, to puzzle over the meaning of the new formula-tion. One thing seems clear: the past teaching is infallible and cannot be abandoned. If we were to abandon infallible teaching even on this issue — which is *most certainly* not at the center of our Faith — all and sundry other issues would come knocking at the door, begging to be changed. The Trojan horse of modernism would have been brought into the sanctuary. Then the gateway to destruction would be opened wide, luring the hope of the godless, who call evil good and good evil.

Marian Coredemption Is Foolish?
Mary Is Not Mediatrix of All Graces?

The Church has for at least a century and a half taught and accepted the notion that Mary cooperated in Christ's redemptive work on Calvary. This cooperative work is sometimes named *coredemption*. This term is intended to signify Mary's work, with and under Christ and in absolute dependence on Him, in procuring by her merit the treasury of graces that are dispensed throughout history. Mary's cooperation in the redemptive work of Christ is distinguished from her cooperation in the distribution of that treasury after her Assumption into Heaven. Although the terms "treasury" and "distribution" are metaphorical, since grace does not exist in a vat in Heaven, the distinction between these two parts of the salvific action is very real. Now, the latter work is Mary's *mediation* of graces. But the Church has also long taught that, after her Assumption into Heaven, Mary mediates *every* grace that God gives to us. The focus of this section is Marian coredemption, her cooperation with Christ's redemptive act in gaining the treasury of graces. What binds all these teachings together is the Church's confession of Mary as mother of all the living.

It should be clear that Mary is able to cooperate with Christ only because *He* empowered her to do so. By His power, while yet on the Cross, He lifted her up to be an instrument (a free one) who, with Him, offered up His suffering and her own so as to procure with and under Him some title to the treasury of graces for all others excluding herself. Thus, the prefix "co-" indicates not only cooperation but subordination and participatory dependence. So much is this the case that we must ascribe all Mary's cooperation to Christ as to its radical source. He gave her the gift of being able to cooperate with Him. Moreover, Christ did not need her help; He chose to lift her up so that she could help.

By making these claims, we extol Christ all the more, since He is the great redeemer who lifted Mary up to cooperate with Him. A redeemer that could not do that would not be so great. What are the sources of our knowledge of Mary's coredemption? Scripture, Tradition, and the Magisterium witness to Mary's work. Assuredly, it is no superficial and easy matter to establish the revealed testimony to this mystery. As with the Immaculate Conception, it requires great care and wonder, not to mention time and patience, to discover this teaching.

Scriptural Sources
In Genesis 3:15, God promises the serpent (Satan) that "the woman" and he will have hostility, enmity toward each other. For the woman to have hostility toward the devil implies not merely privileges passively received but also active participation in a battle. The passage reveals more than the Immaculate Conception, a doctrine whereby Mary benefitted in a passive manner.[651] In that same passage, God indicates that a redeemer will come, her offspring, who will crush the serpent's head. This image

---

[651] See Charles Boyer, "Thoughts on Mary's Co-Redemption," in *Studies in Praise of Our Blessed Mother*, ed. Joseph Clifford Fenton and Edmond Darvil Benard (Washington, D.C.: Catholic University of America Press, 1952), 149–151.

is completed in Revelation 12, wherein the great dragon (Satan) wars against "the woman" and her son. In each case, the redeemer is Christ, warring with Satan. But in each case, also, a woman is engaged in the battle. That woman is Mary. How do we know this? We know for various reasons. For one, the Hebrew word for "serpent" can also mean "dragon." Thus, the imagery of woman and serpent is neatly mirrored by that of woman and dragon. Furthermore, Revelation 12:5 clearly teaches that the woman bore the messianic son, but it was Mary who bore the Mes-siah. Now, some point out, rightly, that Israel is in a collective sense the "Mother" of Jesus and that the Church is the Mother of Christians. This is true. Revelation is polyvalent. But only Mary is *both* the Mother of Jesus *and* the Mother of Christians. And Revelation identifies the woman precisely in this way: having tried in vain to pollute the woman and crush the Christ, "the dragon was angry with the woman, and went off to make war on the *rest* of her offspring" (Rev. 12:17, emphasis mine). The polyvalence and symbolism of Revelation 12 is simply breathtaking. Christ's work against Satan procured our redemption. Battling against the infernal foe with and through Christ, Mary cried out in labor for our coredemption (Rev. 12:2).

Luke, moreover, reveals to us the prophecy of Simeon, who said of Jesus to Mary, "Behold, this child is set for the fall and rising of many in Israel, and for a sign that is spoken against (and a sword will pierce through your own soul also), that thoughts out of many hearts may be revealed" (Luke 2:34–35). Simeon linked the death of Jesus, by which we are redeemed, with the spiritual suffering of Mary.

We know also that Paul drew an analogy between Christ and Adam. Adam the first man worked our condemnation, but Christ the New Man worked our redemption. The theological tradition unpacked the implica-tions of Paul's teaching.

Theological and Magisterial Development
In the theological tradition, the implication of Paul's analogy was drawn out explicitly. In the middle of the second century, Justin described Mary as the New Eve. A few decades later, Irenaeus taught that Mary cut the

knot of Eve's disobedience and became a cause of salvation for herself and the whole world.[652] These themes emerged with greater force in the twelfth century, when Arnold of Chartres spoke of two altars, one for the body of Jesus and another for the heart of Mary. In the fourteenth century, the term "Coredemptrix" was applied to Mary in various places, such as Salzburg and Spain.

For the past century and a half, the Magisterium has taught the substance of Marian coredemption, albeit rarely employing the term. For example, Pius IX wrote:

> Just as Christ, the Mediator between God and man, assumed human nature, blotted the handwriting of the decree that stood against us, and fastened it triumphantly to the cross, so the most holy Virgin, united with him by a most intimate and indissoluble bond, was, with him and through him, eternally at enmity with the evil serpent, and most completely triumphed over him, and thus crushed his head with her immaculate foot.[653]

Pius IX associated Mary's work with Christ's redemptive work on the Cross, by which He conquered the devil. Later, Pius IX taught that Mary associated her suffering with the sacrifice of her Son.[654] These are all affirmations of Mary's coredemptive work.

Leo XIII taught that Mary,

> when she professed herself the handmaid of the Lord for the mother's office, and when, at the foot of the altar, she offered up her whole self with her Child Jesus — then and thereafter she took her part in the laborious expiation made by her Son for the sins of the world.... There stood by the Cross of Jesus His Mother, who ...

---

[652] See Irenaeus, *Against Heresies*, III, 22, 4.

[653] Pius IX, *Ineffabilis Deus* (1854), Papal Encyclicals, https://www.papalencyclicals.net/pius09/p9ineff.htm.

[654] This quote by Pius IX was taken from a letter published as the preface to *Marie et le Sacerdoce* by Msgr. O. van den Berghe (Paris, 1873).

offered generously to Divine Justice her own Son, and died in her
heart with Him, stabbed with the sword of sorrow.[655]

Here, Leo taught that Mary offered up her Son and her own sufferings to
God in reparation for the sins of the world. Such an offering is precisely
coredemptive work. In *Parta humano generi*, the same pontiff declared
that Mary "was made participant in human redemption with her son
Jesus." Clearly, Leo XIII taught the coredemption.

Later, Pius X wrote:

> From this communion of will and suffering between Christ and
> Mary, she merited to become "most worthily the reparatrix of
> the lost world" and dispensatrix of all the gifts that our Savior
> purchased for us by his death and by his blood.[656]

Pius X made clear that Christ has the strict title to distribute gifts and
that Mary's suffering makes it *fitting* for her to share in this distribution.
Similarly, Pius X made it clear that Christ alone is the productive cause
of grace by His divinity and that Mary serves in the manner of a channel
or aqueduct. Then, in a momentous declaration, the pope added:

> Since Mary carries it over all in holiness and union with Christ
> and has been associated by Christ in the work of redemption, she
> merits for us *de congruo* [as they say] what Christ [merited] for us
> *de condigno*, and she is the supreme minister of the distribution
> of graces.[657]

Pius X's teaching is clear. Mary has a role in the distribution of all graces.
This is her role as mediatrix of all graces. But she also had a role in the
redemptive work. As Pius X taught, what Christ merited strictly (*de
condigno*) Mary merits in a fitting way (*de congruo*). There are two things
to notice in this teaching. First, there is a distinction between a strict
title in justice; this is *de condigno* merit. It is distinct from a fitting title,

---

[655] Leo XIII, *Iucunda semper expectatione* (1894).
[656] DH 3370.
[657] DH 3370.

which is merely *de congruo*. Second, notice that the pope used the present tense for Mary and the perfect tense for Christ. Some theologians hold that the pope was simply employing a Latin locution according to which the present tense verb is meant to be read in the perfect tense as well. If this is so, the apparent distinction should not draw our attention, even though it would in no way diminish the claim I am making. If, however, the pope meant to draw a distinction, he thereby showed that Christ's power always undergirded and supported Mary's work. Christ was the foundation, and His work was the presupposition of Mary's; she worked only upon that foundation. In either case, as the pope taught, Mary did gain a title, in a fitting way, to the treasury of grace to be distributed over time. Later, the Holy Office under Pius X approved on more than one occasion calling Mary "coredemptrix."[658]

For his part, Pope Benedict XV affirmed and deepened Pius's teaching. In *Inter sodalicia*, he wrote:

> To such extent did she (Mary) suffer and almost die with her suffering and dying Son, and to such extent did she surrender her maternal rights over her Son for man's salvation and immolated Him, insofar as she could, in order to appease the justice of God, that we may rightly say that she redeemed the human race together with her Son.[659]

Here we see Mary's own suffering in connection with *appeasement of divine justice*. The pope said that she redeemed the human race together with her Son. Precisely such work is what we call "coredemption." Again, Pius XI declared, "The virgin, suffering greatly, participated in the work of redemption with her Son Jesus Christ."[660] The same pope explicitly called Mary coredemptrix on three occasions.[661]

---

[658] See AAS 5 (1913): 364 and AAS 6 (1914): 108.

[659] Cited from Junipero Carol, *Fundamentals of Mariology* (New York: Benzinger, 1956), 59–60.

[660] Pius XI, *Explorata res*, in AAS 15 (1923): 104.

[661] See Pius XI, allocution to pilgrims from Vicenza, November 30, 1933, published *L'Osservatore Romano*, December 1, 1933; Pius XI, allocution

False Mercy

Pius XII taught the substance of the doctrine as well:

Now, in the accomplishing of this work of redemption, the Blessed Virgin Mary was most closely associated with Christ.... For "just as Christ, because he redeemed us, is our Lord and King by a special title, so the Blessed Virgin also (is our Queen), on account of the unique manner in which she assisted in our redemption, by giving of her own substance, by freely offering him for us, by her singular desire and petition for, and active interest in, our salvation."[662]

Mary worked with Christ to procure our redemption. This is nothing other than the coredemption.

From what precedes we see that the doctrine of Marian coredemption is a longstanding teaching of the Church. Unfortunately, this teaching has recently come under fire. Why?

Countering Confusion

We can point to three factors in the confusion.

1. First, we must once again recognize the pernicious influence of Karl Rahner, who came to deny any redeeming role for Mary. For the mature Rahner, Mary was merely a recipient of redemption but not a cooperator in redemption.[663] Of course, since Rahner denied that Christ's death had

---

to Spanish pilgrims, published in *L'Osservatore Romano*, March 25, 1934; and Pius XI, radio message for the end of the Holy Year, published in *L'Osservatore Romano*, April 29–30, 1935. For more, see Theological Commission of the International Marian Association, *The Role of Mary in Redemption* (2017), International Marian Association, https://internationalmarian.com/sites/marian/files/uploads/documents/the_role_of_mary_in_redemption_1.pdf, note 28.

[662] DH 3914. See also Juniper Carol, "Our Lady's Coredemption," in *Mariology*, vol. 2, ed. Juniper Carol (Post Falls, ID: Mediatrix Press, 2018), 423–475.

[663] See Karl Rahner, "Le principe fondamental de la théologie mariale," *Recherches de Science Religieuse* 42 (1954): 509 and 513. See also Karl Rahner, "Zur konziliaren Mariologie," *Stimmen der Zeit* 174 (1964): 87–101.

a causal role in the offer of saving grace, it is no surprise that he denied a subordinate one to Mary as well.

2. Second, the Second Vatican Council did not employ the term "Coredemptrix." Nor did it describe Mary as "Mediatrix of all graces." Some theologians took this silence the wrong way. Among these, alas, was Joseph Ratzinger, who later became Pope Benedict XVI. Shortly after the council, Ratzinger wrote, "The idea of Mary as 'co-redemptrix' is gone now, as is the idea of Mary as 'mediatrix of all graces.'"[664] How should we respond to Ratzinger's remarks?

A. Ratzinger wrote those words as a private theologian. He later stated something similar, albeit less categorically, while serving as cardinal prefect of the CDF. But in both cases, he wrote as a private theologian.[665] So, these remarks have no authority.

B. Ratzinger seems to have concluded from silence. But as we have seen, we may not argue from the silence of a council to the denial of a doctrine. That would be an invalid argument indebted to a hermeneutic of rupture. Moreover, the council document itself announced that it is not a comprehensive statement of all Catholic doctrine on Mary.[666] We must not think that recent magisterial documents must carry the burden of incessant repetition. However, in times of confusion, a little repetition and recollection can help.

C. We know why the council refrained from using the title "Core-demptrix." Those involved in the drafting of the final document indicated that suchlike titles are "very true in themselves" but that the draft did not use them because they might be difficult for non-Catholic Christians to understand.[667] It was a *pastoral*

---

[664] Joseph Ratzinger, *Theological Highlights of Vatican II*, trans. Henry Traub, Gerard Thormann, and Werner Barzel (New York: Paulist Press, 1966), 93.

[665] See Joseph Ratzinger, *God and the World*, trans. Henry Taylor (San Francisco: Ignatius Press, 2002), 306.

[666] See *Lumen gentium*, art. 54.

[667] See *Acta synodalia sacrosancti concilii oecumenici Vaticani II*, vol. 1.4 (Vatican City: Typis polyglottis Vaticanis, 1971), 99.

communication's strategy, not a doctrinal denial. This strategy is understandable and has its strength as a prudential measure of reaching out to a broad audience in a readily acceptable manner. At the same time, this strategy presents a challenge. To refrain from speaking the whole pertinent truth, especially when that truth has come into question, risks giving the impression of denial or doubt. The early (and even the mature) Ratzinger serves as an example. There is a lesson here. When members of the hierarchy remain silent on issues that the world presently doubts or scorns, the faithful can eventually find themselves bewildered.

3. More recently, Pope Francis seemed to some to reject the term "Coredemptrix" in a homily. He stated, "Faithful to her Master, who is her Son, the only redeemer, she never wanted to take anything that belongs to her Son for herself. She never presented herself as Co-redemptrix. No, as disciple."[668] Later in the homily, he referred to a request some had made that he declare this or that Marian dogma. In response, he remarked, "Let us not get lost in foolishness." *Crux* magazine tied the two statements together and concluded that Pope Francis declared the idea of a dogma on Mary as Coredemptrix "foolishness."[669] In a Wednesday Audience, Pope Francis said that "there are no co-redeemers with Christ. He is the only one." He went on to say that Christ entrusted Mary to us "as a Mother, not as a goddess, not as co-redeemer: as Mother."[670]

What are we to make of the remarks of Pope Francis? Regarding the Wednesday Audience, Pope Francis rightly rejected any notion that Jesus' work in the Redemption was lacking. It is also very true that Mary is not a goddess. She is merely a human being. The correct understanding of Marian coredemption perfectly accords with these truths. The correct

---

[668] Pope Francis, homily, December 12, 2019, my translation.

[669] Inés San Martin, "Pope Calls Idea of Declaring Mary Co-Redemptrix 'Foolishness,'" *Crux*, December 13, 2019, https://cruxnow.com/vatican/2019/12/pope-calls-idea-of-declaring-mary-co-redemptrix-foolishness/.

[670] Pope Francis, General Audience, Wednesday, March 24, 2021.

understanding of Marian coredemption affirms that Mary's work depends on Christ's and magnifies it.

Next, let us consider Francis's homily. Three points are in order. First, a fine theologian, Robert Fastiggi, rejects *Crux*'s reading of the homily.[671] Fastiggi notes that the pope did not directly call the term "Coredemptrix" foolishness, much less the notion itself. Still, one wonders what other dogma the pope could have been calling "foolishness."

Second, Pope Francis did not in this homily explicitly teach that Mary is not Coredemptrix. Rather, he claimed that she didn't arrogate that title to herself when she appeared to Juan Diego. So much is obviously true. So, too, the divine Son rarely invoked His own lofty status but instead referred His glory to the Father. Like her Son, Mary rarely acclaimed her privileges, turning instead to the glory of her God and Redeemer. Read along these lines, the pope was pointing to Mary's humility. Now, we Christians would never dare to use Jesus' humility as reason to deny His prerogatives, e.g., His status as Messiah and His eternal deity.

Third, we should distinguish the substance of the Marian doctrine from the use of the title "Coredemptrix." Pope Francis's remarks may pertain to the title more than to the doctrine. In this connection, we should note that fewer popes have chosen to use the title than have taught the doctrine. Still, the substance of this doctrine has long been taught by the Magisterium. Catholics are still bound by the duty they owe to the Magisterium to submit religiously with mind and heart to this substance.

Concerning Vatican II and the Postconciliar Magisterium
The Second Vatican Council and the postconciliar Magisterium actually taught the substance of this doctrine.

1. Vatican II rightly stressed the perennial truth that Mary's work comes from and ever depends on Christ's work. Yet the council was not

---

[671] Robert Fastiggi, "Pope Francis and Mary Co-Redemptrix," Where Peter Is, December 27, 2019, https://wherepeteris.com/pope-francis-and -mary-co-redemptrix/.

silent on her work, declaring that Mary cooperated in a "singular way" in the work of the Savior.[672] That is, her cooperation differs *qualitatively* from ours. We can to some degree cooperate in the *distribution* of some graces from the treasury of grace; that is, we can pray for each other. Because Mary cooperates in the distribution of all graces, her cooperation far exceeds ours. But we did not and could not cooperate in any way in the work of redemption. By contrast, Mary uniquely served the Redemption itself, with and under Christ.[673] The council quoted Irenaeus's startling remark to this effect: "Being obedient, [she] became the cause of salvation for herself and for the whole human race."[674] The council described Mary as "enduring with her only begotten Son the intensity of his suffering, associated herself with his sacrifice in her mother's heart, and lovingly consenting to the immolation of this victim which was born of her."[675] She was at work in the Passion as a sacrifice offered to God. In sum, the council expressed some of the substance of the doctrine without using the words. Still, because of this reticence to express the full truth, the orthodox and competent theologian, Fr. Manfred Hauke, commented, "It was no wonder that this treatment of the figure of Mary resulted in a 'Marian Ice Age,' during which any mention of Marian mediation itself was taboo even among Mariologists."[676]

2. John Paul II authoritatively reaffirmed the substance of this teaching on a number of occasions. He affirmed that Mary offered Jesus up in expiation for all our sins.[677] He made clear that Mary's cooperation pertained also to the very work of redemption, a work *anterior* to the work of distribution. He noted that we cooperate with Christ in the distribution of graces by praying for each other, but he stressed that we do not

---

[672] *Lumen gentium*, art. 61.

[673] Ibid., art. 56.

[674] Ibid.

[675] Ibid., art. 58.

[676] Manfred Hauke, "Mary's Motherly Mediation in Christ: A Systematic Reflection," *Nova et Vetera* 7 (2009): 945.

[677] See John Paul II, General Audience, April 2, 1997.

cooperate in the redemption. By contrast, Mary also cooperated in the redemptive sacrifice itself.[678]

3. As pope, Benedict XVI reaffirmed that there is no fruit of grace that comes to us without Mary's mediation.[679] Moreover, he affirmed that Mary fought against the devil with Christ. The former was an affirmation of Mary as Mediatrix of all graces; the latter was an implicit affirmation of Mary's cooperation with redemption.[680]

4. Pope Francis affirmed the core insight that binds together both Mary's mediation of all graces and her coredemptive work—namely, her universal motherhood. He stated, "Our Lady, who, as the Mother to whom Jesus entrusted us, 'enfolds' us all."[681] Further, it is true that Mary is not a goddess. Nor is she a redeemer on a par with the one Mediator of all, Jesus Christ. She did, however, singularly cooperate in the redemption procured on Calvary.

As we can see, for about a century and a half, numerous popes have authoritatively taught the substance of Marian coredemption. The Second Vatican Council taught this substance as well, even though its documents were crafted with an eye to the world as audience and were explicitly stated not to be a comprehensive presentation of Catholic teaching on Mary. We therefore have no excuse to deny the teaching, and no teaching of the Church is foolishness.

Jesus Not God? Only the Father Is God?

The foundation of the Christian religion is that the Son of God, who is true God from true God, came to dwell among us as a man. We believe that He preached to us the truth and offered us an example of how to live.

---

[678] See John Paul II, General Audience, April 9, 1997.

[679] Pope Benedict, homily for the canonization of Fra Galvao, May 11, 2007, EWTN, https://www.ewtn.com/catholicism/library/homily-at-mass-and-canonization-of-blessed-frei-galvo--pope-benedict-xvi-6216.

[680] See Pope Benedict, Angelus, August 19, 2007.

[681] Pope Francis, General Audience, March 24, 2021.

We believe that He suffered, died, and rose again so that we might have the forgiveness of sins and the outpouring of grace. The divinity of Jesus is the foundation of our religion. Heretics of various sorts have denied the divinity of the Son. One such heresy was that of the Ebionites, who believed that Jesus was a man, a prophet, in whom God dwelled or by whom God (who, for them, is only the Father) spoke to us. The Church rejected this heresy, since Jesus was no mere man but the eternal Word made flesh, and this Word is eternally God. Later, Arius defied the Son of God, claiming that He was only a high and lofty being but still a creature made by God. The Church solemnly condemned these errors in dogmas.

Countering a Confusion

Recently, Eugenio Scalfari alleged that Pope Francis does not believe in the divinity of Jesus Christ.

1. He claimed in 2013 that Pope Francis said to him the following: "I believe in God. Not in a Catholic God; there is no Catholic God, there is God. And I believe in Jesus Christ, his incarnation. Jesus is my teacher and my shepherd, but God the Father—Abba—is the light and the Creator."[682]

2. In the October 8, 2019, issue of *la Repubblica*, Scalfari again alleged that Pope Francis said the following of Jesus: "Although he was an exceptionally virtuous man, he was not God at all."

Some might be quick to interpret these statements as though they really were words of a pope or even papal words. They might take the first citation to claim that God is only one person, the Father, whereas Jesus is merely an earthly teacher and shepherd. The second citation they might take to claim that Jesus is not true God but a mere man.

What should we think of these remarks? Neither of these statements is even a word of Pope Francis. They are only alleged words of the pope. Much less are they papal words. In his papal words, Francis has explicitly affirmed the humanity and divinity of Christ. For example, in his homily of December 24, 2013, he stated, "The grace which was revealed in our

[682] Scalfari, "The Pope: How the Church Will Change."

world is Jesus, born of the Virgin Mary, true man and true God." This is the orthodox and Catholic Faith. Let us all remember that no one has authority to preach to us a Gospel other than that which the Church has always taught. We all believe what St. Paul wrote, "If anyone is preaching to you a gospel contrary to that which you received, let him be accursed" (Gal. 1:9).

Epilogue

We have treated numerous errors and heresies currently afflicting Catholic life. The global error is doctrinal evolutionism, the notion that dogmas last for only a certain time, eventually needing to be replaced, altered, or watered down. We must reject doctrinal evolutionism. We must forever retain all dogmas and infallible doctrines, neither denying them nor watering them down. Newer developments nourish the life of the Church and are to be welcomed, always in continuity with the past. We must likewise remember the whole truth, the precise truth, and the unambiguous truth. Silence is not denial; an ambiguous expression does not cancel an unambiguous one; an imprecise expression does not void a precise one; and an unclear statement does not eclipse a clear one. For a season and a purpose, it may be salutary to speak incompletely and imprecisely before strangers alienated from the Faith. But the members of the household need the full truth taught clearly, lest, in their zeal for bringing the straying home, they find themselves lost, like sheep without pasture or shepherd.

Now, doctrinal evolutionism is the cause and the result of numerous specific errors. Each of the specific errors treated in this book, with the exception of those of chapter 10, centers on the denial of a basic Catholic teaching—namely, that human life is a pilgrimage in which we, through our free choices, journey either toward Heaven or toward Hell. Life is serious. We must keep the memory of death before our eyes. Let us cast into Hell the worm-tongued counsel of those who delude us by the figment of an empty Hell. When these same figures hedge their bets and seek refuge in the heresy of justification through faith alone or the blasphemy of Christ as sinner, let us not follow them. Contrary to their idle dreams, the real Catholic Faith holds that any unrepented mortal sin makes me liable to eternal damnation. How, then, shall I be saved?

Jesus Christ instituted His Holy Catholic Church for the salvation of every human being. He entrusted to her the truth so as to illuminate those who sit in darkness and the saving remedies of grace to wash sinners clean, to feed weary pilgrims, and to guide them toward the refreshing waters of everlasting life. Thus, the Church is the way of salvation. She presents the world with the one true religion that God wills, the only existing religion that God has appointed by which all men are to be saved. Hence, the narrow gate can be found and the hard road to Heaven can be trodden. But who will bear this good news to a hungering world? Evangelization is a necessary task. Catholics are called to share the good news with their neighbors. Although Catholics may not judge anyone's soul, neither may they hide the good news under a bushel to the detriment of their neighbor. If circumstances warrant silence before this person or that, the general call to evangelize remains universal. If we love, we will evangelize, because the greatest good we can will for our neighbor is communion with the Good that does not falter or frustrate, with the Good that holds us in love — namely, the Holy Trinity.

In living out our discipleship as Catholics, we know also that the family is the heart of the future. Many are aware that the infernal foe has marked the family as his final target. Whereas Genesis opens up with the beauty of hope through the cycles of nature that imitate the divine eternity, the devil, in anger and despair wars against all hope. He perverts the purpose of human sexuality. He denies the gift of love by which husband and wife — always and only male and female — cooperate in the divine plan for continuation of the human race, with the ultimate hope of the eternal salvation of their own children. Instead, the devil whispers into our ears that the sexual act is ultimately for the sake of pleasure. Once we accept this lie, we embrace contraception and fight the very end of the act that puts us in touch with all living things on Earth. Having rejected this end, there is no depth to which the human race will not sink, accepting all manner of sordid perversion. As St. Paul preaches, the nadir of this devolution is the embrace of sodomy (Rom. 1).

In the course of this book, we have discussed these and other heresies and errors. It is my hope that this book has strengthened the reader's faith that the Catholic Church is not confused and that the Catholic Faith does not change, even though some theologians, priests, and bishops have deviated from the Catholic Faith. Although many false friends now spread confusion and revel in the mess, the one true Church of Jesus Christ still stands as the spotless Bride, ready to nurse any sick person back to true health.

Hirelings eventually flee. Wolves in sheep's clothing eventually expose their treachery. God shall gain the victory in the end. Meanwhile, may He preserve Holy Mother Church and us from all the opponents of the Kingdom of Christ. May He deliver each of us from our own doubt, confusion, and sin, so that we might walk in His grace now and eternally rejoice with Him in Heaven.

About the Author

Dr. Malloy is married to Flory, and together they have seven children. He teaches theology at the University of Dallas. He has published two academic books and numerous scholarly articles.

Sophia Institute

Sophia Institute is a nonprofit institution that seeks to nurture the spiritual, moral, and cultural life of souls and to spread the gospel of Christ in conformity with the authentic teachings of the Roman Catholic Church.

Sophia Institute Press fulfills this mission by offering translations, reprints, and new publications that afford readers a rich source of the enduring wisdom of mankind.

Sophia Institute also operates the popular online resource CatholicExchange.com. *Catholic Exchange* provides world news from a Catholic perspective as well as daily devotionals and articles that will help readers to grow in holiness and live a life consistent with the teachings of the Church.

In 2013, Sophia Institute launched Sophia Institute for Teachers to renew and rebuild Catholic culture through service to Catholic education. With the goal of nurturing the spiritual, moral, and cultural life of souls, and an abiding respect for the role and work of teachers, we strive to provide materials and programs that are at once enlightening to the mind and ennobling to the heart; faithful and complete, as well as useful and practical.

Sophia Institute gratefully recognizes the Solidarity Association for preserving and encouraging the growth of our apostolate over the course of many years. Without their generous and timely support, this book would not be in your hands.

www.SophiaInstitute.com
www.CatholicExchange.com
www.SophiaInstituteforTeachers.org

Sophia Institute Press® is a registered trademark of Sophia Institute.
Sophia Institute is a tax-exempt institution as defined by the
Internal Revenue Code, Section 501(c)(3). Tax ID 22-2548708.